Wilderness Survival For Dummies®

Cheat Sheet

Improvised navigation

You can use the following methods anywhere on Earth to find general direction. Check out Chapters 9 and 10 for more.

Stick and shadow

1. **Plant a long stick in the ground and mark the tip of its shadow.**

2. **Wait 15 minutes and mark** spot.

   This is the east-west line

3. **Put your left foot on the fir** **and your right on the secor**

   You're facing due north.

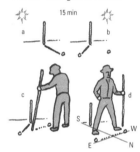

15 min

The North Star

The North Star is located between the Big Dipper and Cassiopeia. This

method for finding North

west
your
you.

The Southern Cross

The Southern Cross lies between the two Pointer Stars and The False Cross. The Southern Cross points perfectly south only when it's standing straight up. Otherwise, use an imaginary point to estimate due south, as the figure shows.

Signaling methods

The following three illustrations show you how to get people's attention with signals.

Ground-to-air emergency code

These symbols are recognized by Search and Rescue pilots as distress signals. Make sure you make these signals a 6:1 ratio so rescuers can see them from the air.

Require
assistance

Require
medical assistance

Proceed
this way

For Dummies: Bestselling Book Series for Beginners

(continued)

Aiming reflector

You must carefully aim your mirror's reflection at the aircraft or vessel you wish to signal, or you may not be seen. You can use a mirror or other reflective items, such as a CD or DVD.

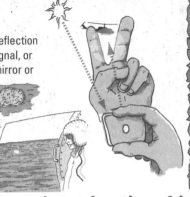

Group splash

If a ring of people all kick simultaneously, the water in the center turns white, briefly, which can be seen against the blue ocean.

Worldwide distress frequencies

The following are distress frequencies used in different parts of the world.

- ✔ **VHF Radio:** Channel 16
- ✔ **CB Radio:** Channel 9
- ✔ **Family Radio Service (FRS) UHF:** Channel 1
- ✔ **Single-sideband and amateur (ham) radio:** 2182kHz, 14.300MHz, 14.313 MHz.
- ✔ **Air band Radio:** 121.5MHz, 243MHz
- ✔ **UHF Radio (Australia):** Channel 5.
- ✔ **Cellphones:** Try dialing 911 on your cellphone, even if you think you're not within coverage. Then try texting someone who you know checks his texts. Text is better than voice in many cases because it can get through when voice can't.

If you have plenty of battery power, send a text, and then leave the unit on as you travel. The unit searches for reception until it transmits. The higher you are, the greater the possibility that your cellphone will make contact with a tower.

- • **911:** U.S., Canada, Central America (partial), Philippines
- • **066, 060, 080, 911:** Mexico.
- • **112:** Europe, Australia, New Zealand, Colombia, India, South Korea, South Africa, Israel
- • **999,120:** China (PRC)
- • **110:** Jamaica
- • **190, 191:** Brazil
- • **1669, 191:** Thailand
- • **113, 115:** Vietnam, Chile
- ✔ SOS in Morse code: . . . - - - . . . (3 short tones, 3 long tones, 3 shorts)
- ✔ International distress signal code word: Mayday, spoken three times

For Dummies: Bestselling Book Series for Beginners

Wilderness Survival
FOR
DUMMIES®

by John Haslett and Cameron M. Smith, PhD

Wiley Publishing, Inc.

Wilderness Survival For Dummies®

Published by
Wiley Publishing, Inc.
111 River St.
Hoboken, NJ 07030-5774
www.wiley.com

Copyright © 2009 by Wiley Publishing, Inc., Indianapolis, Indiana

Published by Wiley Publishing, Inc., Indianapolis, Indiana

Published simultaneously in Canada

For general information on our other products and services, please contact our Customer Care Department within the U.S. at 877-762-2974, outside the U.S. at 317-572-3993, or fax 317-572-4002.

For technical support, please visit www.wiley.com/techsupport.

Wiley also publishes its books in a variety of electronic formats. Some content that appears in print may not be available in electronic books.

Library of Congress Control Number: 2009928733

ISBN: 978-0-470-45306-3

Manufactured in the United States of America

10 9 8 7 6 5 4 3 2 1

WILEY

About the Authors

John Haslett is a veteran expedition leader and adventure writer. He is the author of various adventure books, magazine articles, and academic papers, and his work has been featured in *National Geographic Adventure, Archaeology, QST,* and other magazines. He has spent decades catching unpleasant tropical diseases, explaining himself to local authorities, fleeing from various misguided animals, and putting into practice many of the tenets of this book.

In the 1990s, with the help of an isolated community of Ecuadorian mariners, John built four 30,000-pound wooden rafts and then voyaged on the Pacific Ocean aboard those primitive vessels for hundreds of days. He and Cameron are now preparing their most extensive expeditions to date.

John lives in Los Angeles with his wife, film director Annie Biggs.

Cameron M. Smith's mountaineering, sailing, archaeological, and icecap expeditions have taken him to Africa, South America, arctic Alaska, Canada, and Iceland. In 2004, he made the first solo winter ski crossing of Iceland's storm-lashed Vatnajökull icecap, an expedition televised on the *National Geographic Channel*. He is currently documenting arctic Alaska in winter by trekking on, piloting a paraglider over, and scuba diving beneath the sea ice.

Cameron has written for *Scientific American Mind, Hang Gliding & Paragliding, Archaeology,* and *Spaceflight* magazines and in the books *The Best Travel Writing (2008, 2009), Science under Siege, They Lived to Tell the Tale, The Top 10 Myths about Evolution,* and *Anthropology For Dummies.*

A Life Fellow of the Royal Geographical Society, a Fellow of the Explorers Club, and a member of the Society for Human Performance in Extreme Environments, Cameron is currently writing a narrative of his Iceland expeditions and preparing for balloon exploration of the stratosphere as well as another Pacific expedition with John Haslett. You can track his expedition at www.cameronmsmith.com.

Dedication

John Haslett: This book is dedicated to Annie Biggs, Cameron Smith, Alejandro Martinez, Cesar Alarcon, and Dower Medina — five extraordinary people who know a thing or two about surviving in bad conditions.

And to the boys and men of Troop 100, BSA, wherever you are . . .

Cameron M. Smith: Like John, I dedicate this book to my companions in adventure: namely, John himself; my mountaineering partners, Dr. Chiu Liang Kuo, W. McRee Anderson III, and Jamie Anderson; my flight instructors, Larry Pindar and George McPherson; my diving partner, Todd Olson; Arctic Expedition Coordinator Chuck Sullivan; and Dr. Evan T. Davies. Thank you all for throwing your dice with me. I also dedicate this book to the indigenous people across the globe — the Samburu of East Africa, the fisher-folk of West Ecuador, and the Inupiat of Alaska — who taught me how to survive in places where suburbanites like me would otherwise just vanish.

Authors' Acknowledgments

John Haslett: I would like to send my thanks to my wife, Annie Biggs, for her editing, proofing, scheduling, strategizing, and solid backboned, fighting spirit. I am lucky. I would also like to acknowledge Cameron McPherson Smith, PhD, my coauthor. Not only did he write roughly half of this book, but he also hand-drew some 120 technical illustrations at the same time. Thanks to Literary Agent Matt Wagner at Fresh Books, Inc., who represented this book and who has been exceedingly supportive. I'd like to thank the editor of this book, Chad Sievers, who has been excellent to work with and someone I would work with again, as well as copy editor Danielle Voirol, who made important contributions to this manuscript. Lindsay Lefevere, Acquisitions Editor, deserves credit for believing this would be a worthwhile book. Search and Rescue veterans Gary Cascio and Rick Goodman, both of New Mexico, were generous with their time, advice, and facts. Finally, I'd like to send out my deepest thanks to all the readers and supporters of my previous work — all the letter writers and e-mailers and lecture attendees.

Cameron M. Smith: I thank John Haslett for inviting me aboard one of his extraordinary raft expeditions and for his rock-solid friendship over more than a decade. I am particularly pleased to have the opportunity to thank John's wife, Annie Biggs, for supporting John's expeditions. I thank Literary Agent Matt Wagner for suggesting this project, Acquisitions Editor Lindsay Lefevere for managing it, and our primary editors, Chad Sievers and Danielle Voirol, for deftly improving the text. I thank our technical reviewers for their helpful comments, and like John, I thank my friends and mentors from Boy Scout Troop 616, among whose company I first learned the rewards of an outdoor life. I thank Angela Perri for her limitless patience during this time-devouring project and Search and Rescue Technician Jeff Parsons of the Idaho Falls Fire Department for his technical comments. Finally, I thank my parents, professors Donald E. and Margit J. Posluschny Smith, for granting me the freedom to weave reality from my dreams. There is no greater gift, and I know that the price — their worry while I'm on expedition — is real.

Publisher's Acknowledgments

We're proud of this book; please send us your comments through our Dummies online registration form located at http://dummies.custhelp.com. For other comments, please contact our Customer Care Department within the U.S. at 877-762-2974, outside the U.S. at 317-572-3993, or fax 317-572-4002.

Some of the people who helped bring this book to market include the following:

Acquisitions, Editorial, and Media Development

Project Editor: Chad R. Sievers

Acquisitions Editor: Lindsay Lefevere

Senior Copy Editor: Danielle Voirol

Assistant Editor: Erin Calligan Mooney

Editorial Program Coordinator: Joe Niesen

Technical Editors: Jeffrey Hunt Mantel, Edward Sobey, PhD, Alan Searle, MD

Editorial Manager: Michelle Hacker

Editorial Assistant: Jennette ElNaggar

Art Coordinator: Alicia B. South

Cover Photos: Image Source Pink

Cartoons: Rich Tennant
(www.the5thwave.com)

Composition Services

Project Coordinator: Lynsey Stanford

Layout and Graphics: Melanee Habig, Christin Swinford, Ronald Terry, Christine Williams

Special Art: Cameron M. Smith

Proofreaders: Caitie Copple, John Greenough, Nancy L. Reinhardt

Indexer: Anne Leach

Special Help: Megan Knoll, Jennifer Tebbe

Publishing and Editorial for Consumer Dummies

    Diane Graves Steele, Vice President and Publisher, Consumer Dummies

    Kristin Ferguson-Wagstaffe, Product Development Director, Consumer Dummies

    Ensley Eikenburg, Associate Publisher, Travel

    Kelly Regan, Editorial Director, Travel

Publishing for Technology Dummies

    Andy Cummings, Vice President and Publisher, Dummies Technology/General User

Composition Services

    Debbie Stailey, Director of Composition Services

Contents at a Glance

Table of Contents

Introduction

*W*elcome to the realm of the extraordinary. Survival situations can bring out greatness in some people, and they can also bring out foolishness or terror or spiritual renewal or changes in perspective or sometimes, just enormous gratitude for being alive. We, your friendly authors, have crawled like fleas in the face of enormous winds and waves, and we, too, have experienced these extraordinary states of mind — and many more.

But more often than not, survival situations aren't so romantic: You're on a day hike, 5 miles from a major city — hopelessly lost — and even though you can hear and see signs of civilization, you're still in danger of dying from hypothermia in the next hour. Unfortunately, this situation can kill you just as fast as being lost on an expedition to the North Pole. Perhaps even worse, when you do finally make it out, you don't get an ounce of respect for it from the folks back home! Well, we wrote this book with sympathy for *both* — those involved in exotic adventures and those who just got a little turned-around while taking pictures.

You may worry, understandably, that wilderness survival requires you to bite off the heads of snakes and eat them raw or perhaps leap from a cliff into a raging river. Nothing could be further from the truth. Many survival skills are much more mundane. For example, you can extend the life of your batteries by taking them out of your flashlight and putting them inside your shirt (or better yet, in a plastic bag taped to your armpit) — against your skin. Keeping batteries warm makes your flashlight run much, much longer during the cold and dark night. There. That wasn't so bad, was it? You picked up a basic survival skill and you didn't have to shiver or go hungry. You're already rolling.

About This Book

This book is designed to thoroughly cover the basics of wilderness survival. To compile the information, we've used the most tried-and-true sources, such as *The U.S. Army Survival Manual* and *Essentials of Sea Survival,* by Frank Golden and Michael Tipton (Human Kinetics), but we've called upon our own practical experiences as well. We give you much of this information in a cheerful voice, but we also interject a more serious tone when we have to give you grim news. You can find both voices in these pages.

Conventions Used in This Book

Throughout this book, we use the word *we* when we, Cameron and John, both want to say something personal to you, our reader. This book comes from the combined experiences of two people who've been through a lot of misadventures and who are very close friends. We've been in enough trouble — and scared enough — that we think alike, basically, and therefore we speak with the same voice.

We define the *wilderness* as just about any place out-of-doors. We know from bitter experience that it's easy to freeze to death in places that a geographer wouldn't necessarily think of as "wilderness areas." With that in mind, you should know that this isn't a camping book; it's a book for anyone at risk of perishing from exposure to the elements, whether camping or off on a harmless stroll.

We try not to use too much technical terminology in this book, but when we do offer new vocab, we *italicize* the term the first time we use it. Shortly after giving you the new term, we always define it.

Foolish Assumptions

Although we know that you don't fit every description in this list of assumptions we make about you, our reader, we do assume that you have a least a few of the following characteristics:

✔ You want a basic survival book that gives practical, tried-and-tested advice, whether you're solo or with a group.

✔ You've tried other manuals, but they seem just a little too, well, _dry._

✔ You want a comprehensive survival manual that you can throw in your car or backpack (or carry-on luggage), just in case.

✔ You're already in a wilderness survival situation and you have this handbook nearby.

✔ You've seen a survival show on television and it has intrigued you.

✔ You're not someone who is into _bushcraft_ (at least not yet), which is the art of being completely self-sufficient in the wilderness. You can find numerous, excellent books if you want to live off the land, long term. We simply want to help you survive so you can find your way back to civilization or signal a search and rescue team.

What You're Not to Read

Although we hope you enjoy reading every word that we've written, we also realize that you're a busy person, juggling a career, family, and friends and handling ten other responsibilities. If you just want the bare essentials of surviving in the wild, feel free to skip the sidebars that appear in the gray shaded boxes. The information in the sidebars is additional information, purely for the curious. You can also skip over any paragraphs marked with the Technical Stuff icon, which marks info that's fun or useful but not essential. We hope you read them, but if you don't, you won't miss any vital information.

How This Book Is Organized

Though you can turn to any section in this book and start reading, we've organized the information so that we start with the most basic needs and then work up to the extremes. Whenever we talk about a basic idea that we think has an exception in an extreme situation, we tell you where to look for that exception. We also try to do the reverse: In extreme environments, we frequently send you back to the basics to help you review the foundations of survival. Here's what you can find in the various parts of this book.

Part I: Stayin' Alive: Basic Wilderness Survival Principles

In this part, we start with basic survival protocol — what you should do and in what order you should do it. We show you how to make improvised clothing, how to make fire, how to make shelters, and how to find water and food. We also spend some time showing you how to prepare for the wilderness — what to carry and what to keep an eye out for.

Part II: Eyeing Advanced Survival Techniques

This is the part that we hope gives you the upper hand over your surroundings. In this part, you discover how to navigate, trek through trails and the bush, make sure someone sees you so you can be rescued, handle a bleeding wound, and tie knots and make tools from wood and stone.

Part III: Surviving in Extreme Land Environments

In this part, we address all the special problems (and miseries, frankly) that jungle, desert, and polar environments can present to you, the survivor. We delve into topics such as tropical disease prevention, snake avoidance, cactus eating, and avalanche safety.

Part IV: Surviving on the Seas, Oceans, and Great Lakes

This part takes you from the moment your vessel begins to sink to the moment you make it back to shore and every place in between. It shows you how to abandon a ship safely, how to float for extended periods of time, how to inflate a life raft, and hopefully, how to catch a fish — without accidentally deflating the raft!

Part V: The Part of Tens

In this part, we give you ten fun exercises that you can do to improve your survival skills in the field. We also show you ten scenarios that aren't so much about survival as escape.

Icons Used in This Book

In this book, we place icons, little pictures in the margins, next to some of the paragraphs that we feel need a little extra emphasis.

This symbol gives you a little added info that (hopefully) makes the survival skill we've just explained a little easier. Sometimes, a tip is also a small qualification — a little explanation that tells you when you should use another method.

This symbol is a reminder to do a particular action that makes a survival skill successful, or it makes you think about common sense before you rush out and try something!

This symbol means danger. When we use this symbol, we're trying to emphasize some aspect of a survival situation that can really get you into trouble.

This symbol tells you that we're giving you some background info on the topic, but you don't necessarily need to know the info to be able to execute the actions outlined in the text.

This symbol marks true stories of survival and some of our own accounts of close calls, foolish mistakes, and improvised solutions.

Where to Go From Here

Feel free to start reading this book anywhere you like. The five parts are completely modular, so you don't have to read them in order. However, Chapter 1 is certainly a good place to start because it tells you exactly what to do first if you find yourself lost in the woods.

Part I is a great place to start to get a good foundation for all things wilderness survival. If you're planning on a trip to an extreme environment, you may want to start with Part III. On the other hand, if you're looking for adventures on the sea, you can go straight to Part IV.

Of course, when you're in a survival situation, you can check out the index or table of contents and simply flip to the information you need. If you're bleeding, or if you've twisted your ankle, or if you've been bitten by a snake, check out Chapter 13. Or if your ship has gone under and you find yourself in a life raft, go to Chapter 19.

Part I
Stayin' Alive: Basic Wilderness Survival Principles

"Well, that's just great! We're stuck in the middle of nowhere and all we have to survive on is a rubber chicken, a bunch of balloons, and a squirting daisy?"

In this part . . .

*W*hether you're adrift at sea or lost on a day hike, survival situations throw the same basic questions at you: How can you stay warm overnight? How are you going to prevent dehydration or get something to eat?

In this part, we show you how to prioritize your actions. For instance, we let you know that while you're waiting for rescue or planning your escape, your first priorities are to keep warm (or cool), find water, and take shelter — only then do you start looking for food. We also give advice on psychological preparedness, talk about improvising clothing, and name some practical methods for making fire, building shelter, finding water, and harvesting food from the wilderness.

Chapter 1

Surviving the Wilderness

Knowing the threats you face in the wilderness and the wisest courses of action to take to counter those threats can go a long way toward keeping you alive in a bad situation. If you know in advance what the real problems are, then as soon as you find yourself lost or adrift, you can go to work immediately — and that changes you from victim to survivor.

This chapter serves as a jumping-off point to wilderness survival. Here, we give you an overview of the basics you need to know in practically any wilderness survival situation. We show what the threats are and how to take care of them in the right order. Finally, we take a minute to show you how so many people go wrong and how you can prevent your situation from getting worse — or perhaps how to stay out of trouble altogether!

Being Prepared and Proactive

Every piece of knowledge or equipment you carry with you makes you stronger in the wild. Preparation gives you staying power, and it frequently gives you that little extra advantage you need to stay out of a crisis. Chapter 2 discusses what you can do to be prepared.

Being proactive usually means stopping and getting control — such as slowing your swimming stroke or even floating to conserve your energy. If you're lost, don't react and don't speed up. Stop, sit, and think carefully about your situation for a long time. Take control of the situation instead of letting it take control of you.

Keeping the Right Attitude

Real survival situations feel enormously unfair. Almost all survivors face the feeling of injustice — it's as though the world is conspiring against you or the odds are simply beyond your abilities. To survive this situation, you can't let these feelings take over. You need to have your head on straight and keep a positive outlook. Chapter 3 gives more info on survival psychology.

To keep a positive attitude, the first thing you have to do is size up your situation. Take it all in. This can be very difficult for some people, and it can stand in the way of clear thinking. The truth is that most survival situations are so unexpected that they leave you a little stunned. You have to master disbelief. Many people perish simply because they can't go beyond denial.

The following suggestions can help you keep your spirits up:

✔ **Be resourceful.** Resources and options that you've never considered are available to you. Use rocks as hammers, nails as fishhooks, and belt buckles as reflectors for signaling. Then think of new options and work out more plans. Think of a way.

✔ **Be patient.** Consider that being rescued or working your way out of the problem may take time, but never assume that no one will come looking for you.

✔ **Never say die.** Misery and fear can fool you into thinking you're finished. Don't let your mind play tricks on you. You can keep going long after you feel like you can't. A *lot* longer. Don't give up. Keep a positive attitude, or grit your teeth in grim determination. If you slip into a negative attitude, you'll melt like a candle.

Identifying Survival Basics

When you find yourself in a survival situation, the immediate decisions you make can significantly impact what happens to you. Make sure you address your basic needs in the order they appear in this section.

You may also face a medical situation, which may take precedence over the ones we mention here, depending on its severity. For first aid procedures, see Chapter 13.

Regulating your body temperature

Thermoregulation is the management of your body temperature. It's the highest priority because being too cold *(hypothermia)* or being too hot *(hyperthermia)* are the fastest killers in the wilderness. You have to stay warm in cold environments and cool in hot environments. Here's how:

- ✔ **Cool or cold environments:** Don't allow yourself to get wet. Be careful near streams and rivers, shelter yourself from rain, and keep sweating to a minimum. If night is coming, realize that hypothermia is a threat and construct an insulating shelter.

- ✔ **Hot environments:** You need liquid and shade to cool the body. If your temperature is rising, recognize this and rest or find shade. Waiting too long is the biggest contributor to heat exhaustion. Always stay well hydrated in all situations but especially in hot environments.

The four components that govern thermoregulation are clothing, fire, shelter, and your own actions. The following sections give an overview of them.

Your first line of defense: Clothing

In a survival situation, you have to cope with the entire temperature range of a particular environment, as well as the changes in your own body's temperature. The best way to do this is to dress in layers or to improvise layers. You want to be able to add or subtract clothing. For more on clothing, see Chapter 4.

In many survival situations, people discard clothing that they don't think they need (it's true, honest). Never discard any clothing, under any circumstances. If you take off a shirt or jacket, tie it around your waist or jam it in your belt. Be prepared to carry the layers that aren't currently in use.

If you're in a cold environment, strip off layers of clothing if you start to sweat. You must stay dry. If you're facing a cold night, add insulating layers by stuffing grass, leaves, or moss inside your clothing. You can use other materials, including debris, trash bags, cardboard, or anything that you can attach to or wrap around your body, to make layers and insulation. Remember, trapped air is an excellent insulator, so you can use anything that traps a layer of air next to your body.

In all environments, cover your head. If you don't have a hat, improvise one that covers your head and neck thoroughly. In the cold, a head and neck covering deters hypothermia, especially if you've fallen into cold water, and in the sun, it deters heat stroke.

Warming up to the fire

Starting a fire is crucial because it prevents hypothermia, it boosts morale, and it can be used to send a distress signal. Think overkill when preparing your first fire in a survival situation. Don't rush things. Plan it out and have lots of backups to keep the flame going after it ignites. For info on how to make fire, see Chapter 5.

Gimme shelter

Like a fire, a shelter can help you maintain a sufficient body temperature, which is your first priority. And just like fire, shelter can really boost your morale. Even if you're not a do-it-yourselfer around your home, you should know that anybody can make an insulating shelter, regardless of how much experience he or she has had in the woods.

Chapter 6 discusses how to build general shelters. But if you find yourself in a specific wilderness setting, such as a wintry tundra or a hot desert, check out the specialized shelters in the chapters in Part III.

Regulating temperature in oceans, seas, and lakes

If you're in a water environment, thermoregulation is especially important. Take the following measures to say warm:

- ✔ **Stay as still as you possibly can.** Don't tread water if you can help it. That just makes you colder.

- ✔ **Cover your head.** If you have access to anything that can act as a hat, use it.

- ✔ **Try to keep your armpits closed by holding your elbows at your side, and keep your crotch closed by crossing your legs.** These areas leak a lot of body heat.

- ✔ **Don't take any heat-saving measure that causes your head to go under the water.** You lose more heat from your head than from any other body part.

Check out Chapter 18 for a discussion of staying warm at sea.

Signaling for rescue

The sooner you help others figure out where you are, the better. You need to be ready to signal for rescue at all times. Begin thinking about signaling for help the moment trouble starts. Don't ever believe that no one will come looking for you — someone usually does.

To get potential rescuers' attention, your distress signals need to be huge. Shouting is fine if that's all you can do, but just know that shouting is a very poor signal because the human voice doesn't travel very far. To be seen or heard, signals have to be big — choose large symbols, loud noises, bright colors, or large clusters of objects, such as debris fields or people in groups. Even if you believe rescuers are nearby, make sure your signals are big. Chapter 12 provides info on signaling for help.

Avoiding dehydration

In a hot environment, water can become a life-threatening problem within hours, but in most temperate environments, you usually have roughly three days before the lack of water completely incapacitates you. The minute you think you're in trouble, start practicing *water discipline,* which means you're minimizing your usage in everything you do.

To practice water discipline, no matter where you are, take immediate action in these ways:

- ✔ **Stop consuming diuretics immediately.** These are liquids that make you urinate a lot, like coffee, tea, soda, and alcohol.

- ✔ **Minimize your physical exertion if you can.** Even if you can't feel it, you're losing water through perspiration and heavy breathing.

- ✔ **Don't eat or smoke.** These activities use up your body's water reserves. Try to enforce this measure as long as possible.

- ✔ **Limit your water intake as much as you can.** If you're in temperate conditions or at sea, don't drink anything for the first 24 hours — you'll just lose it through urination. The only exception to this rule is if you're in very hot conditions on land. In these conditions, you have to drink as soon as you feel yourself becoming incapacitated.

Check out Chapter 7 for a discussion of catching water, finding water, treating water, and drinking water in the wilderness.

Staying nourished

Food is the last on the list, by far, because in most cases, you're rescued before it becomes a real factor. You can go a week or more before a lack of food begins to incapacitate you. Nevertheless, finding and eating something can really boost your energy and morale.

Many plants and animals are poisonous. If you're in any way uncertain about a food source, don't eat it — becoming incapacitated is the worst thing that can happen to you in the wild. For more on finding food in the wilderness, see Chapter 8.

Navigating in the Wild

The first and most basic rule of navigation is to know exactly where you are as often as you can. Now, you can't stop every two minutes to look at the map — certainly not all day — but that's not necessary to maintain good navigational awareness.

Make sure you don't allow yourself to get more lost. If you're disoriented, stop and take a moment to remember where you were when you last knew your location. If you're lost, consider staying put — especially if you know someone is looking for you or may look for you in the future. (See Chapter 11 for more on traveling with trails and on what to do when you're disoriented or lost.) This section provides an overview of navigating in the wild with the help of tools and with the sun and stars.

Relying on tools to navigate

You may find this astounding, but many people are rescued every year even though they have a map and GPS in their hands. Satellite navigation and modern map making haven't taken *all* the challenge out of the wilderness — if anything, they've given people a false sense of confidence. Whenever navigating with instruments, make sure they're calibrated and that you're looking at the correct map. Chapter 9 provides in-depth coverage on using these tools to help you navigate in the wilderness.

Looking to the heavens

Finding direction with the use of the sun and stars is really quite easy. You can start with the sun — it rises in the east and sets in the west, and if you're anywhere in North America, Europe, or Northern Asia, it's due south of you at midday. Check out Chapter 10 for specific ways you can use the sun and stars to find your way.

Surviving Injury

When you're in the wild, staying healthy and injury-free can go a long way toward surviving your experience. To do so, keep the following tips in mind, and for more on first aid, check out Chapter 13.

> ✔ **Always be on guard for hypothermia and hyperthermia.** Even if you don't feel the symptoms, someone in your party may be becoming incapacitated, and unfortunately, people don't necessarily cry out when they're afflicted by hypothermia — they just lie down.

✔ **Treat trauma immediately.** If a member of your party has suffered a trauma, you must make sure his or her ABCs are working:

- **Airway:** Check to make sure nothing is interfering with that person's airway.

- **Breathing:** Make sure the subject is breathing.

- **Circulation:** Make sure he or she has a pulse.

Be prepared to administer cardiopulmonary resuscitation (CPR). If you've checked the ABCs and they're fine, put the subject in the *recovery position*, which means lying on his or her side with the head on an arm.

✔ **Stop bleeding.** If you have a bleeding wound on your hands (or anywhere else!), keep in mind that nothing's changed since you were in Boy Scouts or Girl Scouts: Direct pressure for about 10 to 15 minutes does more to stop bleeding than just about anything else.

Avoiding Some of the Causes of Survival Situations

Most survival stories never make the news. This section looks at some of the most common reasons people end up lost in the wild. Use this info to ensure you don't end up in the same situation.

Making errors in judgment

The leading cause of crises in the wilderness, according to various authorities, is *errors in judgment.* This is an exceedingly broad term, but a few examples can do a lot to show you how people commit errors in judgment in the wilderness:

✔ **Not watching out for potential falls:** Be especially careful whenever you're near cliffs or when traveling at night or in low visibility conditions. Watch for ledges and earthen trails that can give way.

✔ **Letting yourself become dehydrated:** You only have to dehydrate by about 5 percent to become physically and mentally impaired by 20 percent. When you add this on top of fatigue and hypothermia, you end up incapacitated.

✔ **Trying to walk too far:** Anytime you or one of your party isn't physically fit, you need to be prudent in estimating how far you can go. If you've missed a meal or have been through an excessively exhausting event within the previous 24 hours, don't push it.

✔ **Continuing to walk long after you're lost:** Doing so just gets you more lost.

✔ **Wearing inadequate clothing:** You should know that wet cold is vastly more dangerous than dry cold. Anytime you face wet cold, take extra precautions. This type of environment causes fatalities. Chapter 4 discusses important clothing information.

✔ **Carrying inadequate gear:** Not having durable or warm clothing and footgear or the tools to start a fire are the prerequisites for a deadly hypothermia scenario. Chapter 2 identifies the equipment to take.

✔ **Relying too much on GPS or cellphones to carry you through rough conditions:** Not watching your maps because you have GPS or ignoring a deteriorating situation because you think can always call for help is a recipe for disaster. Take a look at Chapter 11 for more on this.

Losing it: Behaviors that help you get lost

You can get lost in the wild for an infinite number of reasons, but certain common denominators frequently crop up in statistical surveys of lost persons. Chapter 11 has more info about avoiding getting lost and what to do if you're lost.

✔ **Leaving the trail to take a shortcut:** An inordinate number of people get lost every year because they leave the trail to try a shortcut. Stick to the trail, especially if you're in unknown territory.

✔ **Letting your awareness lapse:** You pass through a tunnel in the foliage, or you're concentrating on your photography or on seeing a particular species of bird, and suddenly you're not exactly sure where you are.

✔ **Walking downslope from a trail:** Whenever you walk down from a trail (descend), you break your line of sight with the trail.

✔ **Being overconfident in wilderness areas where you haven't been in for a while:** You can easily get lost when going back to your old stomping grounds.

✔ **Turning onto false trails:** Keep in mind that the world's wilderness areas are constantly in flux. One good rain can wash away enough earth to make it appear as though there's a new trail.

✔ **Forging ahead:** Many people get lost because they reach a point where the trail fades or is poorly marked and they continue on but can't pick up the trail again. Be on guard for this, and make sure you leave behind your own markers in these areas.

✔ **Going farther than you normally go when hunting, hiking, bird-watching, shooting outdoor photography, or berry- or mushroom-picking:** You leave your normal stomping grounds — you push a little farther, and then when you turn around to come back, you get turned around.

✔ **Falling behind the group:** Parties of friends or social groups get spread out, or one particular person becomes begins to straggle.

✔ **Getting separated from the group:** This can happen when-ever you're transported to a remote area, such as when you're taken to a dive site or a location in the desert.

Chapter 2

Preparing Yourself for a Survival Situation

You can take a quantum leap in self-sufficiency and survivability by making a few preparations before going into the wilderness. In particular, you need to consider the weather and how it can affect your situation. Furthermore, a discussion of being prepared isn't complete without mentioning the importance of having a stocked survival kit in case something happens to you or your group.

In this chapter, we give you some practical suggestions for predicting bad weather and knowing how to handle it, and we show you a practical survival kit and how to carry it.

Being Ready for Mother Nature

Various authorities and surveys can tell you that errors in judgment cause more emergencies in the wild than just about anything else. High on that list of mistakes is being ill-equipped for the environment. Properly judging what you're getting into — and carrying the right gear for the environment — can go a very long way toward staying out of survival situations.

By knowing what weather to expect, you can take precautions in deciding what clothing to wear (see Chapter 4) and when and where to venture. This section helps you get a firm grasp on weather-related issues. Later in this chapter, we discuss some of the equipment you need to take with you to be prepared.

Relying on weather forecasts

Before you head out into the field — and until you build up enough expertise to read clouds and wind — your best bet for knowing what kind of weather to expect is to use the forecasts available to you. Try the following resources:

- ✔ **The local news:** It can give you very detailed, specific info that nationwide forecasts can't.

- ✔ **The Internet:** What doesn't the Web have these days? Check out the following sites:

  - • **The National Weather Service:** This is a part of the National Oceanic and Atmospheric Administration, or NOAA, and it's a great place to start if you're in the U.S. The Web page (www.nws.noaa.gov) is excellent.

  - • **Commercial sources:** Other good sources are AccuWeather (www.accuweather.com), Intellicast (www.intellicast.com), and The Weather Channel (www.weather.com). All these sites have an advisories section that lists watches and warnings of bad weather throughout the world.

- ✔ **Weather radios:** To receive National Weather Service reports in the wilderness, bring along an NOAA radio receiver. These units are very inexpensive.

When checking any weather source, know at least four basic pieces of info:

- ✔ **The 24-hour temperature range:** This one piece of info prepares you more than just about anything else because it tells you how to dress and what gear you need to have. If you get lost, delayed, or injured, you may end up having to endure the entire temperature range — from the lowest to the highest.

If you're planning on leaving your base, such as a road or a campsite, for any length of time, take the estimated temperature range, add 10 degrees to the high and subtract 10 degrees from the low, and then consider the wind in your preparations. The wind can make cold temperatures even more formidable.

✔ **The short-term forecast:** The three-day forecast is usually the most reliable.

✔ **Watches and warnings:** Keep in mind the difference between the two types of advisories:

- **Watch:** A watch is simply the weather service's way of telling you that ideal conditions exist for a certain type of weather — tornadoes, floods, storms, and so on.

- **Warning:** A warning means that the weather phenomenon is known to be occurring at this moment. For example, a tornado warning means that someone actually saw a tornado nearby.

If you're going into the mountains or near a coastline, you need to locate the authority who issues the avalanche warnings or rip current and surge warnings.

✔ **Barometric pressure:** *Barometric pressure* is simply a measurement of how much air is sitting on top of the area you're in. The pressure tells you one of two things:

- If the pressure is dropping, the atmosphere around you is becoming unstable. This means that the weather is probably going to deteriorate.

- If the pressure is rising, the atmosphere around you is stabilizing. Rising or steady pressure usually means good weather or a continuation of the weather you already have.

Watching for weather signs

When you're in the field, you usually don't have a chance to check the Web. However, you can watch out for signs of approaching weather — especially changes that weren't predicted or that had a low chance of occurring. Pay attention to the winds and clouds to help you make weather predictions.

Considering the winds

Keep an eye on the wind you feel now as well as the wind you don't feel yet. If the wind increases or changes direction, conditions around you are changing. If the wind changes radically, that usually means a substantial change in the weather.

To gauge the wind you don't feel, try to size up the terrain around you and then estimate what a big wind would do if it were to come upon you suddenly. Here's what wind can do in various terrains:

- ✔ If you're on an exposed mountainside, a hard wind can cause a drastic drop in temperature.

- ✔ If you have open plains around you, remember that wide open spaces are nature's speedway for high winds.

- ✔ If you're near an exposed cliff, the wind may come in, explode against that cliff, and cause havoc.

Watching the clouds

Two types of clouds signify the coming of rain within a few hours or minutes. Here are the *nimbus* (rain) clouds:

- ✔ **Any dark, low, heavily laden clouds:** Rain's obviously coming, right? These gray, blanket-like clouds are *nimbostratus* clouds.

- ✔ **Tall, dense, fluffy clouds:** Though less obvious, this second type of rain cloud indicates heavy rain and thunderstorms. An anvil head (a *cumulonimbus* cloud) is usually tall, dense (like a large island in the sky), and as puffy as cotton. If, during the day, you see this type of cloud grow very tall in the sky, or worse, start to become lopsided at the top — blown sideways by high-altitude winds — you're seeing an anvil head (see Figure 2-1). These storm clouds usually bring rain, lightning, high winds, and sometimes hail.

If you've received a forecast of 20 percent chance of rain and an anvil head or low, gray clouds are nearby, feel free to increase the chance of rain to 50 percent (or more), all by yourself.

Figure 2-1: An anvil head cloud.

Carrying Survival Equipment

Always carry a survival kit with you in the wilderness. If you spend enough time in the dark and in trouble, as we've done, you find that one little item is almost always what saves you. Being prepared and carrying a survival kit can often turn a bad situation into at least a tolerable one. In this section, we discuss different types of kits. Each list of equipment is slightly more elaborate than the previous one. Sometimes we list a piece of equipment twice because to be fully prepared, having two types of a particular item is ideal.

Five items you need

You need to have five basic items with you at all times, even if others in your party have them, too. Without these items, you're utterly defenseless — naked, in fact. You can put three of these items on a keychain, and four out of the five can fit in one pocket.

Flashlight

You need a flashlight so you can perform complicated tasks in the dark and also so you can signal for help at night. Many times, especially when you have plenty of moonlight, you should try to do everything with your natural night vision; however, you may not have time to adjust to darkness, or you may have to perform a critical task, such as map reading in a dense forest on a moonless night. Luckily, your flashlight options are almost unlimited:

- ✔ **LED keychain flashlights:** This is the bare minimum. These tiny flashlights fit on your keychain or in your pocket, and they use LEDs, or *light-emitting diodes*. Because LEDs use only a tiny amount of energy, these lights last a long time on a single battery.

  Try to buy an LED flashlight with multiple bulbs, as opposed to a single bulb. They give off a lot of light for their size.

- ✔ **Conventional penlights:** These lights also fit on keychains, but unlike LEDs, they use conventional light bulbs and use up their batteries relatively quickly. Although they're generally heavier, they're brighter than LEDs. (See Figure 2-2g, later in this chapter.)

- ✔ **Conventional flashlights:** You can't beat a conventional handheld flashlight in some scenarios. These are still the best if you have to shine a beam a long way or if you simply need a lot of light. Many companies make very good, midsized conventional flashlights that can fit in your pocket.

Fire maker

A fire maker, such as a lighter or magnesium bar, is mandatory because it gives you the ability to make heat, and in most cases, hypothermia poses an even greater threat than dehydration. Dying of dehydration takes anywhere from one to ten days, but you can die of hypothermia in less than 90 minutes.

We discuss fire makers in more detail in the section titled "Building the basic survival kit," later in this chapter. Unfortunately, the fire makers work only if you know how to build a fire. For more on fire, check out Chapter 5.

Penknife, pocketknife, or multitool

You don't have to have a big, impressive knife in the wild (although it sure helps), but you do need to have some kind of blade. Your three main options — all of which have blades that fold down — are as follows:

✔ **Penknife:** The smallest knife, the penknife, fits on a keychain. This little item may be the best purchase you ever make — even if you never set foot in the outdoors. Just make sure you take it off before you try to board a commercial airliner.

✔ **Pocketknife:** The next step up from the penknife is the small pocketknife. You can choose from infinite varieties. Regardless of which type you buy, it should have a hole at one end for a *lanyard*, a string that runs from the knife to your wrist, so you don't lose your blade when you're working. A 5-inch long folding pocketknife with a sturdy lanyard on it is a lifesaver.

✔ **Multipurpose knife or multitool:** The next step up is the multipurpose pocketknife, such as the Swiss Army knife, which has a variety of tools folded into one case (see Figure 2-2e, later in this chapter).

Probably the handiest of the multipurpose knives is the *multitool*, which has blades and other utensils packed into a foldable pair of pliers. You can carry a multitool in your pocket, or better, in a pouch that fits on your belt. We talk more about knives later in "Building the basic survival kit."

Water container

Staying hydrated keeps you strong and running at your peak. Carrying a good container gives you the ability to refill it easily. Keep in mind two ideas when buying and carrying a container:

✔ **Durability and versatility:** An army-style canteen is great, and better still is a water bottle that has a wide-mouthed, screw-off top. This offers you the ability to easily scoop up water or collect rain. If you have nothing else, you can grab bottled water from the convenience store.

✔ **Convenience in carrying:** Many times, unbelievably, people who are lost discard equipment, clothing, water bottles, and so on — you don't want that temptation.

If you're not using a pack of any type, know that water bottles tend to ride better on a crossover shoulder strap when they're full and on your belt when they're empty.

Instruments and electronics

If you have electronics and other related instruments within reach, grab them — even if you think you're going to be beyond coverage. Examples include cellphones, any type of compass (Figure 2-2m, later in this chapter), and a GPS receiver (Figure 2-2n). For more on these types of equipment and how they can help you navigate, check out Chapter 9.

Building the basic survival kit

A good wilderness survival kit is a great asset when you go outdoors. Although some good kits are available on the market, we strongly suggest you make your own because you can be sure of the quality of the items inside it (and it's also fun). The basic kit we discuss in this section weighs only a few pounds, and you can assemble it in a day. You can see a fully assembled survival kit in the section titled "Building the complete kit."

We like to brag that you can fit this little kit into a large zipper-lock bag, but we suggest you find a sturdier container. Look for a container around your house, use an ammunition pouch from a surplus store, or your best bet, get a *dry bag*, a completely waterproof vinyl bag that you can get from a boating store. When you have the container you want, take a permanent marker and write your name and WILDERNESS SURVIVAL KIT in large letters on the container.

A complete fire-making kit

Your complete fire-making kit should contain at least three fire-making instruments and some tinder. Good fire-making instruments include the following:

✔ **Lighters:** Butane cigarette lighters (see Figure 2-2s) are good, but saltwater causes them to malfunction within just a few days. Long-nosed fireplace lighters, which are usually red and black in color, last much longer under corrosive conditions, and they're generally superior to just about any other lighter. Some high-tech lighters claim to work in any conditions, but we take that claim with a grain of salt.

Some of our colleagues swear by Zippo lighters, which are metal cigarette lighters that use wicks soaked in lighter fluid. If you carry one, also carry spare flints and wicks.

✔ **Matches:** Carry two types: Plain, wooden, strike-anywhere matches and wooden waterproof matches that you can get at a boating supply store (Figure 2-2t).

✔ **Magnesium bar (metal match):** This is a tiny rod of metal that, when you shave it forcefully with a knife, produces a small pile of magnesium, which ignites under any conditions — even when wet! On top of the bar is flint, which produces a shower of white-hot sparks when you scrape it with a knife, igniting the magnesium (Figure 2-2i).

✔ **Magnifying glass:** Get a flat, flexible plastic magnifying glass, about the size of a credit card, to focus the sun's rays on your tinder (Figure 2-2r).

Tinder is the highly flammable stuff you carry that starts a fire on the first try — even in wet conditions. A film canister filled with lint from your clothes dryer and treated with a couple of drops of lighter fluid or gasoline is good (Figure 2-2b), as is rolled newspaper dipped in paraffin wax. Some people like to stuff paper egg cartons with straw, pour in wax, and then separate each little pocket to create a set of fire starters. The wax and straw burn for as long as 10 minutes, giving you time to get your kindling started. You can also find prepackaged tinder at the outdoors stores.

Pack your fire-making instruments and tinder in a waterproof container, seal it with tape, and put it inside your survival kit.

Items for clean water, shelter, and sun protection

Pack the following items to help you take care of your basic needs for clean water and protection from the elements:

✔ **Water purification chemicals:** These are usually small tablets of chlorine or crystals of iodine. You can buy them at all outdoors stores. Follow the directions on the bottle, and expect to have to wait an hour or two for them to purify your water (see Figure 2-2w).

✔ **Steel cup:** A small metal cup is invaluable because you can boil water in it — which is still the very best way to disinfect water in the wild (Figure 2-2k).

✔ **High-SPF sun block:** Get the highest rating you can find in the smallest container you can, or transfer some into a separate, clean miniature bottle. Put this in a plastic zipper storage bag so it doesn't leak on everything else (Figure 2-2x).

✔ **Plastic painter's tarp:** In an emergency, you can build a waterproof shelter with this tarp, or you can use it as a ground cloth or a water catcher (Figure 2-2a).

✔ **Space blanket:** A *space blanket* is a large and very thin sheet of plastic, coated with a reflective material that traps body heat (Figure 2-2q). These blankets can be invaluable on a cold night, and you can spread the bright, mirror-like surface out on the ground as a signaling device. We suggest putting two in your survival kit.

Tools for making other things

Wilderness survival usually involves a fair amount of improvisation. You may have to make your own shelter, clothing, or weapons for hunting. Pack the following tools so you can cut, tie, cover, tape, and light your way to safety:

✔ **A second knife:** Even if you already have a small knife or multitool (refer to the "Five items always to have" section, earlier in this chapter), a large knife is indispensable in a real survival situation (see Figure 2-2d). If you get into a serious situation, you have to use this knife to dig, pry, hammer, and do just about everything else.

Look for a substantial knife that you can really punish without having it break. Many folding blades are excellent, but you should consider getting a knife made from a single piece of steel — these knives usually require a sheath.

✔ **Rope and wire:** You frequently have to bind things together or make improvised repairs in the wild, so carry some cordage. Here's what to pack:

- The easiest cordage to carry is the ready-made 30-foot lengths of parachute cord (Figure 2-2j), which you can buy at outdoors stores. This is a lightweight line that has an infinite number of uses.

- A small spool of thin metal wire is also a life-saving, multipurpose item.

- For small jobs, consider carrying a spool of 50-pound-test monofilament fishing line or unwaxed dental floss.

✓ **Plastic garbage bags:** You can use plastic bags (Figure 2-2l) as containers and as improvised rain ponchos. Get three or four bags of the heaviest gauge you can find.

✓ **Duct tape and safety pins:** You can use these items when you have to bind, repair, and seal all sorts of things in a crisis (Figure 2-2y).

✓ **A spare flashlight:** You need a backup flashlight. You can carry a medium-sized conventional flashlight if you have room.

A really good idea is to carry a headlamp, such as a Petzl lamp, with a halogen bulb (www.petzl.com/en). The benefits are threefold: it uses less battery power than a conventional flashlight, it throws off an intense light, and you wear it on your forehead, thus freeing the hand that would normally carry a flashlight.

Reverse the batteries when you stow the spare flashlight in your kit — that way, they won't run down if the light is accidentally turned on. *Remember:* Take plenty of extra batteries. You never know how long you may be out there.

Navigation stuff

The following items can help you find your way — and eventually, your way out (for info on using navigation equipment, see Chapter 9):

✓ **Compass:** Even if you've never used one, this handy item can reveal things to you that nothing else can — namely which way you're going! Like your knife, your compass should have a hole for a lanyard. If you have a choice, opt for an orienteering compass, which is molded into a baseplate (see Figure 2-2m).

- **Map of the area:** Any map is better than none, and practically every map is useful in some way (Figure 2-2o). If you head off into the wild, USGS topographic maps are usually the best. Almost all ranger stations have maps, and the National Park Service (maps.nps.gov) as well as National Geographic (maps.nationalgeographic.com) have some online. International Travel Maps, which you can find at the local bookstore, are also very good.

- **Electronics:** If they're within reach, grab them — even if you think you're going to be beyond coverage (Figure 2-2n).

Tools for signaling

Use these items when the going really gets rough and you have to send a distress signal (for more on distress signals, see Chapter 12):

- **Signal mirror:** Use a mirror to signal for help during the day. You can get a good signal mirror (Figure 2-2h) at an outdoors or boating store.

- **Whistle:** A high-pitched whistle can be heard for miles and is vastly better than using your voice. You can usually purchase a signal whistle in the same place you find signal mirrors (Figure 2-2f).

Building the complete kit

If you have a daypack or a full backpack, or if you're traveling in a car or boat, you can carry a more complete kit (see Figure 2-2).

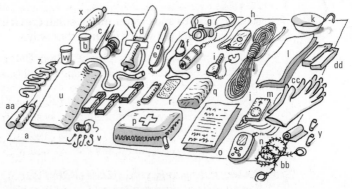

Figure 2-2: The complete survival kit.

Here's what goes in the complete kit. The items on this list are in addition to the basic kit we discuss in the preceding section, and they give you a lot of staying power in the wilderness.

- ✔ **Bivy sack (bivouac sack):** These are fabric bags that work like improvised sleeping bags/tents (see Figure 2-2q). Along with a space blanket or two, they can save your life in the cold.

- ✔ **Heavy duty camel bag:** A *camel bag,* sometimes called a *camelback,* is a flexible bladder that fits on your back like backpack and has a tube that you drink from (Figure 2-2u). These are the very best water-carrying devices.

- ✔ **First aid kit and pamphlet:** Dozens of premade first aid kits are available (Figure 2-2p). Good first aid kits come with pamphlets reminding you how to deal with cuts, burns, infections, broken limbs, and so on. We cover wilderness first aid in Chapter 13.

- ✔ **Map collection:** Collect any map you can. Anything helps — even sightseeing or tourist maps, because each map contains a different type of info. Put your maps in a zipper-lock plastic bag.

- ✔ **Sewing needles, thread, and buttons:** Being able to repair your clothing is important, as is the ability to improvise clothing from scraps of fabric, plastic, and so on. You can carry several needles in a survival kit. We suggest large, heavy needles, at least 2 inches long, with large eyes that are easy to thread with a variety of cordage (Figure 2-2c). Also carry some large buttons, which you can use to repair or improvise clothing.

- ✔ **Flexible straw/surgical tubing:** You can use tubing (Figure 2-2z) to suck water out of small crevices in rocks when you can't get water in any other way.

- ✔ **Candles and spare wicks (Figure 2-2aa):** Before you buy candles, be sure you know how long they'll burn. Some types can burn for 6 hours and are favorites among mountaineers, who know a thing or two about long, cold nights. You can use them for light or to start fires.

- ✔ **Wire saw:** You can buy wire saws (Figure 2-2bb) at outdoors stores. Use these flexible tools to cut off tree branches.

- ✔ **Gloves:** Heavy-duty yard gloves (Figure 2-2cc) can give you an almost superhuman ability in the wild — the only problem is that these types don't have a lot of dexterity.

✔ **Food:** Good old-fashioned granola bars (Figure 2-2dd) can help a lot in a demoralizing situation. Nuts are good, as are packets of soup — just make sure they don't have excess salt in them. If they do, they're diuretics, and they don't help you in the end.

✔ **Mini fishing kit:** These kits (Figure 2-2v) are so lightweight and useful that you should squeeze in a couple of them if you have room. These aren't just for fishing — the hooks and the fishing line have a million and one uses.

You may also want to include an extremely lightweight insulator that you spread on the ground to sleep on. This pad prevents the ground cold from getting to your body and can prevent hypothermia during the night.

Gathering equipment for going out on the water

If you're going to be out on a ship or boat, be prepared with the right equipment. Most importantly, you need a personal flotation device, or PFD, for everyone on board. All PFDs are labeled by type:

✔ **Type I:** These life jackets are the best. They keep you afloat in heavy seas, and they turn you right-side-up if you've been knocked unconscious.

✔ **Type II:** These vests are for near-shore activities, and they don't turn you right-side-up if you're knocked unconscious.

✔ **Type III:** These floatation aids are used when water-skiing or duck hunting. Don't use these in the ocean.

✔ **Type IV:** These are life rings and seat cushions, and they're designed to be thrown to someone in peril.

✔ **Type V:** These are work vests, and they usually look like a harness. They're designed to inflate in time of emergency.

Also, we suggest that you always have a spare propulsion device, such as an extra paddle or oar. Check with your outfitter or the U.S. Coast Guard to see what's required by law to be aboard any vessel you rent.

Chapter 3

The Psychology of Survival: Gaining the Upper Hand

In This Chapter
▶ Understanding your emotions during a survival situation
▶ Understanding how survivors think
▶ Building morale

*M*ore often than not, survival situations catch you off guard. They're nothing like you expected, and the mindset that you always wanted to have in a crisis suddenly seems foreign. There's no background music, like in the movies, and there's nothing heroic about the situation at all. But with a little understanding, perhaps you can find that inner heroic survivor and bring him or her to the surface.

In this chapter, we discuss the mindset you need to get through a survival situation, what you can expect to feel when the crisis comes, and how you can expect others to act — or *re*act — when things go bad. We also show you how you can boost your morale.

Getting into the Right Mindset

The psychological factor — in other words, having the right mindset about the experience — is the most important component in any survival situation. It's more important than training, knowledge, experience, odds, or luck. How you perceive what's happening to you dictates your ability to perform and to survive.

Hundreds of miles from land

In 1995, a U.S. Marine stepped out on the deck of an aircraft carrier for a little air and promptly fell off the boat — in the middle of the Arabian Sea. The fleet sailed away into the night and there he was, with no flotation, no land for hundreds of miles, treading water — a single head in a vast, empty plain of waves. The odds of surviving were off the scale, but nonetheless, he made a flotation device by inflating his pants and then held on for 34 hours — until he was picked up by Pakistani fishermen.

You need to remember one startling fact when facing a survival situation: Many people succumb — they give up and perish — before they're physically overwhelmed. They give up trying to get into a life raft after just a few tries, or they lie down on the trail after just a few days or even hours of misery. Their perception, and therefore their belief, is that the situation is beyond their means or that the struggle simply isn't worth it. If you've ever had the misfortune to see this, then you know, as we do, that it's one of the most bizarre, unfathomable characteristics of humankind.

Just knowing that this problem exists can be a huge advantage for you in a survival situation. Even more, knowing how to summon up some coping mechanisms can help you manufacture — in the field — the mentality that gives you the power to hold out longer, push further, and endure more, which is the essence of survival. This section explains how to develop a survivor's mindset and how to stay focused when you're in a survival situation.

Mastering disbelief

All survival situations are extraordinary — especially when they're happening to you. Many times, the events leave people so stunned with disbelief that they take action very slowly or not at all.

To master disbelief, you need to know that most survival situations feel unfair: You just went for a swim, and now you're 5 miles offshore, dragged out by a current. Or perhaps you're in familiar territory, hiking, and you have lots of experience, but now you're lost and an unexpected cold front is coming in. It's not fair, but it's reality. Some of the most gruesome, incomprehensible stories of survival revolve around not being able to master disbelief.

Make sure you do the following to help you fully accept your situation.

Realize that it's happening to you

Some people simply can't get over the outrage of being put in such a position. Don't let this happen to you. It *is* unfair, but nonetheless, you're in a survival situation, so fair or unfair is irrelevant. Now, that doesn't make the ordeal one ounce more pleasant, but it gives you strength, and the more quickly the idea of what's happening sinks in, the better. Only the inexperienced think this idea is obvious or easy.

Keep in mind that modern ships still sink, people with GPS units still get lost, friends who are just trying to have a nice time still fall into disaster. Realize this immediately and start planning proactive procedures to save yourself and your companions.

Dismiss the odds of surviving

Don't believe that the odds of surviving are just too low. You have to dismiss that type of thinking.

Statistics and odds mean nothing after you go into action. If you spend enough time studying the history of human beings in impossible conditions — survivors — you begin to see that people survive "the impossible" quite frequently. Realize that thousands of people before you have survived these types of perilous situations. These people are just like you — they look like you, they talk like you — they're usually not supermen or superwomen. They're just like you. And they made it.

Working with stress and fear

After you realize you're in a survival situation, you can expect a flood of stress and fear. Stress and fear are necessary because they make you stronger and more alert — but only if you control them. People who don't have any fear get complacent and get themselves into trouble — we know, because we've done it! What's most important is how you channel this emotional response.

You can be scared and still function and still succeed. What you need is self-control; otherwise, your thinking becomes muddled. Here are some methods of controlling fear and gaining the upper hand:

- **Take a deep breath and slow your heart rate.** Simply realize that your heart is racing, and relax. Relax your shoulders — let them sag a bit — and then stretch your neck. Draw in a deep breath through your nose and let it out through your mouth. Your heart rate should slow down a little.

- **Take inventory.** Get a total grip on your situation. Where are you? What are your options? How can you improve your situation? Consider taking a piece of paper and writing down the history of your situation. For example, note when and where you saw the last familiar landmark, as well as what your threats are and your options for dealing with them. Plans and escapes present themselves when you do this, and you gain strength by being proactive.

- **Boil things down to their basics.** Ask yourself what exactly you're facing here. This is a good exercise because it reduces your situation from "the whole world against you" to just one or two problems.

- **Get to work.** Do something — anything at all — to take your mind off the situation.

- **Get angry.** Anger can be super-potent, even in the weakest people. If you need a serious burst of strength, take a moment to get seriously angry. Refuse to accept that some small mistake is reason to lose your life.

- **Get some contempt.** Tell nature and fear and everything else to *shove it*. Refuse to give in. Feel free to be obstinate — it works.

- **Become resigned to the fact that you're in extreme peril.** Many survivors have made it through their darkest hours by resigning themselves to the moment, by taking the attitude that come what may, they're going to keep fighting. Many have looked at death and said to themselves that they don't care if they live or die — but they're not going to give in. This is grim business, indeed, but it has worked in many cases.

✔ **Try the tire-changing mentality.** Instead of flying into frenzied action, act like you're just changing a tire. Just go to work, one thing at time. The no-nonsense body language that comes from this mentality can give you a clear head in an instant — and it has a miraculous effect on others around you. Frequently, when they see you act this way, they adopt this mentality for themselves. Soon, you have a cool-headed group working through a serious problem. We've used this technique in the middle of the night when there was panic all around us and our vessel was in trouble, and it worked.

Planning and taking action

As you calm your stress and fears, you also need to clear your head and think to the future with a clear plan. In stressful situations, your thinking can become muddled. Confusion and bad plans can take over quickly, so make sure you put together a thorough plan before doing anything.

To make your plan so you can take action, keep the following suggestions in mind:

✔ **Eliminate as much physical misery as you can.** Cold, hunger, being soaked, injury — any of these can cloud your judgment. With that in mind, take inventory and try to relieve yourself of some small — or large — misery if you can. You may find that suddenly your mind clears and that making good plans isn't hard after all.

✔ **Observe carefully.** These types of situations can close off your powers of perception. You may have options right in front of your nose that you can't see or haven't even considered. Take time to take it all in, and never, ever assume that you see everything.

✔ **Give yourself an extra choice.** In emergency situations, the either/or decision-making loop can blind you to options that are in fact right in front of your face. We know that not every situation has a wide array of options, but if you have an either/or decision in front of you and both are bad, try coming up with a third — the results may shock you and even give you strength.

After you come up with a third option, continue to expand outward. View the problem from a new perspective. There may be a fourth option you haven't thought of — or maybe even a fifth. Never assume you've thought of everything.

✔ **Keep in mind that survival can be a war of attrition — a fight in which small, persistent actions allow you to succeed.** Your first plans may fail. That isn't a sign or an indication that you're not going to make it. On the contrary, you frequently have to work through several failures before you get to something that works. Just take a lesson from every failure.

If you can't solve your problem immediately, you may be able to improve your position. Small steps can help a lot. Just about any action is better than none, and some small success can lead to another. The more action you take, the more confidence you feel.

Understanding discipline

Much of your chances for survival revolve around how well you stay disciplined and practice self-denial. The more you can conserve, the better. You're in the business of holding out, hanging on, and extending your reserves. Discipline yourself. Tell yourself that using small amounts — of water, food, electrical power, and so on — is going to save your life.

Disciplining yourself is especially important when using signals. Be careful to not let fear run away with the moment. You can easily waste flares that nobody sees or run radios that have only a limited amount of battery time if you're not careful. In a survival situation, those who can discipline themselves are usually the ones who make it out.

Valuing life and home

One way to get in the right mindset is to value living and value your life. In many cases, this simple idea gets lost in the moment. Realize that your life is valuable, that it's worth saving, and that you still have a lot of good living to do.

Group decision-making: Getting people in a crisis to cooperate

Getting a group to be disciplined can be exceedingly difficult. For many people, this may be the first time they've ever had to go on rationed food or water, and they rebel. And food and water aren't the only possible sticking points. Whenever your group has to make a decision — whether deciding when to stop for the night, coordinating your open-sea fishing team, or figuring out which way is north — you have a potential for conflict.

When working with a group, explain everything in full. Try to be as convincing as you can. One of the best ways to do this is to look at the faces around you and make a quick association with those who are cool-

headed and fully functional. Try to get a majority, and try to explain the wisest course of action.

If possible, try not to enforce decisions through power and might. However, you may have to. You may have to guard the water, take dangerous tools and objects away from irrational people, and even physically restrain someone who's doing something that's going to get you killed.

If you have people who simply won't cooperate, you may have to go it alone. Many times, groups go off and do incredibly unwise things. You can always abstain from this; you don't have to go along with a group that's determined to destroy itself.

Keep in mind that people want you to return. Picturing their grief can be a powerful tool in motivating yourself to stay alive. Many survivors have done this. Know that you can cause great suffering to those back home if you don't survive and that you have a duty to them, and to your own life, to stay alive. Picture the faces of your family, your friends. This frame of mind can carry you through when no other can.

Using humor and a positive attitude

Optimism and a positive attitude can turn a bad situation around in a second. We've seen people use positive thinking in the field. The effect really is incredible. Many lifeboat survivors can attest to the fact that a smile and a joke — no matter how strained — can give you hope.

Optimism on ice

Perhaps the greatest expedition leader of the 20th century, Sir Ernest Shackleton, himself a survivor, always maintained a cheerful attitude no matter how bad things got. His results were nothing short of miraculous. He kept all his men alive through a year-long ordeal when they were stranded on Antarctica with no support. He knew that optimism was the highest quality a person could have when facing a survival situation, and he never allowed dark talk or bad attitudes.

Although a humorous comment can alleviate stress and defuse a situation, comments that appear callous can be harmful. Sometimes you have to be sensitive. Pick and choose your moments for levity carefully.

You should try to celebrate sometimes and be proud of yourself. Survival, more often than not, is a clumsy business. You get very few clean successes, and it's easy to see how imperfect your progress is. We've had times when we were making progress in the face of very grim circumstances, but because the progress was small, the pessimists among us used it to show how we were failing. Don't let this happen to you. Survival is about tiny victories. When you win, give yourself credit. It makes you stronger.

Being Aware of Your Emotions

Real survival situations bring out all kinds of spontaneous reactions in you and others that you may have never considered. This section looks at some of the common emotions you and your group may feel and how you can cope with them.

Thankfully, there are practical ways to fight all the emotions we talk about in this section. You can strengthen yourself in the field by taking just a few of the practical steps in the upcoming section "Improving Morale."

Fear

Fear is the most common emotion people in survival situations feel. Fear is a reaction to uncertainty, and it can range from a simmering anxiety to heart-stopping terror. You should expect it and know how to use it to your advantage. We talk about taking advantage of this emotion in the section "Getting into the Right Mindset," earlier in this chapter.

In surveys of lost persons, some fears tend to crop up again and again. None of these will come as a surprise, but knowing that others have experienced these feelings can be reassuring. Here are some top wilderness fears:

- ✔ Being alone
- ✔ The night
- ✔ Suffering and pain
- ✔ The unknown
- ✔ Death
- ✔ Animal attack

Trying to take on all your fears at once can incapacitate you quickly. Any of the preceding threats can come upon you, but you probably won't have to face all at once, and none of them may develop into real threats at all. If you must think about them, take one at a time. Boil down your situation: What are you really facing?

For more on how to cope with fear, check out the "Working with stress and fear" section earlier in this chapter.

Panic

Panic is the most counterproductive emotion you can feel in a crisis. Realize that if you panic, you lose. The most important action you can take is to practice self-awareness, to realize which direction you're going, and to reel yourself back in.

Understanding Lost Person Behavior

Lost Person Behavior (*LPB*) examines case histories of people who've gone lost and tries to find common denominators. Over the years, LPB has revealed some common mistakes that people make when they're lost. Make sure you don't commit them.

✔ **Speeding up:** In most cases, as soon as people suspect they're lost, they speed up. They don't exactly start running; they just start hiking much, much faster, which usually only gets them lost much, much quicker.

✔ **Disbelieving instruments or maps:** This happens with compasses, GPS units, and most especially maps. Trust your instruments and the map.

✔ **Disrobing and discarding equipment:** Never leave anything behind. Find a way to carry it — you'll invariably end up needing it.

✔ **Lying down:** Sometimes the size of the wilderness simply overcomes people, and they lie down and give up.

✔ **Assuming no one will come looking for you:** Don't assume that no one will come looking for you. Be ready to signal.

✔ **Traveling in the direction of least resistance:** When lost, many people take wrong turns on the trail intentionally because a particular part of the trail simply looks easier to walk on. Think through your trail junctions. Another path-of-least-resistance error is to go down a slope, even though it's not the way back.

If you feel an enormous surge of fear rushing over you, or if you feel your body actually speeding up — such as hiking faster or shaking — immediately recognize that you're thinking in the wrong way, and pull tightly on your own personal leash. Self control may feel unnatural, but it makes you very strong in the field, and ultimately, it saves lives.

Some people around you are going to go into a panic and lose their heads. These reactions, such as shouting and screaming, can be severe and very disturbing. Unfortunately, the Hollywood cliché of someone yelling, "We're all going to die!" is all too real sometimes. Expect it. Be ready for it. Some people are unstable, and they explode in the shrillest of fashions in these situations. Don't let it unnerve you or influence you into doing something stupid.

Irrationality

Frequently, people in survival situations act in completely irrational ways — ways that can astonish you. We're not talking about panic here; we're talking about irrational thinking. People sometimes refuse to cooperate even though their lives depend on it, or they sometimes commit acts that put you and your party in even more danger than you're already in!

As soon as you know you have an unstable or irrational person on your hands, you have to be ready for that person to do *anything*. People can sabotage equipment, foil plans, and commit acts that can kill the whole group. Watch irrational people carefully, and never trust them with anything, even if they seem to get better. You may have to restrain them or at least assign someone to watch them.

Anger and blame

Many times, people in survival situations are overcome by guilt for having gotten themselves into such a mess. If you find yourself feeling this way, don't despair; forgive yourself immediately. If someone else caused it, forgive them. Regret, anger, and blame only distract you and waste precious time and energy.

Misery and fatigue

Misery and fatigue can amplify the feeling of despair to the point where it seems that you can't possibly make it. You can gain strength from self awareness and self inventory. Be honest with yourself: You're hot, you're cold, you're hurt, you're fatigued, you're frankly scared. Then admit that these feelings and conditions warp your judgment and make everything seem hopeless.

Some people wilt very quickly. The desire to keep going dies and the will to live or just to save themselves dries up. This reaction can discourage and demoralize you if you misinterpret it. People decline unevenly, but someone else's decline isn't a sign that you have to decline, too. For some suggestions on slowing this decline, or sometimes even reversing it, see the next section.

Improving Morale

 The more you improve your morale, the stronger you become. The situation is serious, but you can give yourself an emotional boost by doing the following:

- **Get ready for night.** Be prepared to face the night, to have to wait it out. Start thinking about coping with the night before it comes — even if it's 3:00 in the afternoon. When the sun goes down, every problem you have is going to be harder to handle, even if you have flashlights. Solve as many problems as you can before the sun sets.

  Also, know that you *can* function in the dark. You may be on a sharp learning curve, to be sure, but you can overcome night paralysis.

- **Assume a positive attitude.** Sometimes improving your outlook can be as simple as stretching a smile across your face when you don't feel like smiling at all. If you have a series of failures, undertake a minor task that you know you can achieve. Doing so can help you regain your confidence.

- **Warm up.** A fire, a hot cup of water, or just a hat or a coat can clear your head. If you're feeling confused or fatigued and you have the ability, do something to warm your body.

- **Clean up.** Try to keep up your cleanliness in the field. It promotes clear thinking and calms you and your companions. Pull your hair out of your face, wash your face, and take a moment to remove irritants. Inspect your body. Look for wounds and clean them if you can.

- **Adjust your clothing.** If your clothes are chafing you, locate the problem and eliminate it. Some small discomfort can take away your strength overnight.

- **Get something in your stomach.** A hot meal or some hot liquid can sometimes give people a lot of strength. Some people decline very quickly when there's nothing to eat. *Remember:* Deciding to eat or drink has to be a judgment call. If water is scarce, don't eat (see Chapter 7 for why you shouldn't eat if you don't have water). Also, worrying about food when you should be trying to figure out how to get out of your predicament is sometimes a dubious decision.

Chapter 4

Survival Style: Keeping Warm or Cool

*I*n any survival situation, you have to know how to warm up if you're cold and how to cool down if you're hot. At home, you control temperature with air conditioning, central heating, sweaters, flip-flops, or what-have-you. But if you find yourself in desolate snow-covered mountains wearing just jeans and a t-shirt, things are going to go bad, fast. Even if you have plenty of food and water supplies, none of that can help you if you succumb to hypothermia.

In this chapter, we cover the basics of temperature regulation in wilderness survival situations. We tell you how to stay warm or cool with certain kinds of clothes (and how to improvise them) and discuss strategies for staying cool in hot environments. (*Note:* We detail shelters for hot and cold environments in Chapter 6.)

Regulating Body Temperature

The human body, tough as it is, is really comfortable in only a pretty narrow temperature margin. Above 75°F (24°C), most people begin to feel too hot, and below about 50°F (10°C), most people start to feel chilly. Figure 4-1 shows specific effects of air temperature on the body.

°F	R E L A T I V E H U M I D I T Y (%)											
	35	40	45	50	55	60	65	70	75	80	85	90
105	118	123	129	135	141	148	155	163	171	180	190	199
100	107	111	115	119	124	129	135	141	147	154	161	168
95	98	101	104	107	110	114	117	122	126	131	136	141
90	91	92	94	96	98	100	103	106	109	112	115	119
85	83	84	85	86	87	88	89	90	92	94	96	97
80	78	78	79	79	80	81	82	83	84	85	86	87

Heatstroke in 10 minutes

Dehydration and high heat cramp risk

Discomfort particulary if humid, working, or resting

Optimal temperatures for moderate exertion for extended periods outdoors with little or no specialized clothing or techniques. (75, 70, 65, 60, 55, 50, 45)

Above 55°F, note that high humidity makes temperatures feel somewhat warmer, and below, somewhat cooler.

°F												
40	36	34	32	30	29	28	28	27	26	26	25	25
35	31	27	25	24	23	22	21	20	19	19	18	17
30	25	21	19	17	16	15	14	13	12	12	11	10
25	19	15	13	11	9	8	7	6	5	4	4	3
20	13	9	6	4	3	1	0	-1	-2	-3	-3	-4
15	7	3	0	-2	-4	-5	-7	-8	-9	-10	-11	-11
10	1	-4	-7	-9	-11	-12	-14	-15	-16	-17	-18	-19
5	-5	-10	-13	-15	-17	-19	-21	-22	-23	-24	-25	-26
0	-11	-16	-19	-22	-24	-26	-27	-29	-30	-31	-32	-33
-5	-16	-22	-26	-29	-31	-33	-34	-36	-37	-38	-39	-40
-10	-22	-28	-32	-35	-37	-39	-41	-43	-44	-45	-46	-48
-15	-28	-35	-39	-42	-44	-46	-48	-50	-51	-52	-54	-55
-20	-34	-41	-45	-48	-51	-53	-55	-57	-58	-60	-61	-62
-25	-40	-47	-51	-55	-58	-60	-62	-64	-65	-67	-68	-69
-30	-46	-53	-58	-61	-64	-67	-69	-71	-72	-74	-75	-76
-35	-52	-59	-64	-68	-71	-73	-76	-78	-79	-81	-82	-84
-40	-57	-66	-71	-74	-78	-80	-82	-84	-86	-88	-89	-91
-45	-63	-72	-77	-81	-84	-87	-89	-91	-93	-95	-97	-98
	5	10	15	20	25	30	35	40	45	50	55	60
	W I N D				S P E E D			(MPH)				

Comfortable conditions if remaining active (40, 35)

Uncomfortable cold if resting and normally dressed. (30, 25)

Frostbite in 30 minutes (20, 15)

Frostbite in 15 minutes (0, -5)

Frostbite in 10 minutes (-10, -15)

Frostbite in 5 minutes (-30, -35)

Figure 4-1: General effects of heat and cold on the human body.

Humidity can intensify the effects of heat, and wind speed can intensify the effects of cold. Note that in the top half of Figure 4-1, relative humidity increases to the right, showing your perceived temperature at different temperature and humidity combinations. For example, at 85°F, with a relative humidity of 85 percent, you actually feel a temperature of about 96°F. In the lower half of the figure, wind speed increases to the right. At –5°F with a wind of just 20 mph, for example, your skin feels a temperature of –29°F.

Zipless at 40 below

In March 2007, I (Cameron) was trekking alone on Alaska's North Slope to learn about the beautiful world of the tundra in winter. One day, while testing a new clothing system, I felt myself getting colder by the minute. My experimental system wasn't working, and I knew that if I felt cold, my body was screaming at me to do something to warm up.

I should have listened, but I pressed on, thinking, "Oh just do another hour. You've been plenty cold before." This was an almost fatal mistake. Soon my body was conserving heat in emergency mode, calling warm blood in from my extremities to keep my core organs warm (fingers, toes, and nose freeze first). Before I knew it, my hands and feet were profoundly numb.

To warm up, I stopped dragging my sled and instantly tried to put on a heavy parka, one that I'd used to bring me back from the brink many times. I knew that if I just got the zipper up, my core temperature would rise enough that my body would let blood back into my fingers and toes.

When I had the zipper halfway up, though, the little metal pull-tab snapped off in my glove. It was a cheap zipper I'd sewn onto my customized parka. I stopped breathing. With my whole chest uninsulated, I was in real trouble, and my hands were so useless that making some kind of repair was unthinkable. Without my hands, I might not be able to set up my tent and get inside, out of the wind, to get warm. This was no spectacular Hollywood moment, but the situation was potentially lethal.

With near-useless hands, setting up my tent took an hour — it normally took about three minutes. Using my teeth and the heels of my mittens as crude clamps, somehow I managed to get the tent up and crawled into my sleeping bag, and somehow I opened my thermos flask to get some hot liquid into my guts. An hour later, the crisis was over as hot blood flooded back into my fingers and toes. Rewarming felt exactly like when you hit your thumb with a hammer, but it went on for half an hour or so, on every fingertip and toe.

My parka is in my closet now, and on my list of things to do before I go back to Alaska is "replace parka zipper with sturdier."

The body's *internal temperature* is different from the air temperature. Internal temperature is normally about 97–98.6°F (36.1–37°C); if it rises above 104°F (40°C), you suffer the effects of *heat stroke* (a form of hyperthermia), and if it dips below 95°F (35°C), you begin to suffer from hypothermia. We introduce these conditions later in this section, and we discuss how to recognize and deal with them in detail in Chapters 17 and 13, respectively.

The sensations of uncomfortable heat or cold are your body's signal that something's wrong! Don't try to just headbang your way though uncomfortable temperatures. If you feel uncomfortably cold or hot, use the techniques we describe in this chapter to regulate your temperature.

The cold continuum: What happens as your body cools

When the body cools below the optimal temperature of 97–98.6°F (36.1–37°C), you begin to feel the effects of hypothermia. *Hypothermia* is a debilitating reduction of body temperature (you can identify hypothermia by the symptoms we outline in Chapter 13). Unless you do something to stop cooling, you can easily slip into a lethal hypothermic coma. It's that serious. Table 4-1 shows you what can happen when your body cools.

Table 4-1	What Happens as Your Body Cools	
Stage	**Body Temperature Range**	**Symptoms**
Mild hypothermia	95–98.6°F (35–37°C)	Shivering, clumsiness
Moderate hypothermia	90–95°F (30–32.2°C)	Loss of shivering; loss of muscular coordination, leading to clumsiness
Severe hypothermia	85–90°F (29.4–32.2°C)	Confusion, loss of vision, apathy
Profound hypothermia	Below 85°F (29.4°C)	Dilated pupils, coma, death

Luckily, you can do plenty of things to stay warm, and we cover them in most of the rest of this chapter.

People have survived many situations that tables and charts, or doctors themselves, would call "clearly unsurvivable." Never give up; however cold you or your companions are, don't write anyone off. Keep at it. Keep trying.

The heat continuum: What happens as your body heats

When the body overheats, the effects can be as lethal as when it cools beyond a certain point. *Hyperthermia* occurs when your body suffers from overheating. You can identify hyperthermia by the symptoms we detail in Chapter 17.

Table 4-2 shows you what can happen when your body heats. Body temperature begins to be dangerous around 104°F (40°C), and by 106°F (41.1°C), brain damage can occur. Around 120°F (48.9°C), your body goes rigid, and soon thereafter you die. But you can do plenty to prevent this scenario.

Table 4-2	What Happens as Your Body Heats	
Stage	*Body Temperature Range*	*Symptoms*
Moderate hyperthermia	104–106°F (40–41.1°C)	Nausea, vomiting, dizziness
Severe hyperthermia	106–113°F (41.1–45°C)	Brain damage
Profound hyperthermia	Above 120°F (48.9°C)	Muscle rigidity, coma, death

Relying on Layering for Warmth

All clothing that keeps you warm works on the same principle; it traps a layer of warm air, normally warmed by your own body, between you and the elements. Layering involves using several garments to trap layers of air (such as wearing three thin sweaters instead of just one thick one), and it's an important basic principle of cold-weather clothing. This section explains the importance of layering to keep you warm and suggests how to layer your own clothing.

Avoiding a cold sweat

You should wear several layers of clothing that you can add to or take off, depending on your activity level. When you start to sweat, you can take off a layer or two.

Sweat is your number-one enemy in cold-weather situations for a few important reasons:

- Sweat deprives you of bodily fluids, leading to dehydration. Dehydration worsens hypothermia.

- As sweat evaporates, it cools your body and brings on the onset of hypothermia much faster than if you were dry.

- Sweat can soak your insulating layers, making them stick together so that they no longer effectively trap a layer of warm air, ruining their insulation properties.

Although a single, heavy layer — such as a parka — definitely keeps you warm, it also makes you sweat, even if you're just moving around camp or chopping wood. But with layers, you can add to them or strip them off according to your circumstances.

If you're breaking up firewood, plowing your way through knee-deep snow, or doing other similar heavy work, strip off a layer or two to prevent sweat from soaking your insulating layers. On the other hand, when you're doing less strenuous work — such as butchering an animal, setting traps, fishing, or washing plant foods — you're best off wearing more layers.

Because keeping warm mainly relies on trapping a layer of warm air next to your body, you should always try to keep your clothes dry in a survival situation. If it's raining, you're going to have to wait before really drying your clothes (unless you're lucky enough to have access to a cave or can use a tarp to protect your fire from the rain). If you're caught in a downpour, use whatever you can (such as the space blanket or a plastic bag from your survival kit) as shelter from the rain and make a fire as soon as it stops raining. If you can't make a fire, you can at least wring out your clothes and hang them in direct sunlight.

Choosing your layers

The good news is that layering clothing is straightforward.
A good layering system for temperatures around freezing
includes the following:

- ✔ **Base layer:** The base layer should be something like long
  johns. Avoid cotton, because of all the outdoor clothing
  you can use in cold-weather environments, cotton has
  the least capacity to trap warm air and keep you warm,
  particularly when it gets wet.

- ✔ **Thermal layer:** Wear wool, pile, or *fleece,* a wool-like
  synthetic material that retains its insulation properties
  even when wet.

- ✔ **Shell layer:** Wear a shell layer to protect you and your
  insulation layers from wind and moisture. Ideally, the
  layer is *breathable,* meaning that it lets sweat vapor out
  but doesn't let water droplets in — that's the main
  characteristic of waterproof/breathable shell layers,
  such as those made of Gore-Tex or its equivalents.

Ideally, your jacket or shell layer should have zippers
along the underside of the arms and along the outside
of the legs. Zipping these openings up or down controls
the flow of air into your clothes, allowing you to remain
properly ventilated so you sweat less.

When you begin to feel too warm, start by taking off the shell
layer, and then, if needed, remove the second (thermal) layer,
still leaving you with the base layer. In many cases, such as
hiking or doing other similar heavy work, you can work with
the shell layer over the base layer, preventing overheating.
When you stop moving, though, you may put a sweater
(thermal layer) on over the base layer and then put the shell
back on as well to give you three layers.

Of course, in wilderness survival situations, you don't always
have the luxury of wearing a perfect three-layer insulation
system. Here's where you have to be creative. If you're
scavenging supplies from some kind of wreck (such as from
a boat, car, or plane), keep your eyes out for any textile not
made from cotton. If cotton is all you have, so be it; but don't
forget, you do much better with something else (just about
anything) if you're trying to keep warm.

Improvising Cold-Weather Clothing

If you don't have access to nice, dry, cold-weather clothing, you have to improvise. You just need to know a few basic skills and apply them with some creativity to improvise with cold-weather clothing.

For improvising cold-weather clothing, the best guides are the native people of the polar regions, who've adapted to various wildernesses for thousands of years. Their invaluable expertise can help you when you find yourself trapped in a place you've seen only on TV. In this section, we describe how to stay warm outdoors, using a lot of advice based on native methods. Figure 4-2 shows the native dress of Arctic Canada and a hypothetical cold-weather wilderness survivor. Note the following items of clothing:

- ✔ A hide jacket trapping a layer of air against the skin (Figure 4-2a)

- ✔ Fur used to block wind from the face (Figure 4-2b)

- ✔ Heavy mittens (Figure 4-2c)

- ✔ High boots for deep snow (Figure 4-2d)

- ✔ Cloth used to wrap the head and neck (Figure 4-2e)

- ✔ Improvised snow goggles (Figure 4-2f)

- ✔ A heavy jacket trapping a layer of warm air next to the body (Figure 4-2g)

- ✔ Mittens improvised from heavy socks (Figure 4-2h)

- ✔ Improvised gaiters/boot covers (Figure 4-2i)

- ✔ Fabric sewn to a coat to provide a sitting surface (Figure 4-2j)

- ✔ Improvised snow shoes (Figure 4-2k)

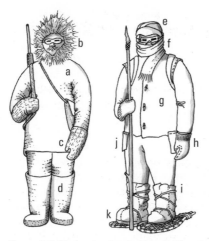

Figure 4-2: Native Arctic clothing (left) and a cold-weather survivor in improvised clothing (right).

See Chapter 16 for info on how to make all the improvised clothing: goggles, mittens, gaiters, and snowshoes. The techniques we describe in this section do require a few basic tools. You can't do much without a knife and some kind of needle and thread (you should have these supplies in your survival kit, which we describe in detail in Chapter 2). You can improvise cutting tools and even needle and thread, but everything is easier if you just always have your survival kit on hand.

Extreme sewing: Using needle and thread to save your life

Improvising clothing requires you to join together pieces of fabric or other flexible material. The best way to do so is with needle and thread. Knowing how to use both is a great outdoor skill that can keep you alive. If you don't have a needle in your supply kit, you can improvise one from a piece of plastic, a splinter of bone or antler, or any one of many other materials (to see how, head to Chapter 14).

After you have a needle, you can improvise cordage (thread) from any number of materials; shoelaces or laces pulled from a hood, wiring ripped from the wreckage of a machine, and dental floss are all acceptable, though they make different sizes of holes in the fabric you're sewing. Natural cordage for sewing includes *sinew* (the tough, stringy tissues stripped from animal joints) and tough vegetable fibers.

To thread your needle, slip the cordage you're using through the eye and pull through a good measure; put a knot in the thread at the beginning of where you'll make your seam to prevent the thread from pulling through the fabric (refer to Figure 4-3a). Join the two fabrics (Figure 4-3b) and end the seam with a final knot to prevent the seam from coming apart.

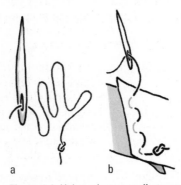

a   b

Figure 4-3: Using a bone needle to sew a flat seam.

Using plastic, cardboard, and other materials for warmth

If you need to improvise and make your own cold-weather clothing, you can look to different materials, such as plastic, cardboard, and so on. These materials are durable and can make weatherproof layers for keeping warm. When you're considering improvising cold-weather clothing, keep in mind the layering principles we outline in the section "Relying on Layering for Warmth," earlier in this chapter.

If you find yourself in a cold setting and need to improvise with materials around you, look at the following items:

✔ **Car seat covers:** They're often made of a flexible plastic, and you can easily cut them away and sew them into an improvised shell layer to protect you from wind, rain, and snow. Use the padding inside these seats as insulation (the thermal layer) by stuffing it inside your outer layer.

✔ **Plastic sheet, tarp, or garbage bag:** You can easily convert one of these plastic items into a poncho simply by cutting a foot-wide slit along a fold, near the center, for your head to pass through.

✔ **Cardboard:** You can sew cardboard together to make large sheets for use as a poncho, though it breaks down in rain after a while.

✔ **Extra sleeping bag:** You can modify a sleeping bag into a heavy insulation layer, but only do this if you have a spare. A sleeping bag is more useful in keeping you alive overnight, when the temperature really plummets; during the day, you can stay active to keep warm.

✔ **Duct tape:** Duct tape is one of the wonders of modern civilization, and it's useful in a hundred wilderness survival scenarios. You can use it to patch holes in your clothing, tape over a cloth hat to make it waterproof, and even tape over sneakers to help keep out rain. Keep some in your survival kit. You can wrap a few yards of it around a cigarette lighter for easy access later.

✔ **Dry grass, leaves, moss:** You can stuff dry grass, leaves, and moss into your clothes, or better, between your layers to make that all important space of dead air that insulates you.

✔ **Newspapers or magazines:** You can crumple up pages of newspapers or magazines and stuff them inside your outer layer. The crumpling helps trap a layer of air inside the paper, which acts as a very good insulator inside your clothing. Whenever you drive into extreme cold or snowstorms, you can keep an ample supply of newspapers or magazines in the trunk of your vehicle.

Putting together animal skins

If your survival situation has you trapping small animals, such as squirrels, you can use their skins to help you keep warm (Chapter 8 explains trapping). You need multiple skins to sew together to create a garment, though a hat may take just a few.

You need to process and preserve the skin before you use it. To preserve an animal skin so you can use it to create a piece of clothing, follow these steps:

1. **Scrape off the loose, fatty tissues from the inside (the non-fur side) of the skin.**

   If you don't, these tissues will rot and degrade the hide. You can de-fat the skin of any mammal with any sharp instrument, such as a knife blade or a broad scrap of plastic. Soaking a hide in water for a day can make de-fatting easier, as can using wooden pegs to stretch the hide flat on the ground.

   Hold the scraper blade across the skin and scrape (don't slice) off the fatty tissues by drawing the scraper toward you; the motion is like shaving your cheek or leg with a razor. This is a messy job, and the fat adheres to the blade; clean it off every few strokes.

2. **When you have enough animal skins prepared, let them dry out; then begin to sew them together.**

   Just let one overlap the other a bit and start sewing to join the overlapping margins. Soon you'll have a towel-sized skin that you can use as a hat or a light cloak. Be creative and make whatever garment you need.

   If you wear the fur on the inside of the garment (next to your skin), you get a warmer garment because the fur next to your body traps a layer of air.

Processed skins stiffen over time. Keep them pliable by bending and wringing them with your hands every day.

Process and store your animal skins away from camp when you're not wearing them, because their odors may attract bears or mountain lions.

Having the right headwear, handwear, and footwear

When you're in a cold setting and not wearing clothing that adequately keeps you warm, you at least want to keep your head, hands, and feet warm. Keeping these body parts warm is particularly important, because

✔ So much heat is lost from the head.

✔ If your feet freeze, you can't travel.

✔ If your hands freeze, you can't even make a fire or set up a camp.

Also take care to keep your wrists and neck insulated; in both places, the skin is particularly thin, and you can lose heat from these regions very quickly. You can use duct tape (or any kind of tape) to tighten your cuffs if they don't already have Velcro tabs for adjustment.

Keep the following in mind about these important body parts:

✔ **Your head:** The first thing to do when you feel cold is get a hat on. The scalp contains so little fat that you lose a great deal of heat though the head. Slowing or stopping that heat loss can keep your whole body warm.

✔ **Your hands:** Mittens are usually warmer than gloves, and they're easy to improvise from a pair of socks. Mittens trap a larger layer of air around your hands than gloves do because gloves wrap only around individual fingers.

✔ **Your feet:** To keep your feet warm, you can take several steps:

- **Loosen the laces on your boots or shoes.** Don't loosen so much that they fall off, but make them loose enough that your blood (which warms your skin) can circulate.

- **Add layers to the inside of your footwear.** This can be as easy as slipping on another layer of socks, being sure to keep your laces somewhat loose. If you don't have the luxury of extra socks, improvise them by making a simple tube of cloth sewn down the side and across the toe-end. This doesn't have to be particularly comfortable; it just has to help trap warm air inside your shoe or boot.

- **Insulate the outside of your footwear.** The padding from seat cushions can be useful as insulation that you layer on the outside of your footwear. Cut the padding into slabs and sew them together, paying particular attention to the toe area. You can also make snowshoes from cordage and flexible, green branches.

Using Other Ways to Keep Warm

In addition to wearing layers of dry, air-trapping clothing, you can keep warm by staying active, covering yourself with blankets or other insulation, and using fire. We cover fire later in this chapter and discuss shelters in Chapter 6. For now, here are some good ways to keep warm.

Staying active

One way to stay warm is to keep moving, which generates body heat. On really cold mornings, you may want to do some jumping jacks, run in place, or windmill your arms (which drives blood back into your fingertips).

However, being active does have its drawbacks. When you're active, you sweat, which can soak your clothes — and then they can freeze solid. (Check out the earlier section "Avoiding a cold sweat" for more on the dangers of sweating.)

During a hard day in the Arctic winter, we constantly adjust our clothing systems to prevent them from being sweated up and freezing solid. If you're going to do some vigorous exercise, remember to strip off a layer before you start, but put it back on soon after you stop moving. The other problem with staying active is that it burns calories. If your food supply is an issue, weigh the pros and cons of having to consume more food to stay active. In the extreme cold, recovering from hypothermia is very difficult, so err on the side of eating more rather than less.

Staying warm when you're staying still

A cold night can turn into an eternal agony; it seems that the sun will never come up. But remember, it will. To help you keep warm, you can try the following options:

✔ **Insulation from cold surfaces:** Never sit or lie directly on the ground. Always use some kind of padding to insulate you from cold surfaces; for example, you can gather pine boughs to make a soft, thick insulating pad that you can sleep on.

✔ **Hot rocks:** If you've had a fire, you can pull warm rocks from near the fire to slip inside your clothes. Be careful that they're not hot enough to burn you, though.

✔ **Huddling with your companions:** If you have companions, huddling with them allows you to conserve the group's body heat by having it all under one cover. Use any type of cover you have as a blanket to stay warm (you should definitely have at least one space blanket in your survival kit; see Chapter 2).

✔ **Candles:** If you have a candle, hunch over it to keep your hands warm and to allow you to inhale warm, dry air.

Cool Threads: Clothing for Staying Cool

We think the best guides to surviving in a hot wilderness are the native people of such areas, and in this case, we look to the nomadic Bedouin folk originally of the Arabian Peninsula. Figure 4-4 shows a Bedouin in native dress, and shows a desert wilderness survivor in improvised clothing. Note the following items of clothing:

✔ A long cloth used to completely protect the head and neck from the sun (Figure 4-4a)

✔ Long, flowing, robe-like clothes that let air circulate next to the skin but shield the skin from direct sun (Figure 4-4b)

✔ Lack of shoes (Figure 4-4c)

Going barefoot is an aboriginal custom you shouldn't emulate. Bedouin folk go shoeless from childhood, and their feet are very tough. Your feet aren't accustomed to going barefoot, so make sure you wear shoes.

✔ Survivor's t-shirt head-garment that completely protects the neck and head (also note use of sunglasses and face mask) (Figure 4-4d)

✔ An untucked shirt to let air circulate (Figure 4-4e)

  ✔ Hand-protecting flaps of cloth sewn to cuffs (Figure 4-4f)

  ✔ Improvised sandals (Figure 4-4g)

Figure 4-4: Shows a Bedouin in native dress(left) and a desert wilderness survivor in improvised clothing (right).

One of the principles of dry hot-weather clothing is shielding from the sun. Although on vacation you may want to get a tan by wearing a t-shirt and shorts outdoors, doing this day after day, all day, can be fatal in a wilderness situation. Instead, you need to wear loose, flowing robe-like clothing as well as a substantial head covering to protect yourself from the sun.

This section takes a closer look at the specific types of clothing you can wear and names a couple of important principles to remember about clothing in a hot setting.

Wearing a hat and eye protection

Exposed to direct sunlight for too long, your scalp absorbs too much heat, leading to hyperthermia. Simply wearing a hat can greatly improve your chances of survival. Try to wear a loose-fitting hat with a wide brim that shields the entire head.

A hat also cuts down glare, which you can also reduce with soot under your eyes or with sunglasses. If you don't have sunglasses, you can improvise them from a strip of stiff cloth, a piece of bark, or plastic. You can protect your face from the sun simply by hanging a handkerchief below the eyes: Pin or sew it to your headgear. Check out Chapter 17 for ways you can improvise your own eye protection and headgear to keep cool.

Considering other clothing concepts to keep cool

As you try to come up with clothing in a hot setting, keep the following pointers in mind. These concepts can help keep you cool:

- ✔ **Select light colors.** If you have the luxury of choosing what color material to wear in the direct sun, wear white or other light colors; they reflect the sun instead of absorbing its rays as darker colors do.

- ✔ **Wear loose-fitting clothing.** Hot-weather clothing should be loose and flowing rather than tight. Loose clothing allows a little ventilation to keep your skin cool, but tight clothing makes you sweat, leading to dehydration. Note the Bedouin's loose, flowing robes in Figure 4-4.

- ✔ **Be prepared to add or subtract layers.** As in cold environments, adjust your clothing according to the conditions. At night, be prepared to bundle up, because hot areas can get very cold, particularly on cloudless nights when there's no cloud layer to trap the Earth's warmth.

- ✔ **Cover your skin.** Improvise a robe-like garment from a blanket or sheet to protect you from the sun.

- ✔ **Use ventilation.** Keep ventilated by unbuttoning your cuffs and shirt neck. Wear your trousers loose, or better yet, roll them up to your knees and wear your improvised robe over them.

- ✔ **Drape yourself with damp cloth.** Wet skin cools much faster than dry skin, and if you have the luxury of excess water, you can keep cool by draping damp fabric over your body while resting in shade. As the water evaporates, it carries excess heat away from the skin.

A Cool Proposition: Working at Night, Resting During the Day

If it's really hot and you're trying to walk your way out of the survival situation, you would do best to travel at night, when it's cooler (deserts may be very cold indeed, but it's easier to keep warm by moving than to keep cool when it's very hot). Sleep in the day, under shelter if you can, and travel and/or do your work of finding water, food, and keeping your temperature regulated at night. We tell you how to work and travel at night in Chapter 17.

Chapter 5

Making Fire in the Wilderness

*Y*ou don't just start a fire — you build one! With that in mind, remember that most people have trouble getting their fires started in the wilderness because they hurry the building process and use a haphazard selection of starter materials. So try to think of your fire as being like a well-designed structure — if you build it right, you'll be rewarded.

In this chapter, we show you how you go about constructing a fire. We also show you some interesting alternatives to matches and lighters, as well as some advice for the toughest task of all: starting a fire in the rain.

Making a Fire

If you find yourself in a wilderness survival situation, being able to build a fire to stay warm may be question of life or death. Always keep in mind that every fire needs three things: heat to ignite it, oxygen to breathe, and fuel to burn.

This section explains what you need to do to get a fire going, including different fire-building options, depending on your situation. The most important thing to keep in mind is that getting the fire going — from igniting it until it becomes self-sustaining — is a critical time for you in a survival situation.

Looking at fire-building materials

To get a fire going, you need the right materials. All wilderness fires require three distinctly different kinds:

- ✔ **Tinder:** This is the first material to be ignited, so it must be the most flammable. Make sure you have plenty of it before you strike your first match. Good tinder includes straw, grass, scraped fibers or husks from trees or dried fruit, lint from your clothing, dry shavings from a stick, dry pine needles or leaves, a ball of dry toilet paper or newspaper (although when paper is damp, it's worse than useless), and even sap from pine trees, which burns hot and bright. Be sure to collect tinder if you see it when traveling.

- ✔ **Kindling:** Kindling is the first real fuel to burn, and it's composed of thin twigs (pencil-thick at most) and/or splinters of wood split with an ax or knife.

- ✔ **Fuel:** This is the main fuel for the fire, usually composed of wrist-thick or larger branches and even logs if you're really lucky. You can also burn dried animal dung, as well as natural tar or oil that seeps from the ground.

Whatever kinds of tinder, kindling, and fuel you use, you light the tinder first, which ignites the kindling, which ignites the fuel. Figure 5-1 shows the process, which we discuss in more detail in this section — after looking at how to light a fire in the first place.

Understanding fire-making basics

Before you start trying to create flames or sparks, arrange your tinder and fuel and have it ready to go. One of the main reasons many people have such a hard time is poor selection of starter fuels. The following tips can help you build a good fire:

- ✔ **Watch out for Mother Nature.** Make sure your fire-building site is protected from heavy winds and rain that can extinguish it or make starting it difficult.

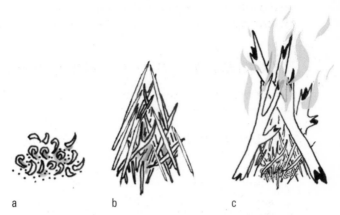

a   b   c

Figure 5-1: Essentials to making a teepee fire: Tinder (a), a teepee of kindling (b), and fuel added to the teepee (c).

✔ **Take time to build your fire.** Don't be impatient. Generally speaking, the easiest type of fire to ignite is the teepee (check out the next section). Take your time making a beautiful teepee. Carefully construct your fire to take full advantage of the fact that fire always burns upward: Put the lightest, driest tinder at the very bottom — wispy-fine fibers are the best — and then build your way up with kindling (twigs) that gradually gets thicker.

✔ **Use the driest wood you can find.** Wood is dry when it snaps cleanly in your hands. You should actually hear a very dry *snap!* when you break it. This type of wood ignites quickly and burns well. *Green wood,* which is wood that still has a little moisture in it, is hard to ignite. If you have to work a stick or twig in your hands to get it to break — or if it holds together by a fiber when you bend it — then it isn't dry enough.

✔ **Use the thinnest possible kindling.** Twigs less than ⅛ inch (3 millimeters) in thickness (thinner than your shoelaces) make the best kindling. When you build a teepee fire, make sure you have very dry tinder at the bottom and then a nice structure of these dry twigs above it.

Have an extra pile of very dry kindling next to you to feed the flame as it arises, because a fire is very precarious when it first starts. You want to make sure you can feed it at just the right speed to really get it going.

✔ **Ignite your fire at the lowest spot you can.** Fire always burns upward, so the lower you ignite it, the better.

✔ **Blow gently on your fire or fan it.** Fire needs oxygen, and the best way to convert a tiny flame into a large one is to give it some air. This is one of the arts of fire making. Put your lips as close to your burgeoning fire as you safely can and blow gently. Doing so can get the fire going more than practically anything else.

Be careful not to blow too hard, because doing so can actually prevent the fire from growing or put it out. A long, gentle stream of air is best.

✔ **Feed your fire.** As soon as your fire ignites, feed the flame quickly and steadily, but don't overdo it; you can smother a burgeoning fire very easily. Keep in mind that fires ignite and burn unevenly. Flames may crop up in places you don't expect. A few twigs, placed well over a burgeoning flame, can get you going.

Considering your basic fire structure options

Different fire structures are useful for different purposes. Knowing the following types of fires can help you conserve your fuel, keep you warm at night, ensure that you have embers ready to relight the fire in the morning, dry out wet fuel, and signal for help. Here are some structures to choose from:

✔ **Teepee fire:** The teepee fire (see Figure 5-2a) is good for a crisis because it starts almost every time.

✔ **Star fire:** When the fuel is really large and hard to break up (as with large logs), push it into a star or cross fire (Figure 5-2b) so that just the tip is burning at any given moment. You can extinguish this fire easily, because all you have to do is pull the star apart by the cold ends of the logs.

✔ **Pyramid fire:** A pyramid fire (Figure 5-2c) built with plenty of fuel collapses in on itself overnight, providing a good pile of embers to use to relight the fire in the morning.

a   b   c

Figure 5-2: The different types of fires.

Whatever fire you make, pile up some dirt, rocks, or vegetation around it, like a screen, just before going to sleep to help reflect the heat into your shelter area on a cold night.

You should have a signal fire structure on standby at all times. For more on signal fires, see Chapter 12.

Striking matches correctly

Lighting a match seems straightforward — until your life depends on it. Then you take your time to think through just what you're going to do. Particularly if you have a limited number of matches, you don't have much room for error.

To strike a wooden match, follow these steps:

1. **Turn your back to the wind, crouch near the tinder pile, and cradle the box securely in one hand, cupping it against any breeze.**

2. **Hold the match in the other hand and stab down deliberately across the striker patch.**

3. **After the match is lit, give it a second (or three) to fully ignite the first quarter of the wood.**

4. **Carefully move the lit match toward the tinder (unless you've struck the match right next to the tinder, which is preferable if there's a breeze or it's drizzling).**

Starting a fire with a dead lighter

Even after your lighter has run out of fuel, you can still get fire from it. The trick is to force the lighter's spark into the very best tinder you find: Lint pulled from cotton socks or some other cotton garment is ideal. Here's how to do it:

1. **Pull off enough lint to make a wad about half the size of golf ball.**

   Make sure the lint is pulled apart as much as possible. Don't compress the lint or roll it into a ball. When you're finished, you should be able to see through the lint. This process is time consuming — it may take you as long as an hour — but it really works.

2. **Roll a tissue or a small length of toilet paper into a cone.**

   You can use any type of paper for this, but tissue is the best. When you have a cone, mount the lint ball just inside the very end of it — think of the shape of a snow cone. This paper apparatus is your fire-starter.

3. **Take a lighter and flick it into the wad of lint at the end of your paper cone.**

The sparks should fly into the wad and ignite it.

4. **If the lint hasn't ignited after a dozen or so attempts, take the metal housing off the lighter and try again.**

If you have a pocket knife or some other straight edge, you can pry the housing off pretty easily. You may have to use your fingernail. Make sure you don't accidentally dislocate the steel wheel or the flint. The wheel and flint shouldn't be attached to the housing in any way, so they shouldn't move when you're taking the housing off. If they move during the process, stop what you're doing and reexamine. After the housing comes off, the lint should ignite on the first few tries.

The lint ignites very quickly, so you need to have everything perfectly prepared beforehand. Have your kindling expertly prepared so it catches properly.

Making fire in wet conditions

When things get wet, making fire is more difficult, but if you're persistent, you may be able to get a fire going. First and foremost, look for dry tinder, kindling, and fuel in the following places:

- ✔ Under rock shelters and in caves
- ✔ Under or inside downed trees or logs (found lying on the ground)
- ✔ Under heavy snow pack (if temperatures are just under freezing, everything above the snow may be dripping with melt water, but deep under the cold snowpack may be colder, dry wood)
- ✔ In animal burrows, such as squirrel or marmot dens

Sometimes you can take sticks that are slightly wet and whittle away the soaked parts to produce somewhat dry kindling.

Also search your clothes and possessions, especially the inside of your wallet, for dry tinder. Sometimes papers or even paper money deep inside a wallet or pocketbook remain dry even though everything else around you is soaked. If you aren't completely soaked through, you can try making a tinder pile using lint from your underclothes. Lint ignites almost every time. The problem is having enough. Making a lint ball large enough to start kindling can take as much as an hour.

In wet conditions, try to build your fire on top of something and under some kind of shelter. Before building the fire, look for a base — a board or a piece of metal is good, and cloth or plastic cloth can work in pinch. Or you can try building on rock; almost anything is preferable to the wet earth. Use anything you can for shelter, as long as it keeps the drops off your fire for a moment.

In wet conditions, consider trying to start your fire without the use of tinder. Many times, when it's wet, tinder is harder to ignite than kindling — especially leaves or paper. If that's the case, make a small teepee of twigs and try lighting the thin stems directly. The kindling must be exceedingly thin, though — the thinnest twigs you can find. A dense teepee made of wire-thin twigs can sometimes ignite when a tinder-fire won't.

Trying Other Ways to Start Fire

You can start fire with many methods. In this section, we show you some of the best techniques you can use if you don't have matches or a lighter.

Starting a fire with common, everyday items

You may be surprised at the wide array of everyday items that you can use to start a fire. Be sure to practice these at home before you go outdoors:

- ✔ **Magnesium bar:** A magnesium bar (also known as a *metal match*) is a block of magnesium inlaid with a strip of flint. This handy item can help you start a fire even when wet! For more on these, see Chapter 2.

- ✔ **Magnifying glass or similar lens**: You can use a magnifying glass to focus the sun's rays onto tinder and ignite it. Doing so is easy, and it takes only seconds to figure out. If you don't have a magnifying glass, you may be able to carefully remove lenses from binoculars or a rifle scope. Check out Figure 5-3.

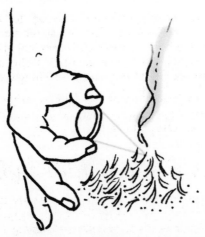

Figure 5-3: Starting a fire with a magnifying lens.

✔ **Stone and steel:** Steel produces a spark if struck against some kinds of stone (including flint and chert). Check the local creek bed for a variety of stones, and then try striking your knife against them. Anytime you're trying to ignite a fire with the use of a spark from metal and stone, try to use the lightest tinder you can find. Lint pulled from clothing is ideal.

✔ **Batteries and steel wool:** Many alkaline batteries (including car batteries and the common 9-volt rectangular batteries used in transistor radios) have enough charge to start a bit of steel wool on fire. Make sure the steel wool is fine. If you're using common soap pads, you have to pull them apart until they're wispy-thin.

Anytime you can connect the two poles of a battery with the steel wool, you have a chance of getting ignition. Here's how:

- **9-volt:** The best thing to do is wrap your steel wool in tinder or toilet paper and rub the 9-volt battery's poles in the wool.

- **Other batteries:** When using any other type of battery, you must pull the steel wool apart and form a cord that can reach both poles.

The steel wool ignites almost immediately, so have your tinder ready.

✔ **Batteries and wire:** If you're lucky enough to have machinery nearby, such as a car or tractor, you can make a spark by attaching a wire to each terminal of a battery and then touching the tips of the wires. Doing so produces a serious spark that you can use to ignite tender.

Be careful not to shock yourself if you're using a car battery. Insulate yourself from the steel wool or wire by holding it with thick, dry cloth.

Igniting a fire, primitive style

Humans have made fire for hundreds of thousands of years, if not a million or more. Still, many aboriginal people prefer to keep a fire going after it's lit rather than building a new one every night. You can discover a lot from them that can help you survive outdoors. This section explains the two easiest kinds of primitive fires most useful in wilderness survival situations.

When making a bow fire or any type of friction fire, you're not trying to get a flame; you're trying to get a coal. After you have a coal, you need to take it and wrap it carefully in the lightest, driest tinder you can find and then blow on it steadily until the tinder catches. It may take multiple tries to get a live coal into your tinder.

Plow fire

A *plow fire* is about as simple as it gets. To start a fire, you carve a *channel,* which is just a long notch, and then run a stick up and down the channel as though you're plowing. Embers then begin to form and embers trickle down the channel, igniting the tinder. See Figure 5-4.

Figure 5-4: Building a fire with a plow fire.

Bow fire

A *bow fire* uses a curved piece of wood, strung with a cord of some kind, to spin a spindle that creates friction. This makes a coal that you can use to light tinder.

The most important part of making a bow fire is selecting good pieces of wood and cordage and then manufacturing good components. To make a bow fire, follow these steps (see Figure 5-5):

1. Use strong, green wood for your bow.

2. Choose the straightest, most symmetrical length of wood you can find for your spindle.

The spindle needs to spin very quickly, so it must be a perfect stick or one carved that way. Even small imperfections can slow the spinning process. An ideal spindle is around 8 to 9 inches (20 to 23 centimeters) long and a little thicker than a quarter. Both ends should be carved to a shallow taper (picture a used crayon — not blunt, but close) to allow for maximum spinning speed and friction.

3. String the bow with shoelaces.

When stringing the bow, the string should be just taut enough to grip the spindle.

4. Carve a shallow notch into the handhold.

The *handhold* is the small piece of wood you use to apply downward force on the spindle. The deeper the notch in the handhold, the more friction you have in the handhold, so you want it as shallow as possible.

You can use leaves or pine needles inside the handhold to dampen the friction. Don't use water or oil because liquids only make the wood swell.

5. Carve a circular notch in a baseboard.

The *baseboard* is a heavy piece of wood split in half.

6. Start spinning your spindle slowly, using your bow, and make sure you have a good groove going.

At this stage, you're just trying to make sure you have a good connection between the spindle and the notch in the baseboard. Try to keep the spindle perpendicular to the line, because that cuts down on the problem of having the spindle slip out of the string (which is the most frustrating part, we know).

7. After you have the connection you want, cut a V from the baseboard's edge to the circular notch.

Put your tinder directly below the V notch in the baseboard. This allows the coal that you make to fall onto the tinder under the baseboard.

8. Speed up your drilling only after you start to see white smoke smoldering from the baseboard.

Embers build in the notch of the base block; they're the beginnings of your fire.

This method is probably the most practical way to make a primitive friction fire. Practice making this type of fire at home before trying it in the wilderness — it can help a great deal.

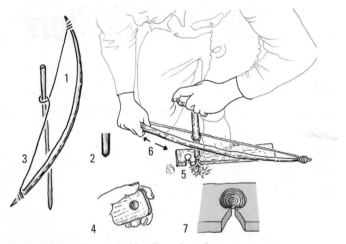

Figure 5-5: Building a primitive fire using a bow.

Extinguishing a Fire

Before you leave camp, you must extinguish all fires. No exceptions. A forest fire can start in less than a minute. You know when a fire is extinguished when you can place naked hands on the dead coals.

To extinguish a fire, use water. If you don't have liquid or are preserving your water supply, bury the fire with dirt built up to at least 1 foot in thickness. Don't use grass or moss, regardless of how wet it is. Then place heavy stones on top of the dirt to make it more difficult for animals to dig up the dirt (animals can smell anything aromatic that has fallen into the fire, such as fat, oil, or food, from a great distance).

Chapter 6

Home, Sweet Hut: Survival Shelters

*W*hen you're in a wilderness setting, getting in from the elements can be a lifesaver. A shelter can keep you warm in cold environments, cool in hot conditions, and dry when it's raining. Sometimes you can take shelter in natural formations, such as caves, but many times you need to build your own haven. That's okay, though, because most survival shelters are easy to make.

In this chapter, we show you the simplest and most effective shelters you can find and make. In Part III, we cover shelters for specific conditions (snowdrift shelters, for example, or desert sunshades and jungle hammocks). For the moment, we look at the simplest ways to take shelter outdoors.

Grasping the Importance of Shelter

Shelter is important in survival situations for physical and psychological reasons. Physically, the human body is pretty frail. A few hours in the sun can burn you severely, and a cold night can incapacitate you. A good shelter

✔ Gets you out of the direct sun, which can prevent sunburn and stave off hyperthermia (such as heat stroke)

✔ Can be warmed, preventing hypothermia and frostbite

✔ Protects you from rain, keeping you warm

✔ Includes an insulating bed that keeps your body heat from being sucked into the cold earth

As for the psychological reasons, everything seems so much better when you can get in from the rain, wind, or storm. If you're fully exposed, heavy weather wears you down, but from inside a shelter, the world and your chances look a lot better.

Taking the time to plan a camp and build a good shelter are proactive steps that remind you that you're working toward survival, not just reacting to things that happen to you. We cover the full importance of the psychology of survival in Chapter 3.

To make a shelter in the wilderness, you can try to make do with natural shelters or build your own. Whenever you're in a survival situation, keep a constant lookout for good natural shelters. If you're pretty sure you're going to be stranded outdoors overnight, finding or making shelter is a top priority. The upcoming sections look at the main natural-shelter alternatives.

Before Making Camp: What to Do

Whether you're going to use a natural shelter or build your own, you need to consider a few things before starting to make camp. In this section, we outline some important ideas to consider when using any outdoor shelter.

Understanding priorities

When it becomes clear that you're going to spend the night out, you should prioritize your actions in getting shelter in the following way:

1. **Decide where you want to locate your shelter.**

   See the next section for why the location is important.

2. **Gather some tinder, kindling, and firewood and put them near where you intend to build your shelter.**

   You don't want to search for these supplies at night. If you can, cover them to keep them dry (even if it isn't raining now, it could be in ten minutes!). See Chapter 5 for more on fire-making.

3. **Build (or find) your shelter.**

   Whatever shelter you use, you should never rest or sleep directly on the ground, because it's always colder than body temperature and it sucks heat from your body. Insulate yourself from the ground with a layer of vegetation, such as pine boughs, or use extra clothing.

4. **Clearly mark your location so you can be seen from the air.**

   Use the methods we describe in Chapter 12.

5. **Settle in for the night.**

   Quality sleep is important to keep up your strength and morale, but psychological factors may make it hard to sleep in a survival situation. See Chapter 3 for ways to proactively cope with stress.

Selecting a good campsite

If you're going to build or find shelter, you need to choose an appropriate campsite. Take some time to select a campsite; a good location can protect you from wind, rain, and other elements. Before you start building or searching, consider the following:

- ✔ **When you're near water, look for higher ground to make your camp.** Cold air flows downhill, so riverbeds and lakesides are colder than slopes that lead down to them, particularly in the early morning.

Beware of *flash floods,* sudden bursts of water that can turn a dry riverbed into a raging torrent. Look for high-water marks, such as water stains on rock faces or vegetation trapped by running water in trees or bushes. Be sure your camp is considerably higher than the usual high-water mark. For more on the dangers of flash floods, and how to spot high-water marks, see Chapter 17.

✔ **When on the spines of exposed ridges, beware of lightning hazards.** Although you may want to build your rescue signals on a ridge, actually camping on such exposed ground is a lightning risk.

✔ **When you're in the mountains, watch out for the telltale signs of avalanche or rockfall.** Either of these can wipe out your camp in an instant. An example of an avalanche area is a treeless swath on a mountainside. An example of a rockfall area is a cone-shaped talus slope at the bases of mountains (*talus* is loose, rocky debris that piles up at the bases of cliffs and mountains). See Chapter 16 for more on avalanche hazards.

✔ **Keep aware of high-wind hazards.** Check trees to see whether they're all leaning the same way or are missing limbs on the same side; these signs can indicate the prevailing wind direction. Set up your shelter in a protected area if you can, because incessant wind really can wear you down psychologically. If you have the misfortune to be camped on *sea ice* (a skin of ice on the surface of the ocean), keep in mind that wind can move sea ice. Look for older, stable ice that has wind-rounded corners and snow on it rather than newer ice that has sharp corners and is free of snow.

Remember that on frozen ocean surfaces (and even some large frozen lakes), *pressure ridges* occur where two large pieces of ice crash together (caused by wind or sea currents). They can be up to 30 feet (9 meters) tall; camping in their *lee* (the side protected from wind) can provide excellent shelter from high winds.

Using Natural Shelters

Natural shelters come in all shapes, sizes, and kinds, but they really boil down to two types: trees and caves/rock overhangs. This section looks at these two shelters and discusses which critters to watch out for before you move in.

Trees

In a survival situation, you can turn to trees for shelter. You can use trees that have been hollowed out by fire or downed for some other reason and rotted from the inside-out. Put down some vegetation, such as leaves or pine boughs, on the floor of the shelter to keep your body off the cold ground. Figure 6-1 shows two examples of tree shelters.

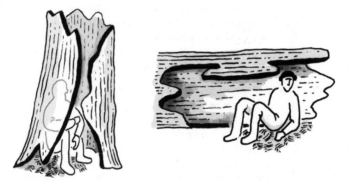

Figure 6-1: Taking shelter in a hollow tree (left) or log (right).

Old logs are often as populated as apartment buildings, crawling with ants, termites, spiders, millipedes, and a multitude of other wonderful bugs. If you're desperate for shelter, you can try to evict these inhabitants by building a fire next to the tree and fanning dense smoke (produced by throwing live branches on the fire) onto the log. *Note:* This is a lot of work that may or may not pay off.

Caves and rock overhangs

A cave or rock overhang is an ideal shelter for a person lost in a wilderness. With *caves* — actual cavities in rock faces — smaller is normally better because small caves are easy to heat up with a good campfire. You won't be looking to warm *rock overhangs* — simple rock shelves that may offer some protection from rain or sun — so they can be large or small. Cave or rock overhangs can exist anywhere you see rock, so keep an eye out for them and look carefully. Figure 6-2 shows an example of using a cave entrance for shelter.

Figure 6-2: A cave can be a great shelter.

If the cave is very deep and you can't find the back, resist the urge to explore by making a torch or using a flashlight. Stay in the first few feet of the shelter, just deep in enough to keep out of the elements. Your objective is simply to survive. You can easily get lost, take fatal falls, or even get trapped by flash floods in a dark cave.

Check for current residents

Although natural shelters can be ideal, you need to make sure no one else calls yours home. For example, does a bear live there? Bears den in caves throughout North America from late September through late May. You can spot some clues near the cave entrance to find out whether the place is vacant; caves occupied by larger mammals often display the following telltales:

- ✔ A faint trail leading into the entrance. (Look at the paw prints in the trail — are they squirrel-sized, dog-sized, or person-sized? Larger prints may indicate a bear.)

- ✔ Food debris, such as bones, shells, and bits of vegetation, scattered at the entrance.

- ✔ Feces *(scat)* present at the entrance or just off to the sides of the entrance.

- ✔ Animal hair hanging on vegetation near the entrance.

- ✔ A distinctive odor, much like a wet dog.

Depending on the environment, snakes, spiders, scorpions, bats, birds, and a dozen other kinds of critters may well live in the shelter, too, so you should check any natural shelter out carefully before moving in.

If you suspect a bear lives in the shelter, back away slowly and then get the heck out of there. It's tough to say how far you should go to stay safe in this situation, but you may want to travel several hours to get out of the bear's territory — even that may not be enough. If it's a mama bear inside with her cubs, you sure don't want to challenge her for the shelter.

In other cases, do the following to determine whether anything lives in a tree:

- ✔ **Use a long and sturdy stick to knock on the shelter.** Be ready for a raccoon, bird, or some other animal to explode out of the entrance.

- ✔ **Creep closer and look closely.** Don't assume there's nobody home, because some animals freeze rather than run when frightened.

- ✔ **Carefully explore the inside of the tree shelter with the end of the stick.** Use the stick like a poker.

A good fire may deter animals from coming back to the shelter at night. Build the fire right at the entrance to the cave or rock overhang. Take care to shield the fire from strong winds near the entrance and be sure to place your fire so it can't be extinguished by rain.

Putting a Roof over Your Head: Building Simple Shelters

If you're going to be out even just one night, building a shelter is well worth it. Doing so is easier than it sounds. You can build a simple and effective shelter within an hour with just a few materials — either found in the wild or carried in your survival kit. In your kit, you should have the following three shelter-building tools:

- ✔ **Knife (or other cutting and chopping implement):** See Chapter 14 for how to improvise knives and chopping tools from stone.

- ✔ **Tarp:** A tarp can help waterproof the shelter. A large plastic bag or three may work in a pinch.

- ✔ **Cordage:** You can use cordage (rope, shoelaces, wire, strips of cloth, whatever you have) to lash wooden parts of a shelter together; parachute cord is ideal. If you're running low, you can cut open parachute cord to get at multiple strands inside it, giving you three or five times as much cordage as you think you have.

By making a temporary home, you can really improve your situation. This section shows a few simple shelters to make.

Making a tarp shelter

A simple plastic tarp is invaluable outdoors. It's probably most useful for making a shelter that can keep you out of the rain, sun, and wind. If you can make a fire near the entrance and block the rear entrance with brush or a backpack, you have a shelter that can keep you alive indefinitely.

If you build a fire in your shelter, always be careful not to light your shelter on fire. Keeping a pile of sand or dirt (or, if you can afford it, a jug of water) next to the fire can help you put out a fire before it spreads.

The basic type of tarp shelter uses a line tied between two trees as the peak of the tarp. All you need are a couple trees about 10 to 20 feet (3 to 6 meters) apart, a length of cordage, your tarp, and a few stakes that you can use to anchor down the corners, as in Figure 6-3a.

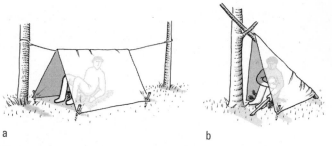

a   b

Figure 6-3: Two types of tarp shelters.

To create this tarp shelter, follow these steps:

1. **Tie the length of cordage between two trees.**

   The tighter you tie it, the better. You want the roof to be straight, not bowing down.

2. **Drape the tarp over the cordage, making the peak of the roof.**

3. **Use stakes to secure the corners of the tarp by hammering them into the ground.**

   Stakes should be green wood cut from living trees, not the more brittle wood you find lying on the forest floor. If your tarp has *grommets* (metal-reinforced holes) on the corners, put the stakes through them to prevent the tarp from tearing under pressure.

If you're in a hurry or are weak and need to rest, you can make an alternative tarp shelter, as in Figure 6-3b. This shelter uses a ridge pole and is simpler to set up, but it's a little cramped, so after the storm passes or you're more fully rested, you may later decide to use cordage to make a roomier, more permanent shelter.

Whichever type of tarp shelter you fashion, use some foliage (such as pine boughs) to insulate the ground so you don't rest directly on the earth.

Building a downed-tree or other A-frame shelter

Downed-tree or A-frame shelters can provide a little more protection from the elements than a simple tarp shelter if the downed tree (or A-frame materials) has a lot of vegetation still on it. Like the tarp shelter, you can supplement these shelters with a tarp for waterproofing. They should always be equipped with an insulated sleeping/sitting area and a fire with a fire reflector. Figure 6-4 shows examples of these types of shelters.

Figure 6-4: A downed-tree shelter and an A-frame shelter.

Both shelters use a *ridgepole* (a pole at the peak of the shelter) flanked by walls. In the case of the downed-tree shelter (Figure 6-4a), the ridgepole is simply a tree trunk that's fallen (you can fell it yourself if you have an ax). Crawl under the tree and cut out tree limbs that hang down to the ground, making a hollow under the ridgepole; you may also want to cut off branches that stick up above the ridgepole to prevent them from catching wind and shaking the shelter.

Here's how to build the A-frame shelter:

1. Gather wood to make the frame.

In the A-frame (Figure 6-4b), the ridgepole is a sturdy sapling supported by about six *uprights;* all of these should be green wood, not dead wood from the forest floor.

2. **Build the frame as in Figure 6-4b.**

   Lash the uprights to the ridgepole at an angle of 45 degrees or more.

3. **Pile branches with vegetation against the ridgepole, at the angle of the uprights, to make the walls.**

In either case, a tarp draped over the ridgepole (and tied down or staked down, as seen in Figure 6-3) can help waterproof the shelter. Build an insulation bed under the shelter and a fire with a fire-reflecting screen of sticks, placed vertically in the ground, to reflect the fire's heat back into the shelter area.

Constructing an insulated shelter

You can make a very simple, very warm shelter by doing the following:

1. **Next to a log or long rock, make a 2-foot-thick (0.6-meter) bed of leaves, grass, moss, pine needles, any other dry vegetation, clothing, or other items that can insulate you from the ground.**

2. **Lean four or five 5-foot-long (1.5-meter) branches against the log or rock, forming a sloping roof over the bedding.**

   This is the frame for your shelter. Don't make it too big. You want this shelter to be tight-fitting so it insulates you almost like a sleeping bag.

3. **Pile a 3-foot-thick (0.9-meter) insulating layer of leaves, grass, moss, pine needles, any other dry vegetation, clothing, or other items on top of the roof.**

   If you have a waterproof tarp, you can tie it to the roof to help you stay dry.

4. **Mark the outside of the shelter so it can be clearly seen and then squirm inside, sealing the opening with a backpack or more vegetation; then try to sleep.**

   Remember, you can improve your morale with just a few hours of good sleep.

Keeping Your Shelter Clean

Remember the old adage: Cleanliness is next to godliness. The same goes for your shelter and campsite. A clean, organized campsite is important because

- ✔ **It's less likely to attract bears, wolverines, or other potentially dangerous animals.** To keep camp clean, designate a butchery and food preparation area 20 or more paces away from your actual shelter (though still within sight).

- ✔ **It allows you to find what you need when you need it.** When you hear a helicopter flying overhead, you're ready to light your signal fires, find your signaling mirror, or turn on your radio or any other electronic device. To stay organized, we suggest hanging signaling gear from lines or branches so you can easily access it when the chopper flies overhead.

A clean and organized camp also gives you some peace of mind. You're not just eking out a filthy, savage existence; you're doing okay. You know what you're doing, you're taking steps toward staying healthy and being found — you're surviving!

Chapter 7

Liquid Capital: Finding Drinking Water

· ·

In This Chapter

▶ Knowing how much water you need

▶ Knowing where to look for water

▶ Collecting rain and condensation

▶ Extracting drinkable water from plants

▶ Filtering and purifying liquids

· ·

*R*egardless of the wilderness setting you find yourself in, finding and storing water is your second priority after you do all you can to protect your body temperature. If you have the problems of hypothermia or heat exhaustion under control, then go to work on collecting and conserving as much water as you can.

In this chapter, we show you the average time it takes for dehydration to incapacitate you in the wilderness — and how to extend that time. We show you how to find water, how to extract it from various sources, and finally how to filter and purify unclean liquids so you can consume them.

Knowing Your Water Needs

You can estimate how much water you need in any situation by starting with the averages. Under average, moderate conditions, you lose from 2 to 3 quarts (2 to 3 liters) of body water per day. If you don't replenish this lost water, you begin to feel the effects of dehydration.

Dehydration usually starts with a drop in your energy level, which is quickly followed by headache, mental confusion, dry mouth, quivering muscles, and then extreme fatigue. If the average human loses water at the average rate and doesn't replace any of it, he or she loses consciousness after three days and perishes after five.

Now that you know the averages, you need to know the extremes:

- ✔ If you're in temperate conditions and you stay in bed all day, you lose only about 1 quart (1 liter) of water per day.

- ✔ If you're involved in normal activities in a hot climate, you lose about 1 gallon (4 liters).

- ✔ If you walk across a desert at midday, you can lose over 5 gallons (more than 20 liters) in one day, which, if not replaced, is fatal.

For more on the special problems of hot climates, see Chapter 17.

You can measure your personal dehydration rate by examining your urine. If your urine is clear and straw-colored, you're basically hydrated, but if it becomes yellow or orange, or cloudy or "thick," or if you don't urinate at all over a 10-hour period, then you're dehydrated.

Your first strategy in a survival situation is to conserve your body's water usage. If you're thorough in the conservation practices, you can stretch your water — and your survival time — significantly.

Stretching your water supply

Your body uses water all the time, even when you're at rest. It leaks out in three ways: urination, perspiration, and respiration (breathing). Though you can't stop the water-leaking process, you can slow it down to a trickle, and in a survival situation, that's your goal. Here's how to do it:

- ✔ **Stop water intake in the short term.** Stop consuming your water supply for a short while. Your body has a reserve supply, and any water you consume before the reserve is used up will be lost through urination. You have to make a judgment call here: Adrift in a life raft in moderate conditions, you can go the first 24 hours without any water at all. In hot desert conditions (or in extreme cold, such as the Arctic), you may not be able to last that long.

✔ **Don't consume any diuretics.** Diuretics are liquids that make you have to urinate a lot, such as coffee, soda, alcohol, and salt water.

✔ **Limit strenuous movement.** Limit your physical exertion to the absolute minimum. Lie still and rest if you can.

✔ **Keep your body cool.** If you're in hot conditions, stay in the shade or erect a covering to make shade. Splash any liquid that you can — even salt water — on your body. Don't lie on hot surfaces like the ground. If you're in cold conditions, strip off layers of clothing when you feel yourself start to perspire.

✔ **Don't eat or smoke.** If you have to eat, try to eat carbohydrates. You need water to digest food in general but especially fats and proteins, as well as to process tobacco.

✔ **Breathe through your nose and limit talking.** Try to limit the loss of your breath's vapor.

✔ **If you're at high altitude, descend.** The higher you are, the harder you breathe, and the more vapor you lose.

Rationing water

You ration water only when you know you're in a real survival situation. If you don't know whether you've reached the survival stage yet, then practice some or all of the water conservation steps listed in the preceding section — this is the first step in your overall strategy.

Base any water-rationing program on your environment. You have to find a balance between extending your life and impairing your physical capacities so much that you can no longer function. For instance, consider the following:

✔ At sea in a raft, the minimum you need is around 1 cup (237 milliliters) per day. This is the smallest amount you can consume and still survive for more than a week or so, and this pertains only to ideal conditions.

✔ If you're on land, especially in hot conditions, cutting down to a cup per day when you have 2 or 3 gallons (7.5 or 11.5 liters) lying around is counterproductive, because you end up physically incapacitated long before you consume your water.

Discuss any type of water rationing with your companions thoroughly. Make sure everyone in your party feels they're included and that they're being treated fairly. You should also discuss plans for finding water, which we cover later in this chapter.

What Not to Drink

You may be tempted to drink whatever fluids you can find during a survival situation. However, some liquids, such as salt water, blood, and urine, cause more trouble than they're worth. Here's why you should stay away from them:

✔ **Salt water:** Salt water increases urination, which makes you even more dehydrated. Although some survival texts claim you can consume salt water, these claims are almost invariably based on faulty sources, or they don't take into account the practical problems (namely, that as soon as you start drinking salt water, it's very hard to stop), or they ignore volumes of research. So we have some simple advice: Never drink saltwater. For more on the problems of drinking salt water, see Chapter 20.

✔ **Blood:** Consuming animal blood causes trouble in several ways: Your body must draw on its own water reserves to digest the protein contained in the blood, so even though you're drinking fluid, you may be depleting yourself. Secondly, animals frequently carry diseases in their blood — diseases you don't normally contract because you cook the meat. Consuming blood also puts you at risk for vomiting, which further dehydrates you. (***Note:*** We endorse only one exception to this rule: drinking turtle blood at sea. For details, see Chapter 20.)

✔ **Urine:** Generally speaking, drinking unpurified urine is highly inadvisable. It's most likely a diuretic, or worse, a poison. And as soon as you begin to dehydrate, your urine only becomes denser and saltier. For more on the bitter controversy surrounding drinking urine, see the nearby sidebar.

The controversy over drinking urine

Of all the issues we address in this book, none is more controversial than the question of whether drinking urine extends your life or hastens your demise. The truth is that some castaways and wilderness survivors have endured extended dehydration times while drinking urine, and some have probably hastened their deaths from drinking it, too.

Each year, a story surfaces in which a person drinks urine and then stays alive well beyond the average survival time. The problem is that knowing what the person could've endured had he or she *not* drunk urine is practically impossible. In some cases, survivors have gone seven full days — an unusually long survival time — without any liquid at all. Some didn't even lose consciousness during these extended times, even though they drank nothing at all. So just because a survivor drank urine *and* had an unusual survival time, while dehydrated, doesn't necessarily mean that urine-drinking and extended times are related.

The argument is divided into three camps: Those who absolutely oppose drinking urine, those who favor it, and those who oppose it but who've read enough case studies to know that the question probably doesn't have an easy answer. This last camp, which consists of some famous survival experts, usually addresses the issue in a highly diplomatic fashion or simply tries to ignore it altogether.

That leaves us with some facts:

- Urine is sterile when it comes out of the body.

- Urine will keep for about two to three days, depending on how it's stored.

- If you're properly hydrated at the start of the survival situation, your first urination would be the purest.

- Drinking urine before you've exhausted all other possibilities is most likely a very bad strategy. You don't know whether you're drinking something that's harmless or something that's a diuretic. There's no use, in the initial stages, in taking a chance.

- The more you dehydrate in a survival situation, the more salty, toxic, and diuretic your urine becomes. If you're cycling your urine through your system, you need to know that this can hasten a shutdown of your renal system.

- In the last stages of dehydration, the uric acid in unpurified urine strips the membranes from the inside of your mouth and severely aggravates the cracks in your lips. Both are exceedingly painful traumas.

Based on this information, we suggest that you avoid drinking urine and look for other water sources. If you have no other water source and you're desperate, consider running urine through a solar still.

If you're in dire straits, you can get drinkable water from salt water or urine through distillation. See "Distilling salt water and urine," later in this chapter, for details.

Knowing the signs of a low-grade or even possibly poisonous water supply is essential. Here's what to watch out for:

- ✔ An acrid, foul, or sewage smell
- ✔ Skeletons of dead animals nearby
- ✔ No plant life whatsoever near the water source
- ✔ Bubbles, foam, or thick green slime on the surface
- ✔ Milky colored water (especially from glaciers)
- ✔ A profusion of cattails or rushes in a stagnant area

You want the highest quality water you can find — before you filter and purify. For more on purifying water, see "Filtering and Purifying Water," later in this chapter.

Finding Bodies of Water

You can find drinkable liquid in almost any environment; you just have to know where to look. After you find that liquid, you may then have to transform it into something you can safely consume. (For a look at cleaning water, check out the later section titled "Filtering and Purifying Water"; for tips on recognizing contaminated water, see the preceding section.) This section identifies water sources and helps you locate water.

Locating water in drainages

One of the first places to look for water is in a *drainage,* which is any place where rain trickles down and collects. Most drainages are at the bottoms of slopes. Valleys and canyons are drainages, as are creek beds, culverts, gullies, ditches, runoffs, and depressions in the land, such as ponds or lakes.

Sometimes the nearest drainage is obvious: It's the raging river right next to the trail. Many times, however, you have to examine your surroundings to determine the pathway rainwater takes after it falls on the ground. Sometimes old sewer pipes can indicate the existence of nearby drainages. Any drainage may hold water for months after the last rain.

If you find a drainage that seems dry, work your way downstream until you find a puddle; in temperate or near-temperate climates, you can almost always find one. If you're in bone-dry conditions, dig for water underneath the drainage.

When heading into an unknown drainage, you must mark your trail or, at the very least, turn around as you descend to make sure you know your way back. Walking downslope from a trail frequently gets people lost because as they walk down, they break their line-of-sight with the trail. For more on marking trails, see Chapter 11.

Knowing other signs of water

You should keep a sharp lookout for signs of water at all times — even before the survival situation occurs. Places to look for water include the following:

- **Where you see a profusion of green vegetation:** This is especially true if the vegetation is bunched in a low spot, such as in a ditch or at the bottom of a valley or depression.

- **Beneath a damp surface, such as damp sand or mud:** This may indicate ground water. You may have to dig down and allow the water to seep into the hole.

- **At the foot of concave banks of dry rivers:** For more on dry riverbeds, see Chapter 17.

- **In holes and fissures in rock faces:** Sometimes rock faces have cracks or deep holes in them that hold water for months at a time between rains. You may have to use a tube or straw made from a reed to suck up the water.

You can also find water by paying attention to wildlife. Most animals drink at dawn and at dusk, so try to track their courses at these times of the day. When checking out animal behavior, look out for the following:

- **Game trails:** Game trails are narrow pathways that animals of the area beat through the grass. Many times these trails lead to water — especially the trails that go downslope or converge.

- **Birds, especially smaller birds:** If they fly low and straight, they're usually headed for water; after they drink, they usually have to fly from tree to tree to rest. Large birds of prey, however, like eagles, hawks, owls, or buzzards, aren't indicators.

✔ **Bees, flies, and ants:** Bees fly to water, as do green flies. Trails of ants crawling up trees frequently lead to pockets of water trapped in hollows.

Catching Rain

All too often, survivors miss their golden opportunity to collect rainwater because they didn't realize that you have to be highly prepared to really take advantage of rainfall. Make sure you get organized before the first drop falls.

To catch rain, you basically want to create the biggest funnel that you can and channel as much water as you can into as many containers as you can acquire. The key is to have a large surface area, or *plane,* to catch the maximum number of drops. A water-catching plane can be (and usually is) a plastic poncho or tarp (see Figure 7-1a), but you can also use metal sheeting, broad leaves (Figure 7-1b), fabric such as canvas, or even wood to channel drops into your containers.

As in any survival situation, containers are king. If you believe rain is coming, collect or build as many water-collection containers as you can. Here are some options:

✔ Look for plastic debris, such as bottles.

✔ Shape paper or heavy cloth, like denim, into cups that last long enough to drink from.

✔ Make large bowls from sturdy half-pieces of bark, sealing the ends with plastic, fabric, or clay.

✔ Use split bamboo canes — they're nothing more than a long row of bowls.

✔ Channel water into natural receptacles that you've widened, such as nearby tree hollows or natural depressions.

✔ Let your water-catching plane serve as your container: Dig a wide, shallow pit and line it with plastic, fabric, paper, or leaves to make a little pond (see Figure 7-1c).

If your collection materials are clean, you can drink the collected rainwater straight, without purifying it.

Figure 7-1: Ways to catch rain.

Collecting Condensation

If water isn't flowing down rocks or falling from the sky, you may have to pull some water out of thin air. The good news is that this process is more science than magic. After water vapor condenses and reverts to its liquid form, you can move in and collect it. In this section, we tell you how to gather dew and collect the water that evaporates out of plants.

Gathering dew

You can frequently collect enough condensation or dew to drink. This water has to be purified only if you think the surface it comes from is somehow contaminated. Here's how to collect dew:

- ✔ Take your shirt off, tie it to your ankle, and walk through the wet grass; then wring out the water into your mouth.

- ✔ Look for puddles of condensation that form in the pits of rock faces and inside bowl- or pitcher-shaped leaves.

- ✔ Soak up the drops on metal or glass surfaces with your shirt or a sponge. You can also use a credit card or something like it to coax the drops into a container.

Dew usually forms sometime during the night, not at dawn. You can maximize the amount of water you collect if you act right after the dew has formed.

Making a transpiration bag

You can get water from plants by using a transpiration bag. A *transpiration bag* is a plastic bag that you wrap around a tree or bush that captures the water that naturally evaporates from the vegetation. Droplets form inside the tightly sealed bag and then trickle down to collect in the bottom.

You can use any plastic sheeting to make a transpiration bag — just make sure you have a tight seal around the vegetation and try to make sure that it's exposed to direct sunlight. If you have a tube of any kind, you can thread it down to the bottom of the bag and just suck up the fluid as it accumulates — that way, you never have to break the seal of the bag and interrupt the evaporation process. Check out Figure 7-2 to see how a transpiration bag works.

If a plant is poisonous, the water you collect from it is poisonous. For more on poisonous plants, see Chapter 8.

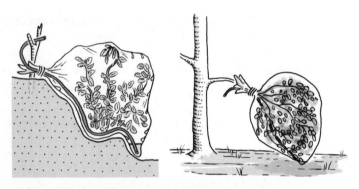

Figure 7-2: Transpiration bags on the ground and on a tree.

Setting up a solar still

A *solar still* is a tightly sealed evaporation unit that allows droplets to form and then trickle down to a collection cup. You can use this method to get water from vegetation; you can also use it to desalinate salt water or purify urine or other contaminated water. Sometimes just the wet earth below the topsoil can be enough to produce drops if you build a solar still over a freshly dug pit.

You can follow these steps to make a basic vegetation still, but this setup (shown in Figure 7-3) also works for all the applications previously listed in this chapter. Solar stills like this produce only a tiny trickle of water, so build as many as you can.

1. **Dig a pit and fill it with freshly cut plants, the wetter and fleshier the better.**

   Poisonous plants produce poisonous liquid in solar stills. Don't put plants that ooze milky fluid or sticky sap in a solar still (with the exception of the barrel cactus — see Chapter 17).

   To purify contaminated liquid, place a container of it in your pit in place of the vegetation. If you don't have vegetation or liquid but the ground is wet, you can simply put plastic over the empty pit, and the ground-water will evaporate into the still.

2. **Put a collection container in the center of the pit, on top of the vegetation.**

3. **If possible, extend a tube from the container at the bottom to the rim of the pit.**

   Using a tube vastly improves efficiency. With the tube in the cup, you can suck up the condensation without disturbing the evaporation process inside the still.

Figure 7-3: A basic solar still with vegetation.

4. **Drape plastic sheeting over the pit; then take a slightly pointed stone and push the plastic down gently to form a slope.**

   This allows the condensation to roll down and drip into the container. You want to end up with a miniature stalactite shape just over the container. You can try canvas if no plastic is available.

5. **Heap sand or stones around the edge of the plastic sheeting to anchor it in place.**

   Make sure you get a good seal around the plastic.

Extracting Water from Plants

You can get the water you need from nearby vegetation, but you have to be on guard for signs of poisonous liquids. This section identifies trees and plants that provide safe drinking water.

Consider any plant liquids that are sticky or milky to be poisonous and unfit to drink!

You can frequently find water in tree hollows and in pitcher- or cup-shaped leaves. Or you can extract water from trees if you know the right methods. Here's how:

- **Palms:** Coconut, buri, nipa, rattan, and sugar palms all contain drinkable liquid. Bend over a flowering stalk of palm and cut the tip off to allow the liquid to drip into a cup. Make a new cut every 12 hours to renew the flow.

- **Banana and plantain:** Cut down the tree and then convert the stump into a reservoir by hollowing it out. The tree's liquid rises and fills this reservoir quickly. Check out Figure 7-4. At first, the liquid is too bitter to drink, so you have to sit through two to three fillings before the liquid is palatable. One tree can provide you with three to four days' worth of liquid.

- **Umbrella tree:** Found in western tropical Africa, this tree has leaf bases and roots that can yield water.

- **Traveler's tree:** Water collects at the bases of the leaves of this fanlike tree, which grows in Madagascar.

✔ **Baobab tree:** Water collects and is stored in the bottle-like trunk of this tree, which grows in Australia and Africa.

Figure 7-4: Cut down a banana or plantain tree to get water in the trunk reservoir.

Other plants that yield water include the following:

✔ **Bamboo:** Green bamboo may contain water. You can either cut the sections open and drain them or bend the entire cane over, cut the top off, and let the water drip into a cup. If the water is clear and doesn't smell bad, you can drink it straight; if it's brown or smells fermented, you have to purify it (see the next section). Brown canes sometimes contain water as well.

✔ **Coconuts:** Drink only from mature, brown coconuts. Young, green coconuts contain an oil that acts as a laxative, and too much of it can cause diarrhea.

✔ **Fleshy plants:** Cut down plants with fleshy centers and then squeeze or mash them to extract the liquid from them. *Warning:* Some varieties of fleshy cactus are poisonous. For information, see Chapter 17.

✔ **Vines:** To extract water from a vine, first cut it at the highest point you can; then cut it at a lower point to allow the liquid to drain down. If you cut low first, the water just runs back up the vine. Don't drink any vine liquid that appears sticky or milky.

Filtering and Purifying Water

In the field, any body of water can contain bacteria, parasites, and toxins, such as pesticides — any one of which can make you ill. Nearly all water-borne diseases involve a violent bout of diarrhea, which only accelerates dehydration. To avoid sickness, consider all water dangerous, regardless of how clear it appears. Filter and purify all your water to the best of your ability. This section explains methods you can use to purify or treat water, starting with the most effective one.

In most tropical situations, it's vastly better to get an organized rain-catching operation going than to mess around with having to filter and purify water.

Boiling water

Boiling water for 10 to 15 minutes is the very best course of action in a wilderness situation. If you have a tin cup or some other type of metal container and you can get a fire going, always boil your water.

Boiling water in a plastic container is possible, but you risk destroying your only container. Put some thought into this procedure before you risk it. If boiling in plastic is your only alternative, proceed slowly and keep a sharp eye on the plastic. It should turn black, but you obviously want to watch for the deformities that indicate the plastic is melting. The key is to suspend the plastic container from a tripod and never allow it to touch hot flames or coals. (For instructions on building a tripod, see Chapter 14.)

Before boiling any water, consider filtering it first to remove larger particles. See the later section "Improvising filters" for details.

Going with chemical treatments

If you can't boil your water, you should use chemicals to purify it. (Preferably after filtering — see the later section "Improvising filters.")

The general rule when using chemicals is to use a standard dosage if the water is clear and doesn't smell bad and to double the dosage if the water is cloudy or foul smelling. When you have access to chemicals, you usually have one of three options, which we present in Table 7-1.

Table 7-1	Chemicals for Purifying Water	
Chemical	*Description*	*Standard Treatment*
Water purification tablets, commonly chlorine or iodine	These are standardized water treatments, packaged in bottles and blister packs.	Follow the directions to the letter — the chemicals themselves are poisonous!
Iodine	This is liquid iodine, which you can find in many first aid kits. You may find iodine swabs in your kit, which you can also use.	3–5 drops liquid iodine (when using a 2% iodine solution) per quart (liter) of water; or drop in the swabs and remove them when you think the water is purified
Sodium hypochlorite	You can find this in household bleach.	2–3 drops per quart (liter) of water

For small amounts of water, you should wait at least 30 minutes for the chemical to kill enough germs to make the water safe. For gallon jugs and larger, wait two hours or more.

Distilling salt water and urine

If you have the necessary tools and time, you can convert salt water or urine into drinkable water by heating it in a metal container and collecting the steam in fabric. Then wring out the fabric into a container. Or you can distill salt water and urine in a solar still. For more on this, see "Setting up a solar still," earlier in this chapter.

Distillation is the only method that makes salt water or urine drinkable. Using water purification tablets doesn't do anything to make salt water or urine safe. Some filters can desalinate salt water, but you must read the label on the package of the filter to make sure it's built to do this highly specialized task.

Using commercial water filters

Commercially made water filters are available at most outfitters. These are usually small hand pumps that force liquid through a cylinder filled with purifying chemicals and dense particle filters. The main thing to keep in mind is that many water makers aren't guaranteed to filter out all harmful germs or to remove the salt from salt water. Read the instructions thoroughly, as well as the warning labels on the pump itself.

Improvising filters

You have access to several types of natural water filters in the wilderness, and though they can remove excrement, leeches, body parts of dead animals, and many other unpalatables, they don't necessarily remove all the bacteria and toxins from the water.

The only time you want to use this last method, *improvised filters,* is as a last resort — or as a precursor to chemical treatments or boiling. Improvised filters are filters you make in the field from natural elements, like sand and grass. This section looks at a couple of options you have.

Using improvised filters is a judgment call. If you're on the verge of being incapacitated and you can't boil your water, distill it, or treat it with chemicals, you may have to try an improvised filter so you can remain conscious and ready to signal for rescue. The water that comes out of the improvised filter may not harm you at all, or it may give you a disease. Most water-borne diseases give you diarrhea, and when your body begins to purge itself, you begin to dehydrate rapidly. Diarrhea can begin as quickly as 8 to 12 hours (in the case of dysentery) after you consume bad water, or it may not start for several days.

Many times, you have access to several types of filters in the wild. You can use any of the following filters, either by themselves or in combination:

> ✔ **Fabric:** You can filter water through a t-shirt or sock (see Figure 7-5, on the left) — just make sure you're not making salt water! If you're near the ocean or if you've perspired a lot and you try to filter a small amount of fresh water through a shirt or sock, you usually taint it with salt.

✔ **Vegetation:** Grasses can make good filters for large particles, as can straw (Figure 7-5c).

✔ **Sand:** You can use sand as a filter, especially in layers (Figures 7-5b and 7-5d).

✔ **Charcoal:** Make charcoal by burning hardwoods. Charcoal neutralizes some toxins and sometimes filters out bad tastes (Figures 7-5a and 7-5e).

You can combine natural filters to make a layered multifilter by using a sock or a tripod, as in Figure 7-5. (If you're unfamiliar with the construction of the tripod used in the figure, take a look at Chapter 14.)

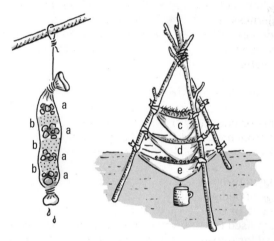

Figure 7-5: Sock and tripod filters using fabric, vegetation, sand, and charcoal.

Digging a seepage basin

If you have no filtering equipment or resources at all, you can try digging a *seepage basin*. This is a pit that you dig next to a pond, creek, or river that allows the water to seep in. The sand between the water source and the pit acts as a crude filter. Here's how to make this basin (refer to Figure 7-6):

✔ **Next to a river, creek, or pond:** If you have any suspicions of the quality of the water, especially in the tropics, dig a pit about 2 to 3 feet (0.6 to 0.9 meters) from the banks of the river, creek, or pond, and use the seepage as your water source.

✔ **Next to the ocean:** You can dig behind the first or second sand dune on beaches. Sometimes the top 2 inches (5 centimeters) of the seepage that fills this basin is drinkable, although it often tastes bad.

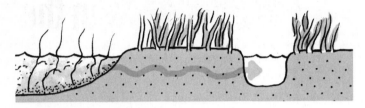

Figure 7-6: A seepage basin.

Chapter 8

Gathering and Hunting to Stay Alive in the Wilderness

*A*fter you solve your most immediate survival problems — maintaining good health, keeping a tolerable body temperature, and securing a water supply — you need to start thinking about food. Although people can and have gone for weeks or even months without significant amounts of food, having the strength to keep up your campsite, signal for help, or start traveling toward civilization all require food.

The good news is that humans have lived off the land for a lot longer than they've been going to the nearby grocery store. Although most civilization-dwellers have forgotten how to subsist on what nature provides, this chapter shows you how to do exactly that: how to find — and get your hands on — food sources even when it seems that there's nothing to be had. You also discover how to clean and cook food.

Managing Food in the Wild

When you find yourself in a survival situation, the first thing you think about is probably food. But despite your immediate desire for food, the human body can go much longer without food than it can without water.

As soon as your water situation is under control, you need to assess your food situation. If you have food on hand, remember the following:

✔ **Don't eat for the first 24 hours.** Your body can handle this time just fine on its own, and you may as well get used to a little hunger.

✔ **Don't eat if you don't have a good supply of water.** Digestion requires water.

✔ **Eat what will spoil earliest first.** Consume spoilables, such as meat, before foods that keep well, like dry rice or any canned or packaged food.

✔ **Arrange your food by dividing it into portions per person per day.** Start by assuming you'll be out for a week (most lost hikers are found well within this time frame). If you're dealing with relatively small quantities of food, say, back-packing meals, lay the food out so you can inspect it visually. Doing so allows you to be sure the food isn't spoiling, and it shows you how serious the situation really is.

✔ **Immediately consider using any existing food as an emergency supply and plan to subsist on what you can hunt and gather.** If you can find food in the wilderness, this leaves your nonperishable civilization foods — such as granola bars or a can of chili — as a reserve that you can count on.

✔ **Consider ways of preserving your incoming food supply.** Keep a supply of food coming into camp and being stored, while eating only a portion. You can rely on that supply if you have to travel or you're injured and unable to check your snares and fishing traps for a while. Find out how to preserve food in the later "Drying and smoking food" section.

Unless you have a tremendous amount of nonperishable food on hand, you should begin to think about living off the land.

Trying new foods

You want to survive, don't you? Then get over food taboos. If you can stomach it without throwing up or setting off your food allergies, you're getting calories to your body, and that's the point. Of course, if you're vegetarian or vegan, you may have some serious philosophical soul-searching to do if you get into a wilderness survival situation. Good luck!

Including Plants in Your Wilderness Diet

When you're stranded in the wild and looking for food, plants are a great food source. The good news is that human beings can safely eat thousands of kinds of plants. All you have to know is which ones are safe to eat. Unfortunately, figuring out which ones you can eat — and their seasonal variations across the planet — would take a lifetime. No worries. We're here to help. This section explains how you can figure out which plants to eat, names some common edible plants, and identifies which types of plants to avoid.

Perusing the salad bar: Where to find a variety of plants

One of your first tasks in finding plant food is to find a decent vantage point, sit down, and take a careful look at the terrain. No matter how uniform the area you're stranded in appears, you can probably find some variations in the landscape (ecological *niches*) where different kinds of plants thrive. Even in a desert, you can find vegetation niches — including open ground (in direct sun) and shaded terrain (under the edges of large boulders) — if you look carefully.

Instead of wandering aimlessly in search of plant foods, systematically search each vegetation niche to increase your odds of finding new kinds of plant food. For example, search carefully near a lakeshore, then on the open plain between the lakeshore and some foothills, and then up in the foothills themselves; you can find different plant life in each area.

Looking at a plant's edible parts

You can divide each plant into segments that you can consider eating. If the flower doesn't look at all appetizing, maybe the leaves are more palatable, or maybe the roots can supply food. This section looks at some common guidelines for consuming different types of plant parts. (For info on cooking and preparing these plant parts, see "Cooking food you can eat now," later in this chapter.)

Fruits

Fruits are the ripened reproductive elements of plants that have flowers. They often contain large numbers of seeds. Fruits are normally safe to eat unless they're

- ✔ Divided into five segments (bananas are an exception)

- ✔ Fermenting (the sickly sweet smell is unmistakable)

- ✔ Moldy

You need to be aware of the poisonous berry varieties in the areas you're most likely to visit — do some research before you go hiking or camping. Remember this fun little saying when deciding whether to eat berries (but to be sure berries are safe, always use the Universal Plant Edibility Test that we describe later in this chapter):

> *Red, white, or yellow might kill a fellow!*
> *Black or blue, that's for you!*

Leaves

You can eat many leaves safely. Although you want to avoid leaves with hairs or spines, even these can sometimes be softened by boiling, as in the case of stinging nettle leaves.

Flowers

Soft flower petals are often edible. They may be bitter, though boiling may help.

Flowers may cause allergic reactions because they're often coated with pollen.

Mosses and lichens

In the Arctic, reindeer (caribou) and people alike eat tundra mosses. These mosses grow in small tufts, often clinging to rocks. *Lichens,* which are technically a combination of algae and a certain kind of fungus, are similarly low-lying; some are edible.

Nuts and seeds

Nuts and seeds are high in calories. Except in the case of fruit seeds, though, they're often encased in hard shells that can take time to process. Some people have nut allergies. Many seeds are poisonous or can at least make you very sick, but cooking many of these is an effective way to make them safe.

Roots and tubers

Roots and *tubers,* which are swollen underground stems, are the plant's nutritional feelers. They can contain quite a bit of water when you dig them up. You can dig out and pry up roots with a stout wooden staff. Try not to take so many that you kill the plant. Some roots and tubers are poisonous, so use the Universal Plant Edibility Test if you have any doubt.

Naming edible plants

You'd have to be a botanist to know the thousands of edible plants available to you in the wild. To help you, this section identifies some of the most common edible plants in various climates. We just scratch the surface here, but this list can guide you to further researching what's available in your area. (*Tip:* Identifying plants can be tricky business, so perform the Universal Plant Edibility Test, described in the next section, if you're not certain of a plant's identity.)

Edible Temperate Climate Plants

Amaranth	Persimmon
Arrowroot	Plaintain
Beechnut	Pokeweed
Blackberries	Purslane/little hogweed
Blueberries	Sassafras

Burdock	Sheep sorrel
Cattail	Strawberries
Chestnut	Thistle
Chicory	Water lily and lotus
Chufa	Wild onion and garlic
Daylily	Wild rose
Nettle	Wood sorrel
Oaks	

Figure 8-1 shows some examples of temperate climate plants.

Figure 8-1: A nettle (a), blackberry (b), and cattail (c).

Edible Tropical Climate Plants

Bamboo	Mango
Bananas	Palms
Breadfruit	Papaya
Cashew nut	Sugarcane
Coconut	Taro

Figure 8-2 shows three examples of tropical climate plants.

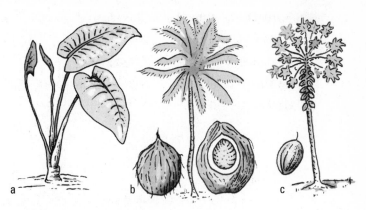

Figure 8-2: Taro (a), coconut (b), and breadfruit (c).

Edible Desert Climate Plants

Acacia	Date palm
Agave	Desert amaranth
Cactus	Prickly pear cactus

Figure 8-3 shows three examples of desert climate plants.

Figure 8-3: Agave (a), acacia pods (b), and prickly pear cactus (c).

Edible Arctic Climate Plants

Crowberry	Rock tripe
Dandelion	Salmonberry
Mountain sorrel	Willow shrub
Reindeer moss	

Figure 8-4 shows three examples of arctic climate plants.

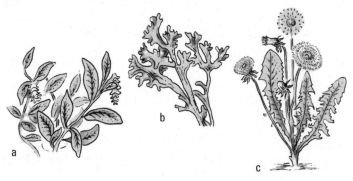

Figure 8-4: Willow shrub (a), reindeer moss (b), and dandelion (c).

Edible Seaweeds

Dulse	Laver
Green seaweed	Mojaban
Irish moss	Sugar wrack
Kelp	

Figure 8-5 shows three examples of edible plants at sea.

Is it safe? Deciding whether to eat an unknown plant food

The preceding section lists some safe plants to eat. How do you know, though, if you're in the wild and come across a plant you're unfamiliar with? In this section, we list some signs you should avoid a plant altogether, and we tell you how to test plants that are still in the running to be your next meal.

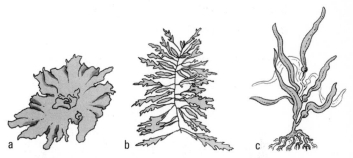

Figure 8-5: Green seaweed (a), mojaban (also known as sargassum) (b), and kelp (c).

Knowing which plants to avoid

To help you figure out which plants not to eat, keep these rules in mind. Don't eat the following:

- Any plant with a milky sap
- White, yellow, or red berries
- Red plants
- Plants with hairs or spines
- Plant bulbs (except onions or garlic); beware that the death camas *(Zigadenus venenosus)* bulb, which looks very inviting, can kill
- Fruit that's divided into five segments (except bananas)
- Any plant food with an almond scent (this may indicate a powerful toxin)

After these rules, what's left? A lot! In fact, you can eat many thousands of kinds of plants. If a plant doesn't automatically score a spot on the forbidden list, you can check your next potential meal by using the Universal Plant Edibility Test, which we cover next.

Taking the Universal Plant Edibility Test

When you're considering eating any unfamiliar plant food, you must carry out the Universal Plant Edibility Test (but don't use the test for fungi, because some are lethal even in small doses — see the nearby "Hold the mushrooms, please!" sidebar). This test determines whether a given plant is safe to eat. The test takes a whole day, and you can only drink water during that day, so it's quite an investment. The return, though — knowing that you can safely eat a certain plant — may well be worth it.

You can find the test in Table 8-1. If you get through a step without having a bad reaction, proceed to the next one. And if you go all the way through without any problems, congratulations! You can consider the part of the plant that you've eaten to be safe to eat.

Table 8-1 The Universal Plant Edibility Test

Step	Test	Duration	Possible Bad Reactions
1	Hold a piece of the plant on the sensitive skin inside your elbow joint or on the forearm.	15 minutes	Rash
2	Touch a small piece of the plant to your lips.	5 minutes	Burning sensation
3	Hold a piece of the plant on your tongue.	3 minutes	Stinging sensation
4	Chew a small piece of the plant and hold the chewed vegetation in your mouth — without swallowing.	15 minutes	Burning or stinging sensation
5	Swallow the vegetation you've been holding in your mouth.	Wait 8 hours	Vomiting or diarrhea
6	Eat another small portion (about ¼ cup).	Wait 8 hours	Vomiting or diarrhea

Hold the mushrooms, please!

However enticing mushrooms look, the species you're hungrily eyeing may be a deadly mimic of the kind you grew up finding in forests back at home. That's why we suggest that you completely avoid mushrooms and other fungi in survival situations. Having said that, if you're in the most desperate straits and have only fungi to eat and can't hold out any longer, three rules can help you stay alive. Don't eat any fungi with

✔ White gills

✔ A cup-like basin at its base

✔ Rings around the stem

Hunting and Trapping Food

Even though getting meat may be more difficult than gathering plants, it's not impossible. Since the beginning of time, native people all over the world have hunted and trapped animals. Instead of running down animals or lunging for them from a bush, you too can make tools that extend your reach and make it sharper. (Or you can pick up some grasshoppers, mealworms, and other little critters that are yours for the taking. See the sidebar titled "Finders keepers: Foraging for food" for details.)

This section helps you find animals you may want to hunt and includes info on how to make and use snares and weapons, such as a bow and arrow, spear, and bola. Finally, we tell you how to get to the meat.

Looking for tracks and critter highways

To hunt or trap successfully, keep an eye open for places where animals often travel, feed, drink, and/or sleep. Animals often travel repeatedly on game trails, which you can spot in many environments. *Game trails* (see Figure 8-6) are faint clearings through vegetation.

You may also notice the trails marked with animal tracks.

Figure 8-6: Look for faint (or distinctive) paths through vegetation.

Finders keepers: Foraging for food

Most hunting-and-gathering aboriginal folk worldwide gather just as much as they hunt or trap. This lifestyle is called *foraging*. Foragers are

✔ **Opportunistic:** Just about anything that flies, hops, swims, walks, or crawls can be cooked and eaten (including mussels, limpets, and clams). For example, a grasshopper, a snail, or a nest of eggs all serve as nutritious food sources. You can also snare the parent when it returns to the nest.

✔ **Observant:** Learn the patterns of the land. See how things change by day, night, and at high- and low-tide (but avoid any shellfish you find above the high-tide mark — they can be poisonous). Think of yourself as a part of the landscape rather than an actor on the stage of the landscape. Think about how other animals make their living out here and envision how you can do the same. If it isn't feasible where you are, you may have to move somewhere else.

Snaring small animals

Snares capture animals that you can later collect and eat. A *snare* is essentially a loop of wire or very strong cordage that an animal gets entangled in and can't escape. If the snare closes around the throat, the animal may die before you reach it. If the snare only snags the animal's leg, you may have to kill the animal when you check your snares. Snares are best-suited to capturing smallish mammals, such as squirrels and rabbits.

Setting up your snares

Making snares is fairly easy; most just require a good piece of wire or very thin cordage. You can strip suitable snare-making wire from cars, airplanes, and other vehicles. You need lengths well over 1 foot (0.3 meters) long. If the wire is sheathed in plastic insulation, strip it off before making the snare.

To create a basic snare, follow these easy steps:

1. **Make a loop about 4 inches (10 centimeters) in diameter (for the neck of a squirrel) or larger if you're trying to snare a larger animal.**

2. **Tie the snare off with a snare knot.**

   To tie a snare knot, loop the end of the line around twice and then thread the end through the first loop. Make sure you pull the knot tight. Check out Figure 8-7 for an example.

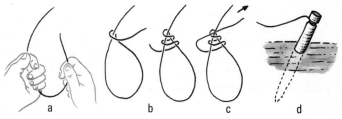

Figure 8-7: A snare knot.

3. **Arrange the snare loop so that it lies right in the animal's path.**

   Take some time to study the game trail or branch on which you're deploying the snare.

4. **Tie one end of the snare wire to a sturdy tree or stake, bury the stake deep, and regularly check on it to see what you've caught.**

When you make a snare, wear gloves (if you have them) to prevent your scent from getting on the wire, which alerts the animal of danger. If you can't do this, you can camouflage your scent by burying the snare wire in dirt for 24 hours before deploying it, using pieces of cloth or socks on your hands to prevent you from scent-marking your snare lines.

Some types of snares you may want to use include the following:

✔ **Branch snare:** Place branch snares in series on branches where you've seen animals like squirrels travel frequently. Figure 8-8a shows a series of squirrel snares; place many of these snares so that one traps the squirrel as it travels on the branch.

✔ **Burrow-hole snare:** You can spot animal burrows in many places, such as near the banks of rivers or under heavy brush. In any case, you can use a burrow-hole snare (see Figure 8-8b), which you place just outside the entrance to a burrow. It traps the animal as it exits or enters.

   When setting up a burrow-hold snare, firmly anchor a strong stake near the burrow. Better yet, anchor the snare to an existing branch, sapling, or trunk so the animal doesn't spot some new element in its environment.

✔ **Game-trail snare:** A snare on a game trail has lightweight brush walls that corral the animal into the snare (see Figure 8-8c). Most animals are unwilling to travel backward, so they run into the snare instead of backing away from it if they spot it.

   You make this snare by suspending a slipknot loop over a trail. Place the wire on two small forked twigs just above ground level so the animal's neck goes into the snare.

Figure 8-8: Different types of snare setups.

You can use bait to lure animals into snares, but we suggest focusing on laying out many baitless snares and checking them often. Baiting is complicated, and some baits alert the animal that something is amiss. If you do use bait, you need bait that the animal is familiar with or bait that's unfamiliar but attractive to the animal.

Checking snares and collecting your catch

Check and maintain your snares regularly. Sometimes the snare kills the animal, which is one reason to check snares often; predators may get to your prospective meal before you do. Other times, you may come back to a snare and find it holding a wounded, desperate, and potentially dangerous animal. Kill a snared animal as quickly and humanely as possible. A sturdy club works fine. (Check out the later section "Going in for the kill with a club.")

Be equipped with a spear (or bow and arrow, bola, or other weapon that extends your reach) anytime you venture away from camp, ready to kill animals you come across while making or checking your snares. We discuss these other weapons in the upcoming sections.

Using a throwing stick

A throwing stick, although not as sexy as a spear or bow and arrow (see the next sections), can be effective for killing small animals such as rabbits and squirrels. A throwing stick is larger than a stone and more likely to hit the target. It's especially useful when you throw it into groups of smaller animals, such as a flock of birds.

Use any 1- to 2-foot long (0.3- to 0.6-meter long) green branch or sapling that's from 1 to 2 inches (2.5 to 5 centimeters) in diameter. Strip it of all bark and whittle away any branches. Try to find a branch that's a little heavier on one end than the other. Throw the stick so that it hurtles through the air horizontally, something like a Frisbee.

Making and using a spear

A spear is a good implement for nearly any wilderness survival situation. You can use a good, sturdy spear for self-defense from animals, as a probe for checking out murky water or thick brush, and for a dozen other things. For hunting, spears can wound large animals enough that, although the animal flees the attack, you can follow its blood trail (the *spoor*) until the animal dies or is so weak that it's an easy kill.

Constructing a spear isn't difficult. Just follow these steps (and Figure 8-9):

1. **Select a green sapling, thicker than a broomstick, and cut it down (Figure 8-9a).**

2. **Strip the bark from the sapling and cut the length to about 6 feet (1.8 meters; see Figure 8-9b).**

3. **Sharpen one end of the sapling with any knife you have available, be it metal or stone, as in Figure 8-9c.**

4. **Harden the sharp end of the spear by holding it over a fire for a while, being sure to rotate it (see Figure 8-9d).**

   Rotating drives some of the water out of the wood, blackening the tip and making it very hard; now it will puncture rather than just bend. *Note:* If you're going to add an armature (keep reading for instructions), you don't have to sharpen or harden the tip with fire.

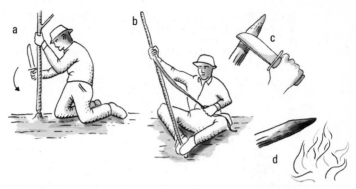

Figure 8-9: Creating your own spear.

If you prefer, you can mount an armature on the end of a spear. An *armature* is any hard, sharp item that can serve your needs. You need to bind an armature carefully and very tightly onto the working end of the spear. Begin by splitting the end of the spear by hammering a knife into the end (see Figure 8-10a). Then slip in the armature (see Figure 8-10b) and wrap tightly around the whole assembly with strong cordage (as in Figure 8-10c); be sure to wrap below the armature to prevent the spear from splitting. You can use any type of cordage, although wire tends to slip.

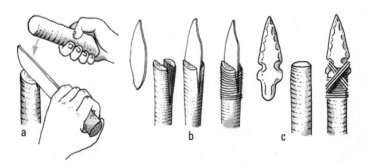

Figure 8-10: Lashing an armature onto a spear.

Good items for making an armature include the following:

  ✔ **A large nail:** Bind a nail to your spear very tightly. A nail is best for fishing, which doesn't put as much stress on the nail as using the spear for self-defense from a large animal does.

✔ **A sharpened sliver of hard plastic:** You can get one from a shattered car-light cover.

✔ **A sharpened splinter of bone or antler:** See Chapter 14 for how to process bone and antler into sharp slivers.

✔ **A sharpened sliver of stone or glass:** These take more time and effort to shape than bone or antler splinters, but they can be very effective.

If you can put notches into the sides of the armature, your cordage has something more to grab, which holds the armature more firmly.

Despite what you see on TV or at the movies, few aboriginal people worldwide actually throw spears at animals to kill them. Throwing your spear will probably just result in a fleeing animal and a broken spear tip. For attacks at range, a bow and arrow, throwing stick, or bola is much more likely to land you some food than a spear is.

Making and using a bow and arrow

People have been using bows and arrows for tens of thousands of years, and they can be very effective weapons against both small and large animals. Making and using them is a fun activity for an afternoon, and it's great practice for anyone contemplating going outdoors. Among other things, practice can show you how far you can expect to be accurate with a bow (for most people — with practice — that's about 10 to 15 yards, or 9.1 to 13.7 meters).

Creating the bow

To make a bow, just follow these easy steps:

1. **Select and cut down a sturdy 1- to 1.5-inch (2.5- to 4-centimeter) diameter sapling with a straight trunk (see Figure 8-11a).**

2. **Strip off the bark (Figure 8-11b), leaving a clean 4-foot (1.2-meter) pole.**

3. **Whittle away the ends of the bow with a knife (as in Figure 8-11c), leaving a sturdy midsection as a handle (Figure 8-11d).**

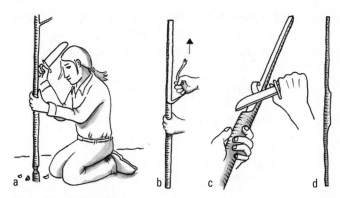

Figure 8-11: Making the bow.

4. **Notch the upper and lower ends to accept the bowstring (Figure 8-12a).**

   Cut about ⅓ of the way into the branch but no deeper. The *heartwood* is the strongest wood, and you don't want to cut into it too deeply.

5. **Tie your string to one end of the bow using the two half hitches knot (as in Figure 8-12b).**

   Use fishing line or some other suitably durable cordage, such as electrical wire.

6. **Bend the bow and attach the other end of the string (Figure 8-12c).**

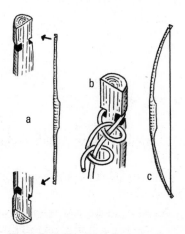

Figure 8-12: Attaching the bowstring.

Making arrows

Carrying about six to ten arrows should be sufficient. Here's how to make each arrow:

1. **Select a thin, sturdy (green wood) branch as an arrow shaft (see Figure 8-13a).**

2. **Strip off the bark (Figure 8-13b).**

3. **Use a knife (or sharp stone) to shave away irregularities and whittle a point on the arrow (Figure 8-13c).**

   At this point, you can harden the tip over a fire as in Figure 8-13d, or you can try to attach a separate point (the armature). Here's how:

   1. Split the shaft on one end and then tie off the shaft below the split (to prevent the split from spreading).

   2. Insert an armature (such as a sharpened splinter of bone or a sliver of glass) into the split (Figure 8-13e). For more on how to make armatures from stone, bone, or antler, see Chapter 14.

   3. Use more cordage to secure the split wood around the base of the armature (Figure 8-13e).

3. **Cut a notch into the base of the arrow for the bowstring and then tie off the arrow above the notch to prevent it from splitting the arrow (as in Figure 8-13f).**

   Your complete arrow should look something like Figure 8-13g.

Figure 8-13: Making arrows.

Practicing the fine art of archery

Here's how to use the bow and arrow (see Figure 8-14):

1. **Stand with your chest at 90 degrees to the target (not facing the target), as in Figure 8-14a.**

   In Figure 8-14b, the archer has dropped to one knee, perhaps hiding behind cover in an ambush or simply seeking a more stable firing position.

2. **Fit the notch of the arrow on the bowstring.**

   In Figure 8-14c, you see the grip you use to hold the arrow in place and draw back the string (*Note:* We show a left hand drawing the bow for clarity.) Use the three upper fingers of the hand (not the thumb or pinky finger), holding the arrow between your index and middle fingers. The other end of the arrow should rest against the bow, not quite resting on your thumb, as in Figure 8-14d.

3. **Lock the arm that's holding the bow straight out in front and aim for the target.**

   In a survival situation, simply aim for the largest body mass visible, such as the abdomen. A gut-shot animal won't die quickly, so you'll have to use your club to kill it.

   To prevent the string from chafing you when you release it, you may want to first tie a patch of cloth to the wrist of the hand holding the bow. Figure 8-14e shows this bracer.

4. **Draw the string only as far back as your chin and then sight directly down the arrow shaft; release the arrow.**

   Pulling the bowstring beyond the ear can cause the string to lacerate your ear and probably doesn't add much more power.

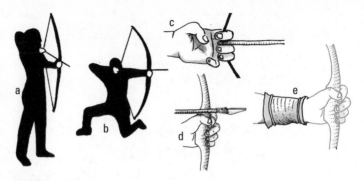

Figure 8-14: Properly using a bow and arrow.

Making and using a bola

People have used bolas for thousands of years to hunt all kinds of animals, including birds and rabbits. *Bolas* are simply strings weighted at one end. When they find their target, they can wrap around and ensnare the legs, immobilizing the prey and allowing you to move in for the killing blow with a club.

Bolas are easy to make; just stick to these steps:

1. **Find three to five smooth, round stones, each an inch or so in diameter; for each stone, cut a piece of cloth or other textile about 4 inches (10 centimeters) square (see Figure 8-15a).**

2. **Wrap each stone in its own cloth (Figure 8-15b) and tie off this cloth tightly with cord (Figure 8-15c).**

3. **Connect all the cords and make a loop for swinging the bola (Figure 8-15d).**

You need to practice using bolas accurately. Whirl a bola well above your head (Figure 8-15e) and then release to send the weapon at the target. Whirling a bola without knocking yourself out takes practice. In the heat of the hunt, whirl the bola only one or two times before releasing so you don't alert the prey.

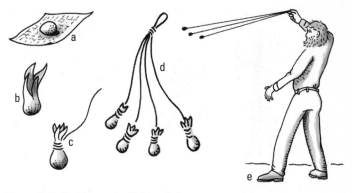

Figure 8-15: Crafting and utilizing a bola.

Going in for the kill with a club

Many animals won't be killed by spear, bow and arrow, or bola. Many times, you have to follow a blood trail to the injured, exhausted animal and then kill it with your club.

To make a killing club, select a 1- or 2-inch (2.5- or 5-centimeter) diameter sapling and cut a 3-foot (0.9-meter) length from it. Strip the bark (which would otherwise decay and skip around like a sheath) and lash a wrist-loop of some kind of cordage around the base so it doesn't fly out of your hand.

Be prepared to attack with a purposeful explosion of energy; just like you, an injured animal will fight hard to stay alive. Use a ruthless, lightning-fast attack, aiming at the neck to kill the animal humanely and quickly.

Don't underestimate any animal's ferocity or the damage it can do even with small claws and teeth! The danger from infection is real.

Butchering your next meal

After you make your kill, you need to take quick action and butcher the animal before it starts to decay. Butcher animals at least 50 yards (45 meters) from your camp, near water if possible, so you don't attract predators and scavengers to your campsite.

Skinning a larger animal

To butcher a larger animal, follow these steps:

1. **Hang a large mammal by the hind limbs, cut deeply across the neck, and let the blood drain away (see Figure 8-16a).**

   You can capture and consume the blood instead of draining it away, but consuming it can carry a heavy risk of infection, and we don't recommend it except in the direst of circumstances.

2. **Cut along the dotted lines shown in Figure 8-16b to facilitate removing the hide.**

   You're not butchering the animal (taking it apart) yet, just removing the hide.

3. **Cut with just the tip of a sharp knife slipped under the skin (see Figure 8-16c) and cut the genitals as shown to prevent infection.**

4. **Remove the hide, cut away the intestines, and generally empty the body cavity (see Figure 8-16d.)**

   Deer have scent glands behind the knee that can smell foul; you can avoid the smell by cutting around the knee rather than through it.

   You're now ready to cut the muscle from the bones and cook it. In survival situations, you want to eat as many parts of the animal as you can stomach: lungs, knuckles — everything but hooves, bones, and hide are pretty much edible (though carnivore livers can be toxic).

Keep the bones (and if available, antlers) of any mammal larger than a small dog. Bone and antler are excellent raw materials for making survival tools (as you see in Chapter 14), as are the hide and *sinews* (stringy tissues that hold the limbs together), which you can use as cordage.

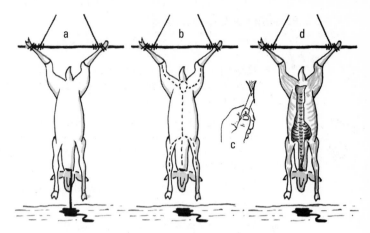

Figure 8-16: Butchering a large mammal, such as a deer.

Skinning a smaller animal

To skin a small animal, follow these steps:

1. **Make an incision though the skin (but not deeper than the skin) across the back, as in Figure 8-17a.**

2. **Grab the two sides of the hide by slipping your fingers under it and pulling outward (see Figure 8-17b).**

   When the skin snags at the paws, you can easily slice it off with a knife. Small mammals don't need to be bled if you're going to roast them whole next to a fire, which is a good way to cook them.

3. **After you skin the animal, remove the meat.**

   For information on getting that meat into edible form, see "The Wilderness Café: Preparing Food Outdoors," later in this chapter.

Figure 8-17: Skinning a small mammal.

Getting Your Hands on Freshwater Fish

In addition to gathering plant foods and hunting, fishing — if water's nearby — is a good way to live off the land. You can often find fish in large numbers, and with some ingenuity (and patience), they can be relatively easy to get your teeth into! This section focuses specifically on freshwater fish, including info on catching them in different ways and how to clean and cook them. (Check out Chapter 20 for more specific information on fishing at sea.)

Locating fish

Before you can enjoy the delicious taste of a bluegill, perch, or some other freshwater fish, you need to know where to catch them. Fish like to take cover in certain places in rivers and streams. You can find them in the following places:

- ✔ In *eddies* (mini whirlpools), where they can rest (Figure 8-18a)
- ✔ Just downstream of rocks or gravel bars, where they can rest (Figure 8-18b)
- ✔ In the shade under overhanging vegetation or logs, where they can hide (Figure 8-18c)

Figure 8-18: Where to fish a stream.

Fishing with a hook and line

Fishing with a hook and line (also known as *angling*) is relatively straightforward. If you have a wilderness survival kit, you may have a line and hooks ready to go; you only have to bait them, weight them, and set them in the water. If you don't have hooks, you can improvise them from many materials, including wire, safety pins, or splinters of bone, antler, or plastic. You can set out as many fishing lines as you have hooks.

Here's how to fish without a reel:

1. **Tie a hook, weight, and float to the line; tie the other end to a 5- or 6-foot (1.5- or 1.8-meter) pole, cut from a living tree.**

   You may want to put the hook at the end of the line, with a weight — any piece of stone or metal — above the hook, or vice versa. The weight keeps the line from pulling out horizontally in a current.

   A *float* — which you can make from any piece of floating material, such as cork — can show you that a fish is taking the bait. Figure 8-19a shows a hook baited with a worm, using a float but no weight. In a waterway with a little current, use a weight, as in Figure 8-19b.

2. **Bait your hook and drop the line in the water.**

   Bait is a topic for a whole encyclopedia, but here we can say that winged insects, worms, and grubs are all good bait.

3. **Check your lines every few hours and bring in your catch by taking in the line, hand over hand.**

   Have a club ready to kill hooked fish, which may flop right back into the water if you're not careful.

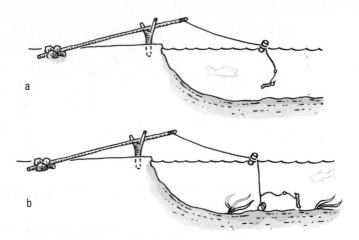

Figure 8-19: Fishing with a hook and line but no reel.

Put out multiple fishing lines and check them often, just like snares. The beauty of this system is that it works 24/7.

Making and using fishing spears

Catching fish with a spear is common worldwide even today. You can master this technique with some practice. To make your spear, stick to these easy steps (and check out Chapter 14 for more on tying knots):

1. **Cut down a long sapling (up to 8 feet, or 2.4 meters) and strip it of bark.**

2. **Cut a notch into the base of the spear to attach a lanyard (see Figure 8-20a).**

   A *lanyard* is a simple leash made of any durable cordage that prevents you from losing your spear in the water.

3. **Use a quick clove hitch to tie your lanyard into the notch at the base of the spear (Figure 8-20b).**

4. **Finish the leash with a bowline knot, leaving a loop large enough to slip your hand in and out easily (refer to Figure 8-20c).**

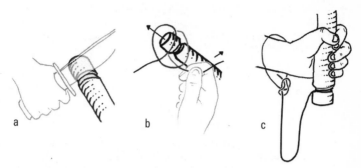

Figure 8-20: Crafting a fishing spear and fastening it to your wrist.

5. **Fashion some barbs from bone, antler, or even hard plastic or wood; attach the armature to the spear.**

   We show you how to attach armatures in the earlier section "Making and using a spear." You should catch fish with barbed spear armatures; these prevent the fish from wriggling off the spear. Figure 8-21 shows a range of possible designs. Because fish are hard to spear, lash several armatures on the spearhead. Make your lashings tight. You can secure lashing with sticky pine *pitch* (sap).

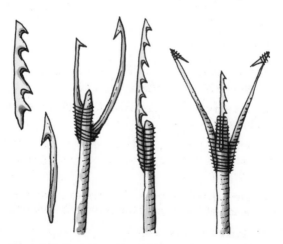

Figure 8-21: Barbed armatures can make spearing fish easier.

Here are some spear-fishing tips:

- ✔ When spear-fishing from a bank (see Figure 8-22), try to keep your shadow under you or behind you to keep from alerting fish of your presence.

- ✔ If you wade into the shallows, don't go deeper than knee-deep and move slowly to prevent splashes that drive fish away.

- ✔ Aim a little lower than the fish appears in the water. This corrects for the water's distortion of perspective; as Figure 8-22, the fish's apparent position (in gray) is somewhat above its real position.

Figure 8-22: Fishing with a spear.

Fishing with a net

Making a net is so laborious (and requires so much cordage) that we don't want to cover it in this book. However, if you come across an old fishing net (you may find one on the seashore), you can use it to catch fish by stretching it across a water course and weighting the bottom. Check the net every few hours.

Creating a fish bottle trap

A 2-liter soda bottle makes a great trap for small fish. To use the bottle, just cut off the top and add some rocks or sand to weigh the bottle down. Flip the top around and insert it backward into the rest of the bottle, as in Figure 8-23. It may hold by itself, or you can sew through the plastic with heavy thread for a few stitches or use duct tape to secure the joint.

Simply place the bottle trap in the water and wait. With the weighted bottle on the bottom of a stream, small fish may enter the opening but find it hard to swim out again.

Figure 8-23: A soda-bottle trap.

Preparing fish to eat

You can boil small fish whole, without bothering with butchery, but any fish larger than the palm of the hand should be butchered. Here's how to clean and cook a fish:

1. **Cut the fish down the belly and remove the guts, either by pulling them out (Figure 8-24a) or by cutting them out with a knife (Figure 8-24b).**

   You can use the guts as bait. Just be sure to store them away from camp.

2. **Decapitate larger fish.**

   You can boil the head for soup and cook the resulting fillet.

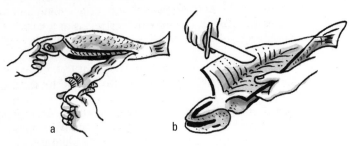

Figure 8-24: Cleaning fish.

The Wilderness Café: Preparing Food Outdoors

You may not have a fancy cutlery set or a stove or a clean kitchen sink, but you can still prepare your food in the wilderness to make it safe and reasonably appetizing. In this section, we tell you how to prepare food before you eat it and how to preserve food for later. (For information on building a fire, see Chapter 5; for directions on lashing together a tripod that you can use to cook over a fire, flip to Chapter 14.)

Whatever animal parts you don't eat can be burned (thoroughly, down to just ashes) or buried away from camp (at least 50 yards, or 45 meters) to prevent attracting other animals.

Cooking food you can eat now

With few exceptions, you should cook wilderness survival food to kill bacteria and parasites. Cooking can also improve flavor and make some foods (like snails) more palatable. This section gives you an overview of how to cook and otherwise prepare foods in the wild.

Plant foods

Although not all plant foods require cooking, you should cook most of them. Microorganisms thrive on plant surfaces as well as in water that plants may be growing in. Boiling, steaming, and otherwise cooking plant foods can decrease their nutritional value, but it's worth knowing that you're not eating the colonies of bacteria that live in a single drop of swamp water.

You can boil plant foods, bake them, or roast them over a flame. Here's how to prepare various plant foods:

- ✔ **Fruits:** Wash fruits before eating them. Most fruits don't need to be cooked, though you can make some (like the *plantain*, a banana-like fruit) more palatable by cooking.

- ✔ **Nuts and seeds:** Wash and shell the nuts and seeds on a large, clean working area, such as the surface of a clean tarp.

- ✔ **Leaves and flowers:** Thoroughly wash leaves before eating them. Flowers must be washed and boiled.

- ✔ **Moss:** Boil moss before eating it.

- ✔ **Roots:** You have to cook most roots to soften them up before eating. Bake them in coals or boil them. When they're softened, you can mash them if you like.

You can bake foods like roots in a ball of wet clay, which you then place into embers until it hardens. When you break off the clay, the root food should be well cooked.

Mammal foods

Although some wilderness TV shows have featured people devouring uncooked (or even living) animals on camera, don't do it. This is just a trick for dramatic TV, and it's a spectacularly bad idea. Cooking kills many potentially lethal microscopic life-forms; it's the main reason that humans cook food in the first place!

You can roast mammal meat on a rack or spit above fire, boil it in water, or bake it in clay or wrapped in thick layers of leaves. Mammal meat should be well-done, not raw or bloody, when you consume it.

You can split open mammal bones with a heavy rock (crush the bone on an anvil stone) to get at the *marrow*, a nutritious, calorie-rich tissue inside. You can also boil bones to extract every possible calorie and nutrient in a tasty broth.

The organs of mammals are normally good to eat, but be aware that the liver of many carnivores contains high concentrations of vitamin A, which can cause death. Don't eat carnivore livers.

Insects and invertebrates

Grasshoppers, snails, mussels, and other critters can be roasted on a rack over a fire or boiled. Some insects are so hard to process, though, that it's best to just crush them into a paste that you boil in water as a soup.

Insects are related to shellfish, so if you have a seafood allergy, leave insects off the menu.

Fish

Although you may get away with eating some fish uncooked (and you may have to if you're stranded in a dinghy!), fish should normally be cooked, like any other animal tissues.

Fish are excellent survival food because they cook quickly and can be dried and preserved for a long time. Figure 8-25a shows how to rack a larger fish next to a fire for cooking (we explain smoking fish and other meat in the next section); be sure to slice small flaps in the meat, allowing the filet to hang on the rack. You can simply skewer smaller fish on a clean stick next to a fire as in Figure 8-25b; when the fish is dry and flaky, it's ready to eat. Or use other methods, as long as you can prevent the body from falling apart when it heats up. Boiling prevents you from losing any of the fish in the fire.

Drying and smoking food

Preserve your survival foods if you're not eating them immediately; the wilderness is no place to waste anything! Dried food is less liable to attract insects and is slightly water-resistant. Store dried foods carefully.

Figure 8-25: Cooking large and small fish.

You can mash fruit flat and spread it (not too thinly!) on a flat surface, like a rock, to dry in the sun. The resulting fruit leather makes a good trail food.

You can dry meat and fish on a rack — just be sure the wood for making the drying rack is clean. Also try to use *nonresinous* wood for smoking foods — smoke from resin, which is present in pine, sours the meat. To smoke fish and meat, follow these steps using a teepee-style rack (see Figure 8-26):

1. **Build your fire and let it die down.**

   You don't need a hot fire with flames to dry meat; in fact, it's better to dry food slowly, over coals.

2. **Build a tripod over the fire.**

   Make sure the branches are sturdy. We explain how to build a tripod in Chapter 14.

3. **After laying strips of meat (either mammal or fish) on the various rungs of the tripod, you can cover the structure with a tarp or even brush to concentrate the smoke.**

Figure 8-26: Smoking meat on a tripod.

Part II
Eyeing Advanced Survival Techniques

The 5th Wave   By Rich Tennant

In this part . . .

As soon as you understand the basics of staying alive in the wilderness, you need to know how to get yourself out and back to civilization. There are two ways to do this: Signal for help, or make the big decision to walk out. In this part, we tell you how to navigate across land, how to use Mother Nature's clues to help you find your way, and how to signal for help with things like fire and smoke. Finally, we cover first aid and give you a bundle of no-nonsense techniques (such as how to tie knots) that can make the difference between just surviving outdoors and thriving.

Chapter 9

Finding Your Way with Tools: Basic Wilderness Navigation

In This Chapter

▶ Understanding the basics of land navigation

▶ Using maps

▶ Relying on a compass

▶ Using a GPS receiver

*N*avigation, like fire building, is a skill you should practice a little when the pressure's off. Later on, when it counts, this small amount of practice can end up meaning as much to you in the wild as a good knife or a dependable lighter.

In this chapter, we show you the basics of *navigation,* or otherwise staying oriented in the wild. We show you how to use a map, a compass, and a GPS receiver. (For information on navigation using the stars and sun, see Chapter 10.)

Grasping Navigation Basics

Whether you're working your way back to civilization, moving toward a water source, or simply trying to figure out where you left your pack, being able to navigate is essential to your survival. You want to know not only where you are but also where you're heading. Even in the era of the GPS, you should keep in mind some basic navigational practices. These principles apply whenever you head into the wild:

✔ **Try to know your position as closely as you can, as often as you can.** Many times, people get lost in the wilderness due to a momentary lapse in awareness. (If you have no idea where you are, see Chapter 11 for tips on what to do when you're lost or disoriented.)

✔ **Navigate for yourself.** Work out as many situations and problems as you can in your own mind, regardless of who "the navigator" is, because nobody's perfect.

✔ **Trust your instruments.** When you're disoriented (and really frustrated!), you tend to ignore what your map and compass are telling you — especially when they don't seem to make sense. Maps and compasses can be wrong, but it's rare.

✔ **Always orient your map.** Keep your map aligned with the terrain around you at all times. Check out the section "Orienting your map," later in this chapter, for more info.

✔ **Be thorough.** Double-check your calculations, and if you're moving through new, unexplored territory, make notes of your movements.

To simplify the whole process of navigation, use your wits and instruments to find large landmarks; then use these large, easy-to-find landmarks to find smaller ones.

Setting a route with waypoints

Whenever you move through the wilderness, you should establish a route made up of a series of waypoints. *Waypoints* are prominent places along your route that give you the ability to know precisely where you are for a moment. You can use waypoints in two ways:

✔ **Beforehand:** You can use waypoints as a way to break up your route into goals — places you want to reach, check off, and then move past. Plot your waypoints on a map or pick them out in the terrain in front of you.

✔ **As you go:** You can use waypoints to record your course, which gives you a "trail of breadcrumbs" so you can make your way out of the wilderness. This is such an important part of navigation that practically all GPS units have a *waypoint function* that allows you to record your waypoints as you're passing them.

If you're operating in an area that doesn't have trails, you can always use handrails. A *handrail* is exactly what the name implies: a sturdy, reliable object or landmark — such as a large rock outcropping or a river or creek — that can guide you. Even if you seem to be going a long way out of your way, moving from large landmark to large landmark is almost invariably the fastest, easiest way to travel in the wilderness.

A handrail is almost always better than a beeline. A *beeline* is a straight line cut across the wilderness, and it often only *looks* like the shortest route. In reality, it's almost invariably the longest — especially when you're dealing with hilly terrain or dense underbrush in a jungle.

Using deliberate offset

Deliberate offset, sometimes called *aiming off*, is a navigation trick in which you intentionally miss a small landmark to hit a large one. Why would you want to do that? Because sometimes the waypoint you need to reach is so small that when you aim right for it, you miss it and go right past.

A lot of navigation in the wilderness centers on trying to use large landmarks to find smaller ones. For example, you can use deliberate offset if you're trying to reach a house that sits near a road. Instead of trying to hit a bull's-eye and land on the front porch, aim a little off — say, a quarter mile down the road (Figure 9-1). When you arrive at the road, you should know which direction to turn because you deliberately aimed a little off, and you can now turn and travel straight to the house.

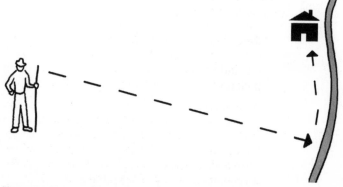

Figure 9-1: Using deliberate offset to find a small landmark.

Map Reading Made Easy

When you head out into the wilderness, you need to be able to read the appropriate kind of map. You may end up using any of the following:

- **State and national park maps:** You usually find these maps at the ranger station or online on the park's Web site.

- **Travel maps:** These maps tend to incorporate detail of both human-made and natural features; they usually cover a large area, such as an entire province or nation.

- **United States Geological Survey (USGS) maps:** USGS maps are usually referred to as *topographic maps,* or *topo maps.* These maps use contour lines to show the shape of landforms, such as mountains and valleys.

To make sense of the map you're using, you need a good foundation in map reading. The map's key or legend can give you the specifics on your map's symbols and colors. Also note the map's scale; sometimes the scale is inches to miles or inches to kilometers. For now, this section helps you figure out what the different parts on your map mean so you know where you are and where you're going.

Deciphering your map's colors

The colors on your map can tell you a lot (as long as you take them with a grain of salt). Table 9-1 lists the standard colors for a map showing the area's physical features.

Table 9-1	A Standard Map Color Key	
Color	**Feature**	**Comments**
White	Open ground	Open ground doesn't mean bald. Many white areas have a respectable amount of vegetation.
Green	Vegetation	The map implies that there's usually more vegetation in these areas, but you don't always encounter verdant, lush growth in areas marked green on your map.

Color	Feature	Comments
Blue	Water	Blue denotes where water usually is. **Warning:** Be especially vigilant if you're in a gully or dry riverbed that's marked as water, because flash floods can come in seconds if a rainstorm hits.
Black	Manmade structures	Keep in mind that manmade structures are rarely drawn to scale. They're much smaller in real life.
Brown lines	Contour lines	These lines tell you what the land looks like in three dimensions. Check out "Using contour lines to identify the shape of the land" for details.
Blue lines	Navigation grids	These grids include latitude-longitude and UTM. For more on these, see "Understanding your coordinates," later in this chapter.

On many USGS maps, trails — which are drawn as tiny channels of dotted lines — are so faint that you need a magnifying glass to see them. Magnifying glasses are molded into the baseplates of most modern land compasses.

Measuring map distances

To read a map and calculate distances, start with the scale. The *scale,* usually located at the bottom of the map, helps you determine the distance between landmarks and how large landforms are in real life (except for manmade structures, which aren't drawn to scale). The scale is expressed as a ratio, such as 1:75,000. What that means is that 1 inch on your map equals 75,000 inches, or 6,250 feet, on the ground. But on a more practical level, the scale allows you to convert inches on a map to miles (or kilometers) on land. The best way to calculate distances is to lay something that bends, such as a string or wire, over the scale at the bottom, mark it at various intervals, and then use it as a measuring stick on the map.

When measuring distance on the map, you're always at risk of confusing the various units of measurement — kilometers, statute (land) miles, nautical miles, and so on. You can stay out of trouble by writing down distances or any other type of measurement on paper rather than trying to work things out in your head.

Using contour lines to identify the shape of the land

To read a topographic map, you need to know how to interpret contour lines. *Contour lines* are the mapmaker's way of expressing a three-dimensional world on a flat map. Each contour line denotes a change in the altitude of the terrain, such as when you have hills or valleys. At the bottom of your topographic map, you can find the *contour interval*, the amount of altitude change that each contour line equals. For example, a contour interval may equate to 500 feet in elevation.

On a topographic map, the closer the contour lines, the steeper the terrain. Densely packed lines (as in Figure 9-2a) may indicate a sharp slope or cliff. Widely spaced lines (as in Figure 9-2b) mean gentle grades, easy slopes, and flatter terrain.

Many times, the contour lines form designs on your map that correspond with certain types of landforms. You can use these recognizable shapes to quickly identify landforms in the terrain around you. Following is a list of contour designs and their real-world equivalents; Figure 9-2 shows how those contour lines translate into 3D.

- ✔ **V-shaped lines pointing toward higher elevation:** Drainages, like creeks, runoffs, washes, and sometimes canyons (as in Figure 9-2c)

- ✔ **V-shaped lines pointing toward lower elevation:** *Ridge lines,* which are long crests, and *spurs,* which are small crests that that protrude from the main crest (as in Figure 9-2d)

- ✔ **U-shaped lines pointing toward higher elevation:** Valleys, usually gentler depressions than canyons (as in Figure 9-2e); densely packed lines near the base of the U usually mean a cliff or sometimes a waterfall

- ✔ **Circles, especially circles decreasing in size:** Peaks and hilltops, as in Figure 9-2f

✓ **Hourglass forms (two U-shapes butted against each other):** Passes in mountains and hills, as in Figure 9-2g

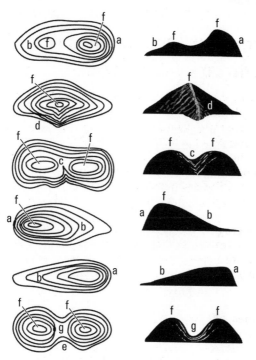

Figure 9-2: Landforms and how they appear on a topographic map.

Understanding your coordinates

Practically all maps are based on a grid of some sort. There are a variety of types of grids, but the two you're most likely to run into are *latitude and longitude* and *Universal Transverse Mercator* (UTM). We discuss both in this section.

Using latitude and longitude

When trying to determine where you are on your map, you can check out the latitude and longitude. These numbers are important because they tell you how far north or south you are or how far east or west.

Latitude and longitude are both measured in degrees, and each degree is divided into 60 minutes. A minute is equal to about 1 nautical mile (about 6,076 feet), which is about 15 percent longer than a statute mile (5,280 feet). (*Note:* If the distance scale at the bottom of your map uses miles, it usually means statute miles unless otherwise indicated). A minute — 1 nautical mile — is always identified by its unique symbol: '.

Latitude lines run horizontally, and they tell you how far north or south you are. There are 90° of north latitude and 90° of south latitude. You can't miss this type of helpful measurement on your map. It's always located along the side margin and is identified by the degree symbol, °.

When you stand on the equator, your latitude is 0°, and when you stand at the North Pole, your latitude is 90° North. If you stand on the South Pole, your latitude is 90° South. Easy, isn't it? A higher number means you're closer to the pole. You don't need a sailor's cap or a parrot for that. If you look at your map and figure out that your latitude is 26°11' North and the Coast Guard tells you over the radio that they're at 26°13' North, you know that they're 2 nautical miles north of you because they have a higher number value. The opposite is true when you're south of the equator — if a location has a higher number than yours, it must be south of you.

Longitude tells you how far east or west you are. There are 180° of west longitude and 180° of east longitude. Instead of starting at the equator, longitude starts at the Prime Meridian, a vertical line passing through Greenwich, England. If you're standing at 118°36' West and you need to go to 118°38' West, then you need to travel 2 nautical miles west, because your destination has a higher number.

If you travel 180° to the west of the Prime Meridian, you hit the International Date Line, an imaginary line of longitude in the middle of the Pacific Ocean. If, on the other hand, you leave Greenwich and travel 180° east, you hit the same line! In this way, the world is divided into two halves: west longitude and east longitude.

Using the UTM grid

If your map has a UTM grid, you can use it to your advantage if you know how to read it. *UTM* stands for Universal Transverse Mercator, a navigation system used by mapmakers all over the world. This system is based on the meter, with grid lines drawn on maps at every kilometer (1,000 meters, or about 0.62 miles).

Using UTM is very easy: The vertical lines drawn on your map are called *eastings*. Eastings are numbered, and their numbers increase as you move east. Moreover, the numbers count meters as they move across your map. For example, if you're near the easting 350000 m.E. and your map shows that the easting 351000 m.E. is near your camp, then you know that your tent is 1,000 meters to the east.

The light blue lines running horizontally across your map are called *northings*. Northings' numbers increase as they move northward. So if your GPS tells you you're located at 411536 m.N and you look on your map and see that the river you want to reach runs along the northing 411000 m.N., then you know that the river is 536 meters to your south.

Navigating with a Map

Many times, you can navigate through the wilderness with just a map — especially if you're on well-marked trails. The problem is that your map can get you lost, too! The basic practices in this section can cut down on the unwanted angst.

Orienting your map

Each time you pull your map out, you have to orient it. *Orienting* a map means physically aligning the map so that it matches the surrounding terrain. If the river is on your left and the hills are on the right, then you should rotate the map in your hands until the map reflects that real-world reality — even if it means turning the map upside down! Why? Because the very essence of map reading is about interpreting spatial relationships — how the real world really looks. If your map isn't in sync with the real world around you, then you're just inviting mistakes. You can orient your map in one of two ways:

> ✔ **Eyeball it.** Look at the nearby features and then rotate the map until it's close.

✔ **Use a compass.** If you have a compass nearby, use it; compass orientation is much more exact. For more on orienting you map with the use of a compass, see "Using your compass to orient the map," later in this chapter.

Keeping track of distance traveled: Dead reckoning

You can find your way in the wild with a map by dead reckoning. *Dead reckoning* is a method of figuring out where you probably are by keeping track of how fast you're going and how long you've traveled. For example, if you walk at 3 miles (4.8 kilometers) an hour and you've walked for about two hours, you can estimate that you've travelled 6 miles (9.6 kilometers).

Ideally, you should dead-reckon every time you go out. Keeping a log, a journal of your travels, is the very best way to dead-reckon, but even if you just make a mental note of the time of day at every important juncture, you're helping yourself a lot.

When estimating how fast you're moving, you have to take into account difficulties in terrain, especially when you leave the trail. The accepted standard of rate of travel by foot is 3 miles per hour over flat terrain. When leaving the trail, your pace usually drops off to less than a mile an hour. One of the most common errors in navigation is to overestimate how fast you're traveling on foot.

When estimating your rate of travel and navigating through the wilderness, you frequently estimate distances to landmarks, even if it's just subconsciously. Here are a few situations in which just about anybody can assume landmarks are closer than they really are:

✔ When looking uphill or downhill (watch out for this one especially)

✔ Whenever a bright light is shining on your landmark, especially a large one, such as a mountain; if the sun is shining brightly on a mountain in front of you, expect it to be much farther away than you initially think

✔ Whenever looking across flatlands, such as a desert, or bodies of water

✔ Whenever the air is unusually clear, such as after a good rain and when the air is cool and crisp

Understanding How Your Compass Works

Your compass gives you the ability to stand anywhere in the world and determine which direction is north. If you know that, you can determine all the other directions relatively easily.

A variety of compass types are out there. You can find highly accurate digital compasses that correct a compass's errors for you, or you can opt for back-sighting compasses, which have what look like gun sights mounted on them to tell you which direction you're currently pointing. But the standard compass for wilderness travel is an *orienteering compass* molded into a clear plastic baseplate, like the one in Figure 9-3. It's *top-sighting*, which means it's made to be mounted below eye-level, or held low, so you can read it by looking over its top. Top-sighting compasses also include many cheap compasses — affectionately called *gumball-machine compasses* — that find their way into survival kits, in glove compartments, or onto keychains.

Orienteering and gumball-machine compasses are the two compass types you're likely to come across in a survival situation. Both are top-sighting, so if you understand how an orienteering compass works, you can figure out how to use the gumball-machine one.

Breaking down the parts of an orienteering compass

Before you can fully understand how an orienteering compass works and how you can use it in the wild, you need to know the parts of a compass:

✔ **Baseplate:** The flat plastic platform that the compass unit sits on (see Figure 9-3a)

✔ **Direction-of-travel arrow:** The large arrow on the baseplate, where you read the bearing (see Figure 9-3b)

✔ **Housing (bezel):** The small plastic dome that protects the compass needle and also has the degree readings on it (Figure 9-3c)

✔ **Orienting arrow:** The red arrow painted on the inside of the housing (Figure 9-3d)

✔ **Straight edge:** Simply the edge of the baseplate; it works like a ruler (Figure 9-3e)

✔ **Needle:** The small, magnetized bar that swivels around inside the housing and always points north (Figure 9-3f)

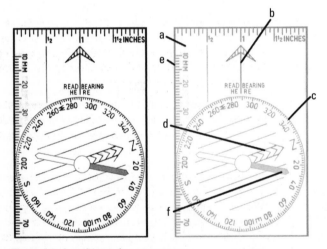

Figure 9-3: An orienteering compass.

Being aware of potential errors

Although a compass is a great navigational tool, it isn't accurate 100 percent of the time. As long as you're aware of the two types of slight error, you can adjust the compass readings to correct the errors and determine what the true readings should be.

Understanding declination (variation)

You probably know the exasperating truth by now: Your shiny new compass probably doesn't point to the North Pole. It points to *magnetic north,* which is an alignment with the Earth's magnetic field. On land maps, the difference between these two spots is called *declination* (on nautical charts, *magnetic variation*). *Declination* is simply the amount of error your compass has in any given area. You have to add or subtract this amount from your compass's reading to get true north.

At the bottom of your map, you can find the amount of declination you need to adjust for in your area. Look for a diagram with the annotations TN, which stands for *true north,* and MN, which stands for *magnetic north,* and then a number, like 13°. The declination may be east or west:

- ✔ **East:** If magnetic north is located to the right of true north in the diagram (as it is on maps of most western states in the U.S.) the declination is east (see Figure 9-4a). Subtract the number of degrees from your compass bearing to get a true bearing.

- ✔ **West:** If magnetic north is to the left (as in most eastern states), the declination is west (Figure 9-4b). Add the number of degrees to your compass bearing to get a true bearing.

To remember whether to add or subtract, just remember a simple rhyme: "East, least; West, best." How does that help you? Well, if your compass claims you're pointing to 90° but you look at the bottom of your map and you see that you have a declination of 13° east, you just remember "East, *least,*" so you subtract 13° and you know that you're really pointing 77° (true bearing).

Any type of compass can have a *declination adjustment,* a feature that corrects the error automatically. The declination adjustment feature usually takes the form of an extra dial inside the main dial of the compass. This extra dial changes the way the compass points — ever-so-slightly — to make the instrument point toward the North Pole. Electronic units do this same trick but with a computer, which you of course never see.

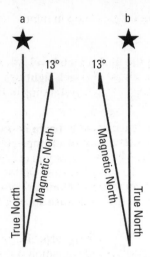

Figure 9-4: Typical east (a) and west (b) declination diagrams.

Interference: Understanding local deviation

Sometimes nearby magnetic disturbances can influence your compass and cause it to have a second type of error: *deviation*. If you have stereo speakers nearby or if you have headphones on or if you have a large block of iron — like an engine, for example — you can expect it to pull on your compass's magnetic needle. The best way to find out whether you have this type of compass error is simply to move the compass around in one area. If you see the needle pulling to one side for no apparent reason, try to get as far away as possible from what you think is influencing the needle.

Navigating with a Map and Compass

Your map and compass can give you more peace of mind in the wilderness than anything else (short of a GPS; look later in this chapter for more on the GPS). However, they can also help you get lost if you don't use them correctly. Map-and-compass navigation usually requires a little practice before you get that wonderful ah-ha experience, so be patient and keep at it.

When using your map and compass, keep in mind a few basic procedural ideas:

- ✔ **Try to hold your compass at stomach-level when sighting (unless your compass is back-sighting).** This usually gives you the greatest understanding of the spatial relationships around you.

- ✔ **When moving across the landscape, try to be flexible in the way you use the compass.** For example, if you're moving on a river and you know where you are, you don't have to be precise in every bearing. On the other hand, if you're approaching a small landmark, you should slow down and be very precise, because small landmarks are so easy to miss.

- ✔ **Write down anything and everything, especially if you're at risk of being lost.** A journal or log or simply a good piece of scratch paper to keep notes on can help tremendously.

This section gives you directions for performing basic navigational functions with a common handheld, top-sighting orienteering compass. If you have a cheap gumball-machine compass, check out the sidebar titled "Stuck with a gumball-machine compass?" for some adjustments you can make.

Understanding common compass usage

The orienteering compass may seem complex, but keep in mind that most of what you do with this compass requires only two or three actions:

- ✔ **Taking a bearing:** A bearing is an imaginary line drawn from your compass to something you see, like a landmark. Simply point the direction-of-travel arrow at something in the terrain, and you're taking a bearing.

- ✔ **Adjusting the housing:** Turn the housing dial, usually while holding the compass stationary on the map.

- ✔ **Using the compass like a ruler:** Line up the straight edge of the compass's baseplate on two points of the map. This is useful because the baseplate's sides are made to run perfectly parallel to the direction-of-travel arrow (more on that later.)

Establishing a field bearing

You can get started moving with your compass as your
guide by taking a field bearing. A *field bearing* is a compass
measurement that gives you the ability to establish an orderly
course in the wilderness and navigate in a straight line. It
doesn't require the use of a map. Check out Figure 9-5 while
you're following these steps:

1. **Point the direction-of-travel arrow in the direction
   you want to travel (see Figure 9-5a).**

2. **Rotate the housing until the red end of the magnetic
   needle is centered above the orienting arrow (the
   magnetic arrow is pointing to north).**

   This is called *boxing the needle.* Figure 9-5b aligns
   north with the compass needle; the bearing to the
   landmark is 258°.

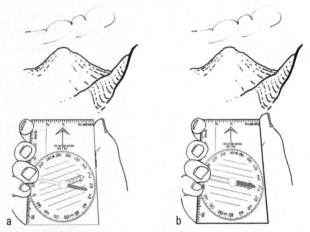

Figure 9-5: Taking a bearing in the field with an orienteering compass.

3. **Read the bearing, in degrees, where the housing
   meets the direction-of-travel arrow.**

   This reading is your field bearing.

4. **Pick out a series of landmarks along this field
   bearing and make note of them.**

You can begin walking toward the first landmark in the series — just don't touch that dial! Leave the housing of your compass alone. You're trying to navigate on a set course now. You want to reach your first landmark, make sure the next landmark lines up on your course, and then continue on.

Your field bearing doesn't need to be corrected for declination because you're simply using your compass as a pointer — you're trying to travel in a straight line, nothing more.

Stuck with a gumball-machine compass?

If you get stuck in a survival situation where all you have is a basic gumball-machine compass, you can still take a field bearing. Simply hold the compass between your thumbs and forefingers. Your fingers should form a triangle in front of you, slightly below chest level.

Now, point your finger-triangle in the direction you intend to go, and then rotate the compass until the needle lines up with north. Read your bearing from right behind where your fingers touch, and walk toward your chosen landmarks.

In this way, the gumball-machine compass works just like the orienteering compass that we use throughout this chapter. All you have to do is use a little ingenuity instead of using sophisticated equipment features. Here's how:

- Instead of turning a housing dial, you rotate the whole compass.

- To box the needle, you center the needle behind the N mark.

- You use a finger-triangle to represent the direction-of-travel arrow of an orienteering compass.

Rotate compass until needle is aligned with "N".
Read bearing from 'pointing' fingers; here, about 300 degrees (magnetic.)

Using your compass to orient the map

Using your compass to orient your map can go a long way toward helping you figure out where you are — especially if you're disoriented or lost. When you use this technique, you can rest assured that your map matches up with the physical features around you. That helps a lot if you're trying to figure out whether the trail is on your right or left — or behind you!

1. **Lay your map on a flat surface and place your compass on it, with the straight edge of the compass's baseplate lined up with any straight edge on the map.**

2. **Rotate your compass's housing until the N, located above the 360° marker, is centered on the red direction-of-travel line.**

3. **Rotate the entire map and compass around smoothly until the red end of the compass's magnetic needle is centered over the orienting arrow inside the housing.**

   You're *boxing the needle.* Your map is now oriented to magnetic north (see Figure 9-6a) — which isn't exactly good enough, because you want true north.

4. **Correct for declination.**

   Now you want to eliminate the error between magnetic north and true north. For example, if you have a 13° east declination, you have to subtract 13° from your magnetic heading, which gives you 347° (360° – 13°). Rotate the housing to 347° and then box the needle by rotating the entire map again. (See the earlier section "Being aware of potential errors" for more on declination.)

When you're finished, your map and compass should look like this:

✔ The baseplate of the compass should be lined up on one of the straight edges of the map.

✔ The red needle should be hovering over the orienting arrow inside the compass housing.

✔ The housing should be set to read 347° on the direction-of-travel arrow (corrected for declination).

When this is done, your map is officially oriented to true north, and it matches your surroundings exactly. Check out Figure 9-6b.

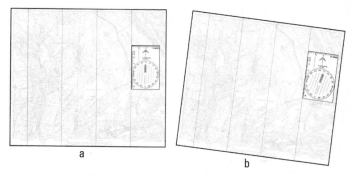

a

b

Figure 9-6: A map oriented with a compass both before (a) and after (b) correcting for declination.

The following sections show you additional ways to use your map and compass. All these methods use this map-orienting procedure as their foundation.

Setting your course from a map bearing

If you know where you are on the map and you know where you want to go, you can take a bearing from the map and then use it to make your way across the terrain. The upshot is that you can navigate toward a landmark that isn't yet in sight. Just follow these steps:

1. **Orient the map (see the preceding section).**

2. **Lightly draw a straight line from your starting position to your destination.**

3. **Place the edge of your compass's baseplate on the line, with the direction-of-travel arrow pointing toward your destination.**

4. **While holding the compass and map firmly in place, rotate the housing until you've boxed the red part of the magnetic needle in the orienting arrow inside the housing.**

5. **Lift the compass from the map while keeping the red end of the magnetic needle boxed over the orienting arrow.**

You're now pointing toward your destination.

After you set your course from a map bearing, you don't need to make any more adjustments to the compass or perform any adding or subtracting. You can begin moving from landmark to landmark.

Making improvised compasses

You can make an accurate compass yourself if you can simply magnetize a small, thin piece of metal. The problem is that some metal won't magnetize! You need iron-based objects for this, which in this modern day means things made of steel. Sewing needles work well, but some are now being made from nickel-plated brass, which can't be magnetized. Paper clips also work, as do some double-edged razors and clips on the tops of writing pens.

To magnetize your needle, you can use

✔ The magnets inside stereo speakers — even the small ones like those found in headphones

✔ Stones containing iron, which usually means stones that are brown or rust-colored

✔ Materials that carry a static charge, such as pieces of fabric and human hair (the best fabrics are silk and nylon)

✔ Batteries and wire

Here's how to make your compass:

1. **Magnetize your "needle."**

Whether using a magnet, stone, or your own head of hair, the trick is to stroke the piece of metal over your magnetizer slowly, repeatedly, and always in the same direction. For example, when using a piece of silk fabric, take your needle and stroke it 100 to 200 times across the silk — but always in the same direction. To use a battery to magnetize a needle, hook up a wire to the poles of the battery and then wrap the wire around your needle like a coil.

2. **Suspend your needle so it can rotate freely.**

You can do this by hanging it from a string, a long hair, or by putting it on a floating object in a bowl of water. Floating objects include cork, wooden matchsticks, and the best of all, leaves. The container has to be nonferrous (not made of iron), like a plastic or porcelain cup or an aluminum mess tin. When free to rotate, the needle should align itself on a north-south axis.

Navigating with a GPS Receiver

The *global positioning system* (GPS) is a network of satellites that send precise navigation data to hundreds of thousands of receivers all over the world. Receivers come in all sizes and levels of sophistication. More and more, they're becoming a standard feature in cars and cellphones. Knowing how the technology can work for you in the wild can go a long way toward getting you back home.

This section familiarizes you with what GPS receivers offer — what they can and can't do — and then shows you some basic actions to make sure GPS works for you in the wild.

What to expect from GPS

When you activate a GPS receiver, the unit makes contact with its satellite network, works out a few calculations, and then tells you where you are. (It usually lets you know by flashing "Position Acquired" on the screen.) The modern GPS system is so accurate that it's rarely off by more than just a few feet.

GPS receivers range widely in sophistication, but all units do one or two things:

✔ They give you your position purely as a series of coordinates, which you then have to transfer to a paper map to find exactly where you are. (See the earlier section "Understanding your coordinates" for info on using map coordinates.)

✔ They show you your position on an electronic map that's installed on the unit.

Most GPS receivers also have a compass function that can tell you which way you're pointing.

Most maps on GPS units lack sufficient detail to help you with navigation in tricky areas, and the compass calculations in GPS receivers sometimes lag behind real time. And like any other electronic instrument, GPS receivers can break down in the field or simply run out of battery power. A great navigational package for the wilderness includes a GPS, a paper map, and an orienteering compass — regardless of what data your GPS receiver can offer you.

When carrying a GPS receiver in cold conditions, put it on a cord around your neck and slip it inside your shirt to keep the batteries warm, which makes them last longer.

Setting your receiver

Before you start trying to figure out where you are, you have to make sure the receiver is giving you the right data! Some GPS receivers give you the right data through default, but you still need to make sure you're set up before heading out into the wild. Check the GPS receiver's settings for the datum, position format, and unit format.

Datum

Datum is the survey information that was used to make a particular map, especially a topographic map. If you're using a GPS receiver that gives only coordinates, you first have to make sure that your receiver sends you information based on the datum used to create your paper map.

To find out which datum was used to make the map you're currently using, look in the margins of the map for one of the following statements or abbreviations:

- ✔ North American Datum 1927 (NAD27)
- ✔ North American Datum 1983 (NAD83)
- ✔ World Geodetic System 1984 (WGS84)

To determine which datum your GPS unit is set to, go to the menu and click on the datum function. Then select the datum that matches your map's datum.

Position format

Regardless of whether your unit gives you a map or just coordinates, you have to set the *position format*. This is your opportunity to choose which coordinate system you want to use to locate your position. Most receivers offer you the choice between latitude/longitude and the UTM coordinate system. Choose the one used by your paper map or the system you feel most comfortable using if the map has both. For more on how these coordinate systems work, see "Understanding your coordinates," earlier in this chapter.

Unit format

Finally, you need to make sure you're using a *unit format* that you understand. The unit format setting is your chance to set the receiver to the units of measurement — miles, kilometers, degrees, whatever — that your map is using in its scale. The GPS unit may do this for you, or it may offer you a choice.

If you're using the latitude/longitude coordinate system, you probably want to use nautical miles as your unit of measurement. If you're using UTM positions, using kilometers is best.

Using GPS in the wild

Probably the most important action you can take with your GPS receiver is to record *waypoints,* places of interest and importance you pass along your travels. The single most important waypoint is your start point. Before entering any wilderness area, bring up the unit's menu, go into the *waypoint feature*, and record your position at that moment. Regardless of where you go afterward or how lost you become, you can now go into the waypoint feature and ask the receiver where this starting point is — and how far away you are.

As you go about your travels in the wild, you can continue to record waypoints. If you do become disoriented, you can go to the waypoint feature and find where the last waypoint was and backtrack. (Record these waypoint readings on paper, too, because GPS units can run down in the field.)

A second function that can go a long way toward keeping you found, not lost, is the track function. After you turn on the *track feature,* the unit automatically makes a record of your travels. The receiver has to remain turned on for this to work, so battery power is always a consideration. But if you have fresh batteries, this is a great feature because it gives you a "trail of breadcrumbs" that can help you find your way back or simply tell you how far you've gone.

GPS receivers can't always communicate with the satellites, but you can solve this problem many times by simply knowing that receivers sometimes have to be in just the right spot to work. If your unit isn't receiving, move it — especially if a cliff or a hill is nearby. If it still doesn't work, move it again. You may have to get creative.

Chapter 10

Looking Up to the Skies: Celestial Navigation

In This Chapter
▶ Relying on the sun to find your way
▶ Checking with the stars

*P*eople have been using the sun and the stars to find their way across land and sea for thousands of years. Sometimes this type of navigation can be complex, but more often than not, using the heavens to navigate is relatively easy.

In this chapter, we show you how to find direction using the sun, the stars, and a little ingenuity. Keep in mind that though these techniques are sometimes incredibly accurate, more often than not, they give you only general direction. Nevertheless, if you don't have a compass or a GPS unit, you should consider the results that come from these methods to be very reliable.

Finding Direction with the Sun

The sun can be a great tool to help you find your way in the wilderness. You can use its position in the sky just like a compass if you know a few easy techniques.

None of these methods are hard to do; just keep in mind that the closer you are to the equator or to the poles, the less accurate these methods are. Luckily, the majority of the world's landmasses — including North America, Europe, and most of Asia — lie at latitudes that make these sun-navigation techniques useful.

You can improve the usefulness of all these techniques by carefully drawing a mock-up of a compass in the dirt or sand. After you find north and south, draw a 90° line to indicate east and west. Likewise, if your technique gives you east and west, draw in north and south.

Finding north and south around midday

The sun rises in the east and sets in the west, regardless of where you find yourself on planet Earth. Just keep in mind that it doesn't always rise at *due east,* or precisely east, nor does it always set at due west. But you can take the dawn's early light to be generally east and sunset to be generally west anywhere in the world.

At midday, if you're anywhere in North America, Europe, or Northern Asia, the sun lies due south of you. For example, if it's lunch hour, say, between 11 a.m. and 1 p.m., you can rest assured that if you turn and face the shining sun, you're facing south. And behind you, over your shoulder, lies north. From this easy technique, you can figure out the other directions, too. If you face the sun at midday in the Northern Hemisphere, east is on your left, and west is on your right.

Likewise, you can use this technique to find north in some of the southernmost parts of the Southern Hemisphere. At midday, if you're in New Zealand, Argentina, or South Africa, the sun lies due north of you. (In the northernmost extremes of Argentina or South Africa, this may not be accurate on a few days out of the year. On those days, the sun appears to be directly overhead at midday.)

Drawing a compass with the stick and shadow method

If you're in the wilderness without a compass or GPS, you can construct a reliable type of compass using the *stick and shadow method.* This direction-finding instrument can be highly accurate, and it works everywhere on Earth.

To create a compass using the stick and shadow method, follow these simple steps:

1. **Take a 3-foot-long stick and plant it in the ground.**

   You can use practically any length of stick, but 3 feet (0.9 meters) is ideal.

2. **Take a rock and place it right on the point where the stick's shadow ends (see Figure 10-1a).**

   This is your first mark, and it represents *west*.

3. **Wait at least 15 minutes and mark the new location of the shadow's point with another rock (Figure 10-1b).**

   During this time, the shadow moves. This second point is *east*. If you don't have a watch, you can simply estimate this time — it doesn't have to be exact.

4. **Put your left foot on the first mark and your right foot on the second mark.**

   You're now facing true north.

5. **Draw a straight line from one rock to the next.**

   This is your west-east line. See Figure 10-1c.

6. **To complete the compass, make a cross by drawing a line through the middle of the west-east line (Figure 10-1d).**

   This second line should be at a 90° angle to your first line. This is your north-south line.

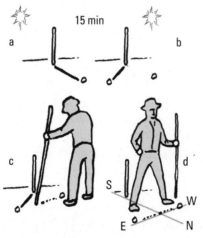

Figure 10-1: The stick and shadow compass.

Finding direction with your wristwatch and the sun

If you have your wristwatch set to local time, you can use it to find direction. This technique uses the sun's position to determine north and south. Although the wristwatch method isn't as precise as the stick and shadow method (see the preceding section), it's much faster because you don't have to wait 15 minutes to find out which way is north or south. Just keep in mind that this method becomes less accurate the closer you are to the equator. But if you don't have the time to wait, just point your wristwatch at the sun and get on your way!

If you're in the Northern Hemisphere, follow these instructions to find directions by using a watch:

1. **Take a sheet of paper and place it on the ground; then put your wristwatch on the paper.**

   You don't have to use paper to mark your directions; you can perform this technique on dirt or sand. The main idea is to be thorough and make sure you have a clear picture of a compass before moving on.

   The wristwatch technique for finding direction uses the hour hand of a watch. But what if your watch is digital? No problem. Simply draw a circle on a piece of paper and then draw in where the hands would be at the current time. This is your "wristwatch" for the next few minutes.

2. **Take a twig and stand it up on the paper so the twig forms a shadow.**

3. **Rotate your wristwatch until the hour hand (the small hand!) points toward the sun and is perfectly lined up under the shadow.**

   If your watch is set to local Daylight Saving Time (DST), you must subtract one hour from the time shown on your watch. For example, if your watch reads 3:00, either temporarily turn it back to 2:00 or simply make sure the stick's shadow falls over the point where the hour hand would be if you did move it back (in this case, 2:00). *Note:* In the United States, DST runs from the second Sunday in March until the first Sunday in November; in Europe, it goes from the last Sunday in March until the last Sunday in October.

4. **Make a mark on the sheet of paper over the 12 at the top of your watch.**

5. **Draw a mark at the halfway point between the shadow and 12.**

   This mark points due south. Take a look at Figure 10-2a.

6. **Take a straight edge and lay it over the watch; make a mark on the exact opposite side of your watch from your due south mark.**

   When you have this second mark, you have due north.

7. **Without disturbing the paper, remove the watch and draw your north-south line; then draw your east-west line.**

When navigating with a wristwatch, you don't necessarily have to use the paper each time you take a reading. If you have a good idea of which way you're going, take readings on the move by just eyeballing the wristwatch.

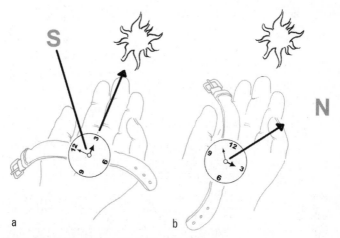

Figure 10-2: Using your wristwatch to find direction in the Northern Hemisphere (a) and Southern Hemisphere (b).

The wristwatch method of finding direction works only if your watch is set to local time. If your watch isn't set to local time, use another technique. See the earlier section "Drawing a compass with the stick and shadow method" for one option.

In due time: Making a portable sun compass

If you're a hands-on type of person, you can create your own portable sun compass to help you in a bind. All you need to make this improvised compass is a piece of paper (paperboard or cardboard work slightly better, because they're slightly tougher than paper, and you have to carry the sun compass with you when you navigate), a stick, and a watch so you can track the time. The only problem with this method is that you need several hours, or even an entire day, to make it right. But if you're facing a long march to safety, it's a good idea to make one of these because it keeps you from having to stop and set up a shadow compass every time you want to find direction.

To make a sun compass, follow these steps (and check out the following figure):

1. **Take a piece of paper (or paperboard or cardboard) and put it on the ground in a place where the sun will shine on it all day.**

2. **Attach a 1- to 2-inch (2.5- to 5-centimeter) stick to the center of the paper.**

   This is your *shadow-maker*. Making your compass consists of simply tracking the shadow's

path across the paper for as long as possible.

3. **Throughout the day, at intervals of every 30 minutes, mark where the stick's shadow ends; write down the time of day next to each mark.**

   For example, at 10:30, place a dot at the very tip of the shadow and write "10:30" next to your mark. Then wait 30 minutes and make a new mark with "11:00" next to it and so on. Look at the following figure. (The time increments in the figure are marked only on the hour for clarity, but you get the idea.)

4. **Stay at it as long as you can.**

   It won't take long to have a long arc of dots streaming across the piece of paper.

5. **When you have enough marks to form an arc, draw an arrow that goes from your shadow stick to the closest part of the shadow line.**

   This line is true north.

You navigate with your sun compass by holding it to the sun and rotating it until the shadow falls on the current time of day. Your arrow will then point to true north. As the day progresses and you're moving across the land, you just keep rotating the compass to keep the shadow on the current time. For example: If it's 4 p.m., turn the sun compass until the shadow falls on the 4:00 mark. The north line you drew earlier is pointing to true north.

Consider your sun compass to be accurate for only a week. After seven days, you have to make another one (by then, hopefully, you'll be out of the wilderness!). Also, try to use as many of the other techniques in this chapter as you can to constantly confirm your direction.

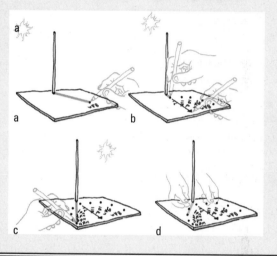

You can find direction in the Southern Hemisphere by using your wristwatch, but you have to modify the technique slightly. It's still very easy, and it works every time. To do so, follow these steps:

1. **Place a sheet of paper on the ground and stand up a twig on the paper so the twig casts a shadow on the paper.**

2. **Place your watch behind the twig so that the shadow falls directly over the 12.**

   The twig's shadow should draw a straight line right down the very center of your watch's face, from 12 to 6.

3. **Make your first mark at the midway point between the shadow and the watch's hour hand.**

This mark represents due north. Look at Figure 10-2b.

Your watch must be set to local time for this method to work. If you're in the Southern Hemisphere and the country you're in uses Daylight Saving Time (DST), then you need to compensate by subtracting one hour from the current time. For example, if it's 4:00 p.m. DST, you want to determine the midpoint between 12 and 3 on the watch to find north.

4. **Take a straight edge and place it so you can make your second mark on the exact opposite side of the watch from your first mark.**

   You can now draw your north-south line. Afterward, you can draw a perpendicular line to represent east and west.

Finding Direction with the Stars

When you're in the wilderness and don't have any tools to help you find your way, you can resort to what men and women have done for thousands of years: Just look up. You can rely on the stars to guide you to safety.

What follows in this section are the easiest methods in the world, and they're a lot of fun to know. Don't be surprised if you find yourself checking every night for your newfound beacons in the sky. Enjoy.

Looking for the North Star

You can count on the North Star, called *Polaris,* to be your most reliable signpost in the sky, because it's the only heavenly body that never moves or sets. (Actually, it does move, but only a tiny bit — so little, in fact, that you'd need instruments to detect its movement.) After you find the North Star, you can easily determine the other directions: south, east, and west.

When you're facing the North Star, west is on your left and east is on your right. If you want to travel west, for example, you simply turn to the left and keep your right shoulder oriented on the North Star as you walk. The North Star lies almost directly over the North Pole, so when you're facing it, you're facing true north, not magnetic north, which is the direction your compass points.

Before you can find the North Star, you have to find one of the constellations that lie on either side of it, the Big Dipper or Cassiopeia. These constellations point the way to the North Star and allow you to confirm that you have just the right pinpoint of light in the sky. The following methods work in any season for everyone in the Northern Hemisphere (see Figure 10-3):

- ✔ **The Big Dipper (Ursa Major):** The Big Dipper appears in the sky just as its name suggests: like an enormous ladle. You can find the North Star by following the pointer stars at the end of the bowl.

- ✔ **Cassiopeia:** This constellation looks like a huge W, although it usually appears tipped over on its side. Find the North Star by following the inside point of Cassiopeia.

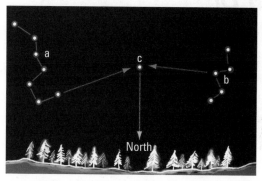

Figure 10-3: The Big Dipper (a), the North Star (c), and Cassiopeia (b)

Finding due south with the Southern Cross

If you're anywhere near the equator or below it, you can see the Southern Cross and use it to find direction at night.

The Southern Cross appears in the sky just as advertised — like a cross — so locating it after nightfall is no problem. Just be sure you have the genuine article! Next to the Southern Cross lies a false cross (see Figure 10-4c). The only way to be sure you've found the right one is to locate the Pointer Stars, two bright stars near the Southern Cross's base. You should think of the Southern Cross and the Pointers as parts of the same body.

You can find south with the Southern Cross; just remember that the Southern Cross doesn't always sit directly over the South Pole. You find due south by using the Southern Cross and Pointers like a ruler. Just draw an imaginary line straight down the center of the Southern Cross (Figure 10-4b) and draw another imaginary line that cuts the space between the Pointers in half (Figure 10-4a); follow these two imaginary lines, and you get a point in space where the lines cross (Figure 10-4d). Directly below this point lies due south.

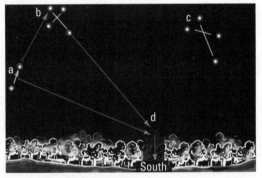

Figure 10-4: The Pointer Stars (a), Southern Cross (b), and false cross (c).

Chapter 11

Trekking over Land

· ·

In This Chapter

▶ Traversing trails

▶ Knowing what to do when you're disoriented

▶ Sitting still or moving when you're lost

▶ Traveling over open wilderness

▶ Handling obstacles

· ·

*I*t's not hard to picture the situation: You've been walking all day on a well-marked trail or in a seemingly familiar area, and now the sun is going down and suddenly nothing seems well-marked or familiar at all.

You can work your way out of this mess, but it'll take time, a clear head, and a lot of patience. This chapter helps you traverse over trails and shows you the basics of traveling through the wilderness, including info on how to cross rivers and streams and what to do if you're lost.

Understanding Trail Travel

You may be wondering how difficult traveling on trails can actually be. You'd be surprised, brave traveler. Any wilderness area you go into is in reality a maze — a labyrinth of trails, false trails, animal trails, and washes. To avoid meandering or even getting lost in the wild, check out the following practical tips for successfully traveling trails. (And see Chapter 9 for the basics on finding direction.)

Before you head out, let someone know where you're going and when you plan to be back. If you don't return as expected, that person can contact the authorities and help set the search-and-rescue teams in motion.

Knowing where you are

When traveling on a trail or doing some other activity in the wild, try to know your position as closely as you can, as often as you can. This deceptively simple principle can do more to keep you from getting lost than just about any other.

Leaving the trail to take a shortcut gets more people lost in the wilderness than just about anything else. Many times, leaving the trail and heading directly for a large landmark seems like a shorter route, but doing so is frequently the start of trouble. Without the help of the trail, even experienced wilderness people sometimes become disoriented.

Another practice that gets people lost is leaving the trail to walk down a slope, such as down to a creek. When you walk down from a trail, you lose sight of it. You can still see signs of it, but many times they can be misleading. If you do walk down slope from a trail, always turn around and look behind you to make sure you know the way back.

People usually get lost in the wilderness due to a momentary lapse in awareness — *part-time navigation.* Many times, people who are bird-watching, berry-picking, or hunting end up lost because they're so concentrated on the task at hand that they only occasionally look up to see where they're going. They frequently find what they were looking for, but then they realize that they've strayed into an unknown area.

Knowing where you've been

Finding your way back is more important than forging ahead. You can stay out of trouble almost indefinitely if you can remember how to get back to where you came from, such as the car, the river, or the trail.

Your greatest survival tool on the trail is the ability to stop, turn around, and look behind you. Always look behind you when you're walking on any trail — even if you don't expect to go back that way. People get lost in the wilderness every year because they get on the trail and think only about moving ahead. When they turn around to go back, the trail doesn't look the same — it has lots of turns they didn't see and lots of landmarks they aren't sure about. The following is a list of problem areas to keep an eye on. When encountering these points, examine the area well enough that you'd know it in the dark or in a driving rain.

- ✔ **Trail junctions and intersections:** Many times, a pathway joins the trail you're walking on and you don't realize it. When you come back down your trail, that seemingly harmless junction is going to be a fork — a fork you've never seen before. When you're hiking, turn around and look at each junction from the direction you'd see it from if you were returning. Stop and make sure your mind absorbs each junction. Let it really sink in.

- ✔ **Old trails, false trails, animal trails, and washes:** Always watch for trail imitators and imposters. A single sudden rain can create a track in the land that looks just like the turnoff that takes you back to your car or the road, but it in fact takes you off to nowhere.

- ✔ **Tunnels through foliage:** These are especially bad because when you emerge from the tunnel after you've had no view for a long time, your sense of spatial relationship is distorted.

- ✔ **Rivers, streams, lakes, landforms, and manmade structures:** If you run into a landmark in the wilderness, keep in mind that it may have a *twin* — a nearby lookalike that can easily fool you in the rain or in the dark. Always look for distinguishing characteristics — shapes of rocks, strange trees, and so on.

- ✔ **An area outside your normal stomping grounds:** If you frequently hike in a particular area but then decide to push your boundaries a bit, look behind you as you leave familiar grounds.

- ✔ **Your old stomping grounds:** Remember that when you go back to your Uncle's old farm, or when you take the trail to your favorite old swimming hole, the lay of the land may have changed.

In the next section, we show you various techniques you can use to find your way back should you become disoriented.

Getting Back on Course When You're Disoriented

If you're disoriented, stop. Plant yourself. Take a deep breath and settle your mind. You can almost always find your way out of the wilderness if you can calm yourself and work the problem thoroughly.

If that seems like simple advice, it's not. More often than not, your instincts tell you to double your efforts, to try harder, to walk more — and to walk faster. But the harder you try, the less you think. The instinct to double your efforts only makes things worse. If you find yourself off course and disoriented, this section can help you get back on course.

Don't backtrack unless you're absolutely certain that you know where you came from. The most important thing to do when you're disoriented is to find out where you are *now*. Sometimes backtracking just gets you more disoriented. If you do backtrack, establish a range and mark your trail. For more on these basic travel practices, see "Traveling in a straight line" and "Marking your trail," later in this chapter.

Reviewing your calculations

If you're using instruments to find your way and you've become disoriented, make sure you haven't made an error in your calculations or measurements (for more on calculations, see Chapter 9):

- ✔ **Make sure your map is oriented correctly.** Incorrectly oriented maps get more people in trouble than just about anything else.

- ✔ **Make sure you're looking at the right map.** Keep in mind that you may have walked off the map or that you may have been navigating all this time with the wrong map.

- ✔ **Check the date of your map.** Your map may be outdated and inaccurate — especially in the category of manmade features, which change all the time.

- ✔ **Check your compass corrections.** Many times, you have to correct for compass error, which is the source of so many mistakes. Make sure your compass isn't being affected by some metallic or magnetic influence.

✔ **Make sure you're calculating with the right units of measurement.** Not all maps use the same units of measurement, and many maps offer the ability to measure distances in two or three different units — miles, kilometers, and so on. When using a GPS receiver, make sure it's calibrated to the units of measurement on the map and to the *datum setting* (the frame of reference that matches the geographic features to map coordinates).

Using your senses to help you find your way

If you don't have maps or instruments with you, or if you've examined them and you still can't make heads or tails of where you are, you can reorient yourself by examining various clues around you.

Stop and observe

Taking a moment to stop and look around can be tough, and sitting still can be excruciating, but stopping to observe your surroundings and thinking through your earlier movements can get you back on the trail. Try the following:

✔ **In your mind, go back to the last point where you were certain you knew where you were.** Make a list of what you've seen and everywhere you could've gone wrong. If you can figure out where you had your lapse in awareness, you can probably get out of trouble.

✔ **In your mind, try to replay your entire hike, from when you left your base to where you are now.** What were the major features you passed? Did you cross a river or stream?

✔ **Examine the features and landforms around you.** Any two landforms can look the same if you only glance at them, so don't assume that you've seen everything on the first glance. You usually can't distinguish one creek bed or hill from another unless you spend a minute contemplating it. Many features appear different in different shades of light.

✔ **Watch for sunlight in thinning forests or scrub.** You may be next to a major trail or road that's only 50 feet away. A major shaft of sunlight can indicate a break in the forest from a road or a trail.

Listen

Sitting in the quiet can be brutal, but it works. The only way to listen is to be still — really still. Hold your breath if you have to. Here are common sounds to listen for:

✔ **River rapids, waterfalls, and surf:** Water noises are among the very best. On some clear nights, it's not uncommon to hear the surf crashing on a beach that's miles away — even on the other side of hills.

✔ **Highways and roads:** One can hear the roar of cars from miles away, but hearing a single car takes a little work. Sometimes people mistake these sounds for water noise.

✔ **Barking dogs:** A steady, single bark usually denotes a domesticated dog. But remember that in most wilderness areas of the world, domesticated dogs aren't the only types of canine.

✔ **Slamming doors:** This noise can be heard from a long distance, but you must be attuned to hearing it. This sound is especially prevalent in state and national parks.

✔ **Laughter:** You can frequently hear people sitting around a campfire from a long distance — if you're listening for them.

Taking action when you're disoriented

If you've become disoriented, your sole priority should be to figure out where you are — not to travel more. If you can't establish your position on a map, do everything you can to understand your *relative position* — in other words, where you are in relation to some nearby landmark. At least you can establish a base, a single point you can work from. After you've established your base, mark that spot.

Plan on returning to your base after you've tried one or both of the following tricks:

✔ **Move to higher ground.** Higher ground gives you the ability to see a lot of terrain and landmarks all at once — this alone can tell you where you are. Move to higher ground only if you know where higher ground is — and you're positive you'll be able to find your way back to your current position.

✔ **Expand out in concentric circles.** Do this slowly. Venture out nearby and look at the lay of the land around your position. Do this in very small increments, and return to base frequently. You may be able to pick up the trail again this way.

Before you move, make sure you'll be able to get back to where are right now. Whether you move to higher ground or move outward in concentric circles, you need to mark your trail very prominently. Check out the later section "Marking your trail" for specific advice.

What to Do When You're Lost

Whether you wandered off trail or your plane had an unplanned, not-so-gentle landing in the woods, it never hurts to admit it: You're lost. In this section, we discuss staying put and waiting for rescue, and we tell you what to do if you make the risky decision to move when you're lost.

Staying put so people can find you

If you're monumentally lost, or if you have good reason to believe that someone is going to come looking for you, stay put. The following is a list of typical situations in which you need to stay where you are:

✔ You're separated from your hiking or tour group.

✔ You've left word saying you'll be back.

✔ You were involved in a crash or any other tragedy that typically mobilizes search-and-rescue services.

✔ You know that search-and-rescue services are already looking for you. Many times, hikers or victims call in a rescue and then move, which is the worst thing they can do. You only have to be a few feet away — only a few feet — to make yourself invisible to search-and-rescue services.

If you have reason to believe someone may come looking for you, your responsibility is to stay alive and healthy so you can signal them. (For more on signaling, check out Chapter 12.)

Even if your current situation is tough, try to do what you can to stay put. Here's how to ward off the cold and make yourself more comfortable as you sit tight:

✔ **Make a fire and stay the night.** If you can get a fire going, you can turn the tables on the wilderness. For more on the fine art of starting a fire, see Chapter 5.

✔ **Make a shelter.** A small, tight-fitting, hovel-like shelter can do much to insulate you. Building a shelter when you know there's a town nearby may seem crazy, but you need to fight hypothermia in any way you can. If you build a good shelter, you can get through the night — which is much better than wandering. For more on building your wilderness home, see Chapter 6.

Anytime you build a shelter, you need to mark it; otherwise, you're building camouflage! You can use brightly colored cloth or reflective metal, or you can break branches or stack rocks to mark your shelter.

Deciding to travel

When you're lost, you may realize the only way you're going to be rescued is to move. In this section, we tell you how to move systematically when you're lost. In the next, we explain how to travel over open wilderness.

Traveling when lost may make you even more lost than you already are. Even worse, you may move out of the area where people are searching for you. Making the decision to travel when lost must be your last resort. Travel only if you must move because of safety reasons or you've logically concluded that no one is going to come looking for you.

Preparing to move

If you're dead set on moving, take the following precautions:

✔ **Above all, make a plan.** Take a bearing on something —
a tree, a rock, anything; don't just walk aimlessly. (For
more on traveling with bearings, see "Traveling in a
straight line," later in this chapter.) If you're leaving
people behind, make a timetable and a schedule of
contacts (if possible) and thoroughly discuss what the
plan of action is.

✔ **Make the necessary preparations.** Carry water, make
copies of maps, and carry as many tools as you can.

✔ **Leave a message at your current location.** Write down,
specifically, the following information:

- Who you are

- What you're doing

- The history of your situation

- What time you left

- Where you went

Then display this note prominently. If someone comes
looking for you, this information may be the only hope he
or she has of locating you. If possible, periodically leave
small notes that searchers may discover along the way.

✔ **Leave bright markers behind you as you move.** Do
everything you can to help search-and-rescue units find
you. If you don't mark your trail, you complicate the
process enormously.

Detecting signs of civilization

You can detect civilization by listening for sounds and looking
for physical signs. For a list of some of these, check out the
earlier section "Using your senses to help you find your way."
Here's a list of ways to find civilization; always look for as
many indicators as you can:

✔ **A glow on the horizon:** Cities and towns glow on the
horizon. Even if a town isn't nearby, look for the glow of
large distribution complexes or trucking terminals in the
countryside.

✔ **Reflections off of low clouds:** Anytime you have a low
sky at night, especially if it's dense, white, and overcast,
you can see reflections from human-made light. Even a
campfire reflects on the underside of an overcast sky.

✔ **Smoke:** You can see smoke from great distances. A single campfire gives off only a tiny black trickle, so scan the horizon slowly and carefully.

✔ **Converging power lines or railroads:** Power lines and railroads are especially useful for finding civilization if they seem to be converging.

Never assume that your troubles are over if you have a road or power line in front of you. Many times, road and power lines go for miles and miles and lead you deeper into the wilderness.

✔ **Frequent, low-flying aircraft:** If you can see aircraft descending or ascending, especially if you see a series of aircraft moving in the same general direction, that may point to an airfield or airport.

✔ **Noise:** Keep your ears tuned for noises that indicate civilization, such as car or snowmobile engines, voices, industrial machinery, and so on.

✔ **Squared land and fences:** If you have a view of the area around you, look closely for squares or rectangles in the distance. These shapes are a dead giveaway for civilization.

✔ **Smells of food or industry:** Food smells and industry exhaust travel long distances. Many experienced navigators have followed their nose to safety.

Following water to civilization

You've probably heard the old adage that you can follow water to civilization, or perhaps you've heard that you should always work your way downstream. Nothing's wrong with this advice, except that it's not a guarantee. Sorry! You can follow a drainage to a creek and then a creek to a river and so on, but you may be traveling for a very, very long time before you hit people.

Don't travel down the bottoms of steep canyons or river drainages — especially if you have no way to get out in a hurry. The water level can rise swiftly, even if it hasn't been raining. We've been on rivers when, unknown to us, the floodgates of a nearby dam were suddenly opened. The water rose 10 feet in 20 minutes.

Blazing Your Own Trail

If you're in the wild and don't have a trail to guide you, you may end up setting out across the open wilderness. This section gives some pointers you need to remember when traveling without a trail and explains what you need to do to orient yourself.

Be realistic when estimating your rate of travel off trail. Even if you're tough, you can still probably travel only about 1 mile per hour in bad terrain. Many times, you go much slower. Just a small amount of underbrush and growth can slow you down to a crawl.

Understanding meandering

When you're moving through territory without the use of trails, maybe for the first time, keep in mind the following unavoidable problems:

- ✔ **Without anything to orient you, you tend to walk in a series of arcs or in an aimless fashion.** Everybody, you included, tends to veer to one side. This has nothing to do whatsoever with being right-handed or left-handed; it has to do with the fact that one leg is always slightly longer (and usually stronger) than the other. (Didn't Mother always say you were special?) This is true for everyone, and it causes a slow and constant turn unless your mind can orient itself and correct for it.

- ✔ **You tend to make arbitrary turns when you reach obstacles you're unsure of.** Many people take the path of least resistance, or they turn down the trail that appears more inviting, or they prefer to turn right or left, even though there's no real navigational rationale for this turn. If you're uncertain, take your time and think through your turns.

- ✔ **You always tend to turn away from irritants.** Irritants include heavy winds on one side of your face, burning sun, briars and thorns, and especially slopes. Whenever you walk on the side of a slope, you tend to want to walk either up it or down it (especially down).

Now that you know some ways you can get turned around, you're ready to try to walk in a (somewhat) straight line.

Traveling in a straight line

To make a straight path, establish a bearing before you set out into the unknown. A *bearing* is simply an imaginary line you draw from your position to a prominent landmark or feature. Even if you can see only 50 feet in front of you, draw a bearing to a tree or a rock. This helps immensely because it cuts down on the meandering and wandering that can cause you to become disoriented. One of the best types of bearings is the type you make with a compass. (For more on compass bearings, check out Chapter 9.)

You can make an excellent bearing by establishing a range. A *range* is an imaginary line that you draw through any three landmarks that line up in a column. To make a range, you have two options:

- ✓ **Connect three landmarks.** Draw a straight line through three landmarks ahead of you, such as a bush, a rock, and a hill (as in Figure 11-1a). Then follow this straight line through a twisting and turning wilderness.

- ✓ **Use a back bearing.** A *back bearing* is simply a line that runs from an object behind you, through your body, and to an object in front of you. This gives you a range because it gives you three things you can line up in a column.

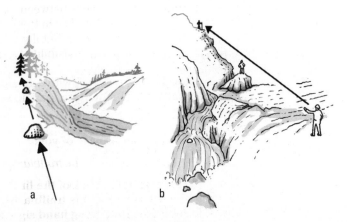

Figure 11-1: Using a bearing (a) and file (b).

Marking your trail

Whenever you're working in uncharted territory with bearings and ranges, mark your trail. Marking your trail, or *trailblazing*, means leaving behind physical signs of your movement through the wild. Just keep in mind that marking the wilderness is something you do only if you're truly lost. Marking your trail does the following:

✔ Gives you the ability to work your way back if you hit a dead end

✔ Allows you to turn around

✔ Prevents you from getting lost

✔ Helps you to maintain a straight line of travel because you can check your back bearing on the trail markers you've left behind

You can mark your trail with just about anything you want — use piles of rocks *(cairns)*, break tree limbs, or tie brightly colored or reflective material to branches. Just make sure your markers are visible from both sides of the tree or landmark, back and front, so you can see them when you look behind you and so search-and-rescue units can see them as they're following you.

In dense jungle, forest, high underbrush, or bad conditions, you may need to shorten the distance between markers down to just 20 feet or less. Patience is the key in these situations. Trailblazing can seem tedious at times, but if you're thorough, this method can save your life in low-visibility terrains.

If you're lucky enough to be traveling with a group, you can blaze the trail by setting up a moving range, known as a *file*. Here's how (refer to Figure 11-1b):

1. **Send two people out in front of you.**

   One is the *aimer*, and one is the *trailblazer*.

2. **If you're standing at the back of the line, use the aimer in the file to line up the trailblazer; then coach the two down the range using hand signals until they're almost out of sight.**

3. **After the trailblazer has gone as far as you want him or her to go, the trailblazer sets a mark — *blazes the trail* — while the rest of the file moves forward.**

Crossing Obstacles in the Wild

When you encounter obstacles in the wilderness, you should generally try to go around them rather than over or through them. All too often, survivors are injured or killed in falls or are swept away in streams and rivers. Sometimes, however, you have little choice. This section focuses on obstacles you may encounter and how to handle them. Before you attempt to climb or go through an obstacle, make sure you've established a bearing on a distinct landmark on the other side. For more on establishing a bearing, see "Traveling in a straight line," earlier in this chapter.

Crossing rivers and streams

If you come up to a river or stream and crossing it is your only option, you need to take some precautions. You can either try to walk through the water or build a raft. This section covers these two choices. (For info on crossing frozen water obstacles, see Chapter 16.)

Wading across

The first step in walking across a river or stream is to choose a place to cross. From high ground or a safe tree, examine the river for possible crossings and look for a ford. A *ford* is a place where the river narrows or becomes shallow. Many times, a little exploration can really pay off. Fords aren't necessarily obvious, and many times you can see them only when you're close to them.

As you evaluate possible crossing places, think about where you'll end up on the other side of the river. The best choice for a landing site is a sandy bank. Know that your landing site will be well downstream. The moment you start to move toward the opposite bank, the current will push you. Don't fight this power; crossing at an angle is always best. Expect to cross a river at a 45° angle.

If you have any type of plastic sheeting with you, take your clothes off and roll them into it, and then tie up the whole bundle with your belt or shoelaces. Then tie the bundle to your wrist and try to hold it above the water. If tied tightly, even the most improvised of packages can keep your clothes dry long enough for you to get across (and help you momentarily float should you lose your footing).

When crossing, you can use any one of the following techniques:

- ✓ **Crossing solo with a pole:** You can use a pole to help break the river's current. Find a strong tree branch or other pole, about 3 to 4 inches (7.5 to 10 centimeters) in diameter and about 7 to 8 feet (2 to 2.5 meters) long, and dig it into the riverbed upstream from your body, as in Figure 11-2a. The pole disrupts the flow so you can walk at a 45° angle to a strong current. Drag the pole along the riverbed, moving it by small increments, and stay behind the break in the current.

- ✓ **Crossing with a group and a pole:** Use a strong pole that several people can hold onto. Have your group form a single column, lined up on the pole, as in Figure 11-2b. This column breaks the flow of water, making it easy for everyone to keep his or her feet. The lightest person should be the one farthest upstream.

- ✓ **Crossing with a group and a loop of rope:** Send the strongest person across first. That person should stay on the inside the loop of rope, with the other two people holding the rope on shore. The second person holds onto the rope as he or she crosses. The third person crosses on the inside of the loop, as the first person did. See Figure 11-2c.

Figure 11-2: Crossing a stream solo (a), in a group (b), and with a rope (c).

You should avoid rapids, but if you find yourself in swift water, try to float on your back with your feet pointing downstream. Escaping rough water is possible as long as you keep your feet in front of you and your buttocks high. Your feet and hands may occasionally graze and bounce off the riverbed like shock absorbers — try to keep this to a minimum, because you want to avoid having underwater rocks or tree roots entrap one of your limbs, and you're trying not to fight the current. Try to float smoothly until you can swim to one side of the river.

Building a raft to cross the water

You can make improvised rafts from one of three types of materials or a combination of all three. We list these raft-building materials here, in order of their practicality:

- **Empty containers:** Anything that holds air can be tied together or put in a bag or tarp and tied up, as in Figure 11-3a.

- **Logs and Styrofoam:** Styrofoam is the best. Always test the floatability of wood — many types don't float very well. Thick bamboo canes are ideal for building fast, lightweight rafts. You can tie logs or Styrofoam together with two pieces of rope and sit in it as in Figure 11-3c. You steer and propel this raft with your hands and feet (it doesn't lend itself very well to paddles).

- **Lots of logs or bamboo poles:** With these materials, you can build a conventional raft using crossbeams, as in Figure 11-3b. Use a simple levering process to tighten the lines. Simply wrap the line around a pole a few times and then pry upward.

a   b   c

Figure 11-3: Your options for rafts to cross rivers and streams.

Here's how to make a trapped-air raft with a plastic sheet (check out Figure 11-4):

1. **Pile 1.5 feet (0.5 meters) of brush, foliage, or plastic containers on top of a plastic sheet or tarp.**

   Don't use foliage that has thick branches for this, because they poke holes in the raft. If you're using a poncho, tie the hood closed and lay the poncho down, hood up.

2. **Tie together two sturdy poles or branches into an X and lay the X on top of your foliage; then pile another 1.5 feet of foliage on top of your X.**

3. **Wrap the edges of your plastic around the foliage and tie them in place using any cordage or vines you can find.**

4. **Place your wrapped foliage package on top of a second tarp or poncho, open side down.**

5. **Wrap the second tarp or poncho around the first and tie the whole package together.**

   Place the entire raft in the water like it is, with the second poncho or tarp on the bottom. The tied part of the second poncho or tarp — the open side — should be face up.

Figure 11-4: Making a trapped-air raft to cross rivers and streams.

Improvised rafts are vulnerable to capsize and disintegration. To cut down on the problem of capsize, build your raft as wide as you can. Small rafts, or long thin ones, are unstable. The best design is a large raft in the form of a square or circle. To avoid having your raft fall apart, overbuild it. Use as much cordage as you can and tie your knots tightly. (For more on ropes and knots, see Chapter 14.)

Going over loose rock and sand

A gentle slope can be just as dangerous to you in the wild as a cliff. Many times, easy-looking hills have gravel and loose sand on them, and as soon as you begin to slide on this type of surface, you can't stop. Before working your way up or down, take a moment to plan a route. If you really examine the terrain before you, you can usually see a possible pathway of ledges, pits, divots, holes, tufts of grass, flat spots you can step on — anything that may support your weight.

When going over loose rock and sand on a slope, you have two options:

- ✔ **The kick-step:** The kick-step is one of the most effective techniques you can use on loose rock or sand. To use this method, take a moment to aggressively kick or dig each foothold with your shoes. Make sure you have a good purchase on the land before you put your weight on the foot you've been kicking with.

- ✔ **The heel kick-step:** This method is excellent for descending a sandy slope. Facing outward, with your back to the hill, take your heel and drive it sharply into a pit or tuft of grass below you. Use your heel like a sharp edge — you want to drive your heel into the earth and form a step that can hold your weight. With a little practice, you can figure out which pits and imperfections in the surface lend themselves to this method.

When using the heel kick-step to descend, keep your downward momentum to a minimum. Dig your heel in, and then stop. Then dig in again, and stop. After you get moving and your confidence in this method builds, your upper body often begins to take on mind of its own — and this leads to slipping and sliding, so take it slow.

Chapter 12

Signaling for Rescue

. . . .

In This Chapter

▶ Understanding the ins and outs of signaling

▶ Choosing the right language

▶ Knowing some tools you can signal with

▶ Using radios and cellphones to signal

▶ Preparing for the arrival of a rescue helicopter

. . . .

You can kick up quite a bit of commotion in the wild and still not be noticed. What seems obvious to you can be completely invisible to a potential rescuer. Understanding what people can actually see and hear — what really gets you noticed — is part of the art and skill of signaling.

In this chapter, we show you ways to get the attention of anybody who's looking for you — and even those who aren't. We show you how you can get attention, how to use a radio to make a Mayday distress call, and how to prepare for the arrival of help from the skies.

Grasping the Basics to Signaling

When you're in the wild and need someone to find you, you send out a *signal* — basically anything that can get you noticed. A good signal is one that not only gets the attention of search-and-rescue units but also gets the attention of those who are *not* looking for you, too — people or passersby who may be able to help you long before the professionals arrive. This section helps you establish a firm signaling foundation so you're easier to find.

Picking a good location

If you're in a situation where you have to begin signaling, take a moment to consider doing it in a place that gives you the maximum visibility. Prime real estate for good signaling is usually

- ✔ The highest elevation you can safely get to
- ✔ A spot that can be seen from all sides; ideally, you want to have 360º visibility
- ✔ An expanse with few natural objects that would distract rescuers; for instance, an open field with no large boulders
- ✔ A wide opening, free from tree lines or cliffs; the wider the opening, the better

If you can't stay at your signaling spot, leave behind a signal pointing to where you are. Large, well-contrasted, and angled arrows make excellent signals. For more on these types of signals, see "Mastering the Language of Signaling," later in this chapter.

Making your signal stand out

The basic philosophy of signaling is *bigger, brighter, different.* These three ideas encapsulate the entire spectrum of signaling. Anytime you can do something bigger, brighter, or different — especially in conspicuous spot — you're improving your chances of being found. This section explains how you can make your signals bigger, brighter, and different.

Bigger

Bigger means anything that makes you, or your signal, larger. A human being is actually a very small thing on this Earth, so whenever you can be a part of something larger, you're making yourself more visible.

If you've been in an accident, stay with your downed aircraft or near the debris field of your damaged or capsized vessel. Debris fields represent a much larger position marker than your body — and search-and-rescue units look for them specifically.

If you're in a group, stay together and form a symbol. If you're in the water, link arms with others in your group.

Brighter

Brighter means a more intense signal. Brighter can mean more light at night, such as more fire or more flares, but it can also mean using the brightest colors you can get your hands on. Here are some ways to make your signal brighter:

✔ Make more than one fire, or make a larger fire.

✔ Put reflectors near anything that puts out light.

✔ Use any types of colored objects, such as clothing, for your signals. If your undershirt is brighter than your outerwear, consider putting the undershirt on over the outerwear.

✔ If you have brightly colored objects that you can lie out on the ground or sea ice, do so. Anything that contrasts with the earth's tones can stand out.

Different

Different can mean almost anything that contrasts with its surroundings or that appears wrong or out of place. Whenever you make something stand out, such as when you fly the flag upside down or leave the hood up on your car, you're signaling.

Nature's lines are curvy and messy, so any line you can make that's straight and clean is good for signaling. Your best signals are right angles and hard angles — these can be seen in the wilderness from great distances.

Being persistent

Unfortunately, getting someone's attention may take a while. Don't expect to be seen easily or on the first try. You should always be prepared to send out multiple, repetitive signals.

It's common for search-and-rescue units or people going about their business to pass right by someone who's signaling frantically. Many times, airplanes or ships change course and only appear to be heading your way. This can be frustrating in the extreme and demoralizing. Continue to signal until you're certain they're coming for you.

Mastering the Language of Signaling

You can always simply shout, "Help!" but in survival situations, you often want to send a message that lasts longer, goes farther, or describes more. A distinct group of words and symbols comprising the language of signaling, known as *distress signals,* can increase your odds of being rescued. These internationally recognized symbols mean only one thing: Someone is in peril.

This section takes a closer look at the language of signaling, whether you're writing, speaking, moving dirt, or sending out sounds or flashes of light. Read on for the basic symbols and words you can use if you need help.

Using three of anything to show something's up

Anytime you use three of any type of signal, you're sending out a strong, universally recognized message. Three loud noises, three bright flashes, three fires built in a triangle — all of these are recognized as distress signals, and they fall into our criteria of "bigger, brighter, and different." (See the earlier section "Making your signal stand out.")

You can use three of anything if you don't know any other types of signals, or you can communicate in more specific terms, such as SOS or Mayday. These are a little bit more complex, but they're very powerful — check out the next section.

SOS and Mayday: Calling for urgent help

You can use SOS or Mayday anytime, anywhere — you don't have to be on the water or in the air, and you don't have to be an official, like a ship's captain, to use them.

Tapping into Morse code

When all else fails, beeps or tones can still be heard — even when there's heavy static and your batteries are virtually dead! Most people know how to sound out SOS in Morse code. After all, it's just three shorts, three longs, and three shorts. But if you need to tell someone your position or medical condition, you need to know more.

Below is the alphabet in Morse code and the digits from 0 to 9. If you can establish contact with a radio operator, you can slowly and carefully say anything you need to say using the code. Thousands of radio operators all over the world understand this code, and if you send it to them slowly, they'll respond, in kind, slowly.

A .-	B -...	C -.-.	D -..
E .	F ..-.	G --.	H ....
I ..	J .---	K -.-	L .-..
M --	N -.	O ---	P .--.
Q --.-	R .-.	S ...	T -
U ..-	V ...-	W .--	X -..-
Y -.--	Z --..	1 .----	2 ..---
3 ...--	4 ....-	5	6 -....
7 --...	8 ---..	9 ----.	0 -----

Use SOS or Mayday only when you're in grave danger and need immediate assistance. These are not the signals to send if you're just tired and want to go home! SOS and Mayday are the biggest, most serious signals you can send.

Spelling or sounding out your SOS

SOS is a traditional distress signal for ships in peril. Over the years, so many people in different situations have used it that SOS now simply means *help*. You can use the universal distress signal of SOS anytime and anywhere you're in peril.

Your SOS can be a visual or audio signal, and you can use either the letters themselves or Morse code. For instance, you can spell out SOS on the ground using large tree limbs or other objects. At night, you can use Morse code flashes from a flashlight. And when you're using a radio or cellphone, you can say "S-O-S," send it as a text, or use a sound or tone to spell SOS in Morse code.

Try Morse code on your radio if your batteries are running low, you have poor reception, or there's a lot of static. Radio operators can frequently hear sharp, piercing beeping sounds through heavy static when no other signals can be heard. These sounds are unlike the sound your voice makes over the radio, and because of that, they're rarely mistaken or confused for something else. (For more on using a radio, see "Sending a distress call over the radio," later in this chapter.)

Anybody can spell SOS in Morse code. It's just nine signals: Three short signals, three long ones, and three short again. In Morse code, SOS looks like this:

. . . ‒ ‒ ‒ . . .

That's it! If you want to know numbers and the rest of the alphabet, check out the nearby sidebar titled "Tapping into Morse code."

Calling Mayday

The most common radio distress signal is *Mayday,* which is the international code word for serious emergencies. Mayday comes from the French phrase *m'aidez,* which means "help me."

You can spell Mayday on the ground or on the roof of downed aircraft or shelters, but its most common use is as a radio signal. For more on how to use Mayday over the radio, go to "Sending a distress call over the radio," later in this chapter.

Sea stuff: Saying Pan-Pan when you're not in immediate danger

Pan is the international code word you use when your situation is serious but not life-threatening. Pan is usually used only on the sea, but it can be helpful in international areas where you don't speak the local language, because most militaries understand it.

Use Pan if you want to send a signal saying your situation is serious but not immediately life-threatening. Generally speaking, Pan is spoken twice, three times in a row. It's pronounced so that it rhymes with swan: "Pahn-Pahn, Pahn-Pahn, Pahn-Pahn."

Using ground-to-air emergency code (patterns)

Large symbols that you make on the ground around you are referred to as *ground-to-air emergency code*, or simply *patterns*. Generally speaking, you make these patterns using debris, colored items, branches, and rocks. Or you can build up mounds of earth — just make sure your patterns are big.

Here are the main messages you may need and the basic patterns:

- ✔ **Require assistance:** V
- ✔ **Require medical assistance:** X
- ✔ **Proceed in this direction:** ↑

Make the lines of your pattern signals six times longer than their width. When you draw your V, for example, the lines should be 3 feet wide but 18 feet long. If you can make each line 4 feet wide, then make the lines 24 feet long. This 6-to-1 ratio makes your signal really stand out from the air. (Check out the Cheat Sheet at the beginning of this book to see what these symbols look like in the proper proportions.)

Using your body to signal

You can communicate with low-flying aircraft and ground units on nearby hills by standing still and forming signals with your arms and body position. Depending on your situation, you basically have four body signals to make in times of distress. They mean the following:

- ✔ **Need help, or pick us up:** Raise both arms into the air, similar to signaling a touchdown in football (see Figure 12-1a). Just make sure you turn your palms forward.

Don't wave at aircraft with one hand if you're in trouble. Waving with one hand means that you don't need assistance. If you're in peril, you must put both hands in the air.

✔ **Land here:** Crouch down and hold your arms straight out, parallel to the ground (Figure 12-1b). Make sure you're pointing toward the specific area where you want the aircraft to land.

✔ **Don't attempt to land here:** This is vigorous waving motion you use to prevent an aircraft from landing in a hazardous area (Figure 12-1c).

✔ **Urgently need medical assistance.** Lie on your back with your arms straight overhead and your legs extended (Figure 12-1d).

You can enhance any of these signals by standing still, with your feet together. When you take that stance, you leave no doubt that you are signaling — not just waving.

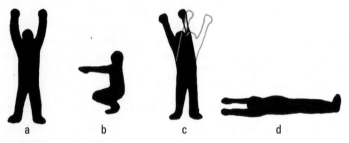

a   b   c   d

Figure 12-1: Body signals.

Mastering Signaling Tools

The more creative your tools, the better your chances of being rescued. However, some tools are much better than others, and these are bound to catch the eyes of searchers. In this section, we take a look at basic tools that have proven very effective in saving the lives of survivors. (For info on radios and other electronic devices, see "Signaling with Electronics," later in this chapter.)

Noisemakers and horns

You can use anything to make audio signals — just try to make your signals unusual. Repeated patterns are the best type of audio signals, and distinct patterns of three sound blasts are usually recognized as distress signals. Here are some good noisemakers:

✔ Whistles of all types

✔ Aerosol-propelled noisemakers, like the type used at sporting events

✔ Gunshots

✔ A steel pot or a metal wing or any other large or hollow piece of metal you can beat on

 Almost any noisemaker we list here is better than the human voice. You can obviously shout anytime you want, just keep in mind that the human voice isn't nearly as piercing.

Mirrors and other reflectors

A mirror or other reflector can sometimes be seen from 50 miles (80 kilometers) away in normal conditions. If you have access to a survival kit, look inside for a signal mirror. If you don't have that luxury, practically anything shiny will work. Here's a list of good reflective materials:

✔ Mirrors in cosmetic cases

✔ CDs, DVDs, or computer discs of any kind (these are very good)

✔ Any piece of glass (a dark backing, like mud smeared on the back, can sometimes increase its reflecting ability)

✔ Plastic space blankets

✔ Glossy book covers

✔ Polished metal lids

✔ A split log with water splashed on (the exposed white wood inside shines when it's soaked)

✔ Flashes on cameras

✔ Belt buckles or buckles on purses

✔ Plastic wrap stretched over a pot

 If you signal with a mirror or some other reflective device, you need to aim your signal carefully. A simple way to aim is to put your hand out before you, line up the mirror so it reflects light on your hand, and then quickly remove your hand. Or you can send an adequate signal by simply moving the mirror back and forth in a tight pattern. Practice before the rescuers get to you — it's harder than it looks! Check out the Cheat Sheet at front of this book to see how to aim your signal mirror.

Even if you can't actually see someone to signal to, continually sweeping the horizon with your mirror or other reflector is a good idea.

Fire

You can use fire anytime as a signaling tool, day or night. However, keep in mind that other fires may be nearby, so yours must be bigger, brighter, or different. In the case of fire, it's almost always best to be different. You can make yours different the following ways, alone or in combination:

- **Three fires in a triangle:** Pilots and search-and-rescue units universally recognize this signal, and it's the very best use of fire as a signal. Try to space these fires at least 75 feet apart.

- **Three fires in a line:** This type of signal isn't as good as fires in a triangle, but if your surroundings hamper you, three in a row works. Again, try to space these fires at least 75 feet apart.

- **A fire that flares up sharply:** Use this technique if you're able to make your fire flare up when ground units or low-flying aircraft are nearby. Oil, gas, or any other petroleum products are good for this, but you can also use paper, leaves, or grass.

- **Large bonfires:** This option is okay if you have no other; just remember that if another large fire is nearby, your fire may not be distinctive enough. Also keep in mind that big fires can quickly get out of control and start forest fires, which can put you in more peril.

For more on starting fires, check out Chapter 5. And for tips on escaping a forest fire, flip to Chapter 24.

Smoke

Smoke is another signaling tool you can use, but make sure you understand that it's very similar to fire (see the preceding section): If you want to use smoke, you have to distinguish it from normal smoke, which can come from any fire anywhere.

The international signal for distress is three columns of smoke. However, simply producing an abundance of smoke that contrasts with your environment can frequently do the trick. You can create contrast and abundance in one of two ways:

- ✔ **Black smoke:** This is your best bet in snowy conditions or when you have overcast skies. Only certain materials can produce large amounts of black smoke, so if these materials are in short supply, you may want to consider building a large fire of other materials and hold your black-smoke producers in reserve. You can then throw these items on the fire when searchers are in your vicinity. Thick, black smoke immediately comes from any of the following:

  - Engine oil, vegetable oil, animal oils, and fats

  - Rags soaked in oil

  - Rubber or rubbery products, like tires

  - Plastic

- ✔ **White smoke:** White smoke is very effective in green forest environments. You can create a sudden surge of white smoke by starting a fire and then partially smothering it. Use any of the following materials for the partial smothering that produces white smoke:

  - Green leaves or grass, or wet leaves or grass

  - Moss

  - Green branches

  - A small amount of water or wet clothes

The torch: Setting an evergreen afire

If you're in the wild and need to signal rescuers, then lighting an evergreen tree on fire — creating an *evergreen torch* — is an option. To make an evergreen torch, cut down an entire evergreen tree or bush, carry it to a large clearing, and pile tinder and kindling in its lower branches. Then light the tinder. Though green, these trees will ignite. The tree's resin, or *pitch,* burns black, and it produces an enormous plume of smoke.

Warning: The risk with the evergreen torch is that it can start a forest fire, so be careful. Do not perform this is in dense forest.

Pitch, sap, or resin — or wood that contains it — can make either white or black smoke, so you have to experiment.

Smoke isn't very effective in windy conditions. If it's windy, consider some other type of signal and save your materials for making colored smoke for when conditions are calmer.

Shadows

You can use shadows to make contrasting patterns that are visible from the air in sunny conditions. Remember that sharp, hard angles get you noticed, especially when using shadow. Always use the standard 6-to-1 ratio when making any pattern. (For more on the 6-to-1 ratio in pattern-making, see "Using ground-to-air emergency code [patterns]," earlier in this chapter.)

Here are some methods you can use to make patterns with shadow:

- **Build up mounds of earth.** This is useful in desert conditions, but the mounds must be substantial. To make this signal stand out, pile up sand or dirt at least 1 foot, preferably more. Keep in mind that what looks obvious to you isn't obvious to others.

- **Tramp down snow.** You can make visible ground-to-air signals with this method; just be meticulous in making your angles and contrasts distinct. In large, flat fields of snow, this kind of signal has to be very sharp and very large. It's not optimal in overcast conditions or gray light.

- **Make piles of branches, foliage, and rocks.** To make this type of signal, you have to be really elaborate. Don't take any chances. This type of signal has to be very large, and the edges must be very well defined.

Dye markers and other color

If you're lucky enough to have a survival kit handy, check whether it contains a *dye marker*. These signaling devices usually look like bulging little packets of tightly packed sand, and they contain about 2 pounds (0.9 kilograms) of food coloring. You usually use this type of signal to mark your position in water. When you open the package, the coloring agent turns the water around you a bright yellow or sometimes yellow-orange.

If you don't have a dye marker, you should still try splashing as much color around as you can. Essentially, you want to use a color that delivers the maximum contrast against your surroundings. Opt for primary colors:

- ✔ **Yellow:** Superb in all conditions except snow

- ✔ **Royal blue:** Very good as well, even sometimes in green forested environments

- ✔ **Red:** Works well on snow or ice

If it's snowy out, you can simply turn over the snow and expose the sod underneath. This makes a good signal because the dark earth contrasts so well against the white snow. You can use charcoal from fire on snow as well.

A good way to signal is to take a bright piece of cloth, tie it to the end of a tree branch, and then wave it vigorously over your head. This is very effective because it gives you motion in addition to color.

Leaving directional signals

You can use branches, foliage, and rocks to mark your trail or lead searchers to your position. The trick is to be obvious. If you break several branches all in the same direction, search-and-rescue units, especially the experienced ones, will pick up on the message you're trying to send.

You can also use rocks to make cairns. A *cairn* is simply a pile of stones built up in a pyramid shape to mark a trail or direction of travel.

The top stone should be an oblong rock that points in your direction of travel.

People frequently use cairns to leave messages for rescuers (such as number in the party, medical condition, equipment condition, available food and water, and so on). Simply write messages on paper and put them into a weatherproof container, such as a zipper-lock bag; then leave them near the cairn's top stone.

Aerial flares

You can use aerial flares in the daytime or at night. If you decide to use flares, take extraordinary precautions when using them. Don't fire flares at random — fire only when you feel reasonably sure someone can see them.

Aerial flares usually come in one of two types:

- **Pistol-fired flares:** These types of flares usually fly only a few hundred feet and burn only for a few seconds.

- **Parachute-type flares, or rockets:** These flares are usually housed in their own cylinders and are sometimes labeled as *rockets*. They can fly to 1,000 feet (305 meters) or more, and they usually burn up to a minute.

If there's a breeze, fire your flare just downwind of vertical. Shoot it at about a 75º angle so it adequately marks your real position without letting the flare come back to land on your vessel.

Aerial flares are basically firearms, and they have the ability to kill people and set survival craft on fire. Old fashioned hand-flares, like the cardboard type found in car trunks and highway emergency kits, have the tendency to drip pyrotechnics. These flares must be ignited well away from the body and should never come near anything flammable or near any important piece of gear made of plastic. These types of flares can sink an inflatable raft in the blink of an eye.

Flashlights and electronic lights

Use a flashlight so it leaves no doubt that you're sending a distress signal. You can use SOS or any other distinctive pattern, like three flashes, or you can tape the flashlight to the end of branch and wave it overhead. This gives the light a wide range of motion and makes you bigger, brighter, and different.

If three flashlights are available, have three people stand as if on the three corners of a triangle and flash in unison. This eye-catching display is clearly different from your surroundings.

Recently, pilots equipped with night-vision goggles were able to detect the light from a survivor's electronic device — his PDA. If you hear an aircraft coming toward you at night, consider moving to a clearing and turning a cellphone or PDA on so that the face lights up. If the pilots have night vision goggles, they can see this from a great distance.

Upside-down flags and other things out of place

You can simply put something where it doesn't belong to get attention (it always got the attention of your mom, right?). For example, you can turn a flag upside down and run it up the pole, you can raise the hood of your car, or you can place a large piece of debris in a clearing.

Signaling with Electronics

Electronics can give you peace of mind in the wilderness, as long as you understand their limitations. Electronic devices and beacons have gone through several changes over the years, so whenever you're preparing to take them with you into the wild, make sure that your equipment is up-to-date and that the frequencies and procedures you've used in the past are still valid. This section delves into the many ways you can use electronics to make contact with potential rescuers.

If you rely on electronics, you're relying on batteries. Try to keep your electronics turned off until you know you need them. Keep your batteries warm and dry. Excessive cold or heat greatly reduces battery life, as does the exposure to corrosives like transmission fluid or brake line fluid (in air crashes and car wrecks) and salt water (in shipwrecks). In extreme cold conditions, place your batteries in a soft pouch with a strap so you can secure the pouch inside your clothing under your armpit or on your belly. This keeps them warm and increases battery life.

Radioing for help

Even in this era of satellite phones, there's nothing like having a good radio around. Many times, the folks who hear your transmission are amateur radio operators and ship captains, and they're great allies when you're in trouble.

Tuning your radio into a distress frequency

In a survival situation, you can use any radio transmitter you have access to, and you can tune it to any frequency to call for help. The law gives you unlimited access to radios and their frequencies when in need of rescue. However, you're much more likely to get a quick response if you send your distress signal on a distress frequency. Here's a list of the radios you're likely to run into and their respective distress frequencies:

✔ **VHF Radio: Channel 16.** VHF radios are those radios you usually see on boats and other vehicles. They tend to be mounted on the overhead dash, with the microphone hanging on a hook at the unit's side. You can expect these radios to have a range of 25 to 40 miles (40 to 64 kilometers) if you're near a U.S. port or a U.S. Coast Guard installation and about a 10-mile (16-kilometer) range when transmitting to other boats on the sea. On land, the radio's range is dictated by hills and other obstacles that the radio can't transmit through. You may have a range of 40 miles or less than 1 mile.

Generally, all distress signals on VHF are sent out on Channel 16. If you receive no response, try Channel 13, especially if you have a large vessel in your line-of-sight or if you find yourself in a shipping lane or near the inbound or outbound lanes near a large port. In some cases, large vessels are legally required to monitor 13.

✔ **CB Radio: Channel 9.** These are radios used by many long-haul truckers. These are short range, usually less than a few miles.

✔ **Family Radio Service (FRS) UHF: Channel 1.** These are handheld units that make up a burgeoning radio network that's becoming popular in the U.S. They have a very short range, usually less than a few miles.

✔ **Single-sideband: 2,182 kHz.** These are long-range maritime radios, and they're only on the better-equipped boats. These radios are usually used for long-range communications, between 75 and 300 miles (120 and 480 kilometers), so they may send a signal that overshoots a nearby station.

✔ **Shortwave (ham) radios: 2,182 kHz.** These radios can transmit hundreds of miles, or sometimes, all over the globe. When using shortwave radios, you can try calling on 14.300 MHz or 14.313 MHz. These are the Maritime Networks for ham radio operators, and they're run by people who will help you anytime you call.

If you don't have a ham radio on your own boat, you may be able to contact people who have a shortwave radio on theirs, and they can perform a relay for you. Generally, the people who operate these types of radios are the most well-trained and experienced radio operators in the world. Distress signals sent on these radios get a very quick response.

✔ **Airband Radios: 121.5 MHz and 243.0 MHz.** These are radios found in aircraft. Military personnel and volunteers monitor these frequencies.

Getting a clear signal

Whenever you use a radio, keep in mind that transmitting a clear signal requires a few physical actions:

✔ Try to find high ground or an area where obstacles won't impede your radio signal. Most radio transmitters are limited in range to *line of sight*, which means they can't send a signal around obstacles or over the horizon. Try to elevate the antenna as much as you can. If you're using a handheld VHF unit, just standing up in the boat helps.

✔ Make sure you know what kind of microphone the radio has: push-to-talk or voice-activated.

✔ Switch to the correct frequency (see the preceding section).

✔ Have your info ready before you send your signal.

✔ Try to keep your radio's antenna perpendicular to your intended receiver.

If you have nothing in sight, try keeping the antenna at a right angle to the ground. Why? Because the antenna doesn't send out energy in an even fashion; it sends out its signal in the shape of a *lobe*, which is a slightly flattened bubble. Check out Figure 12-2 to get an idea of the type of lobe a radio antenna develops.

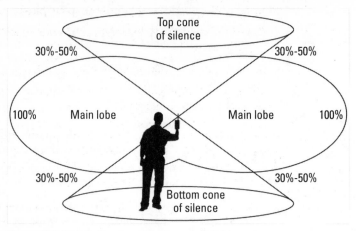

Figure 12-2: The shape of a signal for a radio lobe.

Sending a distress call over the radio

When you send a distress call over a radio, you take a bold step. This type of signal is exceedingly potent, and it sets search-and-rescue units, volunteers, nearby ships, and law enforcement agencies in motion. If you're satisfied that your situation is indeed grave, follow these directions:

1. **Hold the microphone 4 inches (10 centimeters) away from your mouth and speak slowly and distinctly.**

   Don't kiss the mic. The closer your mouth is to the microphone, the more distorted your voice will sound on the other end of the transmission. Give the mic some space.

2. **Call, "Mayday, Mayday, Mayday."**

3. **Say, "This is . . ." and then say the name of your boat or aircraft three times, or just say your name if you're not aboard a vessel.**

4. **Immediately give your position.**

   If you don't know exactly where you are, say that you're giving an approximate position and then estimate how far you are from a prominent landmark and in what direction.

5. **Give the nature of your emergency.**

   For example, "My boat has been swamped and is sinking."

6. **Give the number of people in your party.**

7. **Give a very short description of your vessel, aircraft, or automobile.**

8. **Say, "Over," and then listen.**

   Try to be patient and wait for a response. Sometimes it takes a few moments.

The more calmly and clearly you can talk on the radio, the better. You must say "over" every time you transmit, or the other radio operators won't know you're finished transmitting; they'll wait, which wastes precious time.

If you know your radio signal is weak for some reason, send SOS via Morse code (nine tones or beeps: three short, three long, and three short). On many radios, the button to make beeps or tones is labeled Key or sometimes CW or Tone. (For more on SOS, check out "SOS and Mayday: Calling for urgent help," earlier in this chapter.)

Using cell and sat phones

Cellphones function just like handheld radios. They can send and receive voice and text transmissions only when they're in a *line of sight* with a transmission tower — in other words, they can't send signals around obstacles like hills or mountains or canyon walls.

If you find yourself in a survival situation and you have cellphone reception, dialing 911 is generally best. Even if you haven't paid your phone bill, the system will take this kind of call. (We list emergency numbers for various countries at the front of the book on the Cheat Sheet.) And if you don't know your position, sometimes dialing 911 is enough: With the new *Enhanced 911,* the emergency system receives your exact location whenever you dial 911. This system is replacing the old 911, but it's not countrywide in the United States yet.

If you have no cellphone reception, you have a few options:

✔ **If you're moving and your phone is fully charged or nearly so, send a distress text to someone who checks his or her messages.** After you've sent this text, your cellphone continuously tries to get through to a tower for as long as the phone is turned on. If you're walking, you may briefly pass through an area that — unknown to you — is in line-of-sight with a distant tower, at which time the phone will automatically send the message. This can happen virtually anytime, anywhere.

✓ **If you're moving and the phone doesn't have much charge, text only at the most advantageous spots — like on the tops of tall hills or areas with wide visibility.** After you've texted, turn the phone off, at least for a while, to conserve batteries.

✓ **If you're not moving, have no reception, and are low on battery power, shut off the phone.** Conserve your power and think of a plan.

Satellite phones are becoming more and more popular each year. Despite their popularity, they're like any other electronic device in that they're limited by their battery's life. They also have trouble getting reception when you're in a spot that doesn't have a clear view of the sky overhead. Keep in mind that sat phone technology is still somewhat embryonic. During times of large-scale calamity, like during tsunamis or hurricanes, sat phone networks can be overwhelmed by surges in traffic. However, if you're going on a serious trip where there's no cellphone coverage, you should look into taking a sat phone with you.

Using radio beacons: EPIRBs, ELTs, and PLBs

Radio beacons may look like small, handheld radios, but you don't speak into them. When you activate a *radio beacon,* it simply transmits a distress signal with your exact position to a low-orbiting satellite, which then relays this info to national search-and-rescue units. You register radio beacons so that at the beacon's activation, search-and-rescue services receive info specifically about you (and your vessel) that could save your life. Here are some of the beacons available:

✓ **Emergency position-indicating radio beacon (EPIRB):** This is a small radio beacon used for ships at sea. EPIRBs are usually yellow in color and have a simple activating mechanism that requires you to pull a small cord.

EPIRBs must continuously transmit to be successful; in other words, just pulling the cord and sending a single signal may not be enough. After you've activated your EPIRB, try to keep it in a position that has a 360° access to the sky so the EPIRB can continue to signal its satellites.

✔ **Emergency locator transmitter (ELT):** This is similar to an EPIRB, but it's standard-issue for all aircraft, and most people never come into contact with one. It's activated on impact.

✔ **Personal locator beacon (PLB):** This is a personal, land-based equivalent of an EPIRB that's usually very small and portable. It's for terrestrial applications, such as backcountry hiking. Although PLBs are meant to be carried by a specific person, you can find them in small aircraft and sometimes on boats. Some outfitters now rent these units to hikers headed into backcountry.

In the past, EPIRBs, ELTs, and PLBs transmitted on a 121.5 MHz frequency, but in February 2009, those types of units became officially obsolete.

If you buy a 406 MHz radio beacon, you must register it with the NOAA or your country's search-and-rescue authorities.

Getting a Lift: What to Do When the Helicopter Comes

If you have reason to believe that you may be rescued by helicopter, take precautions to ensure your safety. Helicopters can indeed hover and lower a basket to you, but this is a complicated process. Allowing the helicopter to land and then take you aboard is a safer option. This section discusses preparation for a landing and goes over some copter safety.

Preparing a landing zone

Your first action is to select a piece of ground suitable for landing. The following is a checklist for preparing a helicopter landing zone.

✔ **Choose an opening that's at least 110 feet (37 meters) wide.** This is the *touchdown area,* and it's the bare minimum that the aircraft can enter (see Figure 12-3). The wider the space, the better, especially in windy conditions. Ideally, the touchdown area should have an entrance and exit that allow the helicopter to fly *into* the wind.

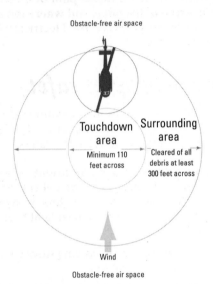

Obstacle-free air space

Touchdown area — Minimum 110 feet across

Surrounding area — Cleared of all debris at least 300 feet across

Wind

Obstacle-free air space

Figure 12-3: Minimum requirements for a helicopter landing zone.

✔ **The *surrounding area,* the area near the touchdown area, needs to be wide, clear airspace if possible.** Some bald ridgelines work well. You want to have several hundred feet around the touchdown area that's obstacle free. Though a helicopter can indeed hover, you want to try to give the aircraft the opportunity to land and take off using forward motion because it's much safer for the aircraft and its crew.

✔ **Find the flattest ground you can.** Helicopters have trouble landing on slopes of more than 5º to 10º.

✔ **Clear the touchdown area.** Remove any object or plant that stands taller than 1.5 feet (0.5 meters) in the touchdown area.

✔ **Remove or hold down all loose items in your landing zone, especially little things like plastic bags.** When the helicopter arrives, it can blow everything that isn't held down into the air, which can play havoc on the whole rescue process. Make sure you've removed all the cardboard, paper, and plastic bottles from your landing zone, and try to stomp down as much loose snow as possible in the touchdown area.

✔ **If you can make contact with the pilot or crew, tell them the direction of the wind and where the nearest power lines or other obstacles are.** Electrical wires are especially hard to see.

Practicing helicopter safety

When the helicopter is on its approach to your landing zone, you need to practice scrupulous helicopter safety. Here are basic points to keep in mind as the chopper lands:

✔ **Stop signaling with mirrors or any bright reflective devices the moment you're sure the helicopter has seen you.** If using a flashlight, don't shine it anywhere near the pilot's eyes. Mirrors and flashlight beams can blind the pilot.

✔ **Put out any fires or smoke-producing devices.** The smoke can obscure the pilot's view.

✔ **Be prepared to be winched if necessary.** If the helicopter can't safely land, one of two devices will be lowered to you:

- **A metal basket:** These float, and all that's required is for you to get inside the basket and make sure you have nothing hanging over the side that could get hung up somewhere during the winching process.

- **A strop:** This is simply a loop of very heavy cordage. Put both arms through the loop, pull it backward until it's under your armpits, and then hold your arms at your sides. Make sure you keep your arms by your side, or you may fall out.

If you're at sea, static electricity builds around these devices, so when they're lowered, allow them to dip into the water first to discharge the static electricity.

✔ **Try not to stand underneath a landing helicopter.** Stay well clear of the aircraft as it lands.

Here's what to do after a helicopter has landed:

✔ **Wait until you're signaled to board the aircraft.** Watch for the crew to tell you that approaching the helicopter is okay.

✔ **Always approach a helicopter from the front.** Position yourself so you're in plain sight of the pilots or aircrew. Never approach the helicopter from the rear (check out Figure 12-4). If you do, you're walking into the pilot's blind spot and are at grave risk of injury. Stay clear of the tail at all times, and never go under the tail boom.

✔ **Never approach a helicopter from higher ground.** The risk of injury from the rotor is too great. If the aircraft is lower than you, stay well away from it until you've walked down to an even elevation.

✔ **Keep long-handled tools out of the way.** Carry long-handled tools like ice axes, ski poles, walking sticks, or digging implements low and parallel to the ground.

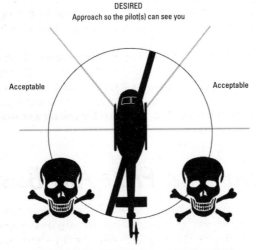

Figure 12-4: Safe helicopter approach zones.

Chapter 13

Administering First Aid

● ●

In This Chapter

▶ Responding to emergencies

▶ Treating major trauma

▶ Treating sprains, fractures, cuts, and burns

▶ Handling bites, stings, and poisoning

● ●

*Y*ou can make a quantum leap in your ability to survive by just knowing a few basic first aid procedures. In a real survival situation, the inability to deal with even minor medical trauma can prevent you from getting back to safety.

In this chapter, you find the step-by-step procedures you need to know when you face trauma in the field. We give you advice for dealing with injuries of all types, including animal attacks and insect stings. Of course, how much first aid you can pick up from a book is limited, so consider taking a course on Basic Life Support or first aid.

Understanding First Aid Basics

Whenever you encounter a person who is injured or incapacitated, you should assume the situation is serious. No matter the circumstances, following the basic responses in this section can help you stabilize the situation. Read on.

Responding to serious trauma

In any crisis, you should work in a sequence of priorities:

1. **Watch for danger to you or the subject and move the subject only if necessary.**

   Be on guard for whatever may have caused the injury — rock falls or other debris threats, dangerous vehicles, poisonous gasses, and so on. If no danger exists, treat the subject in the position you found him in.

   If a threat exists, remove the subject from danger using the *clothes drag:* Grasp the collar at the lowest point you can, and keeping your buttocks low, drag the subject gently out of danger (see Figure 13-1a).

   Moving someone with a neck or spinal injury can cause further damage. Make the best decision you can about which is the greater threat: the immediate danger or the possibility of worsening the injury. If danger is imminent, support the neck with your hands, or better, immobilize the neck with an improvised brace (Figure 13-1b). As soon as the neck is secured, practice the clothes drag.

Figure 13-1: Practicing the clothes drag (a) and immobilizing a neck injury (b).

2. **Make sure the subject's breathing and heartbeat are restored.**

   See the next section for details on checking pulse and breathing and on what to do if you find none.

If bleeding is especially heavy, control it before dealing with the subject's breathing and heartbeat.

3. **Treat bleeding (see "Controlling Bleeding," later in this chapter).**

4. **Protect wounds and immobilize fractures.**

5. **Treat for shock.**

   Check out the "Treating Shock" section later for more info. If you have a subject who has been in the water, look at Chapter 22 for info on cold shock response.

Keep in mind that all the procedures here are for survival situations only. In any of these cases, you should try to obtain professional medical treatment as soon as possible.

Assessing the ABCs

After you remove the subject from immediate danger, you need to make sure the person is breathing and has a heartbeat. Just remember your ABCs: Check the person's airway, breathing, and circulation (see Figure 13-2).

Airway

The first part of the ABCs is making sure the person has a clear airway. To do so, follow these simple steps:

1. **Lay the palm of one hand on the subject's forehead and put two fingers of the other hand under his chin, pulling the jaw forward; then ease the subject's head back a couple of inches (see Figure 13-2a).**

   This procedure prevents the tongue from blocking the airway. If you suspect the person has a broken neck, don't tilt the head back unless doing so is the only way the person can breathe.

2. **Open the mouth gently and examine the airway.**

3. **If you can see anything that's obviously blocking the airway, use two fingers to reach in and pull it out.**

   Things that usually prevent breathing include foreign objects, broken teeth, blood or bloody froth, vomit, the person's tongue, swelling, or kinks in the windpipe. Don't use your fingers to blindly feel around in the person's throat.

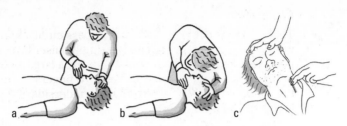

Figure 13-2: Checking the airway (a), breathing (b), and circulation (c).

Breathing

The second part of the ABCs is making sure the person is breathing. You can detect shallow breathing by placing your cheek right next to the person's mouth (see Figure 13-2b). You should also listen for any sucking noises coming from the upper body of the person, which can indicate a punctured lung. For the procedure for handling this injury, go to "Bandaging a sucking chest wound," later in this chapter.

If you can't detect any breathing, follow these simple steps:

1. **Check the pulse.**

   We describe how to take a pulse in the next section. If you find neither a pulse nor breathing, perform CPR.

2. **If you find a pulse but no breathing, pinch the person's nose completely shut and give him two complete breaths by mouth-to-mouth.**

   Blow slowly and steadily twice. Watch for the chest to expand when you're administering these two breaths.

3. **If the torso doesn't expand, check the person's airway again.**

   If you can't find anything, try pushing three to five times forcefully on the subject's abdomen, halfway between his breastbone and belly button. This may eject the blockage.

4. **Repeat the two-breaths-and-clearing process until the person responds.**

People commonly vomit during mouth-to-mouth resuscitation, so be ready for it. If the person vomits, clear it away with your fingers. You can also try rolling the person onto his side so he can expel the vomit or fluid more easily.

Circulation

The third part of the ABC list is to assess circulation. Check whether the heart is beating by taking a pulse. The easiest place to take a pulse is the *carotid artery,* a large blood vessel in the neck. Lightly place your first two fingers on the side of the windpipe just where it meets the underside of the jaw, as in Figure 13-2c.

To measure the heart rate per minute, count the pulses you feel in a 10-second period and then multiply by 6. Healthy pulse rates vary, but you can compare the subject's pulse to these general ranges:

✔ **Children:** 90–110 per minute

✔ **Healthy adults:** 70–90 per minute

✔ **Strong athletes:** 45–60 per minute

A rapid pulse may be a sign of shock (see the later section "Treating Shock"). If you find no pulse, begin chest compressions (see the later section "Giving CPR"). Otherwise, put the subject in the recovery position, as we explain in the next section.

Using the recovery position

If the subject's ABCs are fine but he's unconscious, place him in the *recovery position,* which allows fluids or vomit to drain from the mouth and keeps the tongue from rolling backward and blocking the airway. *Warning:* If you believe the injured person has a neck or spinal injury, don't place him in the recovery position unless you've first immobilized the neck (refer to Figure 13-1b).

To place someone in the recovery position, reach across, grasp the subject's leg behind the knee, and pull the leg toward you. Place the leg at a 90° angle so that it props up the body (see Figure 13-3). You want the subject to end up with the following:

✔ One leg and one arm raised

✔ His head resting on his arm

✔ His mouth free of obstruction

Ideally, you want to place the subject in the horizontal recovery position, with the head below the feet, to help treat shock. For info on shock, see "Treating Shock," later in this chapter.

Figure 13-3: The recovery position.

Giving CPR

Anyone who plans to spend a good deal of time outdoors should know the principles of *cardiopulmonary resuscitation* (CPR), a method of supporting the heart and breathing until rescue crews arrive or until the subject is breathing on his own. CPR is best administered by someone who has received formal training. To find a CPR course near you, consult the Red Cross at `www.redcross.org`.

You should use CPR only if the person both

✔ Has no detectable pulse

✔ Is unconscious and not breathing

If the subject is breathing but has no pulse, do the chest compressions only. Here are the four main steps of CPR on adults:

1. **Place the person flat on his back, making sure his mouth is slightly open.**

   Kneel next to him in such a position that you can perform the chest compressions and breathing without moving.

2. **Locate the spot where you perform chest compressions, and position your hands.**

   Place two fingers at the bottom of the person's breastbone and then place the heel of your hand just above the fingers. Your hand should be near the center of the person's chest (see Figure 13-4a).

   Place your other hand over your first and interlock your fingers. The heels of both hands should now be aligned as in Figure 13-4b. Make sure your hands are well above the subject's sternum (breastbone); otherwise, you're just pumping on the abdomen, which does no good.

3. **Using a straight-armed stance and a steady, smooth motion, lean forward to compress the breastbone down about 2 inches (5 centimeters), and then come back up, releasing pressure (see Figure 13-4c).**

   You should try to do compressions at a rate of slightly more than one per second. A good way to do this is to count "one and two and three and four" and so on.

4. **After every 15 compressions, pinch the person's nostrils together and give two slow breaths (Figure 13-4d).**

   The whole cycle of 15 compressions and two breaths should take you about 15 seconds.

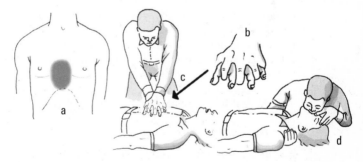

Figure 13-4: Administering CPR.

Continue CPR until the person resuscitates (check the person's pulse and breathing on occasion) or until you're unable to continue. Keep at it as long as you can. In some cases of cold-water immersion or other causes of hypothermia, prolonged CPR has proved successful if the subject was also warmed during CPR.

Controlling Bleeding

When an accident occurs, you can expect to see one or more of the three types of bleeding:

✔ **Capillary:** This is usually superficial bleeding from tiny blood vessels near the skin.

✔ **Venous:** This bleeding comes from the veins, the blood vessels that return blood to the heart. It's characterized by a steady flow of dark red or maroon colored blood.

✔ **Arterial:** This is potentially the most dangerous type of bleeding, and it's characterized by spurts of bright red blood.

This section shows you how to control visible bleeding. Signs of internal bleeding include blood in the urine (though other things can result in bloody urine) or a blue or red discoloration in the skin, but this kind of injury can't be treated without surgery.

Treating capillary and venous bleeding

Capillary and venous bleeding are the two most common types of bleeding. You can control them in the following four basic ways. Think of these techniques as a system, not just individual methods that you have to perform separately.

✔ **Direct pressure:** Apply pressure directly to the wound with a bandage, with some other type of cloth, or with your hand if you have nothing else. Apply pressure for 10 to 15 minutes or more, and resist the urge to look at the wound during that time. If the bleeding doesn't stop, keep up the pressure for an additional 15 minutes and consider applying indirect pressure to a pressure point.

If you need to continue applying pressure but are unable to do so manually, you can apply a pressure bandage. For more on applying a pressure bandage, see "Cleaning and covering wounds," later in this chapter.

✔ **Indirect pressure:** You can apply pressure at one of the body's main *pressure points* (see Figure 13-5). If you can't locate an exact pressure point, experiment by exerting pressure at the joint just above the injury.

✔ **Elevation:** Simply raising the wound so that it's above the heart can slow the blood loss significantly.

Don't elevate a wound in the case of snakebite — in that situation, keep the wound below the heart.

✔ **Holding the blood vessel shut with your fingers:** If you're really in trouble and you have to act fast, you can put one or two fingers over an open vein (or artery). This can sometimes be the only way to stop major bleeding.

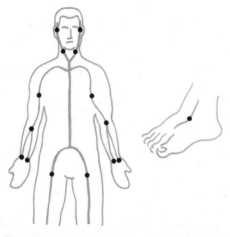

Figure 13-5: Pressure points where you can apply indirect pressure.

Handling arterial bleeding

Arterial bleeding occurs when one of the body's arteries has been injured. You can easily identify it by the extreme amount of bright red blood spurting or pulsing from the body. When this happens, you can

✔ Put one or two fingers into the wound to stop the bleeding. This may be your only option during a crisis.

✔ Try to staunch the flow of blood by exerting pressure on a pressure point above the wound. (Check out Figure 13-5 for where the pressure points are.)

✔ Apply a tourniquet if the situation is dire. A *tourniquet* is a band you apply with extreme compression to cut off circulation.

Deciding to use a tourniquet

Use a tourniquet only when the subject is in clear and immediate danger of bleeding to death. The tourniquet is an absolute last resort! Tourniquets are usually overkill and can cause severe tissue damage, which can lead to the loss of the limb later on. Tourniquets are also very painful, which can cause undue stress and trauma.

Traumatic amputation, such as when a limb is severed or torn off as a result of an accident or an animal attack, doesn't necessarily warrant a tourniquet. The muscles in the remaining portion of the limb may spasm and close the artery. You still have other bleeding to deal with, but you can control this, many times, with other methods. To see those other methods, read the earlier section "Treating capillary and venous bleeding."

Applying a tourniquet

To make a tourniquet, you need a stick (to restrict the tourniquet) and a band, preferably a thick one. A good width is 3 inches (7.5 centimeters) or more. (*Tip:* If you have to use line or wire, wrap cloth under or around the line to reduce the pain and damage from the tourniquet.) The stick should be about 6 inches (15 centimeters) long — you can use a pen or pencil.

If applying a tourniquet is your only option, keep in mind the following instructions and refer to Figure 13-6:

1. **Apply the tourniquet just above the bleeding site and tighten it only as much as is necessary to stop the arterial bleeding.**

   To tighten the band, thread the stick under the band and then twist. Attempt to put a pressure bandage on the wound after the bleeding has stopped (see the later section "Cleaning and covering wounds").

2. **If you know that no help is coming for at least 2 hours, loosen the tourniquet, very slowly, after about 20 minutes.**

3. **If the person is breathing and has a pulse, and if the bleeding is either under control or absent, treat immediately for shock.**

Never cover a tourniquet. Leave it exposed so that emergency personnel can see it if they arrive to help. Take a pen, lipstick, or blood and print *TK* on the subject's forehead so that everyone knows this extreme type of treatment has been given. And of course, never apply a tourniquet to a neck wound.

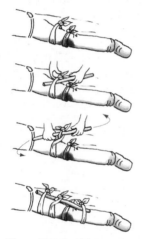

Figure 13-6: Applying a tourniquet.

Treating Shock

Shock is a reaction your body develops as a response to inadequate blood flow. The blood pressure is too low to maintain all the body's functions, especially the brain, and they begin to shut down, which can be fatal. Shock can come as a result of a wide variety of traumas. In any traumatic situation, you should keep an eye out for the following signs of shock:

✔ Cold, clammy skin

✔ Acute anxiety, psychological distress, or disorientation

✔ Bluish lips and extremities

✔ Rapid pulse

✔ Sensation of thirst

Because shock is a reaction to trauma, your first priority is to make sure that none of the subject's traumas are life-threatening. If the patient is breathing, has a heartbeat, and isn't severely bleeding, treatment for shock is as follows (see Figure 13-7):

✔ **Maintain the subject's body temperature.** Place a sheet or blanket under and over the subject to keep him warm. If it's hot out, find shade and try pouring cool fluids onto a rag or sheet and then gently administering the cooling cloth to the subject's body.

✔ **Try to calm the subject.** Stay near the subject and be reassuring, upbeat, and firm. People in shock can benefit greatly from reassurance.

✔ **Lay the subject down and elevate his feet.** The proper position depends on whether the subject is conscious:

- **Conscious:** Lay the person on his back and elevate the feet about 12 inches (30 centimeters) to improve the blood flow to the brain. Don't let the person smoke, eat, or drink.

- **Unconscious:** Lay the person on his side, supporting his neck, and elevate his feet 12 inches. Make sure the subject's airway is clear and that he's breathing. Do *not* attempt to give fluids to someone who's unconscious.

If the subject has a head injury, don't elevate the feet. Just keep him warm and calm.

✔ **Continue to monitor the subject.** Be on guard and ready to treat for shock even if the subject is conscious and doesn't immediately feel pain or other discomfort. If the subject is unconscious, watch for changes in breathing, temperature, and circulation, and try to keep him in the recovery position (refer to Figure 13-3). Anything other than dry, healthy-pink skin and a normal body temperature can indicate the patient is still in shock.

Figure 13-7: Treating conscious and unconscious subjects for shock.

Handling Breaks, Sprains, and Wounds

Any one of the common conditions that follow can debilitate you in the wilderness, and as we tell you at the beginning of this chapter, just knowing the basic procedures can mean the difference between life and death. In this section, we explain how to deal with broken bones, soft tissue injuries, and wounds.

Treating fractures

A *fracture* is a break in a bone, usually from some type of force-trauma. If you don't treat this type of injury, it can cause permanent damage and/or internal injuries. It can also seriously hamper your ability to travel, build, or otherwise move around without causing pain to the injury.

As soon as you believe you or someone else has sustained a fracture (or a sprain), you should assume the injured limb is going to swell. Remove wristwatches, jewelry, or any type of constrictive clothing near the injury.

In treating any fracture, strive to immobilize the part of the body that sustained the trauma. Immobilizing a fracture prevents the broken bone from doing more damage, and it makes transport of the subject possible.

There are two types of fractures, classified according to whether the bone breaks through skin: open and closed. This section explains how to treat them.

Closed

Closed fractures, in which the broken bone doesn't break through skin, can be more difficult to identify. Signs that a person has a closed fracture include the following:

✔ Immediate swelling, usually in the form of a knot or lump

✔ Tenderness at the site of the trauma

✔ A grating sound when trying to move

✔ An unnaturally bent or crooked limb or joint

To immobilize the fracture, apply a splint (see Figure 13-8). A *splint* is simply a rigid support, firmly attached above and below the fracture point. You can use poles, sticks, rolled newspapers, or anything else that's strong and firm as the support for your splint.

Try to use cloth to tie the splint, and try to use square knots or bows that you can easily undo (go to Chapter 14 for more on knots). Always try to align all the knots on one side of the splint.

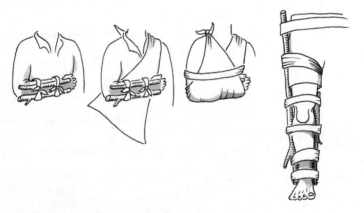

Figure 13-8: Splinting broken bones.

If a limb is bent at such an angle that you can't immobilize the fracture, you can try applying *traction* — a gentle straightening of the limb — so you can apply a splint. Traction should be relatively painless, especially if you perform it before the swelling becomes excessive. To apply traction, gently pull the misaligned part of the limb away from the fracture and move it slowly toward alignment. If this causes any appreciable pain in the subject, stop. Sometimes you can perform traction only in small movements.

After you perform traction on a fracture, you need to check for circulation in at the extremity of the limb. If you feel no pulses, or if the skin is discolored beyond a fracture, you may have to realign the fracture to restore circulation. If circulation is okay, go ahead and apply the splint.

Open

You can quickly identify *open fractures* because when the bone breaks, it pierces the skin.

Open fractures are exceedingly susceptible to infection, so now's the time to put on sterile gloves, wash your hands, wear a mask — do whatever you can to keep things sterile with the supplies you have. Try not to breathe on the wound, and don't touch the protruding bone directly.

Here's how to treat an open fracture (see Figure 13-9a):

1. **Apply traction if necessary (as we explain in the preceding section).**

2. **If bleeding is severe, apply direct pressure to the wound or skin near the break.**

   Try pushing downward on either side of the bone to stop bleeding, but don't put any pressure directly on the bone (refer to Figure 13-9b). For more on applying direct pressure to stop bleeding, see "Treating capillary and venous bleeding."

3. **Pad around and protect the bone before bandaging.**

   You can do this by putting a protective housing over it, such as a clean plastic cup, or you can use rolled gauze (Figure 13-9c). Afterward, apply the proper dressing and bandage. For more on that, see "Cleaning and covering wounds," later in this chapter.

4. **Bandage firmly (Figure 13-9d) and then pinch the limb's extremity to make sure circulation is adequate.**

   The limb is now ready to splint, as we explain in the preceding section.

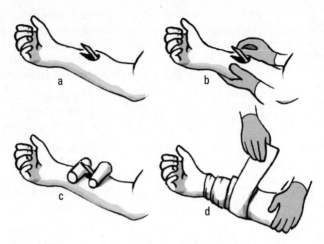

Figure 13-9: Padding and bandaging an open fracture.

Treating sprains

You can think of sprains and pulled muscles as *soft tissue injuries,* which means that the bone hasn't been damaged. You suffer these types of injuries because of stresses on joints, muscles, and damage to tendons. They can be just as debilitating and painful as fractures. In the field, you may not be able to tell the difference between a fracture and a sprain. If you can't tell, put a splint on the damaged site to immobilize it.

To treat a sprain, use the memory tool RICES:

✔ **Rest:** Give the limb at least 72 hours rest, if you can, or it won't heal. Rest can mean simply minimizing motion, although no motion at all is the best.

✔ **Ice (cold therapy):** Apply cold to the injury for 15 to 20 minutes every 3 to 4 hours. Do not apply continuous cold therapy, and don't apply ice directly to the skin; always wrap the ice in cloth.

✔ **Compression:** After applying cold, wrap the injury in a *compression bandage* (any bandage that applies pressure), like an elastic Ace bandage (see Figure 13-10). The bandage should be snug but not constricting.

After you apply the bandage, pinch a finger or toe on the injured limb to see whether the blood is circulating properly. If you don't see a noticeable flood of blood under the skin after you pinch it, you've put the bandage on too tightly, and you have to rewrap the injury.

✔ **Elevation:** Elevate the limb by propping it up about 6 inches to 1 foot (15 to 30.5 centimeters) on something soft. This cuts down on swelling and throbbing.

✔ **Stabilization:** Don't move the injury, and take precautions to prevent an object or person from bumping into or striking the damaged limb. In the case of a sprained wrist or arm, you can use a sling to immobilize it, or you can simply tie the limb to the person's body.

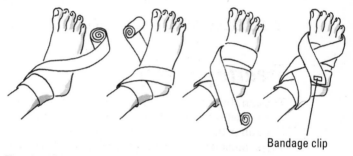

Bandage clip

Figure 13-10: Wrapping a sprained ankle.

Cleaning and covering wounds

You should bandage any wound, no matter how small, to protect it from infection. Take three important steps: clean the wound, dress it, and then bandage the wound. This section explains how to do all three.

Cleaning the wound

Before you start to dress the wound, take a moment to clean it. Cleaning the wound reduces the risk of infection, which could slowly incapacitate you. When cleaning the wound, keep in mind these basic guidelines:

✔ **Operate cleanly.** Try to use sterile gloves when handling a wound. If you don't have them, wash your hands thoroughly with soap and water if possible, or use alcohol or hand sanitizer.

✔ **Irrigate the wound to remove debris.** Use a flow of clean water to wash debris out of a wound instead of removing it with your hands or with a cloth, because your hands usually have unwanted bacteria on them. If clean water is unavailable, you may need to remove grit and dirt with tweezers (make sure your first aid kit has a set).

✔ **Use soap and water.** Washing a wound with common soap and then rinsing it with clean water can do more to prevent infection than anything else. The iodine or antiseptic wipes in most first aid kits are fine, but you should use them only if you don't have soap and water.

Don't use antiseptics on deep wounds. Antiseptics are for small, shallow wounds.

✔ **Clean the wound from the center, outward.** If you clean from the outside toward the center, you risk bringing in dirt and germs from the surrounding skin.

Dressing the wound

After you clean the wound, you're ready to put on a *dressing,* the covering that goes directly over the injured area. Remember the following points:

✔ **Make sure the dressing is the right size.** It should be large enough to extend well beyond the wound's edges.

✔ **Without touching any of the surrounding skin, place the dressing directly on the injured site.** Skin isn't sterile, so avoid sliding or dragging the dressing over the wound.

✔ **If blood soaks through your dressing, don't take the dressing off.** Instead, put another one directly over the first.

✔ **Use sterile gauze if you have it.** If you don't have any, use any clean, nonfluffy material. Fluffy cloth produces a lot of lint, which gets into the wound.

Bandaging the wound

With your dressing in place, you're ready to bandage. When you bandage the wound, keep the following guidelines in mind:

✔ **Use nonfluffy cloth, such as fabric from a shirt, as your
      first option.** If you don't have any, then you can use
      almost anything else.

      If you're desperate, you can reuse old bandages and
      dressings — but only if you boil them in water first.

   ✔ **Make your bandages wide.** Roll the bandage in a wide
      area to spread the friction and force, and tape the
      bandage to itself, not to the skin.

   ✔ **Apply bandages firmly with tape or safety pins, or tie
      them with a square knot directly over the dressing.** To
      see how to tie a square knot, see Chapter 14.

   ✔ **Monitor the circulation.** Keep an eye on circulation,
      because cutting off the blood flow with a bandage is all
      too easy. If blood is flowing properly, you should see a
      rapid return of blood under the skin after you pinch it.

A *pressure bandage*, which you use for continuous bleeding, is
a tighter bandage. To apply a pressure bandage, place a thick
wad of gauze or cloth over the wound so that when you tie
the bandage over it, you apply extra pressure. Always tie the
knot of the bandage directly over the wound. A large knot of
gauze, firmly tied over a bleeding wound, can slowly stop the
bleeding. This bandage isn't a tourniquet, so don't cut off
circulation completely.

Periodically check bandages, and the wounds under them, to
make sure infection isn't setting in. For more on infections,
see the later section "Treating infections in wounds."

Closing open wounds

If you encounter a clean, open wound, try to close it to avoid
infection. There's little reason to sew up wounds in most outdoor situations, but you can essentially tape a wound shut:

   ✔ **Butterfly bandages:** A butterfly bandage is a special
      adhesive strip shaped like an hourglass. Many first aid
      kits have them. When applying the butterfly bandage,
      make sure that the wide parts grab the skin on either
      side of the injury, with the thin part stretched across the
      closed wound.

✔ **Tape:** If you're desperate, you can use strong tape to close a wound. Bring the edges of the flesh *loosely* together with adhesive tape or, in dire circumstances, a safety pin.

Do not close dirty wounds; bandage them and seek help. If you can't close the wound or if the wound is dirty, simply bandage the wound and monitor it for infection.

Bandaging a sucking chest wound

If your subject has had her chest punctured and you can hear air being drawn through the wound, or if you can see bubbles coming from it, you have a special case on your hands: a *sucking chest wound.* If left untreated, this type of wound causes the lung to collapse. Take action immediately by doing the following:

1. **Put the palm of your hand over the wound to seal it shut.**

   This can prevent the lung from collapsing.

2. **Quickly bandage the wound on only three sides.**

   Place sterile gauze over the puncture and then tape it in so that one side is left unattached. In a pinch, you can tape plastic wrap over the puncture.

   The gauze or dressing should lie down snugly over the hole. When the subject inhales, you want the bandage to close tightly over the puncture, like a one-way valve; when the subject exhales, you want the air to escape.

Treating infections in wounds

Despite cleaning and washing, some wounds still become infected. Wounds that have become infected usually display one or all of the following characteristics:

✔ Inflammation, redness, and pain at the wound

✔ Elevated temperature at the wound (the skin feels hot)

✔ Reduction of mobility in the limb

✔ Presence of fluid discharge (pus) from the wound

If you or someone else develops an infection, you can treat the infection with the following treatments:

- ✔ **Rest:** One way to help fight infection is to rest. This may not be possible in a wilderness survival situation, but if you can't rest the whole body, try to rest the infected area as much as possible.

- ✔ **Heat therapy:** Apply very warm, moist bandages over the wound for half an hour, three times daily. A clean, sterile cloth soaked in hot water is ideal.

- ✔ **Daily wound cleaning:** If you collect foreign matter in the wound, or if it appears infected, take a moment to wash your wound with soap and water if possible.

- ✔ **Antibiotics:** Antibiotics can fight infection, but in many survival situations, broad-range antibiotics, such as ciproflaxin (Cipro), aren't always effective. Before going into the field, check with your doctor to find which antibiotics have proven effective for treating infections in the area you're planning to travel in.

Treating Burns

Burns threaten your life in two major ways: shock and infection. When you're burned, your body leaks fluid in response, which you can think of as "clear bleeding." If you're burned over a significant portion of your body, you're going to have the same situation you'd have if you were severely bleeding, and that puts you at risk for shock. Not only that, but burns damage the body's protective layer, and that's where you get the infection. Burned skin leaves you with nothing to fight off bacteria and other germs.

In this section, we tell you how to treat burns, both minor and severe. (For information on treating sunburn, see Chapter 17.)

Handling minor burns

Thankfully, most burns are minor scalds. To treat minor burns, follow these directions:

1. **Remove jewelry and clothing.**

You don't want anything to impede the swelling that accompanies all burns.

2. **Pour cool liquid over the burn site for at least 10 minutes.**

   You can use water for this, but canned soda will do in a pinch.

3. **Bandage the wound according to the guidelines in the "Cleaning and covering wounds" section, earlier in this chapter.**

   Try to be as clean and sterile as you can, because burns invite infection.

Don't break or burst any blister. New skin will form under the blister during the healing process. If you break the blister, you interfere with the healing process and could introduce infection. Cover blisters with a protective bandage, like the type used to protect an open fracture (see the earlier section "Treating fractures").

Dealing with more-severe burns

Some burns are more severe and require different treatment. Generally, in severe burns, the skin is clearly charred or disfigured. Here's the procedure for treating severe burns:

1. **Put a covering on the ground and then lay the subject on it, taking special care that the burned area doesn't come into contact with the ground.**

2. **Douse the burn with cool liquid immediately to stop the burning process.**

   If you're short on water, put some kind of receptacle or dish underneath the subject so that you can catch the poured water and recycle it over the wound. Continuously pour water over the wound as needed for pain.

3. **Check the subject's airway, breathing, and circulation and treat as needed.**

   We explain how in "Assessing the ABCs," at the beginning of this chapter.

4. **Remove constricting jewelry or smoldering clothing near the burn site.**

5. **Apply a sterile bandage.**

   See "Cleaning and covering wounds," earlier in this chapter.

Addressing Hypothermia and Dehydration

In this section, we discuss hypothermia (the cooling of the body) and dehydration. We cover some additional hot- and cold-weather concerns in the chapters that deal with extreme environments, such as the desert (Chapter 17) or tundra (Chapter 16).

Treating hypothermia

When your body cools below the optimal temperature of 97–98.6°F (36.1–37°C), you begin to feel the effects of *hypothermia*. If the human body cools down too much, basic functions shut down and death follows shortly. (Check out Chapters 4, 5, and 6 for tips on how clothing, fire, and shelter can help you avoid hypothermia.)

Hypothermia is a *progressive condition*, which means that the longer it's left untreated, the more dangerous it gets and the more difficult it is to treat. If you notice initial signals of cold, such as shivering, do something immediately, such as putting on an extra layer of clothing or covering your head. Signs of hypothermia include the following:

✔ Extreme shivering

✔ Bluish coloring

✔ Apathy and the desire to lie down or give up

✔ Dizziness, disorientation, slurred speech

✔ A stop in shivering (very dangerous)

If a person who is cold has stopped shivering, or if she lies down after a long bout of shivering, assume that she's in extreme danger. Treat for hypothermia immediately.

To treat for hypothermia, follow these directions:

1. **Try to keep the hypothermic subject horizontal.**

   When dealing with water casualties, try to hoist the subject out of the water horizontally rather than head first. In any case, try to keep the subject's heart level with her head. In extreme circumstances, turning the subject vertical can cause cardiac arrest.

2. **Remove wet clothing.**

   If possible, replace wet clothing with dry clothing.

3. **Rewarm slowly and steadily, monitoring the subject very closely.**

   Rewarming a hypothermia subject too fast can cause the person to go into shock or cardiac arrest, so watch closely and be ready to perform CPR. When treating for hypothermia, it pays to be slow and gentle. Trying to speed recovery can cause more problems than it solves because the dangerously weakened subject can't withstand harsh changes. To rewarm someone with hypothermia, follow these steps:

   1. **Apply sources of warmth slowly, gently, and steadily, starting with the chest.**

      Work steadily by applying warm rocks, hot water bottles, warm hands, or anything else you can to warm the skin of the upper torso. Don't boil your subject!

   2. **Warm the neck and crotch.**

      Don't rewarm the limbs. Doing so may cause the subject's body to divert precious blood to those areas, which can cause shock, stroke, or cardiac arrest.

   3. **Cover yourself and the subject with a blanket, sleeping bag, and/or your survival kit's space blanket.**

A cold person needs rewarming, not just a cover, so get under the covers with the hypothermic person. Give the subject skin-to-skin contact — don't be afraid to strip down.

Never assume that a hypothermia subject is out of trouble after you've rewarmed her. All hypothermia subjects are at risk for *afterdrop,* a continued cooling of the body even after exposure to heat. Don't take your eyes off your subject. Stay with the person and treat for shock and exhaustion.

Dealing with dehydration

The longer dehydration goes on, the harder recovery becomes. As it progresses, dehydration causes fatigue, dizziness, high pulse rate, nausea, and in advanced cases, a swollen tongue, delirium, and death. The only way to treat dehydration is to slow the loss of bodily fluids and to take in liquids that don't dehydrate you further. For a thorough look at getting water, turn to Chapter 7.

If dehydration has already set in and you're lucky enough to have access to water, have the subject take a long series of small sips of water, not big gulps. Large volumes of water can cause complications like nausea and vomiting.

Treating Bites, Stings, and Poisonings

In case of an animal attack, your first priority is to make sure that you and the subject are no longer in danger. Your second priority is to record accurate information. Whenever you deal with bites, stings, or poisonings, you need to immediately gather as much info as you can. That way, you can pass it on to the medical team when you reach professional help. Specifically note the following:

 ✔ **The type of creature or source of poisoning:** For instance, record the color and shape of the spider. Most effective treatments are specially designed for a particular species or substance.

✔ **The condition an animal was in:** Notes on obviously sick animals can help doctors choose treatments or watch for specific signs of disease.

✔ **When the incident occurred:** Some treatments depend on the time that has expired since the bite, sting, or poisoning.

If you can do so safely, capture whatever attacked or bit you. That way, the pros can identify the culprit and test it for disease.

This section provides some basic advice for treating bites, stings, and poisonings when medical help isn't nearby.

Mammal bites

If you're attacked by a mammal, here's what you should do:

✔ **For superficial bites:** These are basic puncture and scratch wounds. Clean and bandage the wound (as we describe in "Cleaning and covering wounds," earlier in this chapter). Mammal and reptile bites, especially deep puncture wounds, also carry the threat of tetanus infection. Make sure your tetanus shots are up-to-date.

✔ **For serious bites and attacks:** In case of a dismembering or deep gouging, concentrate on stopping the bleeding. Cleaning this type of wound in the field is usually counterproductive because getting bleeding under control is vastly more important. Tightly bandage the wound and then get help or transport the subject out of the wild as soon as possible.

Whenever a mammal bites you, you're at risk for *rabies,* a virus that causes severe neurological disorders in all mammals and is fatal if not treated. If you can't safely catch the animal that attacked you and verify that it doesn't have the disease, you may have to undergo treatment for rabies.

Snakebites

Lethal snake venom usually takes several hours to kill a person. However, venomous snakes usually don't inject enough toxin during a strike to kill an adult human. In fact, bite marks don't necessarily mean that the snake has discharged venom at all. But even if a snake isn't venomous, its bite can still cause tetanus and infection, and that makes all snakebites dangerous. You have to take each bite seriously.

You should monitor the subject of a bite for at least 2 hours after she's been bitten. Be on the lookout for the following signs of a reaction to venom:

- ✔ Continuous extreme pain at the bite site
- ✔ Head and muscle aches
- ✔ Dizziness, nausea, and sweating
- ✔ Difficulty breathing and shock

If you've been bitten by a snake in a wilderness situation and you believe the snake is venomous, try to slow the spread of the venom. Here are the steps you should take (***Note:*** In some countries the advice for treating snakebites varies from what we provide here, so check with local experts before you go):

1. **Try to identify the snake.**

   Most antivenins are engineered to work against venom from only one type of snake, so knowing exactly which type of snake bit the subject is critical.

   When trying to identify or catch the snake, keep in mind that a dead snake can still strike from reflex and that the venom is still just as potent.

2. **Make sure the bite is lower than the subject's heart at all times.**

3. **Work to calm the subject.**

   Anxiety makes the snakebite much worse. Any reassurance you can give the person helps.

4. **Wash the wound.**

   Soak up any venom that may be near the teeth marks and then wash the site (with soap and water if possible) and pat it dry.

5. **Apply a pressure bandage.**

   This is a simply a compression bandage that starts above the wound and then winds tightly down to the puncture site. For example, if you're bitten on the ankle, you start bandaging above the calf and work your way down, winding tightly until you reach the bite. This can help stop the flow of toxin through the body. *Warning:* Don't cut off circulation with a tourniquet.

6. **Immobilize the limb.**

In any situation involving a snakebite, be ready to treat for shock and perform CPR. For instructions, see "Treating Shock" and "Giving CPR," earlier in this chapter.

The best treatment for a venomous snakebite is the administration of antivenin, so get to the hospital as soon as you can. The longer you wait before seeking medical help, the more likely that the snakebite will cause complications, and the antivenin will be less useful.

Spider bites and insect stings

Most spider bites and insect stings are merely itchy or painful, but others can cause allergic reactions, paralysis, tissue damage, or death. Avoidance, of course, is the best course of action. (For more on avoiding spider bites and insect stings, see Chapter 15.)

Of the dangerous spiders, black widows, brown recluses, and tarantulas tend to cause the most harm. Brown recluse bites are usually the worst. These bites are painful, and they usually form a large pustule at the bite site; this normally ruptures, and the dead tissue around it falls away in 10 to 14 days. Black widow bites usually cause pain and even partial paralysis, usually for no more than 24 hours; bites are rarely fatal. Tarantula bites are painful, but they're also rarely fatal.

In any bite or sting situation, follow these instructions:

1. **Try to identify the insect or spider.**

   Try to catch the insect or at least make sure you know what color it was and what specific markings it had.

2. **Make sure the subject's ABCs are satisfactory.**

   For a look at these procedures, see "Assessing the ABCs," earlier in this chapter. Be on guard for signs of difficulties swallowing and choking, which are signs of anaphylactic shock (check out the nearby sidebar).

3. **Try to calm and reassure the person who's been stung.**

   Anxiety and high heart rate only amplify the symptoms.

4. **Remove the stinger or mouthparts if they're still in the skin.**

   If the stinger has been left in, scrape it off with a piece of paper or the edge of a knife or credit card. Don't use tweezers for this procedure, which can squeeze the poison sac and just inject more venom.

   A tick anchors itself in your skin with its sucker, which can break off and stay inside you if you remove the critter in the wrong way. To force a tick to release, grasp it at the precise point where it enters the skin, preferably with tweezers, and then pull slowly and steadily. Your skin should rise slightly with the pull on the animal. Hold this pressure. You may have to wait for anywhere from 10 seconds to 2 or 3 minutes, but the tick should disengage and pull its sucker out. When performing this procedure, don't crush or twist the tick's body. You want it to stay alive so it can disengage cleanly.

5. **Wash the sting or bite site with soap and water, and then apply cold compresses.**

6. **Monitor the subject for an allergic reaction or shock, and be ready to give CPR.**

   Regardless of the type, insects pose the greatest threat to you when they inflict multiple stings. Even if you're not allergic, multiple hornet stings or ant bites can cause you to go into anaphylactic shock. Always take multiple sting situations seriously.

Poisoning

Unlike venom, which critters inject, a *poison* is a substance you ingest through your food or water. As always, prevention is best. You can avoid eating poisonous plants by performing the Universal Plant Edibility Test, which we outline in Chapter 8.

The common symptoms of poisoning are

 ✔ Nausea, vomiting, abdominal cramps, and/or diarrhea

✔ Weakness

✔ Sweating

✔ Seizures

If you have a person who has lost consciousness due to suspected poisoning, put him in the recovery position and monitor his airway. The subject may vomit, which can obstruct the breathing. To see the recovery position, check out Figure 13-3, earlier in this chapter.

Note when the subject ingested the poison and how much he took, and try as hard as you can to identify exactly what caused the poisoning. Treatment can vary depending on the substance, so you may have to make a judgment call. If someone has recently eaten a poisonous plant — and he's conscious and coherent — he can put a finger down his throat to induce vomiting and attempt to get it out of his system. However, note that vomiting up caustic substances can burn the throat.

Watching for anaphylactic shock

Many allergens and toxins, such as those found in insect bites and stings, foods, and medicines, can cause *anaphylactic shock*, a deadly allergic reaction. Symptoms usually include difficulty swallowing, dizziness, wheezing, nausea, hives, and swelling of the eyes, face, and tongue.

If you see signs of a severe reaction developing, especially choking and difficulty in swallowing, take extra precautions to maintain a clear airway in the subject, and be prepared to give CPR. Don't put a pillow under the head of the subject, because this can close the airway.

Some people who are prone anaphylactic shock carry medications with them. If you believe you're dealing with a case of anaphylactic shock, ask the subject whether she's carrying medication, or if she can't communicate, look in her backpack or kit. The most common medication is epinephrine, usually carried in syringe called an Epi-Pen. If this isn't available, you can try administering diphenhydramine (Benadryl). Anyone experiencing anaphylactic shock should be evacuated to a medical facility as soon as possible.

Chapter 14

Survive or Thrive? Advanced Methods and Tools

- -

In This Chapter

▶ Tying some basic knots and lashings

▶ Making tools with bone and antler

▶ Using plants for medicinal purposes

- -

Sometimes you need just a little bit more skill to get out of a jam, and sometimes, well, you just want to look good, right? The skills in this chapter make you a little more versatile in the wilderness. They help you change from being an intruder in the wild to, hopefully, being a natural.

In this chapter, we give you a basic primer on rope, knots, and lashings, we show you how to make tools and weapons, and we tell you how to make medicines from plants.

Keeping It Together: Ropes and Knots

Even possessing just a few skills with rope (or *cordage*) can give you tremendous confidence in the wild. This section gives you the lowdown on ropes, including the different types you can use, and then delves into some knots and lashings.

Getting the lowdown on rope

Here are some important principles to keep in mind about the strength of rope:

- ✔ **Shock puts tremendous strain on rope.** When you're estimating whether your rope can hold a certain amount of weight, keep in mind that you need a thicker rope to handle a sudden snap or shock on the line than you'd need if that same amount of weight were applied slowly.

- ✔ **Ropes lose their strength rapidly.** If you have a rope that's been sitting out for a while or one that has lots of burrs and scrapes on it, or if its coloring is faded, consider it to be weakened and vulnerable to breaking.

  You weaken your rope whenever you put a knot in it. The average knot weakens a rope by about 60 percent. Seems kind of unfair, doesn't it?

- ✔ **Braided rope is stronger than laid rope.** Ropes that are *braided,* or woven together, are stronger than ropes that are the same size and made of the same material but are *laid,* or twisted.

Knowing the types of cordage

You usually don't have whole lot of choice of cordage in a survival situation, so you frequently have to improvise. Some ropes are better than others for certain situations, so try to get an idea of what you can expect from the type of rope you do have. Knowing your rope's relative strength and stretchiness can tell you, say, whether you can rely on that rope to hold a raft together, support your jungle hammock, or save you from a fall down the mountainside.

The following list names the main types of rope you're likely to use in your travels, from strongest to weakest:

- ✔ **Nylon:** This fiber is used for climbing ropes and for anchor lines on boats. It's usually white, and it feels soft to the touch, though in climbing rope, it's usually hidden inside a colorful sheath. Nylon is exceptionally strong, and it's very stretchy — almost like rubber in some cases. The stretchiness allows the cordage to act as a shock absorber. Nylon doesn't float.

✔ **Dacron:** This is the type of rope typically found on sailboats. It's very strong, and it doesn't stretch or float.

✔ **Polypropylene:** This is polyethylene's older, stronger brother, and it's usually blue. Not as shiny or smooth as polyethylene, this type of cordage is the strongest of the cheap plastic ropes. It floats and is slow to rot, and you can usually find it aboard fishing boats. It stretches slightly, although nothing like nylon.

✔ **Polyethylene:** This is the type of rope that's usually sold in hardware stores. It's shiny and smooth to the touch, usually brightly colored — most often bright yellow — and it's usually braided. This rope is only slightly stronger than manila or sisal rope, but it rots at a slower rate than those natural fiber ropes, and more importantly, it floats.

✔ **Manila and sisal:** This is the hairy yellow or brown rope that feels raspy in your hands. It's a natural fiber, and if it's thick enough, it's pretty strong. It's very stretchy, and it swells rapidly when exposed to water, which can make it very hard to work with when it's wet. It doesn't float.

✔ **Cotton:** This is the soft white cordage that makes up your clothesline. Don't use it for anything other than to hang up your laundry, unless you have to.

Tying some essential knots

Knots are simply the use of friction to make the rope perform a certain type of job for you. There are hundreds of types of knots. Here, we list several that can get you by in a tight situation.

Whenever you tie any of these knots, take a moment to tighten them — really work them in so that they're locked down. All these knots are designed to lock tightly and then to come out easily when you're finished with them. (*Note:* In the figures, the knots are tied loosely to make them clearer for you.)

Square knot

You use a square knot to tie to two similar ropes together (see Figure 14-1). To tie this knot, follow these steps:

1. **Take two ends of a rope, lay the right end over the left, and wrap it around in an overhand knot.**

This is the same way you start to tie your shoelaces or any other bow, for that matter; just fold the rope around itself.

2. **Take the end in your left hand, lay it over the right, and fold it over once again.**

   You know you have a square knot when it looks symmetrical. If it looks crooked, it's a granny knot — and granny knots don't work very well for anything!

Figure 14-1: A square knot.

Sheet bend

The sheet bend can join two different types of ropes, which is exactly what's required in most survival situations. You can tie any two types of line together with this knot (like nylon to manila, for example), or you can use it to tie any two types of improvised cordage together in an emergency (like if you have to tie a bed sheet to a garden hose or an electrical cord to a beach towel). Just remember that if you're using two dissimilar cordages, the one that is the thickest is the one that forms the bight. To tie the sheet bend, follow these steps (see Figure 14-2):

Bight

Figure 14-2: Tying a sheet bend.

1. **Take the thicker of the two ropes and make a bight.**

   The *bight* is the big loop that the thin line snakes around.

2. **Thread the thin line up through the bight and then wrap it around the head of the bight.**

3. **Thread the thin rope between itself and the bight; then tighten.**

Sheet bend double (Beckett bend)

The sheet bend double is the exact same knot as the sheet bend (Figure 14-2) with one extra step: You just wrap another loop of rope around the bight to increase its gripping strength. Use this knot (Figure 14-3) when you join two things that are really slippery.

Figure 14-3: Making a sheet bend double.

Anchor bend

Use the anchor bend knot (Figure 14-4) whenever you want to attach a rope to a pole or a log or a ring. To tie this knot, follow these simple steps:

1. **Wrap your rope twice around whatever you want it to hold so you end up with a circle of rope around your object.**

2. **Take the free end of your rope, bring it around, and thread it through the circle; then tighten.**

3. **Lay the free end over the rope again and now thread it through this new loop; then tighten.**

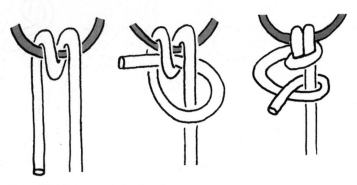

Figure 14-4: Tying an anchor bend.

Bowline

The bowline knot (Figure 14-5) instantly gives you a loop that won't slip. To make this knot, do the following:

1. **Hold the palm of your left hand up and lay your rope on top of it so that you're grasping the rope about 3 feet (0.9 meters) from the end.**

   The 3 feet of line should be hanging down from the heel of your upturned palm.

2. **Take the hanging bit of line in your right hand, reach up, and lay a loop over the line in your left, forming a design that looks like the numeral 6.**

   You should now have a loop of line in your left hand, with about 2 feet (0.6 meters) hanging down from the heel of your upturned palm.

3. **Take the point of the rope, which is called the** *rabbit,* **in your right hand; thread the point up through the bottom of the loop, snake it around the rope on the other side of your left hand, and then thread it straight back down into the loop.**

   This saying can help you remember what to do: *The rabbit comes up through the hole, runs around the tree, and goes back down the hole.*

4. **After you thread the end of the line back into the loop, pull on it to tighten the knot.**

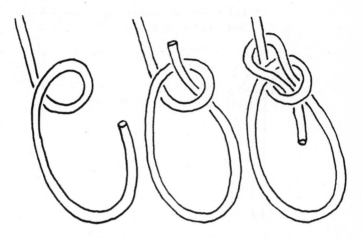

Figure 14-5: A bowline knot doesn't slip.

Clove hitch

The clove hitch (Figure 14-6) is the knot that begins and ends most lashings on wood. To make this knot, do the following:

1. **Wrap your rope around a pole; then wrap it a second time, laying the first wrap over the second to form an X.**

2. **Thread the point of the line underneath the X and tighten.**

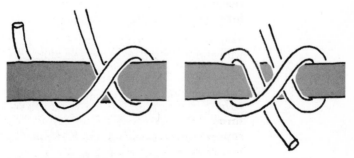

Figure 14-6: Tying a clove hitch.

Two half hitches

You use this quick knot as a finishing knot when tying things down. To tie two half hitches, do the following (see Figure 14-7):

1. **Wrap your rope around a pole and then lay the loose end over the line.**

2. **Thread the loose end under the line lying over the pole; tighten.**

3. **Lay the loose end over the line and thread it through the loop underneath; tighten.**

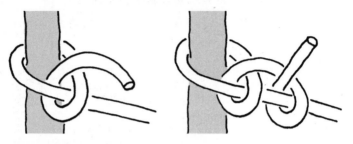

Figure 14-7: Tying two half hitches.

Lashings for loads

If you ever need to secure something, you can use this simple and reliable method to tie something down so it holds. This type of work is called *lashing*, and the lashing we show you here is sometimes called a *trucker's hitch*. We use a luggage rack to demonstrate, but it works on anything — on the back of a truck or on the back of your backpack.

The trucker's hitch is simply a loop and a tensioner. This lashing gives you the ability regulate exactly how much or how little tension you want to put on the line. Check out Figure 14-8 as you read these instructions:

1. **Tie an anchor bend to one pole.**

   We show anchor the bend earlier in Figure 14-4.

2. **Grasp the rope in the middle and pull it up until it forms a bight; then double the bight over itself so that it forms a slip knot.**

   A *bight* is an arc of rope pulled up from the middle of the line. This step gives you a loop in the center of your line.

3. **Wrap the line around the second pole and then return it to feed through your loop.**

   This is your tensioner.

4. **Pull the line through the loop until you have the amount of tension you want; then pinch the neck of the loop with your hand to hold the tension.**

5. **Finish with two half hitches.**

   Tie two half hitches (Figure 14-7) at the neck while holding the tension.

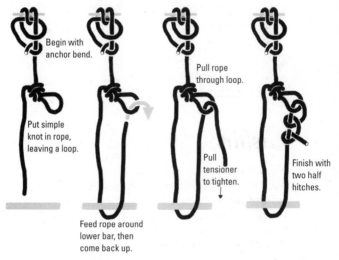

Begin with anchor bend.

Put simple knot in rope, leaving a loop.

Feed rope around lower bar, then come back up.

Pull rope through loop.

Pull tensioner to tighten.

Finish with two half hitches.

Note: Pull all knots tight! These are shown loose for clarity.

Figure 14-8: Lashing a load down.

That's a wrap: Making a tripod

You can use a tripod for a wide variety of purposes in the wild. A *tripod* is three poles, tied together by a lashing, that you can use to make tents, hold pots for cooking, and do a host of other practical things. Refer to Figure 14-9 as you read these instructions:

1. **Start with three thin logs of the same length; place two on the ground, with a space between them, and place the end of the third log between them.**

The poles can be of any length, depending on what you're using the tripod for, but they should be sturdy.

2. **Tie a clove hitch (Figure 14-6) to the end of one of the outer logs.**

3. **Wrap your rope tightly around all three logs as many times as you can.**

   As you're performing this procedure, knead and work each of these wraps so that all the slack comes out and you get a good, firm bond on your logs. Make sure you leave a good deal of rope to finish the lashing.

4. **Tighten the entire lashing with fraps.**

   A *frap* is a wrap that goes between the logs and gathers the ropes into a tight bunch. Take time and care to really tighten your fraps.

5. **Finish with a clove hitch on the log opposite your first clove hitch.**

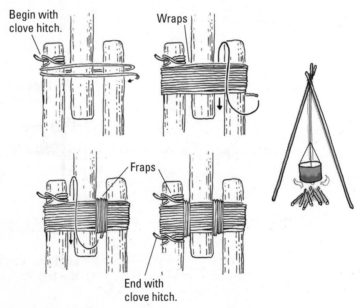

Figure 14-9: Making a tripod.

Making a square lashing

You can use a square lashing to bind one pole to another at a right angle, such as when you're building a platform in the jungle or making any other type of shelter. Refer to Figure 14-10 as you follow these steps:

1. **Put a clove hitch (Figure 14-6) on one pole; then wrap the rope around that pole once to get the lashing started.**

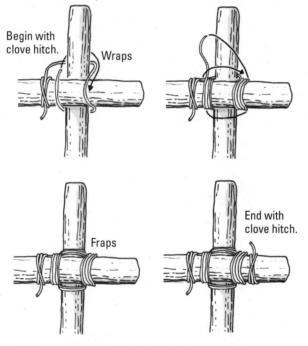

Figure 14-10: Creating a square lashing.

2. **Mount the tied pole at a right angle to the new pole you want to attach it to; wrap the free end of the rope behind the new pole.**

3. **Bring the rope around, pass it over the original pole, and then wrap it around the new pole once again.**

4. **Continue this binding process until you have about four or five wraps; then frap.**

To frap, take the rope and go between the poles, wrapping up only the rope — not the poles. Fraps are for tightening the wraps.

5. **After you get about three fraps squeezing the wraps, finish tightly with a clove hitch on the pole that doesn't have one yet.**

Crafting Your Own Tools

With just a few raw materials, such as stone, wood, and cordage of some sort, you can quickly fashion tools to defend yourself from wildlife as well as to catch food to eat.

This section looks at how to make some basic survival tools almost entirely from natural materials. Keep in mind that it always helps to have your wilderness survival kit handy, containing at least a knife and some cordage (for more on kits, see Chapter 2). You can survive without the kit, but the kit is invaluable in making other tools.

Making stone tools

If you lose your knife, never fear — a stone tool will do in a pinch. This section explains how you can break a stone to determine its type. After you know the type, you can shape it into a tool for various tasks.

Splitting a stone to assess its type

Before you can craft your own stone tool, you need to know about the different stones available and what they can do for you. Superficially, river or beach *cobbles* (baseball to softball-sized round rocks) all seem the same: round, boring, gray rocks. But if you split them open, you find some differences.

To split a stone, take it in two hands and slam it down on another rock. (***Warning:*** At the moment of the blow, close your eyes to prevent being injured by a chip of flying stone. Better yet, wear glasses or sunglasses.) You can simply throw the stone at a cliff wall if you don't want to risk smashing your fingers, but holding the rock can give you a little more control over what you're doing.

After you open the stone, you can assess its grain size and identify what the stone is useful for. Run your thumb over the exposed surface of the rock to assess its grain size. The following are common rock types listed in order of increasing grain size, along with some ways you can use them:

- ✔ **Obsidian:** Obsidian is volcanic glass. It's often black, and when chipped, the edges come off razor-sharp.

- ✔ **Flint and chert:** Flint and chert are smooth, fine-grained stones that have edges that can be very sharp, but they aren't as brittle as obsidian. These rocks are ideal for making spearheads or arrowheads. (If you have access to steel, you may want to save a piece of flint or chert for starting fires — see Chapter 5 for details.)

- ✔ **Basalt:** Basalt is dense, dark rock that doesn't shatter as easily as obsidian. Its edges aren't as sharp as obsidian, but because basalt is more durable, it's great for making tools for heavy-duty work like scraping or chopping.

- ✔ **Pumice and sandstone:** Pumice, an igneous rock, and sandstone, a sedimentary rock, are the sandpaper of the natural world. They're both ideal for abrading wood, bone, and antler into various shapes.

Shaping the stone into a tool

After you have an idea of how fine the grain is, you can begin to shape the stone into the tool you want. Here are the two main tools you need so you can work stone into shapes useful to the survivor:

- ✔ **Hammerstone:** A *hammerstone* is a rock you use to break open another rock. Larger hammers (about the size of a baseball; see Figure 14-11a) are useful for breaking the rock to get good slivers and splinters of rock; smaller hammers (Figure 14-11c) can be the size of a peach pit or a large marble and are used to trim the edge of a splinter of rock with a little more control. In either case, the point is to break the *core* (the main rock) with the hammer and produce *shatter* (Figure 14-11b), bits of stone that have sharp and robust edges that are useful for woodworking or other tasks. In Figure 14-11d, you see a cobble that has conveniently split in half, providing a great hard, sharp edge for chopping wood.

Smash the hammerstone against the edge of a core stone. Holding the core in the hand gives you more control over where your strike lands. This bashing often results in sharp flakes of stone that you can easily use as knives without any further shaping. In most survival situations, you can get what you need just by breaking open lots of rock and picking through the debris to find just the right shape — no pressure flaker required.

✔ **Pressure flaker:** A *pressure flaker* is a piece of metal, bone, or antler, about the size of a pen or pencil, with a robust but sharpened tip (Figure 14-11e); you use it to press hard on the very edge of a flake of a piece of shatter. The pressure flaker allows fine control of the shape of the rock you're working on, allowing you to make shapes as intricate as notched arrowheads (Figure 14-11f) after some practice. To shape a stone with a pressure flaker, carefully trim the edges of a flake of stone into the desired shape.

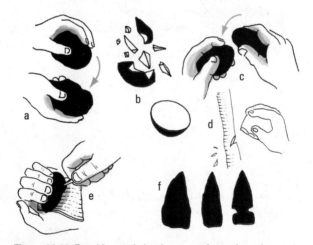

Figure 14-11: Breaking and shaping stone for tools and weapons.

Most of the time, when a stone tool isn't working, the problem is that the rock is the wrong grain size or the hammerstone is too large or small. The only way to figure out these subtleties is through trial and error; experiment in your backyard, and get your hands on a book about basic *flintknapping*.

Carving bone and antler tools

You can carve bone and antler into tools you can use in the wild. In fact, sometimes bone and antler are easier to work with than stone. They flex under impact instead of shattering (which stone does), which makes them particularly good tips for spears.

You can harvest bone and antler from the carcasses of many large mammals. Figure 14-12a shows an elk, highlighting (in white) the very useful antlers and the *metapodials,* the lower leg bones. Don't leave these at a carcass! Collect them, scrape away any tissues, and wash them if you can. Soaking bone and antler in water for 24 to 48 hours can make them easier to work with.

Figure 14-12: Making tools from bone and antler.

Here are the main ways to shape bone and antler:

✔ **Smash them with a hammerstone on an anvil to produce splinters.** To split a bone open, smash down on the bone with a baseball-sized stone or even hit a small wedge of stone into the bone with a hammerstone, as in Figure 14-12b. Many bones (and antlers you may find just lying on the ground, as in Figure 14-12c) are hard to break, especially if the animal died recently. Try again a few days later, when the bone begins to dry out.

✔ **Abrade the splinters with a coarse stone.** Grind away the surface of the bone or antler with sandstone or pumice, just like you do when you use regular sandpaper. See Figure 14-12d.

✔ **Perforate the abraded splinters with a hard item, such as the awl on your knife.** You can instead use a sharp stone splinter to perforate bone and antler, but this is very hard to do. It's much better — as always — just never to be out there without your pocketknife or multitool.

Figure 14-12 shows a variety of bone and antler tools you can make, such as spear tips, harpoons, and fishing hooks. Use your imagination and experiment to find useful shapes.

Making Natural Remedies

When you're in the wild, you may encounter sickness, infection, and other ailments. If you're in a bind and don't have certain treatments in your first aid kit, you can improvise by making your own remedies. This section looks at a few easy and safe medicines you can make.

Using salicin, nature's aspirin

Salicin, or salicylic acid, is one of the main ingredients in aspirin, and you can use it as a cold and headache reliever, as well as a treatment for swelling and inflammation. You can find it in aspen and willow trees. To extract salicin, peel away some bark and scrape off the soft tissue between the bark and the wood. Figure 14-13 shows an example.

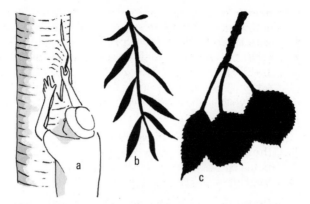

Figure 14-13: Extracting salicin from an aspen tree (a); recognizing willow leaves (b) and aspen leaves (c).

To use salicin, prepare a tea by boiling twigs, buds, or scrapings from the moist layer of wood between the bark and the tree. Steep the materials for a long time, and then mash them into a liquid pudding and drink it. You can also chew on the twigs and use the solution as a topical reliever by smearing it on an inflamed area.

Preparing medicines for wounds, burns, and bowels

You can apply any of the substances in this section to your skin to treat a wound or burn, or depending on the plant, you can ingest them to treat bowel problems or satisfy your hunger.

Tannin

Tannin, or tannic acid, is useful for preventing infection, for treating burns and other skin problems, and for treating diarrhea. You can draw tannin from all types of sources, including just about any tree bark (Figure 14-14), acorns, strawberry leaves and blackberry stems, and banana plants.

To use tannin, prepare a tea by boiling or soaking crushed bark, acorns, or leaves. Steep for a long time, and then add more materials to steep until you have dense tea. Treat burns or wounds by applying cool compresses soaked in the tea. If you're desperate and suffering from a debilitating bout of diarrhea, try drinking a small portion of tea made from white oak bark or other hardwood barks known to contain tannin.

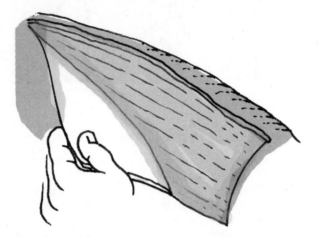

Figure 14-14: The bark from just about any tree has tannin in it.

Plantains

Plantain plants, which come in more than 200 varieties in the tropics, are good for treating wounds of all kinds, itching, and problems in the bowels, such as diarrhea and dysentery. A plantain (see Figure 14-15) is a little banana-like fruit, usually green, flat, and hard like wood.

To use plantain plants, brew a tea of plantain leaves or seeds. Drink it for diarrhea, or mash up the boiled or soaked leaves in the tea and then apply it to irritated skin.

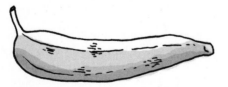

Figure 14-15: Plantain fruit.

Common cattail

Cattail grows at the edge of water sources and is good for treating wounds, sores, and burns. It's also a food source. Check out Figure 14-16 to see a cattail and its roots.

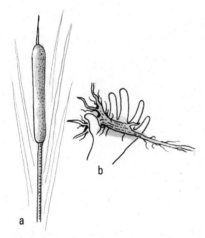

Figure 14-16: Common cattail (a) and cattail roots (b).

To prepare cattail, pound the roots into a mash and then apply the mash to wounds or sores. Cook and eat the green bloom spikes, or peel and eat the shoots raw.

Part III
Surviving in Extreme Land Environments

The 5th Wave   By Rich Tennant

"This looks like a good spot to camp. The ground is flat, we're protected by trees, and this is as far as the extension cord on the DVD player stretches from the RV."

In this part . . .

*A*lthough the basics of wilderness survival are the same worldwide, different environments can pose different problems. How do you build a shelter in the snowy tundra, where the nearest stick of wood is 300 miles away? How do you survive the relentless rays of the sun if you're trapped in the desert? In this part, we cover three main environments: forests (both temperate and tropical), snowy climates, and arid deserts. We tell you how to survive them by looking for food and water in specific places and by making shelter from the materials at hand.

Chapter 15

Special Considerations for Forests and Jungles

- -

In This Chapter

▶ Watching out for dangerous animals

▶ Preventing tropical disease

▶ Taking care of water, clothing, and shelter in the jungle

▶ Making your way through the rainforest

- -

*T*emperate forests offer many resources that make survival a little easier than it is on the open sea or in the desert. Nevertheless, jungles and tropical forests present many problems for the survivor because these areas harbor so many diseases and parasites. Before entering either type of forest — temperate or tropical — make sure you're ready for these situations.

In this chapter, we cover bear safety, insect and parasite awareness, and the dangers of tropical disease. We also give special instructions for dealing with the problem of getting off the floor of the jungle (which is a particularly nasty place) and explain how to use your best friend in the tropics, the machete.

Identifying Hazardous Wildlife in Dry Forests

Knowing what kinds of animal life are nearby gives you an advanced understanding of the wilderness around you. It helps you know where to set traps for food, where to make camp, and where you shouldn't tread. This section points out some dangerous wildlife you may encounter in the woods and how to recognize it.

Preventing bear attacks

Many times, bear attacks occur because a person accidentally stumbles upon the animal when it's feeling vulnerable or territorial. Knowing the signs that bears are nearby can help you remain safe in the wild. Bear paw prints (check out Figure 15-1a) are about the size of a large human hand, and their claw marks are unmistakable on trees — just make sure you're looking in the right place for these marks. Bear claw marks on trees are frequently 8 to 9 feet (2.4 to 2.7 meters) up the side of the trunk.

Whenever traveling in bear country, take the following proper precautions:

- ✔ **Carry bear spray or bear pepper spray:** You can buy it in most National Parks and outfitter stores. Make sure you read the label and follow the instructions. Recent studies suggest that bear pepper spray really works, and you should have it handy — not buried in your pack.

- ✔ **Be exceedingly careful about food smells:** Never keep food in your shelter, not even a morsel. Perfumed soaps and deodorants fall into this category, too. Always place your food at least 100 yards (91 meters) from your shelter. Don't sleep in the same clothes you wear when you cook your food.

- ✔ **Make plenty of noise as you travel:** Many experienced hikers in bear country make constant noise as they hike. Singing, banging metal, or making other such noises lets bears know that you're approaching. Making a noise often causes the bear to move away long before you get there.

- ✔ **Remember which way the wind is blowing:** If the wind is at your back, the bears can smell you coming and usually get out of the way. But if the wind is in your face, you're in danger of startling a bear because your smell is flowing behind you. Make a lot of noise when the wind is in your face.

You should also keep an eye out for three important scenarios in which bear attack is likely:

✔ **Cubs:** If you see bear cubs in the wild, consider yourself in peril. Locate the mother bear as quickly as you can and move away from her. Female bears are known to attack anything near their young.

✔ **Fresh kills:** If you come across a freshly killed animal that has been covered up with some freshly flung dirt, a tree branch, or some leaves (Figure 15-1b), you may have run across a bear's cache, and the animal may be nearby. Get away from this kill site as quickly as possible.

✔ **Hibernation dens:** A large hole that faces away from the wind or at an angle to the wind — especially one that allows snow to build up around its face — may be a hibernation den, especially if you're in bear country between the months of September and April.

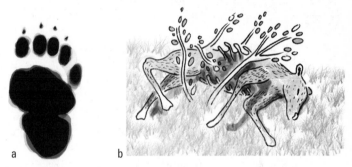

a   b

Figure 15-1: Keep an eye open for bear paw prints (a) and kill sites (b).

If you do encounter a bear, freeze. Talk calmly in a monotone and try to back away slowly. For more on what to do when a bear attacks, see Chapter 24.

Avoiding mountain lions

Mountain lions *(Puma concolor),* or cougars, are big cats that stand about 3 feet (0.9 meters) tall and weigh anywhere from 100 to 250 pounds (45 to 115 kilograms). They rarely attack humans, but attacks have climbed recently to about one per year. Mountain lions usually attack children or the elderly, and they usually do so by lunging for the neck.

Keep in mind that big cats of all kinds hunt for the weakest of the species and that many times, they can tell when you're infirm, especially if you have a limp. (Animal trainers some-times feign limps or infirmity to draw big cats' attention.) If you're infirm and traveling in big-cat country, stay off trails near dusk and dawn and always try to travel with a companion.

If you encounter a mountain lion, don't run. Make yourself appear to be as large as possible. For more on mountain lion encounters, see Chapter 24.

Avoiding woodland snakes

You can avoid snakebite almost indefinitely if you use your head. You should always expect snakes to be under any rock or log. The best way to prevent snakebite is to practice the following:

- ✔ **Wear stout boots.** The taller, the better. Most snakes can't bite through good boots, and most bites occur below the knee.

- ✔ **Watch your step.** Stepping on snakes is a common prob-lem in the wild.

- ✔ **Use a stick and look closely.** Always use a stick or pole to part foliage or turn over rocks or boards.

- ✔ **Check bedding and clothes.** Snakes like to curl up in warm, dark places.

If necessary, you can kill a snake with blows to the head or immobilize the head by using a forked stick to pin the snake's neck to the ground. Table 15-1 lists poisonous snakes in dry forests; antivenins exist for all of these. For information on treating snakebite, see Chapter 13.

Table 15-1	Venomous Snakes in Dry Forests		
Type	**Range**	**Appearance and Behavior**	**Bite Risk**
Rattlesnake	Throughout the Americas	Usually brown and dark brown; 1.5–7 ft. (0.5–2.1 m) long. These animals do *not* always shake their rattles when disturbed or when about to strike.	Rarely fatal if the victim is healthy

Type	Range	Appearance and Behavior	Bite Risk
Copperhead	Mainly in the Eastern United States	Brown and red-brown, with geometric shapes on the back; 2–3 ft. (0.6–0.9 m) long. Timid.	Rarely fatal
Coral	Throughout the Americas; all California wilderness areas should be considered coral country	Beautifully colored red, black, and yellow. Strangely hard to see in most circumstances. Very thin and small, usually less than 3 ft. (0.9 m) long. Timid.	Can be fatal
Water moccasin or cotton-mouth	Mainly in the southern part of North America; can frequently be seen sunning on the side of rivers	Hefty body weight, usually brown, olive, or brownish yellow; 2–5 ft. (0.6–1.5 m) long. Fast swimmers, exceedingly aggressive; they sometimes climb into boats.	Rarely fatal

Evading spiders and ticks

Thankfully, protecting yourself from insects, spiders, and other creepy-crawlies is easy. The problem arises when your mind wanders and you forget the following precautions:

- Always wear a hat.

- Thoroughly shake out all clothing — especially shoes.

- Try not to put your hands in dark places or holes.

Here are some nasty eight-legged creatures you may encounter:

- **Brown recluse:** This spider is brown, with thin legs and a body in the shape of a violin. The bite causes fever, chills, and vomiting for up to 48 hours. It's rarely fatal, but it can cause disfigurement and even lead to limb amputation from tissue death.

✔ **Black widow:** The notorious black widow is generally black with a distinctive red or orange hourglass design on the body. This spider is usually found in warmer environments. The bite, which is rarely fatal, is very painful and can cause temporary paralysis, sometimes up to a week.

If someone is envenomed by a brown recluse or black widow, treat for shock and be prepared to administer CPR (see Chapter 13). Seek medical help as soon as possible.

✔ **Ticks:** You can find many varieties of these tiny arachnids. Ticks carry a wide variety of diseases, including Lyme disease. See Chapter 13 for tips on removing ticks.

Laws of the Jungle: Surviving in the Tropics

We wish we could tell you that you should prepare yourself to fight off a stealthy jaguar or swing from a vine, but unfortunately, the main problem you face in jungle survival is disease. All extreme environments have their own forms of misery, and in the tropics, it's the microscopic creatures that kill.

This section gives you a heads-up on how to survive in the tropics, including info on how to prevent tropical diseases; obtain safe drinking water, clothing, and shelter; and travel specifically in the jungle.

Preventing jungle diseases

Taking necessary precautions is the best way you can avoid major jungle diseases. You can take four basics steps to fend off illnesses that can kill you. If you do them all, the chances of being infected drop significantly. Here are the four methods of prevention, in order of importance:

✔ **Boil water and cook food thoroughly.** Many tropical diseases come from contaminated water and food. Chapter 7 explains how to filter and purify water (or collect rainwater, which is usually fresh if your collecting surface is clean).

- ✔ **Wear proper clothing, sleep under protective nets, and use insect repellant.** Just keeping the bugs off of you goes a long way toward staying disease-free.

- ✔ **Wash and bathe often.** Regular soap and water can do a surprisingly good job of stripping away harmful bacteria and other parasites.

- ✔ **Use vaccines and preventive medication (prophylactics):** These of course must be specific for the environment. Talk to your doctor before your trip.

 We highly recommend visiting the Centers for Disease Control (CDC) Web site at `www.cdc.gov/travel` for travelers' info well in advance of your journey.

Diseases from contaminated water or food

Unfortunately, if you're out there long enough, you eventually pick up something — it is, after all, the tropics. Knowing the signs of disease, when combined with prevention, gives you the best defense. The following tropical diseases are usually contracted from contaminated food or water:

- ✔ **Bilharzia:** You contract bilharzia from contaminated water, either from drinking it or through a break in the skin. A microscopic worm grows in the liver and irritates the urinary tract. The disease responds to medication.

- ✔ **Cholera:** You contract cholera from contaminated food or water. It causes very runny, "rice water" diarrhea, which causes rapid dehydration. It's fatal in the very young, the very old, and the sick. Treatment is large quantities of clean water. A vaccine is available.

- ✔ **Dysentery:** This comes from contaminated water. Dysentery causes severe and persistent bloody diarrhea. Treatment is rest and rehydration. The disease may respond to antibiotics.

- ✔ **Giardia:** Giardia comes from contaminated water. This parasite causes severe and persistent diarrhea, as well as unpleasant burps. Treatment is rest and rehydration. The disease responds to antibiotic courses. No vaccine is available.

- ✔ **Hepatitis:** Hepatitis comes from contaminated water, sexual contact, or contact with urine or feces. It causes nausea, loss of appetite, abdominal pain, and yellowing of the skin (*jaundice*). There are many variations of this disease; some have vaccines, others don't. Treatment is rest and nursing.

✔ **Paragonimiasis:** This parasitic disease, which is prevalent in Southeast Asia, occurs when a fluke worm grows in the lungs. It comes from undercooked food, especially shellfish. Paragonimiasis responds to antiparasitic medicines.

✔ **Traveler's diarrhea:** This is the commonest complaint in travelers to the tropics, and it may be caused by bacteria, viruses, or parasites. Avoiding contaminated food and water is important. Maintaining fluid intake is very important. This condition may respond to Pepto Bismol or antibiotics.

✔ **Typhoid fever:** Typhoid comes from contaminated food. It causes severe intestinal disturbances and pink spots on the chest and the abdomen. Treatment is antibiotics, rehydration, and rest. A vaccine is available.

Diseases from insect and animal bites

Here are the identifying characteristics of the most common tropical diseases that are passed on through insect and animal bites (for more on protection from bug bites, see the later section "Identifying jungle insects and other buggy creatures"):

✔ **Bubonic plague:** You contract this disease from fleas, and it causes fever, persistent vomiting, and painful swelling in the lymph nodes. It's fatal if not treated, but it responds to antibiotics if diagnosed early.

✔ **Dengue fever:** This disease, which you contract through mosquitoes, has been on the rise in areas in the tropics. Dengue fever causes flu-like symptoms and sometimes rashes, especially on the face and neck. It usually lasts a week and is sometimes fatal. There's no vaccine. Treatment is rest. Don't take aspirin or ibuprofen if you think you have dengue.

✔ **Malaria:** Malaria comes from mosquitoes, and it causes weakness, fever and chills, violent shivering, nausea, coma, and death. Preventive medications are effective, but they must be taken up to one week before exposure to the disease and several weeks afterward. Malaria can't be cured, but medicine courses can reduce the severity of the symptoms during the lifelong outbreaks that come after infection.

Malaria is a constantly evolving disease, and older medications become ineffective over time. You must take a prophylactic that's up-to-date — one that's engineered to cope with new strains. Opt for one with a proven record of working in the area in which you're traveling. No vaccine is available.

✔ **Leishmaniasis:** This disease is passed on through sand flies. It causes large sores on the face, neck, and arms that can last for months and frequently disfigure the victim. This condition can lie dormant in the body for months or even years before rising to the surface. It's very difficult to treat, and there's no vaccine.

✔ **Onchocerciasis (river blindness):** Bites from black flies cause worm larvae to infest the victim, which causes tissue damage and blindness. It responds to worm-killing drugs and antibiotic courses. No vaccine is available.

✔ **Rabies:** This viral disease comes from bites from infected mammals, including bats. It causes madness and death. Rabies may respond to a vaccine.

✔ **Yellow fever:** Yellow fever is another mosquito-borne illness. It causes headaches, pain in the limbs, high fever, constipation, vomiting, and yellowing skin after about four to five days. It's sometimes fatal. Treatment is rest and rehydration. A vaccine is available.

Obtaining safe water

The tropical forest is the greatest incubator of disease on planet Earth, and every single body of water presents the possibility of dysentery, hepatitis, and cholera. Consider river and stream water deadly, and make sure you boil all water in the tropics. The clarity of the water in a particular stream means absolutely nothing.

Boil your water for as long as you can. Ideally, you want to bring your water to a rolling boil and keep it that way for 15 minutes. You can sterilize water with water purification tablets, too, but they aren't as reliable as boiling. Whether you use boiling or chemicals, strain your water through a filter first. For more on filtering and purifying, see Chapter 7.

If you don't have the equipment or fire to boil water, start a rain-catching operation. Even a brief rain shower — like the type that comes almost every day in the tropics — can give you more than enough water. You can use broad leaves, like those on plantain and banana plants, as water-catching planes and receptacles. For more on the spine-tingling adventure of catching rainwater, see Chapter 7.

The jungle cover-up: Dressing for the tropics

Frankly, Tarzan was a little underdressed. When you're in a jungle environment, you can think about clothing in terms of *coverage.* You want to cover as much of your skin as possible to prevent bites from insects. Make sure you wear the following pieces of clothing (and Check out Chapter 4 for a basic overview of clothing needs in a survival situation):

- ✔ **Hat:** The most important piece of gear in a tropical forest is a hat. Keep your head covered as often as you can, because spiders and insects can drop from foliage and into your hair.

  Wear a hat even inside a tropical house or hut, even if it has a metal roof. Many insects dwell in the roof of a tropical house or hut, where they have the nasty habit of falling on victims.

- ✔ **Lightweight long-sleeved shirt and long pants:** The material you wear should breathe. Examples of this fabric are ripstop nylon, nylon blends, and cotton. Cuffs, both at the wrists and the ankles, should be snug.

  Ideally, you want adjustable cuffs so you can loosen them during the day and tighten them at dusk. Many outfitters sell lightweight pants and shirts with Velcro on the cuffs just for this purpose.

- ✔ **Boots:** A boot that rises up and meets the pants leg, combined with a snug cuff on the pants at the ankle, can do much to protect you from mosquitoes, fleas, and mites.

In any tropical environment, mold and mildew are serious threats. Mold appears as small black and gray dots on fabric, and it eats through clothing, backpacks, and webbing in just a few days. The best way to defend against this is to hang all fabrics to dry every chance you get. If you've ever wondered why castaways' clothes are always so shredded, now you know.

Avoiding mud flats, sand traps, and dangerous terrain

When you're moving through the jungle, or whenever you're deciding where to camp, be aware of these undesirable types of terrain and move away as quickly as you can:

- ✔ **Stagnant water and mud flats:** Avoid large, open patches of mud and/or stagnant water. They're home to millions of mosquitoes, and when the sun sets, those mosquitoes swarm. They attack by the thousands, and they cause convulsions, shock, and malaria.

    Consider the afternoon sun to be like an alarm: If you're still near mud flats or stagnant water at dusk, you're going to have a problem with mosquito swarms. Don't get caught out in the open at dusk or dark near a mud flat or stagnant pool — try to get away or under a net or some other protection.

- ✔ **Mud holes and quicksand:** These areas are small holes in the ground, usually less than 50 feet (15 meters) across, filled with mud or sand so soft that it can't support your weight. Sometimes you can see these areas, but many times you can't. Quicksand and mud holes won't suck you down and suffocate you, but they can leave you quite stuck. There are many cases of strong people who walked into mud holes and couldn't extract themselves.

    You should carry a large walking stick to probe the ground in front of you — especially if you leave the trail. This can seem cumbersome, but in remote areas, especially if you're alone, you have little other choice. Whenever you begin to sink, especially if you sink past your calf, don't struggle — turn around immediately and go back. For techniques for extracting yourself, see Chapter 24.

- ✔ **Beaches near rivers:** Beaches near tropical rivers are inviting, but you should camp on them only as a last resort. Tropical rivers have a bad habit of rising quickly. This is especially true of the Amazon River and its tributaries. If you do camp on the beach, you have to maintain a good watch at night.

Using a machete

A *machete* is a long metal blade with a plastic handle. They're found in practically every house, bus, and car in the tropics. Sometimes they're called *cutlasses*. Because the vegetation in the jungle is soft and it grows over the trails quickly, you need the unique cutting ability of a machete, as opposed to the harder, blunter cutting ability of an ax. (Sorry, but that beautiful ax you bought at the outfitter starts to lose its value the moment you head off into the Great Green Tangle.)

Choosing and using the right blade

A variety of types of machetes are available. Just know that they can be divided into two categories: those you use to travel with and those you use to work with. If you can, carry both types. Here's when and how to use them:

- ✔ **Use the long blades when you're traveling.** To travel a trail with this type of machete, you use a lazy forehand swing to reach down low and strike the stalks of the plants standing in your way. Try not to flail away at the leaves or stems hanging in your face. Cut the foliage low, at the stalk, using a reaching motion. Done well, you shouldn't have to bend over all day — which is precisely why the blade is made so long.

- ✔ **Use the short blades for work.** When chopping, making shelters, or preparing rafts, use the shortest blade you can. Attempting to use a long blade for work — like when you're doing a lot of chopping — causes fatigue and injury, and it destroys the wood. Always use the short, cleaver-type of machete for work.

A machete isn't a baseball bat or tennis racket; it's not designed to be swung with enormous speed. When working your way through tangled foliage, make your low cuts with a controlled medium-speed motion (which isn't very Hollywood, we know, but there's nothing we can do about it). Wide and fast swings made with a machete eventually result in the blade's coming back and striking you. Even the most experienced jungle people occasionally miss what they're aiming at and strike themselves or someone nearby. Practically everybody we know has a machete scar on his or her leg.

Cutting bamboo

In the tropics, you build just about everything out of bamboo cane, and the act of cutting bamboo cane is a fine art that requires a lot of technique. Generally speaking, you cut at an angle. If you deliver the blow straight down — at a 90° angle to the wood — you just splinter the cane, and as soon as bamboo begins to splinter, it becomes exceedingly difficult to cut through. (If you're in the mood for a bout of hair-pulling frustration, just try cutting bamboo cane the wrong way.) Here's the right way:

1. **Deliver the first blow at an angle slightly higher than 45°.**

   Cut just below the joint, and cut away from the joint, not toward it. The farther you move away from the joint, the harder cutting the cane becomes.

2. **Rotate the cane slightly and deliver another blow, at the same angle, so that the cuts are joined.**

   You want to form one, continuous incision. If the cane is standing, you need to move your body around it to make this continuous incision.

3. **Continue cutting around the joint, lengthening the incision until you've severed the cane.**

   Firm blows made with a slight flick of the wrist at the end of the motion — not heavy or hard blows — are the best. Don't rear back and slam the machete into the cane. This just causes it to splinter. Most of the cutting should come from your wrist at the end of the motion. Experienced jungle people cut cane with a subtle wrist motion at the end of the chop.

Making camp and shelters

When you're in a tropical environment, making camp well before dark is absolutely critical. Keep in mind that there's almost no dusk in tropical areas, especially in the jungle. When the sun starts to drop in the late afternoon, the clock begins ticking for you. Stop what you're doing and set up camp at least two hours before sunset.

When making camp, take extra precautions to get off the ground. Even if you're really in trouble and have no equipment at all, you can make a platform. The platform is an essential tool in the jungle or swamp (see Figure 15-2a). To make one, you want to find three or more stout trees that you can tie poles to. The best poles are usually bamboo canes that are at least 6 inches (15 centimeters) thick. Tie the poles to the trees so you have a rough triangle, and then use branches or other poles as crossbeams. You may have to use vines to make your platform if you don't have rope. When building a platform, use square lashings. (To see how to make a square lashing, go to Chapter 14.)

If you can stand it, consider building a smoldering fire below your platform. The smoke can do much to drive away insects. If you can't build a platform, try to get off the ground and lie in a hammock (Figure 15-2b).

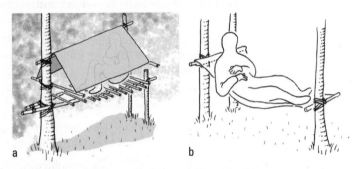

a   b

Figure 15-2: Get off the ground with a platform or hammock.

Identifying Dangerous Animals in the Tropics

Like so many other dangerous animals, those in the tropics can be surprisingly hard to see. You can do a lot to protect yourself by using a long stick to part foliage or probe tangled bushes; this almost always flushes out these animals. This section identifies some of the most dangerous critters in the tropics.

Insects and other buggy creatures

To avoid many tropical diseases — as well as some unpleasant bites and stings — you need to recognize bugs, spiders, and other multi-legged creatures and then take necessary precautions to avoid them. The best line of defense is to wear a hat and not to expose your skin.

The jungle can contain millions of species of bugs, many of which are giant, fairly hideous, and fascinating in a creepy sort of way. But the critters that are most likely to cause you trouble in the tropics can be relatively mundane. Here are the usual culprits:

- **Mosquitoes:** You find these nuisances throughout the world, even in polar regions. They're generally more severe at dusk and then through the night. Never go into a tropical region without a proper net and antimalarial drugs. For info on mosquitoes swarms, see "Avoiding mud flats, sand traps, and other dangerous terrain," earlier in this chapter.

- **Botflies:** Botflies are small, hairy flies found throughout the Americas. They deposit their eggs under your skin, which hatch and grow into a larval sack about the size of a thumbnail. The sacks must be drained in a sterile environment, and a course of antibiotics is advised. Infestation usually isn't fatal, but it's sometimes debilitating.

- **Black flies:** These are small black or multicolored insects with bulbous bodies. They bite hard and spread river blindness (see earlier section "Preventing jungle diseases").

- **Tarantulas (and other spiders):** Large, furry spiders can be found throughout the world, not just in the tropics. The bite is painful but rarely fatal.

- **Centipedes, millipedes, and stinging caterpillars:** These crawling creatures administer painful stings that are rarely fatal. They often have small spine-like hairs on their backs that can seriously irritate the skin and can be next to impossible to get out. Always sweep these animals off your skin in the direction they're crawling.

- **Ticks:** Ticks are widespread in all environments. Always wear a hat to keep them off your scalp, and always inspect yourself each evening. For more on ticks, see Chapter 13.

Jungle snakes

Like snakes everywhere, tropical snakes prefer dark holes or other tucked-away places. However, keep in mind that snakes in tropical areas can be *arboreal* — which means they're fonder of trees than their dry-forest counterparts are. All the snakes we list in Table 15-2 are venomous. Antivenins are available for all of these. For more on treating snakebite, see Chapter 13.

Table 15-2 Venomous Snakes in the Tropics

Type	Range	Appearance and Behavior	Bite Risk
Bushmaster	Central and South America	Large head, brown, with dark brown triangles on the back; usually 6–8 ft. (1.8–2.4 m) long. Nocturnal. Aggressive if cornered.	Often fatal
Fer-de-lance	Northern South America, Central America, and southern Mexico	Brown, gray, or reddish brown, with complex geometric patterns on their bodies; usually 4–6 ft. (1.2–1.8 m) long. Arboreal. A fer-de-lance loops its body over itself shortly before it strikes.	Fatal if not treated
Coral	Central and South America	Beau tifully colored red, black, and yellow. Very thin and small, usually less than 3 ft. (0.9 m) long. Timid.	Can be fatal
Tropical Rattlesnake	Throughout the Americas	Usually brown and black, with diamond-shaped marks on the back and two distinct lines on the neck; 5–6 ft. (1.5–1.8 m) long. Nocturnal. Aggressive.	Sometimes fatal

Type	Range	Appearance and Behavior	Bite Risk
Mamba	Throughout sub-Saharan Africa	Frequently called *black mamba* because the inside of their mouths are sometimes black. Light gray or green in appearance, very slender, and 7–13 ft. (2.1–4 m) long. Live in abandoned rodent nests and are active in both the day and night. Extremely fast.	Fatal if not treated
Boomslang	Throughout sub-Saharan Africa	Green, with very large eyes. Thin body, 3–7 ft. (0.9–2.1 m) long. Arboreal and very hard to see. Inflates its head before it strikes.	Fatal if not treated

Gators, crocs, and caimans

Alligators, crocodiles, and caimans are *ambush predators*. Generally, they strike at short range, trying to catch you unaware. The most dangerous areas are near water's edge, where these animals wait to make their ambush. Also keep an eye out for large clumps of bushes near rivers; these are sometimes used as nests for females laying eggs.

These animals usually don't chase their prey long distances. However, they have been known to chase people in the water, as well as capsize boats. Black caimans in the Amazon and saltwater crocodiles in Australia are the most dangerous. Give these animals a wide berth.

Leeches

Leeches are small wormlike parasites, usually black in color, that live in tropical and temperate waters. They attach themselves to your skin when you swim in streams and rivers; they suck your blood until they've had their fill, and then they fall off. Sometimes leeches can be found on the ground, too, or in dense, water-covered vegetation.

 The best way to avoid leeches is to stay out of the water as much as you can. If you do go into the water, even if you're just crossing a stream, keep your skin covered and the cuffs of your pants cinched tightly around your boots. Leeches can also find their way into the water supply, so as always, strain and boil your water thoroughly. Leeches can make you quite ill in the bowels if accidentally swallowed.

Like ticks, leeches have a way of working into strange places on your body, so take a moment each night to examine yourself thoroughly. You can remove them by applying salt, alcohol, kerosene, or gasoline, or you can burn them off with a lit cigarette or burning ember. Do not attempt to pull leeches off with your fingers — always allow them to disengage and roll away. If you pull them off, the animal's jaws may stay inside your skin and cause infection.

Piranhas

Piranhas are small fish, ranging from 8 inches to 1.5 feet (20 centimeters to 0.5 meters) in length. They're found in the Amazon, Orinoco, and Paraguay Rivers, as well as the tributaries of those rivers. Though they're nowhere near as dangerous as their legendary reputation suggests, they do nevertheless bite humans with their large, razor-sharp teeth, which causes infection.

Piranhas have developed a reputation of being especially dangerous when water levels are low and when the victim is bleeding, although precautions should be taken at all times. Stay out of waters where locals say piranhas live, and be careful crossing shallow streams. Like elsewhere in the wild, we recommend you wear tall, stout boots and long pants.

Chapter 16

The Big Chill: Enduring in Snowy Places

....

In This Chapter

▶ Staying warm when it's cold out

▶ Building survival shelters from nothing but snow

▶ Avoiding avalanches, crevasses, and thin ice

▶ Finding water when you're surrounded by snow and ice

▶ Making tools (like snowshoes) to survive in snowy environments

....

*C*old is simply an absence of heat energy, and you can feel cold in just about any environment on Earth. In this chapter, we focus on snowy environments, which you can encounter in around half of all the land masses in the Northern Hemisphere and somewhat less in the Southern Hemisphere. You can find snow even in unexpected places — both Hawaii and Australia offer snow skiing — so being prepared for cold is always a good idea. In this chapter, we cover methods for surviving in cold, snowy wildernesses.

When you're cold, you have to do something. Don't try to just force your way through the sensation of cold — it's your body's signal that something is wrong, and you may not have much time to solve the problem. Take action.

Staying Warm

Keeping your body warm is your first priority in a cold-weather survival situation. If you become hypothermic in extreme cold or wind chill, survival can become an epic battle. The following are general principles to remember for staying warm outdoors (also be sure to check out Chapter 4 for important info on cold-weather dressing):

- **Breathe through your nose and wear a scarf.** Breathing through your nose conserves body moisture, and wrapping a scarf or other cloth across your nose and mouth can cut the chill so that the coldest air doesn't hit your lungs directly.

- **Stay dry.** Wet clothing cools your body faster than just about anything else, so if you get wet, get under some shelter, make a fire, and dry out your clothes. If you don't have the option of making a fire, try to keep moving — this may help to dry damp clothes, but soaked clothes really need to be properly dried out.

- **Eat and drink.** Keeping the body fueled and hydrated can prevent most cold injuries! If you have food, eat it — eating keeps the body's fires stoked. From your food supply, choose the food that has the most calories. Drinking lots of liquid keeps your body hydrated, which can forestall hypothermia.

- **Get out of the wind.** Wind rapidly sucks heat away from the body, so take shelter when there's wind; if you can't take shelter, try to improvise a windproof layer for your clothing.

- **Loosen your footwear.** Tighter footwear constrains the blood vessels that would normally carry warm blood to the feet, leading to frostbite. So when it gets cold, *loosen your laces*. But be careful to keep the top of your footwear sealed around your calves so that cold air, snow, and ice can't get in. Duct tape or any strong cordage works well.

- **Protect your hands and feet.** These are the first to go when your body gets cold, and because you can't really travel with frozen feet or do anything at all with frozen hands, you have to protect them. Mittens are normally warmer than gloves, something to keep in mind when you prepare to go outdoors in the first place. Gloves under windproof mittens are ideal.

- **Stay active.** If your clothes aren't providing enough warmth, you can temporarily stay active to warm up; but don't do so much that you sweat, which dampens your clothes. Stay out of the wind while getting your heart rate (and heat rate) up.

Cold Comfort: Making Your Shelter in a Snowy Environment

In cold areas, a shelter is as much psychological as it is physical (well maybe not, but nearly so!). One of the first things you notice in a snow shelter is how quiet it is. Coming in out of wind and storm — and into a warm, quiet place — is a tremendous relief. This section first walks you through some general building principles. We then describe three main ways to use snow to make a shelter.

Grasping snow shelter basics

You may think that a snowy landscape provides no shelter, but the snow itself can provide a home. Snow, which is composed of loosely piled granules of frozen water crystals, traps air, which is a good insulator. That's why you can use snow to make a great, warm survival shelter. Just remember these important tips, whatever shelter you build:

✔ **Build your shelter in a safe location.** Stay away from avalanche slopes, and if you're on a frozen lake or sea surface, build on thick ice. Later, in the section "Avoiding avalanche terrain," we cover assessing snowy environments for the likelihood of these catastrophic snow-slides, which can bury your shelter under feet of snow in an instant.

✔ **Keep the shelter as small as is practical.** A large shelter is nice and roomy, but to make it warm, you have to warm more air than in a smaller shelter. Keep your shelter roomy enough so you can sit up, work on gear, and so on, but don't make it much bigger. Opting for a small shelter also saves you work when you're building your shelter.

✔ **Keep your shelter ventilated (see Figure 16-1a).** Burning a camp stove or other fuel in your shelter can lead to an excess of carbon dioxide (a colorless, odorless, lethal gas), so carefully poke several ventilation holes in the shelter's roof with a long pole. A ski pole is thin, so you may need more than eight or ten holes.

Keep your eyes open for the signs of carbon monoxide poisoning, which include a splitting headache, nausea, dizziness, and weakness — if you notice these, get outside fast and then vent that shelter!

✔ **Keep a digging-out tool inside your shelter (Figure 16-1b).** Heavy snow — or in the worst case, avalanche — can trap you inside a shelter, so always store a digging tool in your shelter. You can improvise a digging tool simply from several stout branches lashed together with cordage (see Chapter 14 for tips on lashing), or you can use a helmet, a license plate, or even a cooking pot.

✔ **Block the entrance of your shelter (Figure 16-1c).** Just covering the entrance/exit hole of your shelter with your backpack and perhaps some heavy brush is a great aid in trapping warm air inside; a snow shelter with an open door isn't much better than a refrigerator. Don't block the door until you're satisfied that you have the shelter properly ventilated.

✔ **Make a cold trap in your shelter (Figure 16-1d).** Warm air rises and cold air sinks, and you can use this knowledge to improve your shelter by making a cold trap at the lowest point of the floor. A *cold trap* is simply a basin, trench, or other hole in the snow floor of your shelter that traps the coldest air in the shelter; don't stand in the cold trap unless you want to chill your feet.

✔ **Make your shelter visible.** Snow shelters can blend right into the landscape, so make your position visible to rescue personnel. For example, lay out giant symbols in the snow using dye markers, charcoal from your fire, or sod from beneath the snow. Or securely peg a brightly colored piece of cloth or tarp to the top of the shelter. See Chapter 12 for more on signaling.

✔ **Insulate yourself from the snow.** Never sit or sleep directly on snow; use anything — such as pine boughs, a bed of moss, seat cushions, the fireproof hood liner from a car, or an extra blanket — to stay off the snow (Figure 16-1f). When you're sitting, place a backpack or other insulating object between your back and the wall of the shelter.

✔ **Keep your shelter organized.** At the least, designate a place to store the first-aid kit, your wilderness survival kit (see Chapter 2), and any items you have for signaling passing aircraft or other potential rescuers. Keep these items in the designated places; you don't want to be scrambling around in the dark interior of a snow shelter for your signal mirror when you hear the sweet sound of a helicopter!

You can customize any snow shelter by building in conveniences such as *niches* — little cavities cut in the side of the shelter to store gear or food — and hangers, which can just be sturdy sticks stuck in the walls, on which you can hang equipment. These modifications get your gear up off the floor and make it easier to find what you need when you need it.

Figure 16-1: Snow shelter basics.

Making a snow-cave

A snow-cave is the simplest snow shelter, and it's entirely capable of keeping you warm enough to stay alive indefinitely. A *snow-cave* is basically a burrow inside a snowdrift or a pile of snow. You can either burrow into a naturally occurring snowdrift or build your own mound of snow.

Gas poisoning in the Arctic

A few winters back, I (Cameron) was the sole inhabitant of a remote glaciological research hut on Iceland's Vatnajökull glacier. One night, I heard a machine turn on behind a locked door — an electrical engine activated by satellite control. It was hard to sleep, but finally I did. I'm lucky I ever woke up.

About the incident, I wrote, "A few hours later, I woke with stinging eyes and aching lungs. It felt like someone was standing on my chest. I coughed and hacked and lunged out the door leading to the antechamber. A fierce migraine was slowly slicing my brain in two. Without consciously thinking about it, I was suiting up, and soon I was crawling dizzily out the hatch and gulping fresh air. The first gasps I took in the blast of storm outside collared me and tugged me back from the brink.

"Crouched in the storm just outside the hatch, I realized that the gas-powered generator's exhaust fumes had filled the hut. I hated the thing even more, now, the deep, human hatred of inventions that don't do as they're told. My symptoms were those of carbon monoxide poisoning. I breathed for a minute or so before climbing back in and opening the door to the living compartment. This let in piles of blowing snow, but I didn't care. I had to breathe."

To make a snow-cave shelter, you need a digging tool, such as a helmet, ski, snowshoe, cooking pot, several strong green sticks (cut from a tree) lashed together, or even the glove-compartment door from a car. The best tool, of course, is a *mountaineer's snow shovel,* which is small enough to strap to a backpack (the handle telescopes out) and very strongly built — we won't even travel in snow country without one. The best, made by Life-Link (www.life-link.com), have metal blades that don't break. Plastic shovel blades eventually do.

Consider stripping off a layer of clothing before you start working. Making any kind of snow shelter is heavy work that can make you sweat, and wet clothing quickly cools your body. Also, you'll probably be covered in snow after all the digging that's involved, and that snow can melt from your body heat, leaving you wet.

Creating shelters from natural snow drifts

Wind often blows snow into dunes or drifts, which you may be able to use as a shelter. Before you use a natural snowdrift as a shelter, verify that it's compact enough to hold its shape when you burrow inside. Some snowdrifts are composed of very loose, fluffy snow that's of no use for a shelter.

To test the snow's compactness, dig into the drift a few feet. You may start out in compact snow but then punch through a hard *wind crust* to find loose snow underneath. Is the roof constantly collapsing in like sand? Can you even keep a shape to the cavity you're digging in? If not, move on and find more compact snow.

After you find compact snow, dig horizontally into the drift for about a body-length before burrowing left for half a body length and then right for half a body length, making an L-shaped burrow (see Figure 16-2). You can use the entrance tunnel to store your gear and food and the perpendicular tunnel as your sleeping and resting area.

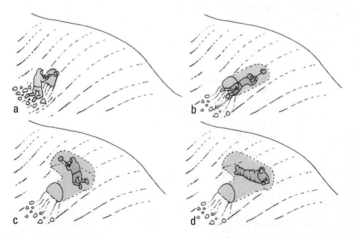

Figure 16-2: Building an L-shaped burrow in a natural snowdrift.

The L-shape of the natural-drift burrow is a strategy for the fact that many drifts aren't deep enough to make a large, round burrow inside. But if the drift is large enough, you can use any shape you like, though we suggest conserving your energy by making it only as large as you need to stay alive and reasonably comfortable.

Don't forget to dig a *cold trap*, which is a trench you make in the floor of the shelter that allows the heavy, cold air to pool or collect beneath you, leaving the rest of the air slightly warmer.

Making your own snow-heap shelter

If you can't find a natural drift, or if the snow is too loose in any drift you find, you can make your own snow heap. This is a lot of work, but it's worth it. To make a snow-heap shelter, just follow these steps:

1. **Strip off a layer of clothing and — using any tool you can — scoop up snow and pile it in a giant mound, up to 6 feet (1.8 meters) wide and 6 feet high (Figure 16-3a).**

2. **Put your layer back on while you let the heap settle for an hour or so.**

   Go and do something else, such as finding a heavy pole or other tool that you can use in the next step.

3. **When you're back at your heap, start to compact the snow by tamping it down hard.**

   Use a large pole or a snow shovel, or even climb onto the heap and jump up and down. You're trying to make the heap as dense as you can, so it may be only 4 feet (1.2 meters) high when you're done

4. **Strip off a layer of clothing again, and start burrowing into the side (Figure 16-3b).**

   Make the door of your shelter face east or a little southeast so you can see the sky lighten with sunrise; this is very good for morale after a cold night.

5. **Hollow out the inside.**

   As you dig in, assess the compaction. Is the roof holding its shape? Is the tunnel collapsing? If not, burrow on! Your shelter is taking shape. After a foot or so, start excavating the interior so you have a round chamber with a flat floor and a dome-shaped roof (Figure 16-3c).

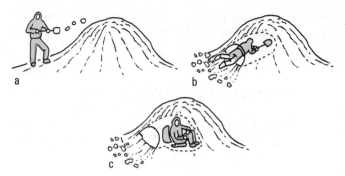

Figure 16-3: Creating a shelter from your own snowdrift.

Making Fire in Cold, Snowy Environments

Cold itself doesn't interfere with making fire. If you can ignite it, fire fuel (such as wood or animal fat) will burn no matter how cold it is. The main fire-making issues in cold environments have to do with finding fuel and getting it to burn without your fire melting into the snow. But don't worry — you can build a fire in a cold, snowy environment with the pointers in this section.

Finding fuel in snowy places

Wooded areas provide plenty of fuel to burn. High in the mountains, though, or on open Arctic plains (the tundra regions), wood may be scarce or absent. You may be able to use the following as fuel:

- **Driftwood:** It may be frozen into a beach, but if you can pry or chop it free, it'll probably burn.

- **Tundra grasses or mosses:** These are under a blanket of snow for much of the year, but by burrowing down, you can find them even in winter; twist them into compact "sticks" or even thick bundles — they burn better than loose clods.

✔ **Dried animal dung:** Caribou, polar bear, musk ox, and wolf droppings may burn.

✔ **Animal fats:** Fats such as seal blubber burn well. If you have the luxury of such a resource, use it sparingly — for example, only to cook or dry clothes but not for warmth unless you really need it. It burns quickly.

Getting any fuel to burn requires the fire-making skills we introduce in Chapter 5.

Protecting a fire from the snow

If you build a fire on a snowy surface, the heat quickly melts the snow and your fire collapses into a wet, smoky snow crater — not what you were after. Building a fire directly on ground you've cleared of snow and ice doesn't work well, either; in the Arctic regions, this ground is usually interlaced with ice, and the heat of the fire melts it into a soggy mess. You can make fire in these situations by using the following methods and building the fire on the following surfaces:

✔ **In or on a piece of metal:** You can use a cooking pot (see Figure 16-4a); any sheet of metal stripped from a car, snowmobile, or airplane wreck (be sure to burn off potentially toxic plastics and paints before cooking over such a fire); or even a piece of tin foil (double it a few times to be sure you don't burn right through it). If you have only one pot, you'll have to find some other container to boil water, but if you're just cooking food, you can roast it above the flames.

✔ **On a wood platform:** Build a flat platform of several layers of branches, each layer laid out at 90° to the last (as in Figure 16-4b). The log platform will catch fire eventually, but by using lots of logs, you can keep a small fire going well enough.

✔ **On a slab or bed of rock:** Exposed rock slabs work fine. You can make a bed of rock by setting small rocks together on a flat snow surface, as in Figure 16-4c.

Figure 16-4: Making a fire on a platform in snowy environments.

Don't Eat the Yellow Snow: Safe-to-Drink Snow and Ice

Locating clean drinking water is essential in any wilderness setting. You may be in a cold tundra with pristine white snow everywhere, but before you grab a big handful and start eating, take a moment to read this section.

Choosing and treating frozen water sources

Microbes can live in the coldest places on Earth, so before you eat snow or drink melted ice, make sure you disinfect it with iodine crystals or the other methods we describe in Chapter 7. Whatever method you use, keep these points in mind:

- **Select clean snow.** You don't want snow that has been discolored by urine or feces (either yours, from around camp, or that of other animals). Snow can be discolored pink *(watermelon snow),* black, brown, or yellow by cold-climate algae. Some people feel nauseous after consuming these.

- **Select non-salt ice.** If you're near frozen seashore, remember that sea ice is salty, but over a period of years, the salt leaches out. Salty ice is gray or white, but blue or glassy ice should be safe to melt and drink.

You can chip off a small piece of sea ice and taste it for saltiness. But be careful — eating ice causes a loss of body heat, so make the pieces small. And choose your ice wisely so you don't have to repeat the tasting process more than once or twice.

Melting snow and ice

Never eat snow in extreme cold unless you're in a warm shelter or have other ways to keep warm beside just your body heat. No amount of snow will provide enough water to quench your thirst, so in cold environments, you have to melt snow and ice to stay hydrated.

Ice is denser than snow, so it yields more water than snow when you melt it. If you can't find ice, then choose snow that's as densely packed as possible. The denser the snow, the higher the water yield. Here are several main methods to melt snow or ice:

- ✔ **In a pot over a fire:** Always use a lid to keep as much heat in the pot as possible.

- ✔ **In a cloth bag next to a fire:** Hang snow or ice in a bundle of porous (nonwaterproof) cloth next to a fire and catch the melt in a container. This works if you have, for example, a plastic container (such as a milk jug or soda bottle) but no metal pan to melt in.

- ✔ **In a container you keep next to your body:** Packing some snow into a bottle that you keep next to your body overnight (inside your sleeping bag or blankets) can yield some liquid water and keeps it from freezing.

- ✔ **In the sun:** If you have a black or dark-colored plastic bag and the temperature isn't too cold, you can pack snow into the bag and leave it out in the sun.

Steering Clear of Cold-Environment Terrain Hazards

Cold, snowy environments present a number of special hazards for the survivor, some of them lethal. With the basic information in this section, however, you can avoid this dangerous terrain altogether.

If you encounter a whiteout and your visibility drops to nearly zero in the blowing snow, you need to stop moving and wait it out. See Chapter 24 for tips on surviving a whiteout.

Avoiding avalanche terrain

Avoid avalanche terrain at all times. You just can't fight tons of snow moving according to the laws of gravity! You don't want to be anywhere near avalanche terrain, and you don't want to set your camp up under avalanche slopes, either. Luckily, it's often pretty easy to assess whether your campsite is safe and whether the snow-slope you're about to try to cross is at risk of avalanching.

An *avalanche* is a mass of sliding snow (and ice, tree trunks, mountaineers, and anything else it picks up) that can move down a mountainside with lethal velocity. It occurs when a new layer of snow doesn't bond well with the snow it settles on. After accumulating for a while, the new layer simply slips off the old layer, headed downhill.

People caught in avalanche are normally killed either by trauma (being swept along until they're slammed into a tree or simply knocked on the head) or suffocation. Suffocation occurs when the snow stops moving and settles; if a person is buried under the surface, the snow can prevent breathing.

The following avalanche-hazard notes apply worldwide (and Figure 16-5 shows these points visually):

- ✔ Avalanches *normally* occur on slopes from 30° to 40° in steepness, but some occur on slopes as low as 20°.

- ✔ Most avalanches occur from 12 to 48 hours after a heavy snowfall (over 6 inches, or 15 centimeters, or so).

- ✔ Many people killed in avalanches trigger the avalanches themselves by walking or skiing in avalanche-prone snow.

If you can't avoid avalanche terrain and you find yourself having to cross a snow slope that you think may avalanche, take some precautions:

✔ Unfasten your backpack buckles so you can cast aside your backpack if needed (it can drag you down in an avalanche).

✔ Zip up all your clothes and pockets (these can fill with snow and drag you down).

✔ Test the slope by listening to the snow under your boot. Is there a *crump* or *whump* sound? If so, get out of there! This may well indicate that one layer is settling on top of another.

✔ Trail a long rope or string so that if you're buried, someone may be able to follow the string to you.

✔ Cross the slope one at a time so that if the slope avalanches, not everyone is endangered at the same time.

Make your way across the slope. Try not to panic; this is very scary. After you reach more solid terrain on the other side, the next person should come across in your footsteps, or a little higher up the slope. As soon as everyone is across, get out of there and don't come back!

For advice on surviving an avalanche, flip to Chapter 24. Finding and digging people out of avalanches is a topic for a whole other book; you can start with detailed advice in *Mountaineering: The Freedom of the Hills* (The Mountaineers Books).

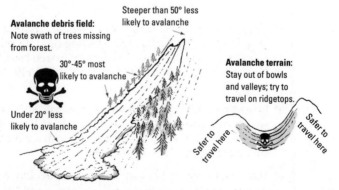

Figure 16-5: Avalanche hazards.

Staying off thin ice

Falling through thin ice (ice over a stream or lake, for example) is a terrible survival scenario. The definitive studies of Dr. Gordon Giesbrecht, at the University of Manitoba, have identified exactly what happens: The body goes into *cold shock*, leading to hyperventilation, gasping reflex, and possible cardiac overload, panic, and death. Every person is different, though. The cold shock response may not come for a few minutes, so use those minutes wisely to get out of the situation (check out Chapter 22 for more on cold shock response).

Do your best not to fall through the ice in the first place. Here's how to avoid this terrible fate:

- ✔ **If you can see how thick the ice is, make sure it's thick enough for your activity.** You may be able to spot the thickness of ice if it's clear, or you may spot some broken ice somewhere. Conditions vary, but here are estimates of how thick the ice needs to be:

    - **Walking:** Avoid freshwater ice that's less than 4 inches (10 centimeters) thick or saltwater ice less than 6 inches (15 centimeters) thick.

    - **Driving a snowmobile:** Avoid freshwater ice that's less than 6 inches thick or less than 1 foot (30.5 centimeters) for sea ice.

    - **Driving a car or truck:** Avoid ice that's less than 1 foot thick.

- ✔ **Keep an eye on the color of the ice.** In Wisconsin, where people spend a lot of time ice-fishing (and therefore wandering around on the surface of frozen lakes), folks say, "Thick and blue, tried and true; thin and crispy, way too risky."

- ✔ **Be extra-careful when the ice is covered with snow, which can mask or hide the ice's true color or texture.** On sea ice, stay away from dark, smooth ice that forms thin plates directly over seawater.

- ✔ **Don't walk on ice without using a probe.** Use a hard pole that you use to test the ice ahead every few steps.

If you need to get someone else out of ice, don't rush to his or her aid! Take a second to think through the situation. Here's what to do:

- ✔ **Calm down.** Take a deep breath. Look for any long item — a rope or pole or branch for example — that you can use to reach the victim. If you have a rope, tie something to the end (to give it a little weight) and throw it to the victim or slide it to that person across the ice. If you don't have a rope and your stick is too short to reach, consider lashing together branches or poles.

- ✔ **If you have to go for the person, get on your belly and slither to distribute your weight over a larger area.** Remember that the two of you are at risk of death, so be extra careful.

- ✔ **If you have several people available, you can reach out to the victim like a human chain.** Each person holds the next person's ankles, all spread out on their bellies on the ice.

After getting out of the ice, anyone who's fallen through must get his or her clothes dry and warm up immediately. Make a shelter and a fire and treat the victim for hypothermia and shock (see Chapter 13 for treatment details).

Avoiding cornices

When you're traveling in snowy mountains, you want to stay on *ridges,* the spines between mountain peaks. That's because avalanches slide down the sides of mountains, and on the ridge tops, you really can't get avalanched. However, when you're on ridges, you want to be aware of cornices and avoid them at all costs. *Cornices* are unstable ledges of snow that can form on ridges. Figure 16-6 shows where cornices form and how to avoid them.

Glacial cracks: Avoiding crevasses

Crevasses are cracks in *glaciers,* which are vast rivers of ice that creep down from mountainous terrain. Crevasses are normally V-shaped, so if you fall in, you continue to fall until your body wedges in tightly at the bottom. Obviously, you want to stay out of crevasses in the first place, and the best way to do that is to stay off glaciers. If you plan to climb on one, you should have extensive mountaineering experience.

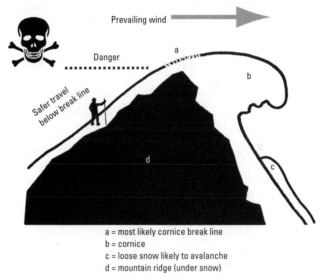

a = most likely cornice break line
b = cornice
c = loose snow likely to avalanche
d = mountain ridge (under snow)

Figure 16-6: Cornices are dangerous places, so steer clear of them at all costs.

If you find yourself trapped on a glacier — for example, if you've crashed a plane on one — your best bet is to stay put and signal for help — you'll stand out against the snow and ice. If you decide to move for some reason, keep the following in mind:

- ✔ **Try to get off the glacier.** Estimate the distance to the surrounding ridges and other rocky terrain and head for them.

- ✔ **Avoid snow bridges if possible.** A *snow bridge* is a natural bridge of snow across a crevasse. These features can be exceedingly risky to cross (however firm they look, they can collapse at any moment, just like in a Hollywood movie), so try to find another way. If you see no other way, wait until night, when the snow is frozen more solidly. Go across on your belly to spread out your weight.

WARNING!

✔ **Don't use a rope to make a bridge crossing "secure."** Tying a rope to someone else while that person crosses a snow bridge will probably (if the snow bridge collapses) just result in both people falling into the crevasse; the first will drag the second in unless you have specialized mountaineering gear and training.

Dealing with snow slopes

If you're in a snowy survival situation and you have to deal with a steep slope, you can use the following pointers to give you a little edge:

✔ **Ascend or descend steeper slopes by step-kicking.** Kick the first third of your boot into the snow with each step. Face the slope and keep three points of contact at all times (at least one foot and both hands).

✔ **Cross steeper slopes by step-kicking carefully with the side of your boot at every step.** Use a staff or pole of some kind to keep your balance, as in Figure 16-7a.

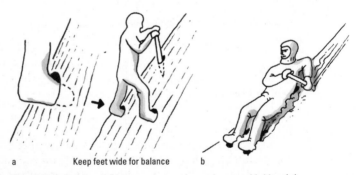

a   Keep feet wide for balance   b

Figure 16-7: Dealing with steep snow slopes by step-kicking (a) and glissading (b).

A slope doesn't have to be steep to cause trouble. If you slip and start sliding down, stopping can be tough — you may fall thousands of feet. The best way to descend a low-angle slope is to *glissade*, or slide down, basically on your hind end. Here are two ideas to keep in mind:

✔ **Control your speed with a very heavy wooden pole.**
A metal rod or a ski pole works fine. Just grasp it firmly
(fit it with a wrist loop) and lean on it as you descend,
as Figure 16-7b shows. Go slowly while glissading — you
may be headed for a cliff!

✔ **Stop sliding if the terrain gets steeper.** Dig in hard with
the pole. If you're going fast, whatever you do, don't dig
in your heels — that just catapults you forward!

Making Wearable Tools for Cold-Weather Survival

If you're in a wilderness survival situation, sometimes the
smallest tool can do wonders for you. And often, these special
tools don't require a lot of extra supplies or work — just a
little patience and ingenuity. The special tools in this section,
which are all clothing-based, can really help you in cold
environments and stack the odds in your favor.

Creating footwear

You can't travel if your feet are frozen, and sinking into the
snow makes walking a cold, wet, exhausting ordeal. In this
section, we explain how to assemble footwear to protect your
feet and help you make tracks.

Making your own snow boots

If you can't loosen your shoes to increase circulation and you
constantly feel your feet are frozen, taking off your shoes and
making your own boots from heavy cloth or any other flexible
material is a good idea. To make your own boots, follow these
steps:

1. **Lay out a square or rectangle of any heavy cloth
   (see Figure 16-8a).**

2. **Place a slab of bark, plastic, or other semirigid
   material on the cloth (Figure 16-8b.)**

   This is the *footbed;* if your shoes really are useless in
   the situation, you can cut your shoes down to supply
   the footbed only.

3. **Wearing the warmest socks you have, place your foot on the footbed; then put dried grass, crumpled newspaper, padding from a car cushion, or any other insulating material under, on, and around your foot (Figure 16-8c).**

   You need a lot of this insulating material to stay warm, so don't be skimpy. Depending on which material you use, you may have to change this insulation frequently as it gets wet or squashed flat.

4. **Draw the sides of the boot up and around your ankle, and tie off with a cord (Figure 16-8d).**

   Don't tie so tight that you constrict blood flow.

These boots are better than nothing, but stay out of water while wearing them, because they fall apart more easily than normal boots.

Figure 16-8: Making your own snow boots.

Making a pair of snowshoes

Snowshoes spread your weight over a large area, allowing you to walk on top of the snow instead of punching through it at each step. Functional snowshoes are easy to fashion from a few sturdy branches, some good, strong cordage, and some patience and creativity. To make your own pair of snowshoes, follow these steps:

1. **Cut two sturdy, green branches from a tree to use as the frame; strip them of bark.**

   These should be about 3 feet (0.9 meters) long and at least 1 inch (2.5 centimeters) in diameter. Cut the wood from living trees, because dry wood breaks.

2. **Assemble the frame as Figure 16-9a shows.**

3. **Select a number of sturdy green branches (at least ¾-inch [2-centimeter] diameter) as crossbars, and lash them across the frame.**

   Use natural places where the sticks branch off to more securely socket the crossbeams to the frame (Figure 16-9b).

4. **Using heavy cordage (parachute cord is ideal), begin lacing across the frame, adding crossbars as needed (Figure 16-9c).**

   Make a kind of web across the crossbeams. This web and the snowshoe frame distribute your body weight across the snow.

5. **Using heavy cordage, make a kind of sling to tie your boot to the frame.**

   A sturdy loop over the toe section may be all you need (Figure 16-9d). Keeping the heel free allows for a more natural walking motion, though while getting used to snowshoes, shuffling your feet is easier. Don't tie your boot so tightly to the snowshoe that it cuts off your circulation — this causes frostbite.

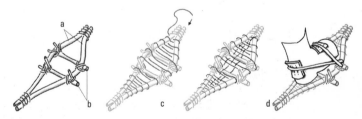

Figure 16-9: Making your own snowshoes.

Snowshoes can be difficult to get used to, but they're worth it; half an hour of *postholing*, going thigh-deep at each step, through deep snow will tell you that in a hurry. While you get used to your snowshoes, you may well want to use a pair of wooden poles, one in each hand, to keep your balance. After a while, you won't need them.

Boot wraps: Making and wearing gaiters

Gaiters are garments that wrap over the top of your boots to prevent gravel, dirt, and snow/ice from getting into your boots; in snowy environments, this can be particularly important because you really want to keep your feet dry and warm. You can create your own by following these steps:

1. **Cut a piece of heavy cloth, flexible plastic, or even cardboard to the shape and size in Figure 16-10a; puncture two holes in the tabs on the lower margin.**

2. **Roll the fabric into a tube and sew up the loose ends.**

   Make sure the tube is big enough around that you can slide it up to your knee and that it fits over the top of your boot (Figure 16-10b).

3. **Take off your boot and slip the gaiter up your leg; then put your boot back on.**

4. **Slip the gaiter down and over the boot-top; tie a length of cordage under the boot, connecting the two tabs, to keep the gaiter from coming off (Figure 16-10c.)**

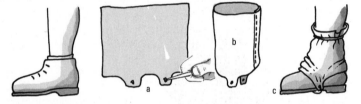

Figure 16-10: Making your own gaiters.

Insulating your clothing

Air is a good insulator, and anything that you can use to trap air next to your clothing can keep you warmer. Insulate clothing by adding a second layer to any garment and stuffing the gap between them with loose material, such as bunched up grasses, crumpled paper (though this becomes useless if it gets wet, so replace it as needed), or crumpled pine needles. These hold the layers of the garment apart, allowing a pocket of air between them.

Protecting your face and eyes

Snow is white because it reflects nearly all the light that strikes it, and all those bouncing rays of sunlight can cause sunburn and damage your vision. In this section, we tell you how to make tools that reduce the glare and protect your face from the sun, wind, and cold.

Sunblock is extremely important in polar regions because the sun reflects off the snow and ice, quickly causing severe burns. Be sure to carry sunblock (or improvise it, as we describe in Chapter 17), even in cold weather.

Making a balaclava

When improvising headgear for the cold, make a *balaclava*, a head garment that's snug around the face and entirely covers the head and neck. You can make one from the leg of a spare pair of pants or stitch together any sheet of plastic or cloth, as we show you in Figure 16-11.

Figure 16-11: An improvised balaclava.

Carving snow-glare goggles

Light reflecting from snow can temporarily blind you; this can happen on an overcast day as easily as on a sunny day. Always wear eye protection in snowy terrain. *Snow blindness* (retinal sunburn) is very painful. The main symptom is extreme pain in the eyes, as though hot sand grains have been packed under your eyelids. The cure is to rest with the eyes closed, perhaps wearing a blindfold. Twelve to 48 hours of rest should be enough, allowing you to see again.

You can avoid snow blindness by always wearing sunglasses and/or goggles in snowy terrain. If you don't have goggles, you can make them very easily from a piece of cardboard, leather, heavy cloth, or pliable plastic, using the steps here:

1. **Cut a slab of bark, plastic, cardboard, or other semi-pilable material into a bar about 8 inches (20 centimeters) across and 1 to 2 inches (2.5 to 5 centimeters) high (Figure 16-12a).**

2. **Cut slits into the material, about eye distance apart (Figure 16-12b).**

3. **Tie a headband onto the goggles by perforating the ends and tying cordage through them (Figure 16-12c).**

Figure 16-12: Improvising snow goggles.

Making mittens out of socks

If you have spare socks, you can make mittens to keep your hands warm. Mittens are normally warmer than gloves and are easy to improvise. Simply cut a slit in the sock for the thumb. Then sew up the slit so that the thumb has its own compartment.

Chapter 17

Staying Alive under the Sun

. . . .

In This Chapter

▶ Protecting yourself from the dangers of sunlight and dehydration

▶ Finding or building shelter in the desert

▶ Finding food and water in the desert

▶ Safely crossing desert terrain in the cool of the night

. . . .

*Y*ou face unique challenges in hot desert regions. Dehydration is always a threat because water is scarce and the heat makes you sweat. But deserts aren't always just hot. Believe it or not, you have to be ready for very cold nights as well, which make you hypothermic in short order. These regions are also home to some hard-to-see animals that strike quickly with dangerous, sometimes lethal, poisons.

In this chapter, we show you how to protect yourself from the sun, make shelter, find food and water, and avoid certain critters. We also show you how to hike your way safely across desert terrain in the dark, when it's cooler.

Knowing the Dangers the Sun and Heat Pose

Your body reacts to overheating by sweating and dilating your blood vessels to expel more heat from your system. If the body becomes so hot that these methods can no longer dump excessive heat, injury can occur. Overheating can be just as deadly as hypothermia (excessive cold).

The heat and sun can threaten your well-being in three ways: sunburn, heat exhaustion, and heat stroke. This section helps you grasp what the sun and heat can do to you if you don't take action.

If you have a good supply of water with you, you can prevent most heat injuries simply by drinking an adequate quantity of liquid.

Going skin deep with sunburn

Sunburn is a common heat malady that can become debilitatingly painful. You can easily prevent sunburn by wearing the correct clothing and using sunblock (see the later section titled "Wearing Sun Shields").

If you do get sunburned, treat the burn by draping a cloth soaked in water over the affected areas. Juice from the aloe vera plant can sometimes give you relief from the pain, although some evidence suggests that aloe vera can slow the healing process.

Overheating your body with heat exhaustion and stroke

Heat exhaustion and heat stroke are forms of *hyperthermia,* an excessive heating of the body. Heat exhaustion can turn into heat stroke, which can lead to brain damage and death. Here's how to recognize and treat these problems.

Recognizing the symptoms of hyperthermia

Heat exhaustion is indicated by one or all of these symptoms:

- ✔ Pale and perhaps clammy skin
- ✔ Racing pulse
- ✔ Dizziness and/or headache
- ✔ Nausea and/or diarrhea

A person with heat exhaustion isn't always sweating profusely; the body may have already used up its water supply prior to reaching heat exhaustion.

Heat stroke is a more dire condition than heat exhaustion, and it's indicated by the following:

- A red, flushed look to the skin
- Shock
- Extreme mental disorientation or unconsciousness
- Very dark urine
- Body temperature over 103°F (39.4°C)

Use your first aid kit thermometer to take a rectal temperature and monitor it carefully; anything over 103°F is potentially life-threatening, so keeping the body cool, wet, and rested is critical.

Cooling off

If the person has heat exhaustion or heat stroke, do the following to treat it:

- Get the person out of the sun.
- Loosen the clothing.
- Cool the body with liquid. Applying warm to tepid water to the skin and then fanning it may be the best course of action. You can substitute alcohol or soda if water is scarce.
- Fan the body vigorously, or if you're the victim, fan gently to avoid overexerting yourself.
- Massage the body to keep the blood circulating.
- Rehydrate the exhausted person with cool water.

When the body temperature is below 102°F (38.9°C), you can stop the cooling with water treatments (both applying it to the skin and drinking it), but be sure to monitor temperature carefully, because a person may go back into heat stroke.

If your survival situation doesn't allow you copious amounts of water to cool a heat-stressed person, you have to decide what's more important: long-term water conservation or saving the person right now.

Wearing Sun Shields

The first step in protecting your body from the sun is to dress appropriately. You should also cover your exposed skin with some kind of sunblock, whether you've packed some SPF 50 lotion or have to improvise some from your surroundings. This section tells you how to wear your sun defenses.

Cool clothes for hot times: Dressing for desert survival

Your first thought may be to strip down while in a desert to avoid overheating, but actually, you have to shield yourself from the sun's rays. Dress yourself from head to toe in clothing that shields you from the sun. You can find out how in Chapter 4 and with the tips we show you here (see Figure 17-1):

- ✔ **Hat or head covering:** To improvise a head covering to keep your brain from cooking, you can use a t-shirt: Simply put the neck of the upturned t-shirt on your head and drop the rest of the t-shirt behind your head, fully protecting your neck and ears. Alternately, you can sew stiff fabric, cardboard, or even pliable plastic, cut to shape with a knife, into a ball cap.

- ✔ **Sunglasses or goggles and a mask:** Sunglasses or even goggles protect you from becoming sunblind. If you don't have sunglasses or goggles, you can improvise them (see Chapter 16). You can also improvise a cloth mask to keep the dust and sand out of your lungs (see Chapter 4).

- ✔ **Shoes or sandals:** These protect your feet from hard stones, sharp thorns, cactus spines, and hot sand and rocks. You can improvise footwear from many materials, such as wood, hard plastic, or rubber. You may be able to protect your legs from snakebite by making a pair of gaiters (that come to the calf) from heavy cloth or even cardboard (see Chapter 16 for more on making gaiters).

Don't ditch your warm clothes! Deserts get cold at night (or they can), and then you face the risk of hypothermia.

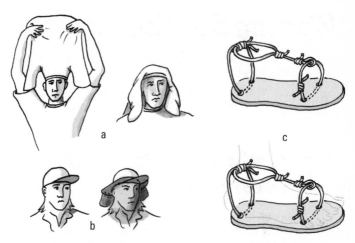

Figure 17-1: Improvised hot-weather clothing for the head and feet.

 If you have the luxury of extra water, keeping a wet cloth wrapped around your head can keep your brain cool. If you're short on water, you may as well use urine's cooling potential. Yes, that's right: *Urinate on your hat and then put it back on.* Hey, we never said any of this wilderness survival business was going to be pretty. Urine is sterile when you first urinate, and in a desert survival situation, it evaporates before bacteria become problematic.

Slathering on the sunblock

You can protect yourself from the sun with any cream or other paste that stands between your skin and the rays of the sun. If you're venturing into hot terrain, always carry a tube of sunblock. If you don't have any on you, you can improvise sunblock from the following:

- ✔ **Mud or clay:** Pigs and rhinos have the right idea when they wallow in the mud. Smear either mud or clay on the skin.

- ✔ **Charcoal:** Grind it up (after you've made a fire) and smear it on your face, mixing it first, if possible, with water or motor oil.

> ✔ **Used motor oil or axle grease:** These materials, which you can find in cars or other vehicles, can be effective sunblocks.

Unless you want to cook yourself in the sun, don't use baby oil, vegetable oil, mineral oil, or any kind of butter (such as cocoa) as a sunblock.

Finding Shelter in the Desert

Getting out of the sun and under a shelter is particularly important in a desert setting because the sun's direct rays can burn your skin, and the heat dehydrates your body. Shaded areas may not feel cool, but they're normally 10–20°F (5–10°C) cooler than areas in direct sunlight. Check out this section for more details.

Building a sunshade

You can make your own desert survival shelter as Figure 17-2 shows. All you need are two large sheets of cloth or plastic (such as a tarp and a space blanket from your wilderness survival kit — see Chapter 2). To make this shelter, follow these steps:

1. **Using a sturdy stick or flat rock, dig a trench in the ground, at least 1 foot (0.3 meters) deep, to get below the hot surface.**

   This trench needs to be big enough to lie in; you must never rest directly on the hot surface.

2. **Pile rocks to hold up the corners of your sheets.**

   Pile the rocks so they hold the sheets off the ground and trap a layer of air between the two sheets. With this construction, the sun beats on only the upper sheet, and the space below it keeps the heat from blasting through and reaching you.

   Using a space blanket as your top layer both deflects the sun's rays and creates an instant signal to any passing plane or car.

3. **If possible, pile up sand and/or rocks to make a shelter against wind.**

Wind can be strong and prolonged in desert areas, preventing sleep and wearing you down.

In windy conditions, your shelter tarps may blow away, so weight them down securely.

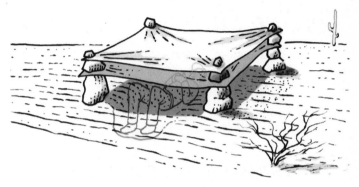

Figure 17-2: A desert shelter.

Looking for shady places

If you don't have the resources to make the desert shelter we show in Figure 17-2, look for the following shady spots:

- ✔ **Bushes and rock overhangs:** Before you find shade, always evict snakes, scorpions, or other critters from the bush, rock overhang, or boulder by first pelting it with rocks or prodding it vigorously with a stick. Animals want that shade as much as you do.

The animals you find, such as rabbits or snakes, may be edible, so always be prepared to kill with a club (see Chapter 8).

- ✔ **Wrecked vehicles:** Make sure all the doors and windows are open so breezes can blow through. Otherwise, they act like ovens.

Anytime you're stuck in a survival situation with a disabled car, be sure to leave the hood propped up, 24/7; this signals *help* to anyone who sees it.

The surface of a desert is normally about 35°F (19.4°C) hotter than the air a foot (30.5 centimeters) above the surface, so you never want to sit directly on the sand or rock. Instead, tip over a rock — watching out for snakes, scorpions, or other critters, of course — and sit on the side that was shaded. Or sit on a bundled-up jacket or your backpack.

Warming shelters overnight

Whatever shelter you use, be sure to make a fire in the late afternoon if you're staying put for the night (if you plan to travel, see later section "Traveling at night"). Collect wood, brush, and other fuel before it gets dark, so you can see what you're doing.

Do not burn wood from species of the genus *Euphorbia* (milk bush or pencil-tree) — the smoke is toxic. Before venturing into desert terrain, look up the milk-bush and see what they look like — there are many kinds!

If you're short on fire-starting equipment, such as matches or lighters, pile on heavy fuel throughout the night so you're always creating more coals, which you can use to restart the fire in the morning. Even in the desert, you should keep embers ready to make a smoke signal (see Chapter 12), and you can use a fire to cook food and purify water. For more on making fires, see Chapter 5.

If you can't make a fire — for whatever reason — you can use rocks heated by the sun to stay warm overnight. Slip some sun-warmed rocks inside your clothes before you turn in. These can keep you warm through a night. As soon as they cool down, though, toss them out; otherwise, they suck heat from your body.

Finding Water in the Desert

Though deserts may lack flowing water, every desert does have some moisture — moisture you need to keep cool and slake your thirst. You just need to know where and how to find it. This section gives you some water-finding methods that are particularly useful in deserts. Chapter 7 covers general methods to collect and purify water (including info on gathering dew, which can work in a desert).

In the desert, dehydration can kill you in hours. You must prevent dehydration at all costs, even at the risk of getting a water-borne disease. Even in hot, arid places, we advise you to filter and purify all water you find in the wild. However, if you're on the verge of perishing from dehydration and you have nothing to purify your water with, just drink unpurified water. Purifying water usually requires you to boil it (which may boil away all that you have in the desert) or put chemicals in it (chemicals you may not have). Unpurified water can give you a wide variety of diseases, but if you're facing death by dehydration *right now,* you'd better just take your chances.

Discovering standing water

When looking for water, one of the best places to start with is standing water. *Huecos* are holes in rocks or the ground that contain standing water. Even in the driest-appearing deserts, you can usually find such water in three main areas:

- ✔ **River courses:** Wet mud or sand, and even pools of water, can stand for a long time wherever rock or canyon walls hang over the riverbed. ("Squeezing water from mud or sand," later in this chapter, shows how to extract water from mud or sand.)

- ✔ **Under the shade of boulders and in caves, where shade may prevent evaporation:** Don't venture too far into a dark cave, though, or you could get lost or fall into a hole.

- ✔ **In solution pockets:** *Solution pockets* are bowl-like depressions in rocks that catch rain and may contain anything from a cup of water to hundreds of gallons.

A *mirage* is an illusion created by heat rising from the ground, and you can see plenty in desert terrain (they can also occur on open, snowy plains). A common — and frustrating — desert mirage is that of a distant pool of water, shimmering on the horizon. Don't change your course to head toward an oasis you think you see on the horizon unless it's accompanied by lots of thick, green vegetation.

Locating water underground

You may be able to discover some water in river courses that appear dry. Figure 17-3 shows you where you may be able to find water. Dig in the outside bends of turns in the riverbed — the outside bend often undercuts the riverbank, providing shade and preventing all the water from evaporating.

Flow

Figure 17-3: The most likely place to find water in an apparently dry riverbed.

Sometimes, palm trees can indicate the presence of water as well. You can often find water about 3 feet (0.9 meters) below a palm tree of any type.

To access underground water, dig down several feet, using a stick, a flat rock, or some other tool to preserve your hands. If you find wet sand, wait awhile; water may seep into your excavation, filling it like a basin. If the water doesn't seep into the excavation, you can either try digging deeper or in another spot, or you can try to squeeze water from damp sand or mud.

Squeezing water from mud or sand

You can extract water that remains frustratingly locked in sand or mud. Simply pile some wet sand or mud on a cloth, and then roll the cloth around the sand or mud before twisting it and catching the water in a receptacle (refer to Figure 17-4.)

Figure 17-4: Squeezing water from wet mud or sand.

Unearthing water from cracks in rock

You can get water from narrow cracks in rocks or very shallow pools by sucking water through a tube. Surgical tubing is ideal, as is a long straw (see Figure 17-5). If you don't have tubing, sometimes you can use a hollow reed.

Figure 17-5: Using a tube to get water from a rock cranny.

You may have to suck vigorously a few times to get the water going. Don't drink the water when you suck it from the cranny unless you're on the verge of succumbing to dehydration. Spit the water into a receptacle and then use some method to filter and purify it. This, however, may be impractical. You may have to simply take your chances and drink it unpurified.

Making a desert solar still

You can use a solar still to recycle urine (or any other impure water) and make it into drinkable water. Chapter 7 discusses how to make a solar still. To repurpose your urine, place a receptacle of urine in the bottom of the still, next to the collection receptacle (see Figure 17-6). The heat evaporates the water from the urine, leaving behind the impurities; the clean water condenses on the plastic and drips into your water collector, from which you can suck up the water with a tube or straw.

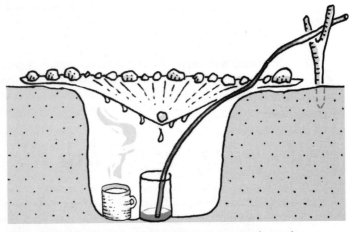

Figure 17-6: A desert solar still for distilling pure water from urine.

Collecting water from a cactus

Hollywood cowboys often cut open cacti to drink, but only one cactus is really safe for this method: the barrel cactus. The best cactus for drinking is the fishhook barrel cactus (see Figure 17-7), which normally stands about 6 inches (15 centimeters) high and has distinctive, fishhook-like thorns.

Figure 17-7: The safe fishhook cactus.

To get water from a fishhook cactus, cut it open with a heavy knife, mash the inside with a stick, and scoop out the fleshy tissue onto a piece of cloth. You can then squeeze the water out using the method we describe in the earlier section "Squeezing water from mud or sand."

 When drinking the fluid out of a barrel cactus, take your time and make sure you can digest it. Some of these cacti are very alkaline, which can make you ill, even if you put the fluid through a solar still. For more on solar stills, see Chapter 7.

Finding Food in the Dry Places

Only after you've protected your body from the sun with clothing and shelter and have secured some water (or thought out how you're going to get it) can you turn your thoughts to food. You can go weeks without food, so water always comes first.

 Food requires water to digest, so if you don't have water, too, don't eat. Some experts even recommend throwing away or destroying your food if you don't have water to help you avoid the temptation of eating! This is a pretty extreme measure, though — a decision best left to the circumstances and your judgment.

This section considers the different types of food sources you may find in the desert as well as some to avoid at all costs.

Fruits of the desert: Eating cacti and other plants

The fruit of any cactus is edible. Just cut off the bulbs and peel the fruit, being very careful of the spines, which can be as fine as peach fuzz. Boiling is the safest way to consume the fruit.

You can eat the tender, young pads of the prickly pear cactus. Just peel and cook them.

The leaves, stems, roots, and flowers of many desert plants are safe to eat, but many species can sicken or kill you. For instance, species of the genus *Euphorbia* (commonly known as milk bush or pencil-tree) are poisonous. So before you eat any plants, check them with the Universal Plant Edibility Test in Chapter 8. **Remember:** Some fungi do grow in the desert, but don't eat them or use the Universal Plant Edibility Test on them — they can be toxic even in small amounts.

Eating insects

Insects are excellent survival foods. Here's how to prepare them:

- ✔ **Ants and termites:** You can collect ants and termites one by one and eat them raw (they're one of the few survival foods that are safe without cooking). Or you can mash them into a paste if you have a lot of them.

- ✔ **Grasshoppers and beetles:** The wings and legs of grasshoppers and beetles are a choking hazard, so remove them before cooking. You can boil these animals in water to make a soup, or to save water, broil them next to a fire.

- ✔ **Larvae:** If you find beetles, you may find beetle larvae — white, grub-like animals — under or inside logs or other pieces of wood. Simply cook and eat them as you do for beetles.

Stay away from bees and hornets because of their painful stings — you may be allergic, leading to a serious and sometimes life-threatening reaction.

Choosing poultry and eggs

All birds are edible, and so are their eggs. Remember that birds don't just nest in tree branches; they may occupy a cavity in a cactus or tree trunk, or their nests may be under a bush on the ground, in a cave, or on a rock ledge. Boil the eggs, and broil the birds after plucking off the feathers.

Catching desert mammals

Small mammals, such as mice, are common in many deserts. They can be tough to catch, though — they're so small that snaring them would require a very small, delicate snare. You can sometimes trap mice by placing a can of water or other bait in the bottom of a 2-foot (0.6-meter) deep, steep-sided hole. At night, mice are attracted by the smell of food or water, and as soon as they fall into the hole, they can't get out.

Larger desert mammals include foxes and various herbivores, such as antelope. You may be able to snare these animals as well, but insects, snakes, or small mammals are much easier to catch. If you do catch a mammal, you can butcher and cook it in ways we cover in Chapter 8.

Dining on lizards and snakes

Many lizards and snakes are harmless. If you do decide to hunt them, make sure you know what you're hunting. We don't recommend hunting snakes because some have lethal bites, but if you do come across one and feel the situation is manageable, there's no reason not to kill and eat it. What is a manageable situation, with respect to a potential killer (like a rattlesnake), is up to you. Your decision depends on how hungry, well-armed, strong, and confident you are. (See the next section for more on venomous reptiles.)

If you choose to eat snakes and lizards, here's how to process them:

1. **Cut off the head by cutting at the neck, several inches down from the base of the skull.**

The poison glands are in the head, and this gets them out of your way. This works for snakes as well as the poisonous lizards, such as the gila monster and the beaded lizard.

Snake heads can still bite 24 hours after death, and lizard mouths are breeding grounds for bacteria. Bury the head away from your butchery and eating spot and mark the burial spot with a pile of stones so you don't accidentally dig it up.

2. **Strip off the skin.**

   Start an incision, lengthwise, down the body from where you removed the head, and then pull the skin off like a sheath.

3. **Cook it properly.**

   Broil the carcass next to a fire or bake it underground, under the hot coals. When the meat is flaky, white, and dry, it is edible.

Avoiding Dangerous Desert Animals

In deserts, keep your eyes out for the following creatures, especially in shaded areas or at night, when desert animals are most active.

Gila monsters and slithering snakes

Most desert lizards aren't toxic, but beware of the bite of the large Gila monster (see Figure 17-8) and Mexico's very similar beaded lizard. Both lizards are around 1 foot (30.5 centimeters) long and are unlikely to attack unless provoked. Unless you have a weapon that you can use to kill the lizard so you can eat it, your safest move is to just walk away.

Many desert species of snakes can sicken or kill you with a lightning-fast bite. Especially stay away from the rattlesnake, which has a diamond-shaped head that's fatter than the neck, as in Figure 17-8. These snakes have a lethal bite, and they make a distinctive *Sssss* sound with their tail-rattles as a warning. Many poisonous snakes don't have diamond-shaped heads, though, so be cautious around any snake.

Figure 17-8: The distinctive head of a rattlesnake and a gila monster.

You can sometimes scare snakes away by making plenty of noise as you walk. Sturdy boots and heavy trousers can protect you from a bite. You can also use *gaiters*, which are fabric covers that seal the space between the trousers and the boots. To see how to improvise these, take a look at Chapter 16.

Stinging scorpions, centipedes, and spiders

Arthropods are critters with hard shells and lots of little jointed legs — and sometimes some pretty nasty bites and stings. You do have to watch out for wasps and ticks as you do in temperate environments (see Chapter 11), but you may also run into some scorpions, centipedes, and desert spiders. In this section, we tell you what to watch out for.

Scorpions and centipedes

What they say in the movies is true: The big, burly scorpions sting hard, but the small ones can be lethal. Meanwhile, centipedes can deliver a very painful and occasionally debilitating bite, to which some people can have a severe allergic reaction.

Scorpions (Figure 17-9a) and centipedes (Figure 17-9b) are tough to avoid in deserts, but you can take some precautions:

✔ Be vigilant with every rock you turn over — use a stick.

✔ Never put on a piece of clothing (such as a shirt or a shoe) without first checking it for scorpions and centipedes. Shake all your clothing and foot gear before putting it on — and we mean shake it vigorously so the fabric makes a *pop!* sound.

✔ Be especially careful between sundown and the next noon — that's when most scorpion stings occur.

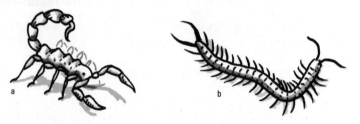

Figure 17-9: Watch out for scorpions (a) and centipedes (b).

Scorpion stings feel like bee stings, and less than 1 percent of scorpion stings in the U.S. are fatal. The symptoms of a serious sting, however, include the following:

✔ Dilation of the pupil and twitching of the eye

✔ Difficulty swallowing

✔ Heart palpitations and sweating

Treat scorpion stings and centipede bites simply by washing and then keeping the wound clean. Painkillers may ease the pain. There are antivenins for scorpion venom, but they must be administered by a doctor.

Spiders

The world is home to almost 40,000 spider species, some of which live the in desert. Most are harmless to humans, but some can be lethal. Dangerous spider bite symptoms include

✔ Dizziness, nausea and vomiting

✔ Fever

✔ Cramps, especially in the abdomen

Chapter 13 covers spider bite treatment. Avoid spiders by checking under rocks and shaking out clothing.

Wind and Water: Watching Out for Desert Weather

Deserts seem so calm most of the time — little wind, not much weather to speak of other than the relentless sun. But there are two real dangers you have to keep an eye out for, outlined in this section.

Staying high and dry during flash floods

A *flash flood* is any unexpected arrival of water on a landscape, and strangely enough, this is a big danger in deserts. A big storm can drop millions of gallons of water 100 miles away — while you're being blistered by the sun — and suddenly the dry riverbed you're staggering along, or sleeping in, turns into a raging river!

To avoid flash flood dangers, walk along the rim of a dry river while you assess the danger, remembering a few tips:

✔ **Look for high-water marks.** High-water marks (refer to Figure 17-10) include stains on rock walls or piles of vegetation snagged in tree limbs adjacent to watercourses, where vegetation floating on a prior flash flood rose up and got caught. Stripes in the rock may not be high-water marks — they may be natural rock layers — so look for stranded vegetation and other signs of flooding.

✔ **Before venturing into a canyon or dry riverbed, look at the horizon all around for clouds.** If you see low, dark clouds that look rainy, get back up on higher ground. The flash-flood water may be pouring down way over there, right now — just an hour from where you are.

Figure 17-10: High-water marks in a dry riverbed mark this canyon as a dangerous place to walk.

Taking shelter from sandstorms

High winds can pick up mass quantities of sand and blow them across deserts with tremendous force in what's called a *sandstorm*. Some sandstorms can actually strip the paint off a car. If you see a giant, sand-colored wall on the horizon (for once, it looks just like it does in the movies!), prepare yourself by covering your mouth with a cloth (to filter out some sand) and finding some shelter. If you have to, build a wind-shelter from rocks. A circle or semicircle of stones large enough to lie behind may be enough to break some of the wind, but you still get covered by sand every few hours. Don't put a tarp over the shelter if the wind is strong — it'll just blow away.

Dense, blowing sand can interfere with radio transmissions, and will ground rescue aircraft anyway, so if you have a radio, save your batteries and wait until the storm ends to begin signaling again. Sandstorms can last for days.

Finding Your Way in the Desert

The decision to travel in a survival situation is a big one that we cover in Chapter 11. If you do decide to move in the desert, the main thing to keep in mind is that you need to have a plan and stick to it. Determine the direction you want to travel, prepare your gear, and then stick to your plan, day after day — or as we suggest in this section, night after night. The good news is that in a desert, you can see a long way, allowing you to plan your trek, take compass bearings, and navigate more efficiently than in, say, a dense jungle. (See Chapters 9 and 10 for more on navigating.) This section helps you travel in the desert both during the day and night.

Whenever you make the decision to travel, be sure to leave a note or signal at the place where you first became lost. And as you travel, leave notes behind updating your progress. Put messages in trees or under conspicuous piles of stone so people can find them easily. Indicate the following:

- ✔ What direction you're headed and why
- ✔ Who you are and what happened to you
- ✔ What supplies you have
- ✔ The date that you're departing

Traveling at night

If you've committed to traveling to get out of your wilderness survival situation, traveling at night is a good tactic for dealing with hot country. Temperatures are cooler and sometimes downright cold in deserts at night, so your body uses less water — about half the water it needs when traveling in daylight.

For navigation, you can use the stars, which — after you know a few basics — are nothing less than a vast compass in the sky (and the stars never lie, thankfully). Chapter 10 tells you how to navigate by the stars.

Spend plenty of time during the day making your plans before traveling at night. Get to the highest point you can safely reach to give you a better vantage point, and then study the terrain, locating the features that can act as landmarks.

Seeing in the dark

To travel at night, you have to use night vision, which you can acquire by letting your eyes adjust to darkness. In the space of an hour of sitting in darkness — with no campfire or any other artificial light — your pupils dilate to their maximum, which allows your eyes to gather more light.

When using night vision, you have to maintain strict light discipline. Don't use a flashlight or even light a match after you start traveling, because these lights will ruin your night vision.

If you have a red lens filter on your flashlight, you can use it to read maps at night without destroying your night vision. A *red filter* is simply a red-colored translucent plastic cap that fits over your flashlight bulb housing. If you don't have a red filter, improvise one by taping red fabric over your flashlight.

Using a staff to probe ahead in darkness

When traveling at night, make sure you use a walking stick or staff to feel the ground in the darkness and help you keep your balance on uneven terrain. Using one in each hand, like ski poles, is also effective.

You can also use a walking stick or staff to prod bushes or other obstacles (or better yet, go around them) when you suspect they may be home to a snake or other potentially dangerous animal. Remember, a lot of desert animals come out at night, when it's cooler.

Confronting drop-offs

Walking at night can pose potential dangers, such as the inability to see that canyon in front of you. If you're on rocky ground, beware of sudden drop-offs.

If the ground goes completely black in front of you, stop and feel with your walking stick or staff. You may have to go around an obstacle, or you may be able to judge how far a drop-off is by probing with a walking staff. If you can feel that solid ground is just a few feet down (and, by throwing a stone into the darkness, you can tell that it's not just a little ledge leading to a high cliff!), you can proceed. But don't jump down the drop-off — that's crazy! To clamber down a 3-foot (0.9-meter) cliff, do the following (see Figure 17-11):

1. **Probe the ground at the bottom of the drop-off with your walking stick.**

2. **Turn to face the land you're walking on and kneel down.**

3. **Hold onto the edge and shove your legs over.**

4. **Slide/lower yourself down, using your arms for support.**

Figure 17-11: Checking height and clambering down a 3-foot drop-off.

Traveling in daylight

We don't believe there's any good reason to travel significant distances in deserts in daylight in a real survival situation. You may as well wait for cooler hours of dusk till dawn, when you'll consume less water and you're at less risk of heat exhaustion or heat stroke. However, if you're forced to travel in the day (we can't really think why, but it may happen):

- ✔ **Watch yourself and your companions for the symptoms of heat exhaustion and dehydration.** We discuss these earlier in "Knowing the Dangers the Sun and Heat Pose."

- ✔ **Protect yourself from the sun with the proper clothing.** See the earlier section "Wearing Sun Shields."

- ✔ **Drink plenty of water.** If you have the water, drink at least 1 gallon (4 liters) a day. You may need up to 5 gallons (19 liters) a day.

- ✔ **Rest in shade and up off the ground for at least 10 minutes every hour.** This gives you a few moments to cool off.

> ✔ **Breathe through your nose rather than your mouth.**
> You want to minimize water loss from exhaled vapor.

Better yet, avoid all these problems by traveling at night.

Crossing Desert Terrain

The vast, open terrain of deserts can be deceptive, making distant hills look three times closer than they really are. Don't get frustrated. Stick to your plan even as you encounter these obstacles:

✔ **Sand dunes:** The wind can blow sand into mountainous heaps. Dunes present no real immediate dangers, but they're dangerously exhausting to climb. You either have to slog over them — sinking back with each step — or go around them, which may cost miles. Tough call.

✔ **Rocky terrain:** Crossing rocky terrain requires shoes or boots. Sturdy soles protect you from heat, sharp rock, and thorns, and high cuffs prevent the dreaded twisted ankle and may stop a snake attack.

✔ **Wadis and lagas:** Dry watercourses — termed *wadis* in Arabia and *lagas* in East Africa — are riverbeds that flow in the spring (when mountain snows melt) but are dry the rest of the year. They can be the home of flash floods in the springtime, so beware of this danger. They may have water in them, though (see the earlier section "Locating water underground").

✔ **Gallery forests:** These are vegetation stands that run along the banks of river courses that are dry most of the year but flow with spring meltwater. They can be a great source of water — because tree roots and other vegetation trap water in their vicinity — but remember that a lot of nonhuman animals (such as African lions) like to take shelter in the shade of gallery forests, just like you do.

Part IV
Surviving on the Seas, Oceans, and Great Lakes

The 5th Wave   By Rich Tennant

YEAR 1 - GET RESCUED
YEAR 2 - GET RESCUED!
YEAR 3 - GET RESCUED!! NOW!
        (FOCUS MORE)
YEAR 4 - GET RESCUED
        (SCREAM LOUDER!)
YEAR 5 - BUILD GOLF
        RESORT

"My thinking has changed a little this year."

In this part . . .

Survival challenges on the water are so unique that we've dedicated an entire part to this topic. How do you protect yourself from hypothermia if you fall into one of the Great Lakes? How can you satisfy your thirst on the ocean when you're surrounded by salt water? Which foods are safe to collect from the sea? Can you fend off sharks and other dangerous animals? And how are you going to get to land — or even find land in the first place? In this part, we answer these questions, and we show you the skills you need to know when you head offshore.

Chapter 18

Staying Afloat and Warm

● ●

In This Chapter

▶ Coping with a sinking vessel

▶ Abandoning ship

▶ Floating after a sinking

▶ Preventing hypothermia

● ●

*I*f you get into trouble while at sea (or on a large lake), your
ordeal begins, most likely, in one of two ways: You get
separated from your boat in some way, or your vessel sinks.
Neither are pleasant thoughts, we know, but you can use
plenty of good strategies to make it through.

In this chapter, we look at scenarios in which life rafts aren't
involved. (Chapter 19 covers life raft procedures as well what
to do if your vessel is disabled.) For now, we show you how to
recognize a ship or small boat is in trouble, how to cope with
that situation, and how to stay alive in the minutes and hours
after the sinking — with or without a life jacket.

Recognizing When Your Vessel Is in Trouble

If you spend any time studying the harrowing history of
tragedies at sea, you quickly see a clear pattern: Those who
recognize what's happening immediately — as it's happening —
usually have the highest rate of survival. This section shows
you some of the causes of sinking and the warning signs that
the vessel you're aboard, whether large or small, may be in
danger.

Overloading

If you find yourself aboard a vessel that you feel is overloaded, try as hard as you can to stay above deck; go below only if you have to. If danger comes — such as heavy weather — an overloaded vessel is going to get into trouble quickly.

Over the years, island-to-island ferries and river ferries in many countries have developed a reputation of being constantly overloaded, which has caused some tragic *capsizes* (overturning). But danger from overloading can happen anytime and anywhere — even with canoes and rowboats on lakes and ponds.

If you haven't yet boarded the boat, here's how you can tell whether it's overloaded:

- ✔ **Check the freeboard.** The *freeboard* is the amount of the boat's hull that's above the surface of the water. If the rim *(gunwale)* of the vessel is too close to the water, even a small wave could sink it. Check out Figure 18-1.

    Keep in mind that some vessels have naturally low freeboards, especially the ones on the big rivers, like the Amazon in South America and Mekong in Southeast Asia. The best thing to do is to compare the freeboard of the vessel you're about to board with other vessels, loaded and unloaded.

- ✔ **Look for empty spaces.** All vessels should have empty spaces in them, places where no person stands, no equipment rests, no cargo is stored. Few boats are designed to be stuffed to the brim. If a vessel appears full and has little or no freeboard, be on guard.

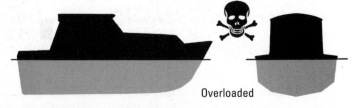

Overloaded

Figure 18-1: Identifying overloading.

Poor trim or listing

If a vessel you're traveling on suddenly leans in the water, this is called a *list,* and it may be a sign you should be planning your escape. This is especially true if the boat is rolling. If the vessel rolls one way and doesn't roll back, this is a definite sign that something is wrong.

All boats should remain *trimmed* in the water, which means they should sail along in a balanced fashion. Even sailboats, which lean over (heal) naturally, should still be trim — in other words, they should lean over in a straight and organized fashion. Many vessels start out their voyages poorly trimmed, and like overloaded vessels, when they get into trouble, bad things happen quickly. Figure 18-2 shows trimmed and poorly trimmed boats.

Small boats swamp quickly. *Swamping* means that the boat floods almost to the brim. This happens when an enormous mass of water comes over the side, or over the back *(transom)*, of the boat.

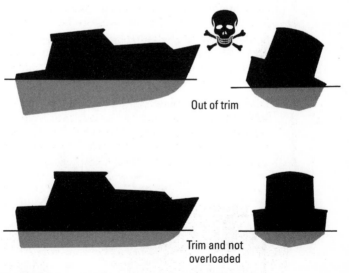

Out of trim

Trim and not
overloaded

Figure 18-2: An out-of-trim vessel and a trimmed vessel.

Bad weather and heavy seas

The vast majority of vessels come through bad weather without any problem at all. But if the vessel you're aboard labors heavily in bad seas, especially if the boat loses power, start thinking about your plans for survival. Most vessels are designed to allow water to come aboard and then drain off. If more water is coming aboard than is draining, be prepared to act.

All waves aren't created equal. Many times, great mountains of water on the sea do nothing but create a lot of foam at the top, and they're much safer to deal with than small waves that fling their tops forward.

When you're in any boat, but especially a small boat, you're vulnerable to the *plunging breaker,* a wave that flings an enormous amount of water in front of it. You can see a perfect example of these curling waves near the shore because the surf is often made up of plunging breakers. However, plunging breakers can develop anywhere. Remember, size isn't the main factor here; a wave can be only about 6 feet tall, but if it plunges, it's dangerous (see Figure 18-3).

Although waves of any kind can cause problems, if you're aboard a small boat and plunging breakers are nearby, be prepared for serious problems like flooding and capsize — another reason to wear your life jacket when going through a heavy surf, or even better, a good reason to avoid the surf altogether!

Figure 18-3: A plunging breaker.

Collisions

The oceans are big, but ships and boats still find ways to run into each other or submerged objects every day. Knowing how collisions occur can give you the added edge of a few extra seconds or minutes to plan your survival. In this section, we tell you how to avoid running into things, whether you're on a lake or the ocean.

Understanding collision courses with other vessels

Collisions between boats usually occur in marinas, ports, entrances to ports, or places with bad visibility, but they can occur almost anywhere. Here's what to do whenever you see another boat (check out Figure 18-4).

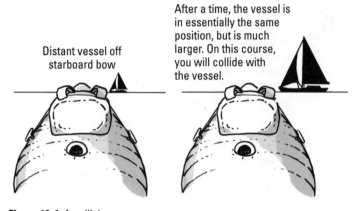

Distant vessel off starboard bow

After a time, the vessel is in essentially the same position, but is much larger. On this course, you will collide with the vessel.

Figure 18-4: A collision course.

1. **Align your view of the other boat with some object of reference on your vessel.**

   Line up a nearby object with the faraway vessel, just like looking down a gun sight. For example, if you're on a sea kayak and you see a sailboat in the distance, make a mental note that the sailboat lines up with, say, your backpack's shoulder strap. In Figure 18-4, the sailboat is off your kayak's *starboard* (right) bow.

2. **After a few seconds, check the alignment again.**

If the sailboat is still aligned with the same object on your sea kayak but the sailboat is much larger — in other words, much closer — the two of you are moving toward the same point.

In a few more seconds, you may take your sighting again, and now the sailboat is so large that you can see the person who's steering it — but it's still at the same sighting point, over the same sighting object: You're on a *collision course*.

3. **If you're on a collision course, take action to get away or turn very sharply.**

   Or if you have no control of the vessel — such as when you're on a charter or ferry, begin taking the steps we show you in "Knowing What to Do If Your Boat Starts to Sink," later in this chapter.

Anytime you're sailing or motoring in waters where there are Jet Skis, Sea-Doos, or any other sort of personal water crafts (PWC), be especially vigilant. These small motorcycles-on-water are involved in a lot of collisions.

Watching out for underwater obstacles

The second type of collision is the type that occurs when the boat you're on strikes a fixed object, or a submerged one, like a reef or rock. Maintain a very sharp lookout for the following:

- ✔ **Any signs or buoys that have large red diamonds on them:** These signs can vary from country to country, but in North America, they mark danger.

- ✔ **Any foam near the shore:** This usually means that a rock is just right under the surface (awash).

- ✔ **Any long lines of rocks extending from land:** Where these long, rocky peninsulas stop is only the start of danger. These rocks usually continue just under the surface.

Fire

Fire burns well on the water because you're in an open space with lots of oxygen. Fire burns so aggressively on the water that the flames and the heat frequently make it impossible for the crew to maintain control of the vessel, which puts you at the mercy of the waves and the sea.

If you see a fire on a cruise or charter, notify the crew immediately. Though you should always try to let the crew of the vessel perform the fire-extinguishing duties, know that on most boats, fire extinguishers are available.

Hatch failure and ship damage

Loosely speaking, a *hatch failure* occurs whenever a previously closed opening breaks and lets water into the boat. Doors can be left unsecured, allowing water to pour into the vessel, and large waves can break windows on boats quite easily. Heavy flooding in these cases happens in an instant, so be ready for it. Some vessels can pump the water out, and some can't.

Many tragedies at sea give warnings in the form of sounds or bad vibrations. The water itself can make horrendous noises against a boat's hull without causing any damage whatsoever, but when a ship strains, the sound is significantly different. The ship groans, metal twisting on metal. All ships make these sounds when laboring, but listen for them, and try to develop a sense of what's unusual. The best way to react to loud or violent noise is to be vigilant, but not panicked.

Knowing What to Do If Your Boat Starts to Sink

As soon as the boat you're on starts to sink, you need to take action. If you keep calm and take a few steps in a timely fashion, you greatly increase your chance of survival. This section takes you through the important immediate steps you need to take if your ship is in trouble and starting to sink.

Radioing for help

If you can get to a radio and your vessel is in grave and immediate danger, you need to signal for help. The law states very clearly that anyone, regardless of experience or licenses, can operate *any* radio he or she has access to if sending a distress signal. The single stipulation to this law — and it's a serious stipulation — is that to signal SOS or Mayday, you must be in "grave and immediate danger" of death or loss of significant property. If your situation isn't that bad, consider signaling Pan, which is for smaller problems. (For directions on how to send a Mayday or Pan signal, check out Chapter 12.)

If you've made radio contact with someone and your distress signal has been sent and completely received, make a *schedule.* Tell the radio operator on the other end that if you lose contact, she should listen again at a specific time for another signal. If radio contact is very good — for example, if you've made contact with a U.S. Coast Guard radio operator or with one of the ham radio networks (such as the Maritime Mobile Net) — then after making your distress call, make your schedule, confirm it, and then shut off your transmitter or cellphone. Good battery discipline can give you the upper hand on your surroundings.

If you know you're going to leave the vessel — in other words, if the boat is sinking and you know there won't be a second contact — tape down the button on the microphone so that the radio continues to transmit for as long as possible.

Putting on a life jacket

Faced with a deteriorating situation, you should put on a life jacket. If the captain or one of the mates of the vessel you're on doesn't give you a life jacket, you may have to find one yourself. Life jackets usually live in the dark. If you're in trouble, look in the darkest places of a boat:

- ✔ Under the seats, in the seat lockers
- ✔ In the *forepeak,* the dark place at the very front point of the boat
- ✔ In the *lazarette,* the trunk at the very back of the boat
- ✔ In the closet behind the *bridge,* the room from which the boat is steered

If you have time and the water is cold, put on as much clothing as you can before putting on your life jacket. Forget all those Hollywood movies where the hero strips off his shirt to dive in. Clothing traps water near your body, which is then warmed by your body, forming a protective layer. Extra clothing usually doesn't hinder you so much in swimming that you should discard it.

If you can, try to find life jackets — and the places where they're stored — while you're still at the dock. Choose the thickest life jacket you can find. Don't go for style — you want puffy and bulky. However, that doesn't mean an *oversized* jacket. The perfect life jacket is one that fits you snugly, like a glove, but with a lot of puffy flotation in it. The ones labeled Type I are the very best (check out Chapter 2 for the lowdown on the types available). Put the life jacket on before you go into the water — you won't have time later! If you're wearing the type that inflates, put it on but wait until you've entered the water to inflate the jacket.

Tighten all straps until the jacket feels like it's actually gripping you — but don't overtighten; if the jacket is too tight, you'll have trouble swimming. Snug is right. Many times, when you abandon ship, the life jacket's buoyancy forces it to rise up and fly over your head — which means you're now in the water, struggling to put it back on. Sometimes it simply shoots up and knocks you in the chin. The crotch strap is the most effective way of keeping the life jacket on, so anytime a jacket has a crotch strap, use it.

Here's the only exception to the rule of putting on your life jacket before you go into the water: if you're surrounded by burning fuel or if you have to submerge your body to swim to safety. Submerging your body long enough to swim under burning fuel or out of a sunken boat is practically impossible when you're wearing a life jacket. If you face this type of situation, try throwing your jacket beyond the flames and then make your underwater escape.

Preparing to abandon ship

If the vessel is sinking, make abandoning it cleanly your first priority — you don't want to be pulled down with the sinking ship. But in the seconds and minutes between when you first realize that there's danger and when you have no choice but to leave, you can take advantage of your surroundings.

As soon as you know the boat is in trouble and is at risk for sinking (and after you've put on your life jacket), take the following precautions — but only if you're sure you have the time. We list these in order of importance:

✔ **Put on a hat.** If you have access to wool, grab it. Having a covering on your head can double your survival time in some cases.

✔ **Protect your cellphone.** If you have access to plastic, wrap up your phone. A woman's handbag can function as a sufficient dry-bag — put the phone in and roll the bag tightly around it.

✔ **Gather signaling materials.** You need to be able to signal for help when you're in the water. Chapter 12 lists items you can grab to make signals.

✔ **Collect water and/or containers.** Even just a small amount of water can help. Your ability to survive long term on the sea, many times, comes down to your ability to catch and store rainwater. (For more on fresh water at sea, see Chapter 20.)

If you can, make sure water containers have a little air inside them so that they'll float well in the waves.

Abandoning ship: The how-to

If you have the choice, stay with the vessel for as long as you can. It's large and easier to see than a life raft, and it's where search teams will start looking for you. It may float, partially sunk, for a very long time. If, however, the vessel is leaving the surface and you can step straight into a life raft, boarding the raft is preferable to releasing the life raft and swimming for it. (For more on using life rafts, see Chapter 19.) The rest of this chapter deals with situations in which you don't have a life raft.

A sinking vessel is a body in motion. Just because the boat is oriented one way right now doesn't mean it's going to stay that way. Expect the boat to roll or pitch heavily. The following are procedures for abandoning a sinking ship or boat:

✔ **Leave from the side on which the wind is blowing (upwind).** If you jump off the boat on the other side (downwind), you run the risk of having the boat blown over you.

✔ **Enter at the lowest point.** Ideally, you want to slip smoothly into the water — slowly. Doing so can help to prevent cold shock response (see Chapter 22 and the nearby sidebar). Jumping from height can also cause injuries as you hit the water.

✔ **If you must jump into the water, assume the following position:**

- **Fold your arms across your chest and grasp the lapels of your life jacket with your fingers before you jump.** Hold your jacket down strongly. Remember, when people lose their life jackets, they usually lose them over their heads because the buoyancy makes the device shoot up while the people are plunging down.

- **Cross your legs tightly at the ankles.** You do this to cut down on becoming entangled in lines and cables and to make your body a solid unit.

✔ **Above all things, part company cleanly.** Stray lines and fishing gear, cables and railing, masts — all these things can grab you. Abandon, and swim away quickly.

Coping with cold shock response

Members of polar bear clubs may get a thrill out of the gasping breaths and racing pulses that come from plunging into cold water, but cold water is no friend to the survivor. Unlike hypothermia, *cold shock response* kills by causing cardiac arrest or stroke or by incapacitating you so much that you drown or are unable to perform physical tasks, such as climbing into a life raft. If you enter the water and you're surprised by how cold it is, you're at risk.

Entering the water slowly and gradually — if you have that luxury — can go a long way toward preventing cold shock response. Another way to help yourself is to gently swim to something nearby that you can hold onto, or just float in your life jacket, and wait until your heart rate normalizes. This usually takes from 7 to 10 minutes. Of course, if you're in extremely cold water and in danger of hypothermia immediately and a lifeboat is nearby, you obviously don't have the luxury of waiting.

You should know that if you have cold shock response, holding your breath for any length of time becomes very difficult. If you're expecting to have to hold your breath for any amount of time and you have cold shock, be very still and wait patiently for your heart rate to go back down. After this happens, you should be able to hold your breath for almost as long as you normally can.

After the vessel has sunk, and you're sure it has sunk, return to the sight of the sinking and begin working through the debris field. All vessels disgorge odd and ends when they sink, any one of which can save your life later on. But you must act quickly. Debris disperses incredibly fast. Scan for jugs, bottles, sheets of fabric, anything.

Coping with sharks

When you're in the water, sharks can be a problem. You need to practice shark attack safety and prevention. Keep the following pointers in mind:

- ✔ **Keep blood out of the water, if possible.** Tend to any wounds as best you can.

- ✔ **Don't swim erratically.** Swim in smooth powerful strokes. Avoid weak or fluttering strokes, and don't thrash about in the water.

- ✔ **Don't urinate or defecate in the water if sharks are nearby.** Sharks have a keen sense of smell and may be attracted to the scent.

- ✔ **Stay in a group.** Most sharks are scavengers and are looking for easy targets. Larger may be better.

In case you're forced into fighting sharks, we offer the following methods, in the order in which we think they're effective.

- ✔ **Pull your knife out and be ready to use it:** Put your knife on the end of a pole — if you're lucky enough to have one or find one floating in the debris. You can use this weapon to scare them away. For more on this procedure, check out the nearby sidebar.

- ✔ **Shark repellant:** You can find shark repellant in many life rafts — just know that it's a one-time-use-only agent. After you open the package, the repellant works for a very short time.

- ✔ **Strike a shark in the eyes or gills.** Try to dig them out with your fingertips or your knife. People have tried this with varying degrees of success. It's certainly better than doing nothing.

✔ **Slapping the water or screaming underwater:** There are, admittedly, two schools of thought concerning this method: Some say it drives sharks away, some say it can attract them. Again, you may have to use trial and error.

Organizing your shark defense

Years ago, when we were drifting on the open sea and were surrounded by thousands of sharks, we devised a method for coping with these animals that was crude but effective.

Our vessel was sinking, and the only way to repair it involved spending a lot of time in the water, so we needed some way to chase away the sharks. To do this, we behaved in a highly territorial fashion and made the sharks believe that they had to leave. The key to success seemed to be to attack several sharks in rapid succession — as many as we could in the shortest amount of time possible. Using a sharp pole or spear, we'd come in from above and behind and jab them sharply in the back, an area that they couldn't easily defend. When we did this, we'd also scream loudly under water.

Whenever we made an attack on one shark, most of the others seemed to take notice — they'd jump as though startled or would suddenly begin swimming much faster than normal. They seemed to register the fact that something had attacked one of their own and would begin to clear out, leaving for better grounds. They seemed to have a short memory, though. A pack would scurry away after an attack, disappear into the ocean, and then slowly reemerge a few minutes later. We frequently needed repeated attacks on a school to drive it away permanently.

Keep in mind that we got these results under very limited conditions:

✔ We were fighting small animals, less than 8 feet (2.4 meters) long.

✔ We were working in water free of blood.

✔ We had four people, were organized, and had time to perfect our methods.

✔ We had pointed weapons and experience using them.

We don't know whether this method would work on larger animals, and we don't believe that it, or any other type of method, would be guaranteed to work in waters filled with blood. However, we did experience good success under the limited conditions we had, so we don't hesitate to recommend this technique. If you're desperate and you're organized, and if you have something that you can use to stab the sharks, then acting territorial in an organized fashion is a proactive method that may give you the upper hand.

Staying Warm as You Float with a Life Jacket

Floating with a life jacket seems pretty straightforward, doesn't it? You just float there and the jacket does all the work. But you may be shocked: Floating the correct way can improve your survival time by 100 percent in some cases! This section gives you the details.

What to do in the water

Regardless of how you end up in the water, you now have to survive in a life jacket, and the first and greatest problem you face is hypothermia — the slow draining of your body's core heat.

If you enter cold water, perform as many sophisticated tasks as you can, as soon as you can. Cold water causes impairment: As your body gets colder and colder, you have more difficulty performing sophisticated tasks — like removing things from bags or closing difficult zippers.

To slow the onset of hypothermia, use the following strategies:

- **Be as still as you can.** This action is the most effective you can take to prevent the hypothermia in the water. Contrary to popular belief, swimming, treading water, or generally moving around makes you much, much colder: You're moving warmed water away from your body and constantly bathing your body in colder water. The less water circulating around your body, the better.

  Whenever you go into the water, you develop a boundary layer. A *boundary layer* is the water next to your skin; your body heats it a little, and it protects you from the colder water.

- **Use HELP.** HELP, or the *Heat Escape Lessening Position,* is a body posture you use to close off your main heat leaks. Check out Figure 18-5, and remember to protect the following areas, which are some of the main places where your body leaks heat:

- **Armpits:** Hold your elbows near your sides to close the armpit area.

- **Crotch:** Squeeze your thighs together so that your crotch is insulated and protected.

Losing heat from the top of your head is worse than anything else, so don't use a heat-retaining position that would cause your head to go under the water. Ideally, you want to end up with your armpits and crotch sealed and your head above the water. If you can, keep as much of your body out of the water as possible; pull your chest up onto a piece of floating material.

Figure 18-5: The HELP heat-saving position.

Staying warm in groups

If you're with a group, huddle together for support and extra warmth. Doing so can increase survival times dramatically. Just put your arms around your companions and have them do the same. For a demonstration on the group huddle, see Figure 18-6.

Just as important, staying together in a group makes you a bigger target for search and rescue to see. For more on being seen, check out Chapter 12.

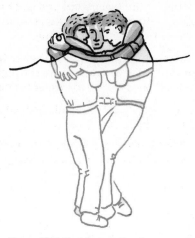

Figure 18-6: Huddle together in groups to keep warm.

Floating without a Life Jacket

As the years pass, more and more incredible stories of people surviving long-term floating experiences come to light. It's no doubt a frightening thought, but many have survived this ordeal. If you ever find yourself in this situation, this section can help improve your chances of survival.

If you're involved in a sinking and you don't have a life jacket on, swim through the debris field after the vessel has sunk. In many cases, you can find extra life jackets or floating debris that you may be able to make into a raft.

Inflating your clothes

If you don't have a life jacket, you can create a provisional float from your own pants. Your success partially depends on the fabric your pants are made of. It doesn't work at all with shorts. The technique is simple (see Figure 18-7):

1. **Remove your pants and tie knots at the bottoms of each leg.**

   In our experience, tying each leg separately works best. Try to tie the knots just as closely to the ends as you can, and tie them very, very tightly.

2. **Take the pants by the waistband and put them behind you — behind your shoulders — as though you were going to use them as a cape.**

3. **In one swift motion, throw them over your head, catching and trapping as much air in the legs as you can, and end with a *whop!* on the water in front of you.**

   To increase the amount of air inside, exhale into the waist band to fill the legs.

4. **Quickly cinch the waist closed with the belt, or if you don't have a belt, hold the waist closed with your hands.**

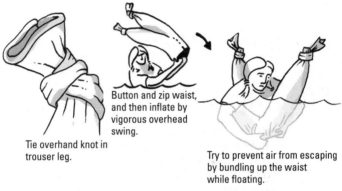

Tie overhand knot in trouser leg.

Button and zip waist, and then inflate by vigorous overhead swing.

Try to prevent air from escaping by bundling up the waist while floating.

Figure 18-7: Making a PFD out of your pants.

You may need several tries before you get hang of it, but the process does work. You have to reinflate the pants anywhere from every 5 to 20 minutes, but done well, you can hold out for a long time this way.

Understanding long-term floating

You can actually float for days — as long as you can remain conscious. But you need to think about conservation of energy. The position that uses the least amount of energy is called *drown-proofing* (by the U.S. Armed Services) or the less appetizing term, *dead-man's float* (by many old-timers).

Essentially, *drown-proofing* simply requires you to take a deep breath, hold it, and allow your body to settle to its normal position, which means face down; this usually requires less effort than floating on your back. Your lungs and buttocks are the two parts that float the best, so after you achieve this position, maintaining it takes almost no energy. There are dozens and dozens of stories of people who have gone into this position and floated for two to three days.

When drown-proofing, you must look up often for search and rescue units. One of the false assumptions that many people make in these situations is that no one is going to come looking for them. In some cases, search and rescue helicopters hovered right over a floating person, but subject failed to respond and the helicopter never saw that person! Don't make that mistake.

Don't drown-proof in cold water. If you do, you end up with your head in the water, which is the worst thing you can do. This causes hypothermia faster than anything else. If you're in cold water and you have no flotation whatsoever, tread water very slowly and gently. You must keep the top of your head out of the water. If you have no flotation, see the preceding section.

When floating long term, maintain a sharp lookout for groups of jellyfish. Many of these animals are translucent, and unless you're really watching for them, you can drift right into the center of a group (we know — we've done it, and a close friend once wandered into a group and ended up sucking some of them down his snorkel!). If you feel a little sting, look around immediately. It's a heck of a lot easier to swim around a group of jellyfish than to look up from your floating position and find yourself in the center — having to swim out!

Chapter 19

The Great Drift: Aboard Life Rafts and Disabled Vessels

*I*n most survival situations at sea, you end up on a drifting vessel, such as a raft or disabled boat (it happens on lakes and rivers, too). *Life rafts* are small inflatable pods, used the world over, for survival situations. They're what you usually find yourself in if you have to fend for yourself on the ocean.

However, most cruise ships have two types of survival craft: Life rafts and *lifeboats*, which are small, rigid boats, many times with motors on them. When the captain orders abandonment, the crew usually tries the lifeboats first because they're motorized. But if you're aboard a ship that begins to lean to one side, or *list*, your only chance of escape may be the rafts. As the ship leans, the crane-like arms *(davits)* that hold the lifeboats frequently can't launch them, so the life rafts, which are launched by hand, are the only way off the ship.

Having a realistic understanding of what you can expect when dealing with a life raft can go a long way toward saving your life. This chapter covers the basics of how to deploy life rafts, how to keep them afloat, and other relevant info concerning a life raft at sea. This chapter also explains what you can do if you're in a small vessel that loses power.

Getting from Ship to Life Raft

Unfortunately, you have no guarantee that the captain or crew of the boat you're on will be conscious or even alive when the time comes to launch the life raft. You may have to activate the raft and get into it by yourself or participate in these actions in some way. In this section, we give you the how-to on inflating and using life rafts. Before going aboard any vessel, you also need to know how to put on a life jacket, which we cover in Chapter 18.

Locating the life raft

Before you even leave port, make sure you know where the life raft is on your boat. Although life rafts usually come in containers, those containers unfortunately don't shout, "Here I am!" On small yachts, they may even be buried in closets or under a lot of equipment. Life raft containers come in three basic varieties:

- **The valise:** A *valise* is heavy bag like a large gym bag. It looks like an oblong cube, with a carrying strap sewn on it. Valises are usually very heavy, so if you grab something you think is the valise and it's light in your hands, it's probably not the life raft.

- **Cylindrical canisters:** These containers are made of metal or fiberglass and look like beer kegs or barrels. They can be any color, but many times they're white. These types of cylindrical canisters sit in a *cradle*, or holder, like a large, sturdy bracket.

- **Flat canisters:** These types of canisters look like the typical modern luggage rack found on the top of an automobile. They can be any color but are usually white, and they're usually strapped into a cradle.

All these containers should have a *painter,* the raft's main rope (bow line) — protruding from them. This line keeps the raft attached to the sinking ship or boat as you're launching, and it also activates the automatic inflator. The painter usually ends with a loop, which is called the *eye.*

Whatever floats your boat: Making a DIY life raft

If your sinking vessel doesn't have a life raft, you need to act quickly. You can work the debris field and collect floating items and tie them together. When boats sink, they almost always disgorge items that float.

Always maintain a lookout on the sea for debris or flotsam of any kind. A lot of stuff is out there — Styrofoam, entire trees, and so on — and you can use any of these things to make a raft. Look for garbage patches and snarls of line and buoys. You can use plastic bottles if you find enough of them. It's not a bad idea to start collecting them when you're in trouble. You need only about 25 to 50 plastic bottles, wrapped in a tarp, canvas, or netting, to make a raft that supports a human being.

When building your raft, anything goes, but here are a few structural ideas that may help you:

✔ The closer you can get to a square or circular shape, the better. Oblong or rectangular rafts are more prone to capsize than wide ones.

✔ The wider you spread out — in other words, the more stuff you tie on — the more stable your craft becomes.

✔ If you can rig rigid poles, such as bamboo canes, to floating flotsam, you can make a very stable raft.

Knowing when to abandon ship

Life rafts aren't pleasant. They're made to keep you alive when other options aren't available, so you want to use one as a last resort. Basically, you deploy a life raft only if

✔ **The boat you're in is completely sinking.** If the boat sinks only partially, stay with the vessel. It's probably easier to see from the air, it has equipment that you can salvage, and it may float for a long time.

A partially sunken vessel can sink suddenly, which could take your inflated (or *un*inflated) raft down with it or damage the fragile little craft. In case of a partially sunken boat, have the raft ready to inflate at a moment's notice and be ready to be cut free of the sinking boat.

✔ **The ship's crew can't get you into a lifeboat.** Sometimes even a competent crew becomes overwhelmed. In these extreme cases, you may have to consider fending for yourself. Generally, if you're aboard a boat or ship that has a crew, they control the abandonment; they direct you to the lifeboats, or they deploy the rafts themselves, and you simply their follow instructions.

Launching a life raft

Letting the crew operate the safety equipment, especially the life rafts, is your best choice. Launch the life raft yourself only as a last resort.

You have to launch the life raft correctly, or you end up with a disaster on your hands. Take your time and make sure you're acquainted with these steps before disaster strikes. That way, you're prepared in case you have to abandon ship. Here's the basic procedure:

1. **If your raft isn't already in place, carry the raft to the side of the vessel.**

   If your raft is in a flat or cylindrical canister, you often have to release the canister from its cradle before you can deploy the raft. There are two ways to do this:

   • **Wait for the automatic hydrostatic release to activate.** The *hydrostatic release* is a device that automatically releases the raft if the boat sinks to a depth of between 10 to 15 feet (3 to 4.6 meters). If you wait for the vessel to sink and for the hydrostatic release to release the canister, you may end up in cold dark water, trying to find the life raft.

   • **Pull the quick release, which is located near the hydrostatic release.** The *quick release* is usually a pin or a button. When you pull or push the quick release, the life raft may roll off into the water, or you may be able to pick the entire canister up and move it to a safer place to launch.

   If you can't release the raft, the hydrostatic release should activate after the boat has sunk, so be on the lookout for the raft to come up in a hurry, and don't let it get away.

2. **Make sure the painter (the raft's main line) is secured to something strong on the boat.**

When the raft inflates, it's just like a kite, and if it's not attached to something strong, it flies away — just like a kite! You may find that the painter is already secured to the *weak link*, which is a fitting designed to break if the boat has sunk and the raft has inflated underwater. Weak links are usually made of lightweight wire. If you think the painter is secured to a weak link, leave it alone. The weak link is strong enough to hold the raft near the boat while you get aboard. If the painter is not attached to a weak link, attach the painter to something solid, like a railing.

3. **Throw the raft overboard.**

No exceptions: You always hurl or push the raft into the water before you inflate it. If you inflate it aboard the boat, it usually hits a sharp edge and bursts, or it gets wedged in a spot where you can't get it out. This happens fast, and you can't stop it after it gets going.

Throw the raft downwind from the vessel if you can. If you throw it into the wind and it inflates, the wind just pushes it right back against the boat, where it deflates against the boat's sharp edges.

Sometimes cradles are made so that when you release the canister, it just rolls right into the water. If the boat is leaning too far over, you may have to give the canister a good kick to get it to roll overboard.

4. **Inflate the raft in the water.**

You inflate a life raft by pulling sharply on the painter. Painters commonly range from 20 to 60 feet (6 to 18 meters) in length, but they can be much longer, and they activate the raft's inflation device only when you reach the end of the line. You may have to pull out a lot of line before you reach the firing point. When the slack stops coming, you yank very sharply, and the raft begins inflating. The inflation takes between 30 and 90 seconds. The overhead canopy (see Figure 19-1a) is the last part to inflate.

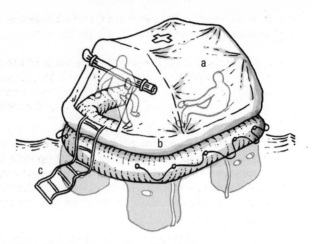

Figure 19-1: A typical modern life raft with a canopy (a), inflated bulwarks (b), and a boarding ladder (c).

Entering a life raft

In the ideal scenario, you enter the life raft directly from the sinking vessel — you never enter the water. However, doing so may not be easy, because the life raft has to be held closely to the sinking vessel, which means the raft can be punctured or dragged down when the boat finally sinks. To enter from the sinking vessel, try to climb down the side of the boat and enter gently. You probably won't have access to a ladder to do this, so the process can be clumsy. Make sure you don't injure someone who's already in the raft or damage the little craft by barging in with all your weight.

If there's any chance that the life raft could come into contact with sharp edges from the sinking boat — any chance at all — you have to keep the raft away and enter it from the water.

Don't jump into a life raft. Jumping in is likely to injure you and anyone already aboard and possibly damage the life raft.

Entering a life raft from the water can be difficult. You have to lift yourself over the raft's walls (see Figure 19-2), and you're usually hampered by fatigue, waves, and a life jacket. Keep in the following ideas in mind:

- **Get your upper torso on top of the walls of the raft.** If you can get your chest on top, or even just close, you can usually roll in or be pulled aboard by other survivors. Fling your body up and forward using all the momentum you can muster.

- **If your raft has a submerged boarding ladder, step on the rungs (Figure 19-2a), pull yourself up with your hands, drape your chest over the raft's opening, and start heaving yourself in.** If you're almost there, throw your head forward as aggressively as you can and try to roll or wallow in.

    If you're almost there, throw your foot up to hook the opening, and then use the extra leverage to work your way in. Flight attendants practice this technique when they train.

- **Some life rafts have a *boarding platform* that resembles a common air mattress and floats right below the opening; you have to fling yourself aboard the platform first and then pull yourself into the raft.** Fling your body up and forward.

- **Using wave action can help.** If a lot of waves are moving around the raft, you can sometimes use the ocean to get you started — to lift you a little higher — maybe just high enough to get your torso in. Watch how the waves rise to the opening, and then try to time one to correspond with your physical efforts (Figure 19-2b). Momentum counts.

- **Allow the strongest to go in first and then have them help the others into the raft.** If you go inside first, kneel on the floor of the raft and reach over the inflated walls to haul survivors aboard. If someone else is inside the raft, have him go to the other side to prevent capsizing the lightweight craft while you're hauling aboard the struggling survivors (always avoid bunching around the opening, which can cause the raft to turn over). For a firm grip, reach over the sides and grab the boarding survivors by the upper arms, or better, the armpits (Figure 19-2c).

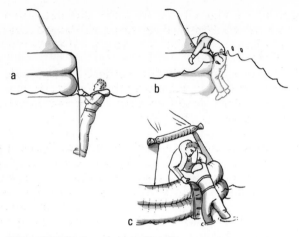

Figure 19-2: Getting aboard a life raft.

Adjusting to Life Afloat

When you're inside an inflated life raft, you're not out of danger. You and your fellow raft-mates have lots of work to do — which is good, because in a bad situation, staying busy is sometimes the best medicine. This section walks you through what you need to do while in a life raft and discusses possible scenarios.

The first ten minutes in a raft

As soon as you're inside the raft, the first few minutes are important for ensuring your safety. Locate the raft's knife immediately, and be ready to cut the painter if the sinking boat goes down. The raft's knife is usually in a pocket in the overhead canopy, near the entrance. Knives in life rafts are squared-off, not pointed, to keep them from puncturing the raft. They have plastic handles that float, and they're usually orange in color. You can still bring aboard survivors after you've cut the raft loose.

A sharp object can sink your only hope in two seconds. Most modern inflatables are strong, but we've seen rafts, hard ones, sliced-through like butter. When you're in your raft, quickly probe for sharp objects or protrusions among your

companions: Check for purses with metal latches or orna-
ments, belt buckles, earrings, snaps with jagged edges, and
even ballpoint pens. Make sure your pocket knife is folded.

When people come on board, they tend to congregate near
the entrance, which unbalances the raft and can cause it to
capsize. Tell people to spread out, and start assigning maintenance jobs. Here's what to do:

- ✓ **Address immediate medical concerns.** We discuss first
  aid for problems such as cold shock response, hypothermia, and near-drowning in Chapter 22, and we cover
  general first aid in Chapter 13. A few inches of water present a drowning hazard for anyone who's unconscious,
  so make sure no person is lying face down in the bottom
  of the raft. If water accumulates as people board, assign
  people to bail it out.

- ✓ **If the boat you've abandoned has sunk completely,
  scavenge the debris field.** Ask yourself whether any
  equipment you can grab — containers, sheets of plastic,
  anything — is floating nearby.

- ✓ **Gather the equipment together and tie it down, especially the inflation pump.** As time passes, the raft
  deflates a little, so you have to reinflate it.

- ✓ **Check the pressure-escape valves, and check the seams
  for leaks.** The escape valves usually hiss for a little while
  to release excess gas. This is normal. If you do find leaky
  seams, look to see whether a repair kit is in the raft's bag.
  If there isn't one, watch the leak carefully and try not to
  put undue stress or weight on it.

- ✓ **Activate the ballast bags if necessary.** These are bags
  under the raft that fill up with water to stabilize the craft
  (Figure 19-3d). Many times they fill on their own.

- ✓ **Deploy the drogue when the raft is clear of the sinking vessel.** The *drogue* is a small cone or parachute
  that drags in the water on a long line that keeps the raft
  headed into the waves (see Figure 19-3a). Some drogues
  have a *recovery float*, a piece of Styrofoam that connects
  to the drogue and makes it easier to haul out of the water
  (Figure 19-3b). Some drogues automatically deploy, and
  some don't.

If you find a cone-shaped bag in the center of the raft, it's probably the drogue. Attach it to the outside of the raft at a location away from the entrance. The drogue is going to be under tremendous strain, so check it periodically for wear and tear.

You want the drogue to float away from the raft on as long a line as possible. It should reach the trough between the waves when the raft is up on a peak of a wave. If you can get it to extend to two or three waves away, try it.

If the drogue seems to be hurting the raft, try using a *sentinel*, a weight that you put on the drogue's line to make the line sink (Figure 19-3c) — this acts like an enormous shock-absorber. You can use anything you have handy as a sentinel, as long as you're not chafing the drogue line.

✔ **Inflate the raft's floor.** Usually, the automatic inflating cylinder doesn't inflate the floor. Look for the valve that accepts the nozzle of the hand pump. An inflated floor helps prevent hypothermia.

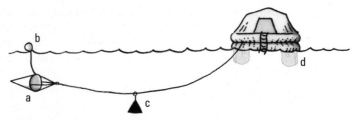

Figure 19-3: Deploying a drogue and sentinel to stabilize your life raft.

Inside the raft: Giving order to the chaos

As you can imagine, being on a life raft at sea can be quite a traumatic experience. You need to prepare for at least one emotional explosion from someone. Sometimes it's panic, recrimination, blame, or indignation at being put in the situation. If someone does have a meltdown, let the person blow off some steam in a benign way. For more on these problems, see Chapter 3.

In this section, we explain how you can organize your raft-mates to increase your chances of rescue, and we name a few ways you can keep everyone a little more comfortable while you're still adrift.

Organizing operations

Most rafts are small, so people are going to be sitting on each other, which can cause injury. It also may be dark inside. Having a plan — and assigning specific functions that people can focus on — can help everyone stay relatively calm.

Try to get everyone to listen and organize, or take a look around and figure out whom you can make an alliance with. Who looks like they can function? They may not be the ones you expect. Begin discussing life raft operations with them rationally, just like you're operating any other piece of equipment. If you can get just two to three level heads working the problem with obvious rationality, this can have a tremendous effect on organizing the others.

Here's how to organize your crew, however small it is:

- ✔ **Start a watch-keeping system immediately.** A *watch team* is a person or persons temporarily on guard. These people look for ships and tend the raft while others rest. Have each watch team go through all the maintenance procedures we list earlier in "The first ten minutes in a raft." When the team is changed, the new watch performs them again.

- ✔ **Organize your bailing operation.** Raft bailers are notoriously small, so use a boot if you have one, and make sure you bail water downwind. Bail out the last drops with the sponge you find in the raft's kit.

  If you have two sponges, only use one for bailing. Keep the other clean for collecting fresh water dew to drink later.

- ✔ **Take stock of your equipment and how much food and water you have on hand.** Discuss each item thoroughly with your companions. For more on collecting and rationing food and water at sea, see Chapter 20.

- ✔ **Make sure everyone's ready for multiple capsizes.** If the waves are big and the wind is strong, you may have to get out of the raft and right it again and again. Familiarize yourself with the procedure we discuss later in "The flip-out: Righting a raft."

✔ **Make yourself visible.** Have your signals, like aerial flares, smoke, or mirrors, ready to go (for more on signals, see Chapter 12). If other rafts are nearby, consider tying them to yours to make you a bigger visual target. Don't do this is rough seas, though, because the rafts will beat against each other and cause damage.

✔ **Watch for land (or search-and-rescue teams) and discuss navigation.** Make sure you start writing everything right away — especially your last known position. For more information on finding land, see Chapter 21.

Increasing your safety and comfort

Life in a raft is uncomfortable at best. Here are a few ways to keep everyone a little less cold, wet, and miserable:

✔ **Dry off.** If you're in wet clothes, take them off and wring the water out, over the side, and then put them back on. Have everyone remove wet cotton clothing, because wet cotton causes them to cool quickly.

✔ **If you're in cold conditions, or if you're trying to keep the seas out, close the canopy.** If you close it using ties, use bows or slipknots so it can be opened easily later on.

✔ **Stay with the raft.** If you have to leave the raft to do something, tie a tether to yourself.

✔ **When someone starts to become seasick, anticipate a bout of vomiting.** Try to move the sick to the opening, because even a small amount of vomit in the raft can make others ill.

✔ **Know that sea creatures like to bump against life rafts.** These creatures include dorados (mahi-mahi), sharks, and turtles. This is largely harmless, but it can be annoying and unnerving.

✔ **Treat sea-related ailments.** Be prepared for sunburn, seasickness, and the like. We discuss treatment in Chapter 22.

The flip-out: Righting a raft

Life rafts are some of the lightest vessels in the world, used in the very worst conditions, such as strong winds and big waves. That's why life rafts capsize all the time, especially right after you've inflated them. Make sure you're ready to handle a life raft that has capsized. If you're with companions, get them to cooperate, because righting a raft while people are still inside is exceedingly difficult.

All life rafts have handles on the bottom to enable you to flip them right-side up. To right an upside-down life raft, do the following (see Figure 19-4):

1. **Swim to the downwind side.**

   This side is where you have a *wind shadow* — in other words, you're behind the raft, and the raft is acting as a wind break.

2. **Brace your knees or feet against the raft and act like you're trying to climb up the handles.**

   When you start to pull on the handles, the other side will rise, catch the wind, and help you turn the raft over. This climbing force causes the raft to flip backward and on top of you — this works, and it doesn't usually cause injury.

3. **Board the raft (as we explain in the earlier section "Entering a life raft").**

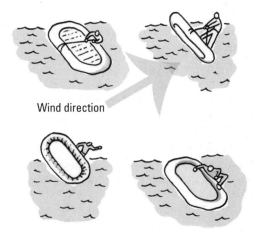

Wind direction

Figure 19-4: Righting a life raft.

Controlling Drifting Vessels

If you find yourself aboard a small or medium-sized boat that has lost power, you have to act fast to gain control of the vessel. This is where you enter the realm of the Lost Opportunity. Slow reaction time is the hallmark of these needless disasters. Most of the tips in this section also pertain to handling life rafts.

Taking action with depowered boats

Boats that have lost power are vulnerable to filling with water or capsizing because instead of driving through the waves, the waves overwhelm the boat. Even on a small lake, large boats can motor by and create waves big enough to sink a small disabled boat. The moment your boat is disabled, take action immediately:

✔ **Try to get some kind of propulsion going, quickly.** Organize a paddling operation immediately. Keep the boat pointed into (toward) the waves, and watch for unexpected waves. If you're with others, quickly explain why they need to paddle or row, or you'll end up with an uncoordinated group. Paddle with anything you can; even your hands will do in a pinch.

✔ **Be ready to bail.** Many times, a wave plunges in and fills the boat halfway, and then shortly afterward, a second wave sinks the craft entirely. Acting quickly can keep this second wave from finishing you off. Organize your bailing operation before you need it.

✔ **Balance the boat.** If the boat is tilted to one side, vmove some weight to the other side. If the back end is squatting down, move some weight forward. If your motor is out of gas, take the motor off the back and stow it in the lowest part of the boat and as near to the center as you can.

✔ **Consider throwing heavy equipment overboard.** If your boat is close to being overloaded and has lost power, you may have to heave something overboard to save your life.

✔ **If you're being blown in a way you don't want to go, employ a drogue.** A *drogue* is a weight that you stream off the front of the boat on a line (or off the back of the boat) that slows you down. If you're near the shore and you're being taken out by the wind, try throwing out a drogue to slow you down. For more on drogues, see "The first ten minutes in a raft," earlier in this chapter, and "Traveling with current and sail," coming up next.

✔ **If you're by yourself in an inflatable boat, sit on the front (bow) and paddle by pulling the water toward you (see Figure 19-5).** The process may seem clumsy at first, but you'll get the hang of it.

Figure 19-5: Paddling an inflatable boat by yourself.

Traveling with current and sail

Beyond the use of paddles, the only other means of moving your disabled vessel or raft is to use the water's current or to use the wind. The key is to pick the one that's going the direction you want to travel and harness it.

To use the water's current, you can simply put a paddle or a drogue into the water and let the water pull you. If the wind is blowing you in a direction you don't want to go but the current is flowing the way you want to go, drogues can many times pull you against the wind. Traveling against the wind in a raft is entirely possible if you can figure out the current. For more on using drogues, see "The first ten minutes in a raft," earlier in this chapter.

You can erect a sail out of just about anything. Two paddles and a shirt will do. The higher your sail is, the better — just make sure you can handle the sail. If the wind really gets strong, be ready to take the sail down. Keep in mind that all life rafts travel in the direction of the wind, with or without a sail.

The wind usually cycles near land. During the day, the wind blows toward land, and at night, it blows away from land. This isn't a sure thing, though. For more on winds and currents, see Chapter 21.

Restarting outboard motors

If your outboard motor won't run, you can take several simple actions that may get it running again:

- ✔ **Let it dry out.** If the motor is wet from water, or if it's flooded with gas, many times just taking the cover off during the day and letting the motor sit under the sun is enough to get it going. Put the cover back on before sundown to prevent condensation from accumulating. Sometimes this drying process takes several days.

- ✔ **Make sure everything is clean.** The fuel or the fuel filter could be dirty and/or clogged.

- ✔ **Make sure debris hasn't fouled the propeller.** Examine below the water line. If anything is tangled, get down there and pull it out before restarting the motor.

Chapter 20

Food and Drink at Sea

- -

In This Chapter

▶ Employing an effective water plan for survival

▶ Collecting and purifying water

▶ Fishing from a life raft

▶ Finding alternative food sources in the sea

- -

*N*ot surprisingly, the challenge of finding food and water becomes life-or-death business within just a day of being adrift in a life raft or lifeboat. It's a terrible irony that at sea you're surrounded by water you can't drink and by food you can't see. The good news is that you can find the food and water you need on the sea by using generous amounts of ingenuity and patience.

In this chapter, we show you the minimum needs you have to fulfill to survive on the ocean, and we look at your options for getting fresh water and food at sea.

On the Water Front: Improving Your Chances for Survival

If you find yourself lost at sea, expect thirst to be a problem very quickly and prepare accordingly. To enhance your chances for survival at sea, take the following actions immediately:

✔ **Master disbelief.** Believing that you can actually die from thirst in this modern, high-tech era is kind of difficult, isn't it? But you need to recognize immediately that the risk is real. Come to grips with this unfair situation and go to work right away on your water plans.

✔ **Expect water to be a problem even if you're within sight of land.** The ocean current can still take you out to sea within a matter of minutes.

✔ **Concentrate on finding and taking any water you can from the sinking or disabled boat before it's lost.** Try to make sure the water containers have a little air inside them so they float well in the waves.

✔ **Scan the *debris field*, the area around the sinking vessel, for important resources you can use later.** You may be able to find containers or sheets of plastic you can use for your water-storing needs.

✔ **Take stock of the water you have and secure it.** Tie all your water containers to yourself or your life raft.

In addition to these immediate actions, you want to conserve and ration the water you do have. The following sections explain your situation and highlight what to do.

Understanding your body's dehydration limits

Without any liquid, the average human begins to lose consciousness after about three days on the sea and perishes after about six (slightly longer time than on land, usually). We don't like these numbers any more than you do, but they provide the foundation for your hydration goals, so knowing and understanding them is key to your survival.

First, take heart: Those numbers are only averages. Many people have survived much, much longer. And here's another factor to take heart in: If you take steps to conserve your body's natural water supply, you need only a small amount of liquid to stay alive. We discuss these important steps in the following sections.

If your body is in the water, such as when you're adrift in a life jacket, death from hypothermia is a much greater threat than dehydration. If you're floating in a life jacket and you're suffering from advanced hypothermia *and* dehydration, try to drink as much fresh water as you need. For tips on staying warm at sea, flip to Chapter 18.

The cup (or half-cup) of life

In 1956, a group of scientists in the UK published a remarkable scientific paper called "The hazards to men in ships lost at sea." The study was drawn from the experiences of thousands of sea survivors in World War II, such as downed air pilots or sailors from torpedoed ships. It was the largest such survey ever taken.

One of the most revealing statistics to come out of the study was that if a human received just 8 ounces (0.25 liters) of water per day while adrift on the sea, his or her chances of living through the ordeal were actually very good — just 8 ounces. However, at the other end of the scale, the study revealed that if the survivor's water ration was cut down to below 4 ounces (0.12 liters) of liquid per day, the chance of death was very high. This area, between about 4 and 8 ounces of water per day, was clearly a deciding factor in whether a person survived or perished.

Even more compelling was the comparison of people who had drunk salt water to those who had not. Those groups who drank salt water were roughly 13 times more likely to die on the ocean than those who didn't.

The first line of defense: Conserving your body's water

As soon as you realize that you may be entering a survival situation on the sea, begin conserving your body's water. The more you conserve, the less you'll need to consume to stay alive. Fresh water is always scarce on the open sea, so you have to cut your needs down accordingly.

Take the following steps to conserve your body's internal water supply:

- ✔ Don't drink anything for the first 24 hours.
- ✔ Don't drink diuretics, such as alcohol, soda, salt water, or urine (which also contains toxins).
- ✔ Avoid perspiration; soak rags in seawater and put them on your body to stay cool.
- ✔ Avoid any type of excessive effort, and breathe through your nose.

✔ Try not to eat protein; many types of seaweed are edible and contain carbohydrates.

Chapter 7 discusses the importance of conserving your body's water in more depth.

Rationing your water

Controlling the amount of water you consume, or *rationing*, can improve your chances of survival at sea. A small amount of drinking water can last you a long time if you consume it efficiently. A human can survive for a short time on as little as 6 to 8 ounces of fresh water per day. That's a daily ration of about 1 cup of water, or 0.25 liters. If fresh water is really scarce, you can get by for a short time, perhaps a week or longer, on this ration.

Take inventory of your water and try to determine how much water you can afford to drink per day. You can't determine when you'll be rescued, so think long-term. Aim for survival, not comfort or perfect health. Here are some rationing guidelines:

✔ If you have little water, limit your intake to 1 cup (0.25 liters) a day. You may have to drink even less than that, but know that a ration of less than $\frac{1}{2}$ cup usually doesn't extend survival time.

✔ If you have an adequate water supply, you can afford to go on a larger ration. If your water inventory isn't so small, a ration of 2 cups (0.5 liters) per day can keep a person alive for many weeks.

✔ If you find yourself sitting on a 50-gallon (190-liter) drum of beautiful drinking water, 1 quart per day (1 liter) is ideal.

Take care to keep in mind that this is a water ration *at sea*, and it doesn't apply to other environments, especially deserts.

Take your ration in several increments rather than all in one swallow; doing so relieves the agonies of dry mouth more often. When taking in your ration, hold it in your mouth for as long as you can to soak the membranes inside cheeks and gums to lessen the pain of dehydration.

Before you begin a water-rationing program, talk to your companions. If they aren't well-versed in survival at sea, take a leadership position and explain how best to conserve water. Then get everyone to agree to the rationing scheme you've developed. Designate one person to distribute the water and one person to assist and keep track of who has gotten a ration. Don't assume these positions yourself, because you, the leader, will be called on later to arbitrate any disagreements. This issue is sensitive, and the more you make it a group project, the better.

Avoiding salt water

Consuming salt water only causes you to further dehydrate, so don't do it. Drinking salt water increases your need for fresh water. If you drink 1 pint (0.5 liters) of salt water, your body will drain at least 1 pint of fresh water from your tissues just to get rid of it. The net effect is to worsen your fluid balance.

Even worse, drinking saltwater is closely linked to delirium and hallucinations on the sea. The old warning that "salt water makes you mad" probably has some truth in it. There are so many case studies on the books that show castaways becoming mentally unbalanced after they drank large portions of saltwater that you can't ignore this danger.

The hallucinations linked to drinking salt water probably occur because of *hypernatremia,* an electrolyte imbalance in the body. Usually, this condition occurs due to an advanced state of dehydration, but drinking large portions of salt water can cause it as well.

The dangers of drinking "a little" salt water

No matter how thirsty you become at sea, don't drink even a little salt water, because after you start, you can't stop. People in survival situations often begin to drink salt water very slowly because they think that if they take just a few sips, it won't matter. It does matter, and you'll get into serious trouble.

Drinking salt water only makes you thirstier. If you drink a few harmless gulps of salt water, you feel satisfied for only about 10 minutes. When your thirst returns, it comes back with a vengeance. You'll be on a vicious cycle, needing to drink more each time.

Kon-Tiki and the Heretic: Survival stories to take with a grain of salt

In 1947, a Norwegian adventurer named Thor Heyerdahl crossed the Pacific Ocean on a giant wooden raft, which he called *Kon-Tiki*. Heyerdahl was trying to demonstrate to the world that primitive mariners possessed the ability to travel from South America to Polynesia in ancient times. His voyage was one of the most significant expeditions of the 20th century, and whenever the question of drinking salt water comes up, many people point to this famous story of men drifting on the ocean.

Heyerdahl and his crew reported that during their time on the sea, they drank great quantities of fresh water mixed with salt water. What most people don't realize is that Heyerdahl and his mates weren't facing dehydration. On the contrary, they were hungry for salt. Fighting the sea day-in and day-out made them perspire very heavily. Although they had plenty of fresh water aboard their raft and drank pure, fresh water until their stomachs were bloated, they still felt a lack of something: salt. Their saltwater cocktail was brewed to replenish their body's lost sodium, not to remedy dehydration.

Shortly after the voyage of the *Kon-Tiki*, another raft voyage came along — one that seemed to present absolute proof that you could drink salt water for long periods of time on the sea. In 1952, a French doctor name Alain Bombard crossed the Atlantic Ocean in a small inflatable raft. Bombard claimed that he had carried no water during his voyage and that he had survived on little more than salt water and the fluid he wrung from fish. He had undertaken his voyage to prove his theory that most survivors in rafts die of despair, not from dehydration or starvation, and that if you could keep your spirits up, you could survive almost anything. He also believed that the claim that drinking salt water was suicide simply wasn't true. This was a highly controversial position, and accordingly, Bombard named his little rubber raft *The Heretic*.

Though Bombard survived several months at sea, his claims simply can't be proven. The French doctor didn't keep accurate or complete records of his exploits. To complicate the matter further, Bombard drifted through regions where rain showers are really quite frequent and collecting adequate fresh water is entirely possible. Important questions of how much salt water he actually drank, how much rainwater he collected, and how much water he was given by passing ships were never fully answered. In the end, Bombard proved his theory that castaways need not die of despair, but his brave voyage didn't prove that a human could survive by drinking salt water.

There are other cases like these that are reported from time to time, or that are rumored. Under careful investigation, however, most of them have mitigating circumstances. Worse, these cases do little to address the risk of delirium. There are hundreds of documented cases, sadly, that show a strong relation between the drinking of salt water and the onset of short-term psychiatric affliction and death.

The salt water–drinking scenario can happen even to the most disciplined. A downed U.S. Air Force pilot once admitted, after being picked up in the Gulf of Mexico, that he had begun to drink salt water after the first day and that after that he "just didn't care anymore," gorging himself on even more salt water. Shortly afterward, he vomited, further dehydrating himself. This particular survivor was lucky to be picked up. Most aren't so fortunate.

The dangers of mixing salt water with fresh water

Don't consider mixing salt water with fresh water and drinking it. If you mix salt water with fresh, you'll most likely be creating a diuretic. You're better off concentrating on getting liquid in other ways rather than polluting what little good fresh water you have.

Making Fresh Water on the Sea

You have a variety of ways to acquire drinkable liquid on the sea, and all these methods have one thing in common: They require immense patience and persistence. Some of these methods in this section may give you only a mouthful of water or just a few drops, but every little bit helps. The history books are filled with survivors who, after a little practice, were able to get enough liquid to keep them going.

Take extra steps to safeguard your fresh water supply at sea. Life rafts and other small vessels pitch and roll violently and in the most unexpected of ways.

Collecting and drinking rainwater

Collecting rainwater is harder than it seems. Most showers last only a few minutes, so before the first drop falls, adopt an aggressive, proactive program to catch every drop you can. We cover rain collection in Chapter 7, but here are some notes on gathering rain-catching supplies:

> ✔ Gather containers first. Scan the debris field and recover anything that can hold water.

> ✔ After containers, sheets of plastic or fabric are of the highest priority. Hold onto any item that you can use as a rain-catching plane.

Shortly before a shower comes, make sure your rain-catching plane — the mouth of your giant funnel — is fully extended, and then rinse off all the surfaces with seawater. The seawater rinse cuts through the salt crust that develops on all things within just a day or so on the sea.

If possible, designate a container to hold only the initial rainfall. Then quickly put that container aside and concentrate on collecting water in another container for your main rain-catching operation. Most of what you collect in the first 20 to 30 seconds of a rain shower at sea is slightly fouled by salt, even if you've rinsed your collection surfaces. Sample this water later to determine whether it's drinkable. If not, use it next time for rinsing collection surfaces.

The biggest problem in collecting rainwater at sea is keeping all the components in place. Violent flapping of the rain-catching plane in the wind can make getting collected water into a container difficult. Develop a rain-catching plan that involves everyone, and use it as a team-building exercise.

If you catch your water in clear or translucent jugs, such as milk jugs, try to store them out of the sunlight. Sunlight makes algae and mold grow in these containers.

Collecting condensation

You can collect condensation from the surfaces of your vessel and use it for drinking purposes — but only if it's free of salt, which is rare. You can sometimes use a cloth or rag to soak up the moisture, but the results can be meager. Sponges are better for this.

Maintain a close watch on all your water-collecting surfaces. You may have a surface that's relatively free of salt. You may be able to maximize the amount of water you collect if you act just as the condensation is forming during the night.

Using water makers

A *reverse osmosis* water maker is a small pump that forces water through a filter, making the water safe to consume (though not all are designed to remove salt from seawater, so check the capabilities of your device). The water maker looks like a small bicycle pump, and if you come across one in a life raft or abandon-ship bag, check immediately for a package of spare filters and put them in a dry, secure place. Most small cylindrical water makers require you to change their filters at regular intervals, although new types use ceramic filters that must be cleaned.

Always attach a cord to your water maker and then tie the other end to your body or to your vessel. As with all tools on the sea, the water maker has a good chance of slipping out of your hands and sinking to the bottom of the ocean or simply drifting away from you. Even if you have good hands and are conscientious, things slip. We can't stress this point enough. Why? Because we've lost a lot of good equipment to the deep blue!

If you have enough containers, use one to hold salt water in the bottom of the boat. Then pump this water through the unit into another container. This system reduces the risk of losing equipment overboard.

Setting up a still at sea

A *solar still* at sea is simply a clear container that uses the sun's rays to heat and evaporate water; the still then condenses the water vapor and collects the fresh water.

A variety of commercially manufactured models (see Figure 20-1a) are available, but they all work on the same principle: You pour salt water (or anything containing water) onto a piece of dark cloth or into a reservoir made of black plastic, and then you put the cloth or reservoir under a little tent of clear plastic. When you put the tent in the sun, the seawater evaporates — but it leaves the salt behind. Droplets of purified water soon form on the inside of the tent, and these trickle down into a receptacle at the bottom of the still.

If you have the materials and the time, build as many solar stills as you can. And take your time with the construction, because craftsmanship counts. Solar stills, especially improvised stills, produce only a tiny amount of drinkable water per day — and this only in calm conditions.

Here's how to build the basic still using odds and ends at sea (remember the debris field you were in?). This type is a variation on the land-based solar still (see Figure 20-1b):

1. **Glue or tape a cup at the bottom of a medium-sized bucket.**

2. **Use a plastic sheet to form a dripper over the cup.**

   The dripper is basically a stalactite-in-a-bucket. To make the dripper, just drape a plastic sheet over the top of your bucket and place a weight in the center of the sheet, which sags down over the cup.

3. **Secure the plastic with string or a rubber band.**

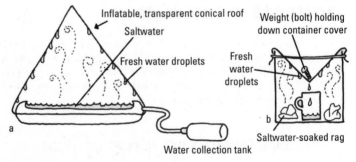

Inflatable, transparent conical roof

Saltwater

Fresh water droplets

Weight (bolt) holding down container cover

Fresh water droplets

Water collection tank

Saltwater-soaked rag

a

b

Figure: 20-1: A commercially manufactured solar still (a) and an improvised design (b).

Try to have good seals around the still the outer perimeter of the still so that you get an air-tight evaporation unit. You may be able to stabilize your solar still at sea by attaching a handle to it and suspending it from a boom or ceiling. Commercially manufactured solar stills usually have weights in their rounded bottoms to make them stable on the bucking ocean.

Using a solar still on the sea can try your patience to the breaking point because everything is in motion, and getting the little drops to fall into the right receptacle can be a nightmare. If your first efforts to distill water yield meager results, look for ways to improve your methods. It takes practice.

Removing salt with desalination kits

Desalination kits use chemicals and filters to convert seawater into drinkable liquid. Usually the kits require you to pour one or two chemicals into a pouch full of seawater and then allow the seawater to pass through a filter. Even the larger kits can't produce much water, many times only a few pints, but they can save you in a pinch. If you're lucky enough to run across a chemical desalination kit, save it for a cloudy day — when your solar still won't work (the preceding section explains solar stills). Try to concentrate on getting liquid from other sources first.

Considering Living Sources of Water

You can supplement your rain-catching and saltwater-distillation activities by drinking the bodily fluids of fish or the blood of turtles. Draining the juice from sea creatures may sound unappetizing, but many castaways owe their lives to these techniques.

Drinking the juice of fish

You can consume bodily fluids of fish to get extra water intake while on the sea. The key here is to use only the fluids that don't contain protein: the spinal fluid and the eyes. *Note:* Try not to drink the fluid in the meat of the fish. This juice contains protein, so your body has to use water to process it. Of course, you have to catch fish before you can wring the juice from them! See "Fishing at Sea" later in this chapter.

A modern castaway's story

On a windy night in late March, 1980, a close friend of ours, a Colombian fisherman named Joaquin Cuellar, went lost-at-sea off the coast of Colombia. He had gone out in a small boat to run an errand with two other men, and unbelievably, his shipmates had managed to get into a childish shoving match and had knocked the boat's outboard motor into the sea. Without power, the tiny vessel drifted away from land and into the vast Pacific.

For nine days, Joaquin drifted on the open sea. His thoroughly unlikable shipmates all but gave up. But he didn't. His will to live was incredible. He tenaciously clawed at every opportunity that came along, and instead of falling into despair, he became defiant. He loved life, and he was going to live. Though it was distasteful, he drank the fluid from his prescription earache medicine. At one point, he found a piece of drifting bamboo and tried to drink the

fluid sloshing inside, but quickly had to spit it out. It was fermented.

On the fifth day, Joaquin managed to snag the leg of a passing sea turtle with a fishing hook. He hauled the 50-pound (23-kilogram) animal aboard and then quickly slashed its throat with a screwdriver he had sharpened. "There was so much blood," he later told us. "It was incredible."

The others in the boat wouldn't drink the turtle blood. But Joaquin did, and it gave him strength. Like so many other mariners, he reported that the blood was not salty but "very sweet."

Drinking the turtle's blood was something of a turning point for Joaquin. It gave him strength and it renewed his determination. With a favorable wind now upon the little boat, he fashioned a sail from plastic and sailed to land, and safety, saving himself and his foolish mates.

Some fish are toxic and you shouldn't consume them or drink their juices. For more info, check out "Knowing which fish aren't on the menu" later in this chapter.

Here are two methods for extracting the spinal fluid from fish:

- ✔ **For large fish:** Cut an incision along the back of the fish and then suck the fluid out, or turn the fish vertical and allow the spinal fluid to flow down into a container. Sometimes, if you're careful, you can use this method to simply remove the backbone altogether.

> ✔ **For small fish:** Make an incision in the spine near the tail
> fin and then turn the fish's body until it's vertical. Either
> allow the spinal fluid to drip out or simply suck it out
> with your mouth.

You can chew or suck fish eyes to get the fluid from them.
They can be very bitter, and some castaways have gagged
when doing this. Even so, juice from fish can sustain you
when you have nothing else.

Drinking turtle blood

To get water intake, you can also safely drink turtle's blood
to save your life. This method has saved many castaways.
Technically, the blood has protein in it, so it would seem to
violate one of the rules of water conservation. But because
this last-ditch source of liquid has saved so many, including
friends of ours, we don't hesitate in recommending it.

Sea turtles are slow-moving animals and you can easily catch
them, either by snagging them with hooks or gaffs (hooked
poles) or by catching them with your hands. For information
on catching turtles, check out the section titled "Identifying
Other Delicious Things to Eat in the Sea" later in this chapter.

After you have a turtle in your possession, you have to extract
the blood. Here's how to do it for best results:

1. **Turn the animal on its back and step on or hold
   down its beak and claws.**

2. **Take a pointed knife or spear and cut the arteries
   where the neck joins the body, near the animal's
   backbone.**

   The severed veins will spurt blood, so you need to be
   ready with your containers.

3. **If possible, turn the animal upside down and allow
   the blood to drain into a container.**

   You may be able to collect as much as 2 quarts (2
   liters) of the sickly sweet liquid.

4. **Drink the blood within about 1 minute of draining it;
   otherwise, it will coagulate.**

Sea turtles are endangered and are important to their respective ecosystems — besides being remarkable creatures. Kill one only if you're at risk of death on the open sea.

Fishing at Sea

After you take care of your water needs, you can begin to take food from the sea. Fishing for survival at sea is a completely unique experience. You usually have to fish from a flimsy craft that's close to the water — a craft that a large fish can damage or destroy. You're probably in crowded conditions, so when you bring the fish aboard, it's like being trapped in a closet with a wild animal. So you have to rethink fishing. You can make a huge leap in thinking by simply reminding yourself that you are now *hunting on the sea*.

Keep the following pointers in mind when fishing at sea:

- ✔ **Always use stealth when fishing.** A fish can see you on your raft, and it can hear many of the noises you make. Even more than that, it has a very strong sense of vibration. Try to be as quiet as possible when you fish.

- ✔ **Maintain a sharp watch on all your lines every second they're in the water.** After you put them in the water, try to keep a hand on every line at all times. If you allow your vigilance to lapse, the fish will surely get away.

- ✔ **Maintain a disciplined fishing time, just before dawn.** Get ready to fish every morning in the same way you'd get dressed for your job on land. Don't be late! Have all your gear in the water before dawn — this alone can save you. Fish for as long as you can every day but especially during this critical time window.

- ✔ **Make plans ahead of time for bringing your fish aboard.** Ocean fish can easily get away — even after you have them aboard — or they can deflate your life raft or cause personal injury, so plan ahead. For details on how to board fish, see "Bringing in Your Catch" later in this chapter.

This section focuses on some specific fishing-related pointers if you're lost at sea. You can also check out Chapter 8 for more-general fishing techniques.

Tackling hooks and lines

You need hooks, line, and bait or lures. Almost anything works, but for a rundown on improvised hooks and lines, see Chapter 8. The best substance for bait is freshly butchered fish meat or entrails. Generally speaking, lures made from white cloth or some shiny object, such as aluminum foil, work best.

When you're at sea, you usually fish with hand lines, and you should fish with the strongest tackle you have first — the strongest and best lines, best hooks, and so on — especially at dawn, when the big fish are hitting. If the fish steal your bait, reduce the size of your hook.

Fishing tackle can save your life on the open sea, but it's very hard to hold onto. Lines break and precious hooks are lost all the time, so take precautions to safeguard your equipment:

- ✔ Stow your tackle in a container that's attached to the vessel.

- ✔ Service your tackle — such as tying on new hooks — only when you have the boat's bottom below you, never over the side.

- ✔ Fish with an assistant if possible. People lose gear or have other minor disasters usually because they're overwhelmed.

- ✔ Maintain the lightest touch possible on a hooked fish. Never fight a fish on the sea if you can help it. Give the fish as much slack as it can handle and wait for it to tire.

Salt crystals develop on fishing lines, and when a big fish pulls sharply, it can turn the line into a cutting instrument — not something you want inside a life raft. When fishing from an inflatable craft, always tie your fishing lines to the exterior grab lines, never to something inside the raft.

Using a spear

Spearing a fish is well within the ability of even the most die-hard of landlubbers. Spears are immensely useful and can be good weapons for killing violent fish in the water (which is better than doing it in your raft or boat, because that can be a dangerous, clumsy process). You can stab dorados in the spine to paralyze them or sharks in the eyes to produce the same affect.

Craft spears by sharpening wood that you find on the open sea (like split bamboo cane) or from metal (such as rod from an outboard motor that's run out of gas or the frame of a backpack). Make spear tips from odd and ends you find in your drifting boat, such as broken oar locks. All you have to do is grind these metal parts on other metal until you form a point, a process that usually takes about two days. You can attach the metal tip as we show you how to do in Chapter 8, or if you have access to wire (perhaps from dead electrical devices or outboard motors), you can simply bind the two together, wood and metal, as we show you in Figure 20-2a.

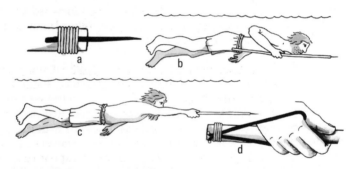

Figure 20-2: Fishing with spears.

If you're using a spear, be extra careful. A spear can deflate your raft or cause injury very quickly! Never underestimate this crude weapon. Treat it like a loaded gun.

Always keep in mind that fish on the open sea like to congregate. In the first few days you're adrift, you may see only the types of sea creatures that swim too fast to be speared. But after a few days, a community of fish will spring up, including the slower swimmers, such as the slow gray groupers, which are meaty and easily speared. Here's how you do it:

1. **Enter the water with a rope tied from the boat or raft to your waist or ankle.**

Doing so helps you avoid getting separated. You also want to have a loop of string that goes from the spear to your wrist so you don't lose your new tool!

2. **Float quietly and wait for a slow fish to come near, or drift casually over to the fish without making any hurried movements.**

3. **Grasp the spear at the halfway point so that it's balanced in your hand; then cock your fist under your armpit (see Figure 20-2b).**

4. **When you think you're close enough, thrust straight out, from armpit to fish.**

   Because you're horizontal, this feels almost like you're pushing the spear directly over your head (Figure 20-2c). This is the fastest motion your arm and the spear can develop underwater. No other way works.

5. **After you spear the fish, reach forward and hold the struggling animal with your other hand, and return to your raft or boat.**

You can construct a slightly more effective fishing spear, called a *Hawaiian sling*, by simply attaching a length of bungee cord, rubber tubing, or elastic, to the butt end of your lightweight spear. After you've done that, just put your thumb through the loop of elastic, reach forward with the same hand, and grasp the spear about three-quarters of the way up. This stretches the elastic and makes the spear ready to fire (check out Figure 20-2d). When you thrust forward, release your hold on the spear for just a moment so that it travels slightly farther and much faster. This weapon is very effective on small fish that congregate within a few feet of rafts.

Using nets

You can use nets, fashioned out of clothing and other fabric, to capture small fish near your raft for use as bait. Submerge your net in an area where smaller fish may be schooling, and then be prepared to pull up sharply. This is an exercise in patience and quiet. Keep in mind that successful fishers who use nets do so with the help of lots of equipment. You may find net fishing impractical, and you may find it better to move on to other methods.

Advanced fishing for the hungry

You may want to consider trying a couple of advanced fishing methods to augment the basics. These methods include the following:

- **Get flying fish to jump in your boat.** You can catch flying fish on the sea at night sometimes by simply turning on a flashlight or a lamp, or better, flashing the light on some background, like a sail or a piece of plastic. These tasty fish many times fly out of the water and land aboard your vessel. They make good eating, but they're sometimes better used as bait. Put a hook in one and toss it out on a line. Larger fish are fanatical about flying fish.

- **Fish with a gaff, a pole with a *very sharp* hook on the end of it.** You can make hooks for this, but large, barbed fishhooks are the best. To fish with a gaff, drop your pole into the water, hook end down. When a fish swims over the hook, jerk the gaff sharply upward. Be careful, though: Like spear fishing, this is also a good method for accidentally sinking a raft.

Catching small sharks by hand

One of the easiest ways to get food from the ocean is to catch small sharks by hand. When you carry this out in an organized fashion, it's safe, and it's a sure thing. This method also doesn't require you to risk your fishing gear to the sea. When you're a castaway, you suddenly notice that you lose fishing tackle at an incredible rate through day-to-day usage: Lines break or hooks are lost or fall overboard. So if you're short on equipment — or have no equipment to speak of — this is a good method to practice.

Use the barehanded method to catch only small sharks; don't try to catch anything longer than about 3 feet (0.9 meters). To catch a shark, simply wait until the creature swims past. Then swiftly reach into the water and grasp the thinnest part of its body — just in front of its tail — and yank it out of the water smartly.

The Baileys' shark-catching operation

Hand-catching sharks may take you a couple of tries, but it's well within the physical abilities of most fit adults. Maralyn Bailey, a 98-pound (44-kilogram) tax accountant from Southampton, England, was frequently able to pull these animals aboard her dinghy during her famous 1973 survival voyage of 117 days, saving herself and her husband, Maurice, from starvation. During the operation, Maurice usually stood by with a towel to throw over the shark's head as soon as Maralyn pulled the animal out of the water. She was so good at it that Maurice eventually had to tell her to stop. We, your friendly authors, have used variations of this method to catch dozens of sharks during the voyage of the *Manteño II* without endangering ourselves in the slightest.

Don't grab a shark by the tail if you can help it. Grasp the thinnest part of its body — right where the tail joins the body. Some sharks have sharp tails that can cut you severely. Also, never attempt to use two hands to grasp a shark (or a turtle) in the water; use one hand for the fish and the other hand to hold onto your vessel.

Turn the shark upside down as soon as you can and throw something over its eyes, such as a shirt or towel. After doing so, hold the shark by the tail until it dies. Alternatively, if you've a cleared spot inside the raft and you have the shark upside down and blinded, you can do this inside. Otherwise, hold the shark on a reinforced area near the entrance to your raft. You may want to club the fish.

Keep in mind, when you start out, that even the very smallest of sharks seem fantastically strong. They fight, wriggle, and twist and writhe violently in your hands. Be aware that sharks writhe violently for as long as 5 minutes and can still bite even after they seem dead. Be patient.

Shark meat tastes of ammonia when first caught. To improve the flavor, let the meat sit out in the sun or overnight. The ammonia taste usually subsides significantly after just 8 hours. You can also rinse it in fresh water or slightly fouled fresh water if you have precious liquid to spare or in salt water if you're desperate.

Bringing in Your Catch

Before you catch fish at sea, you need to have a plan for bringing your fish aboard your vessel. Many fish are essentially pointed animals, and they can deflate your raft or cause injury. They're spring-loaded, too: Most fish have the ability not just to flop but also to jump — sometimes several feet into the air — after they're aboard a raft or boat. You have to make sure the fish can't jump back into the water.

The following is a list of strategies to consider when bringing your catch in:

- ✔ **Get organized.** Discuss thoroughly with your fellows exactly how you'll bring the fish aboard and keep it aboard.

- ✔ **Estimate the pathway that the fish will take when you pull it from the sea and put it in your vessel.** Reinforce this area with anything you can and make sure there are no vulnerable points in the spot where you intend to land the fish.

- ✔ **Kill or stun large or aggressive fish while they're still in the water.** To do this, stab the fish in the eye or just behind the head with a spear — grim business, we know, but you need to be certain.

When killing or stunning a fish in the water, it's best *not* to use a spear that has your pocketknife for a spearhead. Your knife is irreplaceable. Use some other type of spear for this operation if you can.

- ✔ **Be ready to guard the exits when the fish is aboard.** Get between the fish and the sea.

- ✔ **Throw a piece of cloth or canvas over the fish's eyes.** Doing so can sometimes calm it after it's aboard.

- ✔ **Be ready to club the fish after it's aboard.** This can be grim business as well, like the stabbing, but you need to get yourself fully prepared to overpower the fish.

Don't use a spear when the fish is aboard the life raft under any circumstances. That operation is way too clumsy — you'll most assuredly miss and damage the boat.

Preparing and Eating Fish

After maybe a few false starts, we hope you're starting to bring in the catch. Now you have a new problem: How do you eat it? In this section, you find out how to prepare and dry raw fish. We also include some notes on identifying fish that aren't fit for consumption.

Setting up the sushi bar

After you've killed the fish (see the earlier section "Bringing in Your Catch"), you can fillet it if you like, but many times it's easier simply to peel the skin back and then cut the meat into long strips for drying. This is especially true in the case of large fish such as dorado (mahi mahi) and tuna. Here's how to prepare and dry large fish like these:

1. **Cut a large triangle in the fish's skin.**

   Start your triangle just behind the gill and narrow it down to a point at the tail fin.

   If you have no blade, you need to improvise. Anything that's made of metal works; a close friend of ours once cut open the armor plating of a turtle with a sharpened tin can. Unfortunately — or fortunately, depending on how you look at it — you have lots of time on a raft.

2. **Start at the point and peel the skin toward the gill.**

3. **After the meat is exposed, slice off long thin strips.**

4. **String a line from one side of your raft or boat to the other, and hang the strips over it to dry.**

Tuna is the only fish you shouldn't dry in this fashion. Tuna is easy to distinguish because of its shiny silver body and the bloody meat that comes out of it. Consume this meat quickly, or it spoils within just a few hours. Save the entrails for bait.

Knowing which fish aren't on the menu

When you're fishing at sea, you need to know that not every fish you catch is edible. A few varieties of fish flesh can actually poison you. Most of these fish are found near reefs, although there's no guarantee that you won't catch them on the open sea. The following is a list of these toxic fish:

- ✔ **Puffers:** Consider any fish that can expand its diaphragm, or puff up, or any fish covered by spines, to be toxic and inedible. These include

  - Puffer fish (Figure 20-3a)

  - Porcupine fish (Figure 20-3b)

  - Cowfish (Figure 20-3c)

- ✔ **Barracuda:** Larger and older barracuda (Figure 20-3d) have developed a reputation over the years for carrying the toxin that causes *ciguatera,* or seafood poisoning. This is especially true in Polynesia.

- ✔ **Triggerfish:** The general rule with triggerfish (Figure 20-3e) is to consider those species near reefs to be poisonous and those on the open sea — the ones around your raft — not poisonous. If you want to give yourself added protection, you can approach the triggerfish around your raft in the same way most indigenous people do around the world: strictly as a bait fish.

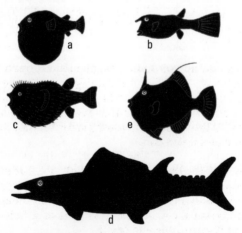

Figure 20-3: Fish with poisonous flesh.

Other fish should be considered dangerous not because they're toxic but because of their various defense mechanisms. For more on fish with nasty spines and stings that can cause injuries at sea, check out Chapter 22.

Identifying Other Delicious Things to Eat in the Sea

Beyond fish, you can find other creatures and plants to eat in sea. You can eat all these foods raw, like fish, although they're invariably more edible when dried in the sun. This section lists some of the more common foods you can eat at sea.

If you're susceptible to deadly bouts of anaphylactic shock from seafood, abstain from eating, at least in the short term. You can try seaweed if faced with starvation, but perform the Universal Plant Edibility Test first (see Chapter 8). You need to know, however, that plankton can attach to the broad leaves of seaweed, and these hard-to-see creatures could cause a reaction, even if the seaweed itself doesn't.

Turtles

Turtles are among the easiest animals to catch in the sea because like sharks, they frequently bump up against your life raft or small boat. To catch a turtle, simply grasp its hind flippers and haul it aboard. It may be possible to turn the animal over on its back and haul it in upside down, which makes controlling it vastly easier.

Sea turtles may appear to be benign animals, but they're more than capable of sinking your inflatable raft with their sharp beak and claws. They're exceedingly strong. You need to have a good plan and be well-organized before you begin to board the animal. Wrap heavy canvas or plastic around this animal's head and claws if you can.

If you can't pierce the turtle's hard shell, you can still cut out its forequarters and hindquarters. On large turtles, this can provide you with as much as 30 pounds (13.5 kilograms) of meat. Handle the meat same way as with large fish — in other words, cut it into strips and dry it.

Birds

You can catch the sea birds that inevitably land on your life raft or boat, many times by hand. We've had many birds land on our rafts, as have many castaways. All bird flesh is entirely edible, although it has a tendency to glow at night due to the bioluminescence of the fish in the birds' diet.

Sea birds can administer nasty bites that can become infected almost immediately. Put on gloves, if you got them or you can make them, when catching birds.

Barnacles

Barnacles, which begin to grow almost overnight on any hull, are the little brown creatures that cling to the undersides of boats or rafts. They appear as long brown tubes, usually with white shells at one end. These critters are crustaceans, related to lobsters and crabs, but they aren't nearly as appetizing. We can tell you here that the good news and the bad news are the same: They're completely edible. You can eat them raw, so feel free to pull them off with a satisfying snap. *Bon appétit!*

Seaweed

Seaweed is unappetizing but edible. Generally speaking, you're looking for seaweed with broad, flat leaves. Kelp is good, and it contains carbohydrates and fiber, which are hard to come by on the sea. You can find many other broad-leaf species floating in the open ocean. To see what the edible types of seaweed look like, go to Chapter 8.

Thin, threadlike seaweed can be acidic and irritating to the stomach. Also, keep in mind that eating too much seaweed (rarely a problem) can cause diarrhea and dehydration. You should use seaweed to supplement your diet, not as a main staple.

Dry seaweed in the sun before eating it. Rinsing it in fresh water helps tremendously if you have that luxury. You probably shouldn't eat seaweed if it's salty, because that dehydrates you.

Chapter 21

Emergency Travel and Navigation at Sea

In This Chapter

▶ Traveling in the water without a raft

▶ Using nature's indicators to navigate for long-term drifting

▶ Coming ashore in hazardous conditions

*R*egardless of what circumstances you find yourself in — whether floating, swimming, drifting in a disabled boat, or castaway in a raft — a few good decisions can help get you back to land. We hope to show how a little wily observation, combined with some decisive action, can help you walk on the shore again — drenched, to be sure, but alive and well.

In this chapter, we discuss how to size up your situation at sea and what signs to look out for — just in case you're in the mood for some dry land. At the end, we give you a few pointers on how to make your landing a little smoother.

Swimming Back to Land

When you're in the water, getting back to land, or just back to the safety of a good vessel, becomes your most important goal. And you don't need us to tell you that it's heck of a lot harder than people think. But if you can measure a few things — if you can use some knowledge and techniques to eliminate chance — you can, like so many survivors before you, give yourself that little edge.

In this section, we talk about getting your bearings, considering a current's direction and speed, and measuring distances when you're in the water. We also tell you how to decide whether to swim or float and give you advice on getting out of a rip current.

Measuring distance to shore

Estimating the distance you must travel to get back to land can be tricky. Land has a nasty habit of always appearing to be a lot closer than it really is. This is especially true when sunlight shines on large landforms, such as large rocks, peninsulas, or mountains near shore. When the sunlight is shining on these types of landforms, expect them to be much farther than you initially estimate. (For more on the funny business of estimating distances, see Chapter 9.)

When you're in the water (either in a life raft or bobbing in a life vest), your ability to see land is diminished because the water interferes with your line of sight. Nevertheless, here are some general guidelines for estimating distances to land:

- ✔ **Within a mile (1.6 kilometers) of shore:** You can clearly distinguish the limbs on humans or the individual branches on trees.

- ✔ **Roughly 2 miles (3.2 kilometers) out:** You can distinguish individual windows on houses or buildings.

- ✔ **More than 3 miles (4.8 kilometers) out:** You can't distinguish exactly where the surf strikes the land.

This last distinction is probably the most important, because if you're in the water and you're more than 3 miles out, you should try getting to land by drifting, not swimming. We talk about the decision of whether to swim or drift later in this chapter.

Figuring out where the current is taking you

You can do a lot of things in life, but you can't swim against an ocean current — at least not for long. You have to work with the current, and that takes patience and faith. Regardless of your predicament, you save a lot of energy and frustration by knowing which way the water is moving before you start making swimming plans.

Debunking some myths about ocean currents

To really understand how currents affect you, consider these truths:

- ✔ **The current isn't necessarily going with the waves or swells.** So even though you may feel as though you're being pushed one way, you may be drifting another.

- ✔ **Tides aren't currents (usually).** Generally speaking, when the tide is flooding onto the land or ebbing away from it, the current actually flows parallel to the shoreline. This isn't always true, but it helps to point out that the current isn't necessarily rushing toward the beach or hurtling out to sea during the tides — it may be just running down the coast.

Determining the direction and speed of a current

So which way is the current really going? Here's one way to be sure: If you can see land, you can use a range. A *range* is simply an imaginary line drawn through two objects on land (see Figure 21-1). Using a range is an exceptionally accurate way of determining which way you're moving — vastly more accurate than using the waves as a measurement.

When you're in the water, take a look at the lights or landmarks on land and try to find two that are in line with each other — such as two large trees, or perhaps the glow from a village and the hill behind it. The line through these two landmarks is your *range*. In a few minutes, you should be able to detect that the linear relationship between the two landmarks has changed. **Remember:** You're moving in the *opposite* direction of the closest landmark.

Figure 21-1: Using a range to tell which way you're drifting.

Another way to figure out the current's direction is to look at a buoy. Most river mouths and bays have large navigation buoys anchored to the riverbed. If you're near a river mouth or a bay inlet, you can simply observe which way the buoy is leaning — that's the direction the water is headed. A buoy that's leaning at a 20° angle indicates a pretty strong current.

Whenever two large rivers converge, or whenever a powerful river emerges into the ocean, the water is pushed up so that you get very dangerous, turbulent seas. The large, standing waves can cause havoc for you when swimming. When making your way back to land, avoid these places at all costs.

Also, beware of *riptides*, or rip currents, that lead back out to sea. This current exists very close to the shoreline and causes a lot of drowning. For info on handling this special type of current, see "Swimming out of a rip current," later in this chapter.

Moving in the water: Float or swim

When you're in the water, you have a decision to make: float or swim. Either mode of transport can get you where you need to go — you just need to know which is better in your situation. In all but a very few cases, it's better to drift with the current. Because the current is doing all the work, you may be able to travel as much as five or ten times as far by drifting than by actively swimming.

In this section, we cover floating and swimming as a means of *travel* toward land. Before you do any type of swimming, either for travel or just to escape from a burning vessel, you should take a look at Chapter 18 on staying afloat.

Letting yourself float

Many floating survivors have been picked up or have reached a distant shore that was well beyond their swimming abilities. If you're without a life jacket, using the *dead-man's float*, or *drown-proofing*, may give you the ability to float for as long as two days. For more on floating, see Chapter 18.

Do not drown-proof in cold water, because floating like this makes your head go under, which makes you lose too much heat.

Swimming slowly

The most critical factor when swimming back to land is *conservation of energy*. In practical terms, that means that you need to relax and take your time. Swim more slowly than you want to — much more slowly, because that keeps your heart rate down, doing more to prevent fatigue than just about anything else. Swimming slowly can try your patience and make you feel as though what you're doing is futile, but it's the best way.

If you're wearing a life jacket, consider doing a slow, easy dog paddle. This type of swimming stroke requires very little energy and gives you steady progress.

If you don't have a life jacket on, keep in mind that the more you fatigue, the less efficiently you swim. One way to cut down on fatigue is to use a variety of strokes, sometimes referred to as *relief strokes*. The three strokes usually recommended for swimming long distances are a lazy backstroke, the breast stroke, and the sidestroke. Alternating among these three is your best bet.

You swim best when your body is horizontal, with your legs more or less behind you instead of below you. As you tire, your body begins to turn upright, and your legs sink below you. This creates more and more drag (check out Figure 21-2). Again, the only way to avoid this is to take your time and try to relax.

Figure 21-2: Swimming failure.

If you feel yourself becoming fatigued, you should drift rather than swim. When you're fatigued, swimming starts to become counterproductive. You can also check to see whether you're moving toward the coast or away from it. If currents are moving you away, stop wasting your energy. Many people have survived by drifting until they were picked up. Also, after you've drifted awhile, your strength may come back.

Swimming out of a rip current

As you approach shore, watch out for riptides. A *riptide* is an area near the surf line where the water is flowing quickly down an underwater trough. You can usually see this phenomenon because it looks like a calm stream or creek flowing through the surf. The surface is usually flat, and sometimes it has an outline of debris or flotsam around it. More often than not, it runs perpendicularly to the main surf. (***Note:*** This effect can influence the course of boats, too.)

When you're in a riptide, you should be able to notice that you're moving away from shore. You may also notice that you've sped up — that the land is leaving you in a hurry!

To get out of a riptide, swim at a right angle to the flow of the water, parallel to the beach. Don't swim against it, toward land. It may take you a long time to get out, maybe as much as half an hour, and you may end up a mile or so offshore — but this is the only way. Don't panic — just realize you're in a rip, and swim to the edge. As soon as you're out of the rip, swim to shore.

Improvised Open-Sea Navigation for Life Rafts

What happens if you're out on the ocean and you can't actually see the land? In this section, we talk about long-term navigation, such as the type you have to perform when you're in a life raft, life boat, or aboard a disabled boat, adrift on the open sea. (For info on actually steering or propelling your vessel, flip to Chapter 19.)

If you're out of sight of land, start writing down as much information as you can (if you haven't already started), such as estimated rate of travel, sightings of ships or signs of land, and so on. This is your log, and it's one of the best safety devices you can have because it helps you put all the pieces of the navigational puzzle together. Even if you're lucky enough to have a GPS unit, you quickly realize that navigation is best when it's the product of a combination of many factors.

Getting your bearings

If you can get you bearings at sea, you can estimate where land lies. Even if you don't have a map, you still usually know where the world's continents lie, and you may have a good idea of where a large island is. So developing a sense of direction can help you guide your craft to safety, or at least help you to know how long you may be drifting, which helps when figuring out what your food and water rationing program should be.

The following sections discuss improvised navigation methods that are unique to the sea. For a basic course on navigation, including instructions for correcting compass errors, see Chapter 9. For info on finding directions by using the sun and stars, see Chapter 10.

Finding direction with compasses and charts

When you're at sea, the most common instruments for navigation are compasses and nautical charts. If you have access to a compass, take a moment to see whether any metal or electronic device may be influencing it — simply move the compass around and watch the needle carefully. Metal items can cause errors by pulling the needle toward them. The best thing you can do is to try to locate the interference and move as far away as you can.

If you have access to a nautical chart, the compass-error info is called *magnetic variation* — not *declination,* as it's called on land maps. These two terms mean precisely the same thing. Magnetic variation simply tells you that your compass will always be in error by a certain amount in the area of the chart. So if your chart says *VAR 10 W,* the needle is always pointing 10° west of the true direction. If it says *VAR 10 E,* the needle points 10° east of the true direction.

Whenever you measure any distance on a nautical chart, you must use the latitude scale on the side of the chart. This scale may be delineated in minutes. A *minute* is equal to 1 nautical mile, which is about 15 percent longer than a terrestrial (statute) mile.

If you think you're located somewhere in the middle of the chart, simply go to the latitude scale nearest your position, take a piece of string, and measure out a minute (a nautical mile). You can then take this string and use it to measure how far you have to go from your position to get to land. If the latitude scale nearest you is in degrees, keep in mind that there are 60 minutes (60 nautical miles) in a degree.

For more on correcting compass error and using latitude and longitude, see Chapter 9.

Determining direction with waves

If you don't have a compass or any other type of navigational instrument, you can use the direction of the waves (and swells) as a rough guide to help you steer your boat or raft throughout the day. At dawn, when you know the sun is rising in the east, study the prevailing direction of the waves. This can give you a general sense of direction throughout the day — until late in the afternoon, that is, when the sun is obviously pointing west, and you'll have to measure the waves' direction again.

This method of orienting with the waves is only useful if you understand that at least two wave systems are usually around you:

- ✔ **Swells:** These are the largest masses of sea and are usually very constant. In other words, if at dawn you see that the swells are moving to the southwest, you can be pretty certain they'll continue to do so all day. These are the best to follow, because they're so constant.

- ✔ **Waves:** These aren't usually exactly in sync with the swells — they're smaller masses of sea that come along a little faster than swells. Sometimes the waves can be in sync with the swells, though watching swells is almost always better.

You need only about an hour of careful observation to see which is which and which way they're moving. Give it a try. If you combine this method with the navigation method of using the sun and stars that we describe in Chapter 10, you should be able to figure out which way you're moving without too much trouble.

Estimating current at sea

If you're far out to sea (you can't see land), it's virtually impossible to establish the current's direction and speed unless you have sophisticated navigational instruments, like a GPS or a sextant.

As a default, you can assume that most of the world's ocean currents move at a speed of between 0.5 and 0.75 miles (0.8 and 1.2 kilometers) per hour. But keep in mind that this is a generalized assessment — many currents move much faster, and some move much slower. If you're drifting off the coast of South America, for example, you can expect to move at about 1 mile (1.6 kilometers) per hour. In the Gulf Stream off the coast of Florida or South Carolina, you can sometimes speed along at 5 miles (8 kilometers) per hour — even though it feels like you're not moving at all! But 0.5 to 0.75 mph is a good baseline to estimate your speed, if you have no other way to judge.

Understanding signs of land

With heightened awareness, you can find your way to land — even if you can't see it and you don't have a compass or chart. Land gives all kinds of clues, but many of them are subtle, so you have to pay close enough attention. In this section, we name some of the signs of land.

At sea, the height of your eye or your antenna or your signal means everything. So when you're looking for land, try to get in as high a position as you can — just standing up for a few minutes in a raft can make all the difference in the world.

Signs of civilization

Some signs point you not only to land but, sometimes even to civilization:

- **City glow:** This can be more subtle than you think. Many times a city's glow shows up as a very light gray semicircle way out on the horizon.

- **Navigation lights:** Many are very hard to see, especially because they often blink only about once a minute — and then only in red! Sometimes, finding a navigation light can be like finding a certain comma on this page.

- **The courses of small airplanes, helicopters, and small boats:** Watch which way these small boats are traveling — if you see a civilian helicopter moving in the same direction, an offshore platform may be nearby.

- **Nautical bells and horns:** Nautical bells are rarely bells at all; they're long, heavy bass tones. They can be heard at night from immense distances, but you have to be on guard — you can easily miss them if you're not paying attention.

  We hate to tell you this, but many times foghorns are deactivated because someone finds them annoying or because they need repairs. This is a common problem. If a foghorn is listed on your chart but you can't hear it, that doesn't necessarily mean it's not there.

If you're out to sea or in heavy fog, you can use an AM radio to find land. This is an easy and reliable technique:

1. **Open the antenna and point it toward the horizon.**

2. **Tune the radio to any station you can, no matter how poor the reception.**

   You're not trying to hear what they're saying on the station — you're just trying to pick up a signal.

3. **Slowly pivot your body while keeping the antenna pointed at the horizon.**

4. **When the station disappears completely, you've hit the *null* — the quiet spot where the station suddenly goes silent or gets very faint.**

   When this happens, you're pointing directly at the transmitting tower — and land!

If you have an AM radio with an internal antenna, you have to take the housing off and find out which way the antenna is pointing. The antenna is simply a metal rod with a lot of wires coiled around it. When you find the antenna, point it toward the horizon and start your pivoting procedure.

Hints from the birds

Sometimes the flight paths of seabirds can point you toward land. The general rule when using birds to find land revolves around understanding what they're doing out at sea. Each day at dawn, they leave the land and fly offshore to hunt for fish. Then, in the afternoon, after they've eaten their fill, they begin steadily gaining altitude. When they reach a certain height and spot land, they tend to immediately fly in a straight line, and often in a V formation, to their home.

Watch for groups of birds coming out to sea at dawn and then leaving in the afternoon or at dusk. If you see birds behave in this manner, especially in groups, that's a pretty good indication that the direction of their flight leads to land.

The idea that all birds must eventually return to land is a myth. For some unknown reason, this idea still persists today, even among some serious mariners. This is false. Many birds stay out and sleep on the ocean — often thousands of miles out to sea.

The problem with identifying birds is that so many varieties exist, so it's easy to mistake land birds for those that sleep on the sea. The most reliable land-returning birds are the following:

- ✔ **Boobies and gannets:** Boobies and gannets have two important distinguishing characteristics: long, thin wings and tails like arrowheads. Their tails aren't split, blunt, or flat-edged — they look just like a sharp triangle or a spearhead. If dusk is coming and you see a group of these birds, watch carefully to see which way they fly away.

- ✔ **Frigate birds:** Identify these birds by their split tails, which are long, thin, and forked, like swallow tails. Frigate birds return to land near dusk.

Other land signs from the water, wind, and air

There are other signs of land, ones that the great Polynesian navigators have used for centuries. Now, you can't master all of these overnight, but you'd be shocked at what you can see if only you pay attention:

- **Sea breeze/land breeze:** On many shorelines around the world, the wind's direction frequently changes with the time of day. Here's the standard pattern: The wind blows toward the land from about noon until sundown, and then it reverses, blowing out from the land from early evening until just before dawn. If you record these types of wind changes in your log, they're probably coming from land. Land will most likely be in the direction from which the night breeze is coming.

- **Smells, pollen, or brown or gray air:** Land has a very distinctive smell, especially at night, when the wind tends to blow offshore toward the sea. If you have allergies and your nose starts to run just after the wind switches direction, the wind is probably coming from land. Also keep in mind that off the coasts of North Africa, Chile, and even Southern California, when the winds get things stirred up, the sky turns brown with dust from the desert.

- **A stationary cloud:** Most islands — even islands that aren't in the tropics — tend to develop puffy cumulus clouds over them during the day (see Figure 21-3a). If you see a single, puffy cumulus cloud that stays in the same spot while all the others are drifting by, this is almost always a dead giveaway that an island is underneath.

- **Discoloration of flat-bottomed clouds:** Low-lying, flat-bottomed clouds reflect whatever is directly under them. If these types of clouds are over an island, they appear distinctly green underneath.

- **Long, curved waves:** If you see long lines of straight, parallel waves moving in the general direction of the wind and then you suddenly notice a distinct curve in the waves (a long bend that extends from one horizon to the other), an island is probably somewhere downwind from you. The island is bending the waves, and you're seeing the first sign of it.

✔ **A sudden, confused wave pattern:** When ocean waves
hit islands or ricochet in and out of gulfs and large
bays, they develop a distinctive crosshatch pattern (see
Figure 21-3b). The sea suddenly becomes exceedingly
turbulent — which means the waves have been hitting
something solid and reflecting. You're close to land.
Unfortunately, this crosshatch pattern usually means
you've already passed the island — although you may
still be able to navigate toward it.

Figure 21-3: Stationary clouds (a) and wave patterns (b) indicating land.

✔ **Walls of white mist on the horizon:** Some very low
shores — like many of the beaches around the Gulf of
Mexico — are so low that they're hard to see, but you
can see the mist that their multiple lines of heavy breakers
kick up. Look for a wall of mist on the horizon that
doesn't evaporate as the day gets hot. You may hear this
before seeing it.

✔ **Water color:** Generally, deep water is blue and shallow
water is green or turquoise, although there are exceptions.
This is another reason to keep your log — if you can
combine clues, you can put together a pretty good
picture of what's going on around you.

✔ **Increase of flotsam:** Random debris floating on the
surface (such as tree trunks, coconuts, garbage, and
so on) usually indicates the presence of land nearby —
especially if the wood or vegetation is still fresh.

✔ **Butterflies and other insects:** There are no insects on the sea, so unless they've stowed away on your raft, they're coming from land.

We hope that all these indicators help you find your way back to land. Just know that when you get there, you still have some surviving to do.

Coming Ashore: A Dangerous Ordeal

Make no mistake about it: As good as land seems after you've spent a perilous time at sea, coming ashore is almost invariably unpleasant. You face heavy surf, coral, rocks, and vicious currents, all of which can drown you and your companions. Everyone wants to go ashore, but the act of landing may be the most dangerous part of your ordeal.

Basic landing principles

Before you think about landing, consider the following facts, which can mean the difference between life and death:

✔ **If you have stormy conditions, stay offshore and wait until things calm down.** In storms, generally speaking, the closer you get to land, the more violent the waves become. If you have a sea anchor, a drogue, or the ability to paddle, deploy these defensive measures to hold your ground until things calm down.

✔ **If it's dark out, try to wait until dawn to land.** Going ashore in the dark is excessively dangerous. Waiting for dawn takes a lot of discipline, but this alone can save your life. (We know. We can remember nights when we really wanted to come in to land but didn't — because it was suicide!)

✔ **If you know the tide cycle, try to land when the tide is coming in.** When the tide is going out and opposing incoming waves, the seas peak more sharply, making a landing more dangerous.

✔ **Try to land on the leeward side of an island or peninsula or near a headland or jetty that breaks up the**

waves. The *leeward* side is the area of land located in the wind's shadow; it's where the wind is *not* directly blowing on shore. A *headland* is a bulge of land, and a *jetty* is a finger of land, and they both protrude from the main shoreline. Usually, neither of these landforms has as violent a surf as a beach.

✔ **Try to avoid any area where you can hear the breakers *before* you can see them — especially if you see a high wall of mist over the breaker line.** These are signs of excessively violent conditions.

✔ **Look for a lagoon, bay, or sandy beach that has less wave energy.**

  • **Lagoons on volcanic islands:** Generally speaking, lagoons on volcanic islands have inlets that face the wind. This would be the only time you'd want to approach land on the shore where the wind is blowing. Ideally, you'd like to sail and paddle through the inlet and into the lagoon.

  • **Lagoons on coral islands:** Generally speaking, lagoons on these types of islands are on the leeward side. If you're on the approach to a low-lying tropical island — especially if you can hear the surf and see a veil of mist around the surf line — you must do everything you can to navigate around it and come in for your landing on the back side.

Procedures for landing

We hope you manage to get to land, and we hope that your landing does nothing more than give you a fine old war story, but the truth is that landings are usually not romantic or fun at all. So get ready:

✔ **When you know you're going to land, heavily reinforce your paddles and bailers.** These are the most important objects in your raft, and they're most likely to break just when you need them. Use tape or rope or anything you have to do this.

✔ **Dress yourself in every piece of clothing you have for protection against the landing.** Use anything you have handy as extra protection. If you're barefoot, tape cardboard, wood, or metal to your feet. If you have duct tape, now's the time to use it all.

✔ **Tie down all objects inside the boat, and tie important electronics, wrapped in waterproof plastic, to your body.** You still need to be able to swim, no doubt, but if you land on an uninhabited coast; you want to land with a stripped-down collection of your best gear, intact and functioning.

✔ **Deflate the overhead canopy of the life raft.** That way, you won't be trapped below during capsize.

✔ **If you're in a small, rigid boat, consider backing in.** Simply tie a line to something heavy (such as a big battery or a tire) and hurl it over the front (bow) of the boat. This gives you a drogue that keeps the front of the boat pointed toward the surf while you're landing. The surf has more than enough power to slowly push you — backward — onto the land. This is a safe, common method used by mariners throughout the world.

✔ **On approach to any shoreline that has steep land nearby, such as a cliff or a mountain, be ready for the wind to die.** High cliffs frequently block the wind and cause a vacuum near the shore. If you're using sails to guide your craft to safety, these areas can mean serious trouble. Be ready with your paddles, and have the paddling chores already assigned.

✔ **Be ready for multiple lines of breakers.** Many times it looks like you have to get through only one line of big waves. Watch out — you may face two or more.

✔ **Stay with the raft or disabled boat for as long as you can.** You'll most likely get stuck — hung up on a rock or some kind of coral. Try to stay with the vessel; the ocean has the nasty habit of hammering boats, and hopefully, it will hammer you ashore. Don't get caught between the boat and a rock or shore.

✔ **Cut your drogue or sea anchor only as a very last resort.** If you stall and you're still far offshore, you may have to cut it free.

Ideally, you want to wash up on shore and quite literally crawl out onto the sand. That may sound crazy, but that's a safe landing!

Chapter 22

First Aid on the Water

. . . .

In This Chapter

▶ Understanding the risks of hypothermia, cold shock, and drowning

▶ Treating typical sea illnesses

▶ Dealing with dangerous sea creatures

. . . .

*E*ven just a little knowledge and ability can make a big difference when you're trying to survive emergencies on the sea. Knowing the signs of danger — and some of those signs are only visible if you know exactly what to look for — can save lives, including your own.

In this chapter, we show you how to respond to cold water immersion and near drowning. After that we show you how to handle the medical problems you may encounter when you drift in a life raft, as well as how to treat bites and stings from sea creatures.

Responding to Water Casualties

In any survival situation on the water, you face four major threats. Most people know about *drowning,* but you should know that anytime you go into the water — especially when you go into cold water — you're also at risk for the following:

✔ Hypothermia

✔ Cold shock response

✔ Near drowning

In this section, we first tell you how to get people out of the water so you can treat them, and then we show you how to deal with these dangers separately.

Getting someone out of the water

When rescuing someone from the water, always try to *reach or throw* something to the person in the water, so you can haul her in. This is almost invariably better than going into the water yourself, unless you're trained in lifesaving, because the weight and movement of the person in peril can easily overwhelm you. Here's how to get to someone out of the water:

- ✔ **Reaching:** Remember to plant yourself firmly. Use one hand to hold onto the vessel and one hand to extend a long stick or pole to the person in the water. Expect a heavy tug when the person grabs on.

- ✔ **Throwing:** The best thing to throw is a coil of line or a *life ring,* a circular flotation device found on practically every vessel in the world. When throwing, remember to use a long, swinging forehand (don't throw it like Frisbee — this never works!), and always hold on with your other hand. Going overboard is very easy because of the momentum your body develops when you hurl the line or ring.

- ✔ **Getting in water:** If you do have to go into the water, tie a tether to your body so you can get back safely.

For pointers on how to help someone into a life raft, see Chapter 19.

Understanding hypothermia

Hypothermia is the progressive cooling of the human body, which leads to mental and physical impairment and later, death. If you're in the water, hypothermia can kill you much faster than on land, because it can incapacitate you so much that your mouth falls below the water's surface, thus causing drowning — long before you actually perish from the cold.

Hypothermia can occur even if you're in tropical waters. It can sometimes take days, whereas it can take only minutes in frigid seas, but enough heat can eventually leave your body to cause hypothermia.

Anytime you've been exposed to a water environment, be on guard for one or more of the symptoms of hypothermia:

- ✔ Extreme shivering

✔ Bluish coloring in the lips or skin

✔ Apathy and the desire to lie down or give up

✔ Dizziness, disorientation, slurred speech

✔ A stop in shivering (very dangerous)

If you or one of your companions exhibits the symptoms in the preceding bulleted list, treat for hypothermia. Here are the main points of treatment:

✔ **Try to keep the subject from exerting himself to the point of tiring.** Climbing out of the water can put an enormous strain on a person with hypothermia. Assist the subject as much as possible.

✔ **Try to keep the subject's body horizontal, even when pulling him out of the water.** After he has cleared the water, elevate the feet slightly, and, if possible, put him in the recovery position (which we cover in Chapter 13).

✔ **Warm the subject slowly, especially if he has been in the water for a long time.** Warm the torso and neck first. Don't warm the limbs. You may have to hold the subject close to your body to transfer heat.

✔ **Monitor the airway closely, and don't allow him to inhale vomit.** Be prepared for *afterdrop,* which is a continued decline of central body temperature after the rewarming process has begun.

Turn to Chapter 13 for a detailed explanation of how to treat hypothermia, the most deadly of conditions.

Treating cold shock response

Cold shock response is a sudden incapacitation of the human body due to cold water immersion. It can incapacitate you so suddenly that you can't swim, inflate a life vest, or climb into a life raft. Signs of cold shock response include the following:

✔ Accelerated heartbeat

✔ Dizziness and disorientation

✔ Hyperventilation

✔ Motor skill impairment

Anyone immersed in water that's less than 50°F (10°C) is considered at risk for cold shock response.

When subjects perish from cold shock response, their core temperatures aren't at the level necessary to cause death from hypothermia. Cold shock deaths usually come from the inability to move (the muscles don't respond) or sometimes cardiac arrest, either of which may lead to drowning.

Treat cold shock response the same way you treat hypothermia, which we discuss in the preceding section. If you're with someone who's at risk of cold shock response, monitor the person closely (don't leave the person unattended) and be ready to perform CPR.

Studies have demonstrated that humans, if exposed to cold water often enough, can build up a tolerance to cold shock. If you're accustomed to crossing cold rivers or swimming in cold seas but you're with someone who isn't, be ready for the possibility that your companion will go into cold shock response, even though you don't feel any effects yourself.

Handling near drowning

Drowning is death due to asphyxiation from fluid in the lungs. Unfortunately, you can't do anything for those who've expired. But many times people inhale enough fluid simply to lose consciousness, become incapacitated, or have difficulty breathing. This condition is called *partial drowning* or *near drowning*.

Reviving near-drowning subjects

You can revive some near-drowning subjects through resuscitation. Treatment involves performing CPR and allowing gravity to withdraw as much fluid out of the lungs as possible. Follow these steps:

1. **Remove the subject from the water, trying to keep the head, especially the mouth, lower than the rest of the body.**

   This prevents the accidental inhalation of water that may be in the throat.

2. **Lay the subject down on the ground and check her airway, breathing, and circulation (ABC); perform CPR if the subject isn't breathing and has no pulse.**

   Continue CPR until you're exhausted. The only good thing we can say about long-term cold water immersion is that sometimes it slows the body's functions down to such an extent that people survive for a very long time, even after they've lost consciousness.

3. **If the subject is breathing and has a pulse, place her in the recovery position, and make sure the mouth is free of obstructions like grass or clothing.**

   Water and vomit should be able to drain freely from the airway.

4. **Monitor the subject (as we explain in the next section).**

For more on the ABCs, CPR, and the recovery system, flip to Chapter 13.

Monitoring someone after near drowning

Even just a small amount of inhaled water can cause the lungs to become swollen and congested, a deadly process that can take anywhere from a few minutes to a couple of hours. More often than not, death occurs after the subject has been pulled from the water and seems to be recovering. Watch near-drowning subjects for the following signs:

- Incessant coughing
- Coughing up water, froth, or bubbles
- Shortness of breath
- Lightheadedness and disorientation

If you or someone around you exhibits these signs, go to the nearest medical facility. If that's impossible, be ready to perform mouth-to-mouth resuscitation or CPR. Putting the subject in the recovery position can help.

Treating Common Sea Ailments

Most of the problems we talk about in this section aren't deadly by themselves, but they can become deadly when they're combined with other conditions, fatigue, or demoralization.

Dehydration is also a serious concern at sea. For information on collecting and rationing water, go to Chapter 20.

Seasickness

Seasickness, or simply *motion sickness,* occurs when a vessel's rolling motion irritates your sense of balance. It usually begins with a bout of yawning, followed by headache, nausea and finally, vomiting. Seasickness usually lasts no more than three days, although in severe cases it can be persistent. It's unfortunately very common in life rafts.

You can take medications to prevent seasickness, but generally speaking, you have to take the medicine before the onset of the symptoms. The most common over-the-counter medicine is dimenhydrinate (Dramamine), which is sometimes in first aid kits. One effective prescription treatment is the transdermal patch of scopolamine. A *transdermal patch* is a dime-sized adhesive gauze that sticks to your skin and releases medication into your body over a period of days.

Prevention and treatment are basically the same thing when dealing with seasickness. Your goal is to try to relieve the irritation as much as you can. The following list includes the most reliable methods for preventing and treating seasickness — experiment with each method until you find one that works for you:

- ✔ **Look at the distant horizon.** The distant horizon is the only thing at sea that doesn't move, and looking at it can prevent your sense of balance from being irritated.

- ✔ **Try not to sit down.** Sitting only makes seasickness worse. When you stand, you allow your body to compensate a little for the boat's motion. In a life raft, you may not have any choice, although you can always try to kneel.

✔ **Stay active.** Give yourself something to do to take your mind off of being seasick.

✔ **Change the motion of the vessel.** This may be impossible to do in a life raft, but if you're in a vessel you can steer, try turning to a new course so the vessel has a different motion in the waves. Some rolling motions are easier to take than others.

✔ **Change your location on the boat or raft.** You may be in a position where you're getting a bad motion, one that's making you sick.

✔ **Get some rest, or even better, some sleep.** Seasickness and fatigue are buddies — wherever you find one, you usually find the other. When resting, lie on your back with your face up and your eyes closed.

✔ **Eat ginger.** Take ginger capsules the moment you feel the symptoms. If the symptoms are advanced, and especially if you're about to vomit, try nibbling on sugar-coated ginger pieces. Many consider ginger to be ineffective, but we've used it with great success.

✔ **Drink something.** If you're vomiting, you're dehydrating, and that weakens you. If you're not dehydrated, consider a clear soda, if you have access to it, to settle your stomach.

Sunburn and heat maladies

Sunburn is a serious threat on the sea. When combined with other problems, it can cause you to go into shock. Do everything you can to stay out of the sun, and keep in mind that the sun's reflection on the water can burn you, too. Try to keep every inch of your skin covered. Use sunblock if you have it, or try making improvised sunblock from mud, charcoal, or used motor oil. You can relieve pain with any type of anti-inflammatory, such as aspirin, ibuprofen (Advil, Motrin), or naproxen sodium (Aleve).

If you're in a life raft at sea, you also have to guard against the typical problems that heat can cause — heat exhaustion and, worse, heat stroke. These two conditions come from *hyperthermia,* or the overheating of the body. For symptoms and treatments of hyperthermia, go to Chapter 17.

Water-glare blindness

Though rarely a permanent condition, *water-glare blindness* is a very painful eye irritation, somewhat like sunburn in the eyes, that comes from the sun's reflection on the water. It can cause your eyes to become bloodshot and severely swollen.

To prevent water-glare blindness, wear sunglasses or make improvised sunglasses (see Chapter 16). You can also apply dark coloring under the eyes to divert the sun's rays. A large stripe of dark paint, charcoal dust, or used oil can absorb harmful rays away from your eyes.

Treat advanced cases of water-glare blindness by bandaging the eyes with sterile dressings. Don't use salt water to cool this condition — use cold packs for pain relief if you have them.

Skin chafe and saltwater sores

Of all the unheroic injuries, *skin chafe* has to be the most painful. Anytime skin rubs continuously on any surface at sea, you're going to have a problem — no exceptions. If your skin is rubbing on a surface like the side of the raft, try to change your body's position or try to protect the skin. If left unattended, skin chafe quickly degenerates into saltwater sores.

Saltwater sores are small pockets of inflammation that form in breaks in the skin. They usually start out as pea-sized ulcers, but they can widen to become dime-sized or larger.

To treat saltwater sores, scrupulously clean every break in your skin with soap and water if possible. Bathing in fresh water can help tremendously, but if none is available, use salt water. Soap doesn't make suds when used with salt water, and salt water also irritates the sores a little, but it's better than not cleaning them at all.

Treating Bites and Stings

We wish we could tell you just to *avoid* the dangerous animals of the sea, but unfortunately, the sea has a way of throwing them in your way, regardless of what you do. This section tells you how to treat injuries from these creatures of the sea.

Jellyfish

Jellyfish stings occur when you brush against the animal's membranes and it releases venom into your skin. All stings are painful, but some are fatal. The white, translucent *box jellyfish,* which inhabits the waters north of Australia, is probably the most deadly. An animal that looks like a jellyfish, but is actually a colony of small animals, is the clear, purple *Portuguese man-of-war,* which is present in all the world's oceans. Reactions to serious stings include nausea, vomiting, shock, and cardiac arrest.

To treat jellyfish stings, follow these procedures:

1. **If you have access to vinegar, pour it on the tentacles; otherwise, use seawater.**

   This neutralizes the stinging mechanism.

2. **Remove the tentacles using tweezers, sticks, or gloves.**

   Don't touch the tentacles with your hands.

3. **Apply shaving cream, baking soda, or even mud to the wound, and then shave the area with a razor or a knife.**

4. **Apply more water or vinegar (or seawater) to the wound to dilute the poison.**

   If the tentacles have gotten in the eyes, irrigate liberally with fresh water. If in the mouth, rinse with a solution of one part vinegar to three parts water.

5. **Treat the wound like a sprain and use the RICES procedure (see Chapter 13).**

Keep in mind that if you or one of your companions has been stung, CPR may be necessary.

Sea snakes

Sea snakes usually live out their entire lives on the sea. Most strikes don't envenomate the subject enough to cause serious harm; however, you should consider all sea snakes to be dangerously venomous. The symptoms of being envenomed don't always show up immediately after a strike. The first sign is usually a headache and aching muscles. You treat a sea snake bite like you treat other snakebites, which we detail in Chapter 13.

Stinging fish and stingrays

Fish stings can damage large portions of tissue and be exceedingly painful — the pain can sometimes last for days or even weeks.

Never try to handle any fish that has spines, points, spikes, or bristles. Never handle a fish that's spotted, that looks like a stone or a rock, or that has zebra stripes or tiger stripes. And never wade near a reef barefoot.

Anytime you believe stingrays may be nearby, keep your feet off the seabed. Stingrays swim across the seabed, and if they feel threatened, they may sting you with the barb on the end of their tail, which is sometimes fatal. If you hook a stingray while fishing, consider cutting the line rather than boarding the ray.

If you get stung, wash the wound immediately with soap and water if possible. If you have access to hot water, immerse the wound in the warmest water the person can handle without being scalded. Repeated immersions in hot water should help. Be prepared to treat for shock and administer CPR.

Cone shells and terebra shells

Cone shells are small gastropods that look like miniature, brightly colored pine cones, between 1 and 4 inches (2.5 and 10 centimeters) in length. You can find them in the Indian and Pacific Oceans, and they frequently travel across the seabed, usually at night. Don't handle cone shells, because they can be lethal — they have a venomous barb that they use like a harpoon to kill their food.

Terebra shells also live in the Indian and Pacific Oceans. They're thin and usually 4 to 6 inches (10 to 15 centimeters) in length. Like the cone shell, the terebra shell has a stinging barb and should be considered very dangerous, although the stings are rarely fatal.

Like ray stings, you treat shell stings by immersing the wound in hottest water the person can stand without scalding.

Part V
The Part of Tens

The 5th Wave   By Rich Tennant

"The scenery here is just magnificent. The
trees, the plants, and I've never seen as
many soaring eagles in one place."

In this part . . .

In this classic *For Dummies* part, we give you ten-item lists to boost your survival power. The best way to increase your chances of survival is to practice a few techniques so that when you need to use them in a crisis, you're not doing them for the first time. Another good idea is to be ready to escape some common — or uncommonly dangerous — situations before they get worse. In this part, we tell you which ten techniques are best to practice and how to get out of ten desperate situations, such as escaping a sinking plane or surviving an encounter with a bear.

Chapter 23

Ten Ways to Practice Wilderness Survival Skills

• •

• •

*A*s you can imagine, many of the skills we talk about in this book require some practice before you can do them every time. However, performing many of these just once is a quantum leap that can boost your confidence considerably.

This chapter covers several skills you may want to practice, including building tools, finding direction, and performing CPR. We start with the fire exercises because they're the ones you should master first. (*Note:* When working on a fire-building exercise, have a garden hose or other fire extinguisher at the ready, don't build next to anything flammable, and be sure to check into local regulations regarding *campfires* or *open fires* before you start building one!)

Make a Fire with Two Matches

Your ability to start a fire can mean life or death in cold conditions, so practicing your ability to successfully ignite a fire and keep it going is the cornerstone of being able to survive in the wilderness. One great practice exercise is to take two matches into the backyard and see what you can do to make a fire. Remember, you get only two matches to get the whole thing started, so overbuild everything. Get as much of the following as you can:

- **Tinder:** Try to use the wispiest of fibers, like a dense wad of hair-thin scrapings from the inside of a dry piece of bark. A dense wad of dry, dead grass works well, as does straw. You can also try something more substantial, like thin wood shavings or leaves.

- **Kindling:** Only use wire-thin twigs that snap cleanly in your hands — that indicates they're completely dry. The largest kindling in your arsenal should be pencil-sized sticks that are so dry that they snap cleanly. *Snap!*

- **Fuel:** Use thumb-sized sticks and larger.

Build the fire meticulously before you start, and make sure you build a wind break around it. Hold the box of matches firmly and stab down. Give the match a few seconds to really start burning, and then ignite your tinder at lowest point possible. You get only two tries. For more on fire craft, see Chapter 5.

Make a Fire with a Magnifying Glass

To start a fire with a magnifying glass, you need pretty strong sunlight. Here's how to light your fire:

1. **Find a spot where you can hold the magnifying glass so that direct sunlight can reach it (that is, out of any shadows).**

2. **Build your fire as in the preceding section.**

   The fire-starting method using a magnifying glass (or sparks) requires you to use exceedingly flammable tinder, such as a golf-ball sized wad of lint collected from your clothes. This tinder ignites fast and burns for only two to three seconds, so you have to use it to ignite secondary tinder, like bark scrapings, dead grass, straw, wood shavings, or leaves.

3. **Hold the magnifying glass in the sunlight, a few inches over the primary tinder, until a bright white spot appears on the tinder; when this happens, adjust the distance from the magnifying glass to the tinder until the spot is as small as you can get it.**

Now it's at its hottest, and in a few seconds the tinder should catch fire.

4. **Use the primary tinder to ignite your secondary tinder; use that, in turn, to light your kindling.**

Make a Fire with a Bow Drill

Making a bow drill is a fun afternoon activity that can help you figure out a lot of info that's valuable outdoors. By making and using your own bow drill, you can discover

- ✔ What kind of cordage does — and doesn't — work for the bowstring (long, tough boot laces are good; however, although the drawstring from sweatpants may work, it's perilously fragile, and it slips)
- ✔ How to use a branch to make the bow
- ✔ The feeling of the right type of friction you need to make an ember

Chapter 5 outlines the how-to to make a bow drill fire.

Make a Flotation Device from Your Pants

You can use a swimming pool for a few hours to figure out how to make an improvised life preserver from a pair of trousers (as we show in Chapter 18). Here's how:

- ✔ Start in the shallow end of the pool (standing in chest-deep water) to see how the inflation process works. Tie tight knots in the bottom of each pant leg and grasp the pants by the waistband. Hold the pants behind your head. In one quick motion, swing the pants over your head and down onto the water, trapping the air inside. Cinch the waist tightly with a belt.
- ✔ After you see how your pants inflate, try going through the whole process in the deeper end of the pool, where you have to take your pants off while floating and/or treading water. If you have a lot of trouble removing your

shoes and pants while you're treading water, you can take a good lungful of air, try to float calmly as you can, and then (very gingerly) untie your shoes and slip off your trousers.

If you're not a good swimmer, obviously the deep-end practice session can be lethal, because you may get tangled in your clothes and drown. Don't try it unless you're very confident and competent in water.

This is a very realistic simulation, and it's one of the best survival practice sessions you can do. If your pants don't inflate well, try submerging for a moment and blowing air up into the partially inflated pants legs.

Find North with the Sky's Help

If you know which direction is north, the rest of the directions are easy enough to find. If you face north, east is on your right, west is on your left, and south is behind you. To locate north, just look to the sun and stars for direction (Chapter 10 covers these methods in detail):

✔ If it's lunchtime — midday — and you're in North America, Northern Asia, or Europe, the sun is due south of you. Put the sun at your back, and you're facing north.

✔ Use a wristwatch to find north in the daytime. (If you have a digital watch, you can draw a simulated watch face, with the current time, on a slip of paper.) If you're in the Northern Hemisphere, point the hour hand of your watch directly at the sun. Due south lies halfway between the hour hand and the 12. When you're facing due south, north is directly behind you. (*Note:* If you're on local Daylight Saving Time, you have to adjust your watch by subtracting an hour. You can either wind it back manually, or you can simply estimate where the hour hand would be if you were to set the watch back.)

✔ Use a simple stick-shadow compass to find your east-west line, and then derive north from that. Place a 3-foot (0.9-meter) stick in the ground and mark the end of its shadow. Fifteen minutes later, mark the end of its shadow again. Put your left foot on the first mark and your right on the second, and you're facing north.

✔ Go out on a clear night and locate the Big Dipper and Cassiopeia. Between them lies the North Star. This method only works in the Northern Hemisphere; if you're in the Southern, you want to look for the Pointer Stars and the Southern Cross to find due south.

Make a Tripod

You can use a tripod of stout poles to hang a pot over a stove, to use as a rack for drying clothes or food by a fire, and to smoke food. In the wilderness, you'd make a tripod from three saplings, stripped of bark and each about 2.5 inches (6.5 centimeters) in diameter. At home, you can simulate these with broomsticks or other similar poles.

Most people need about three tries before they understand the amount of tension they need on the lines to make the tripod work. Use whatever kind of cordage you can scrounge up at home (such as electrical wire or clothesline) to simulate the realities of having less-than-ideal materials in a survival situation. Chapter 14 covers cordage and lashing in detail.

Make a Bow and Arrow

A bow-and-arrow project makes for a fun afternoon. The main obstacle to making a bow in the city is finding a piece of green (living) wood to carve into the bow. You need a sapling about 1.5 to 2 inches (3.8 to 5 centimeters) in diameter. After you have this, the rest of the elements are relatively straightforward, as we outline in Chapter 14. Find a safe place to practice shooting a bow — the local park isn't good because you could injure or kill someone! Call your local police station for advice on where you can shoot your bow and arrow.

A good bow and arrow is lethal, and you shouldn't try to build anything less than that. You want to develop the skills to make something you could use to hunt in the wild. This is a real weapon, so don't point it at anyone.

Make a Transpiration Bag

Water is a major concern in any survival situation, and you should know several places to find it outdoors and several ways to extract it from wilderness resources (such as plants). Chapter 7 addresses the actual how-to directions on making transpiration bags, tools you use to collect water from plants.

A *transpiration bag* is simply a large bag (preferably plastic) that you wrap around the bushy end of a tree or bush limb. The resulting assembly should be about the size of a beach ball, and you should fit it with a drinking hose. As water naturally evaporates from the plant tissues, it collects inside the bag.

Beware that covering a whole plant with a bag can kill it; try to cover no more than 20 percent of a plant's leaves every time you use a transpiration bag.

Use a CD to Practice Signaling

You can practice signaling for help by taking an old CD (and a friend) to a park on a sunny day. Without blinding anyone, try to use the CD to flash the sun at your friend from across the park. Have your friend wear sunglasses to prevent light injury.

Sight directly through the hole in the center of the CD: Put your friend "in the hole" and then tilt the CD very slightly to put the sun on the target. To help you aim, frame your target between two fingers held up like a V. Have your friend raise an arm when he or she sees the distinctive flash so you can tell the method is working.

To make the exercise more fun, have your friend stand in various places. Then see how fast you can get at spotting your friend and then picking the CD off the ground and signaling successfully. Or try a moving target: Signal your friend while he or she walks.

Practice CPR

At home, you can practice *cardiopulmonary resuscitation* (CPR) simply by going through the motions of finding the right place press on the chest, lacing your fingers in the right way (to do the compressions), and figuring out how to get the rhythm of compressions and breaths down. Doing this is a good idea because it builds memories that you can refer to if you end up in a bad spot. *Remember:* When practicing, don't actually do the compressions or breaths; just practice the motions and the rhythm. Of course, taking a course from the Red Cross is the best way to practice CPR, and it's inexpensive. For more on CPR, see Chapter 13.

Chapter 24

Ten Quick Escapes

In This Chapter

▶ Escaping from cars and planes in the water

▶ Getting out of some tight spots in the wilderness

*W*hen you get home, you can tell everyone how you cobbled together a shelter, built a fire, and finally flagged down your rescuers. The most dramatic part of your story, however, usually comes when you have to tell how you made your great escape. In this chapter, we tell you how to get out of ten high-adrenaline situations.

Escaping a Sinking Car

Whether an accident sends your car into a river or a flash flood sweeps you off the road, here's how to escape if your car ends up in water:

1. **Brace for impact.**

   Put your arms up in the shape of an X to protect your face and grab the shoulder strap of your safety belt.

2. **The moment you strike the water and stop moving, roll the windows *down* (not up) and unlock the doors.**

   A flooded electrical system prevents electrical locks from unlocking or windows from coming down.

3. **If no water is flooding through the window yet, unbuckle your seatbelt and go out the side window right away; if water is already pouring in, stay buckled up and wait.**

If the water is flooding in or you can't get the window to roll down, keep your seatbelt buckled. The flooding water can overwhelm you and push you around in the car, disorienting you. Also, as the car floods, it will most likely roll, and staying in the seat helps to keep you oriented.

4. **Wait until the water reaches your chin and then take a deep breath and hold it.**

   You can probably hold your breath for about 45 seconds, which is plenty of time to make it out alive.

5. **If you've gone down fast and you can't roll down the windows or open a door, use a heavy object, like a flashlight or hammer (you can carry one under the driver's seat) to break a side window; don't try to break the windshield — it's too strong.**

Many companies manufacture survival tools specifically made to both cut seatbelts and knock out a window. Every car should have one convenient to reach, and everyone should know how to use it.

6. **Swim out through the window if it's down; if not, try the door.**

   You must wait until the car floods and the pressures are equalized — inside the car and out — before you can open the door. Even when the car is flooded, getting the door open is difficult, but you can do it.

If you're disoriented when you reach the outside of the car, follow bubbles; they tend to go toward the surface.

Escaping a Small Plane in Water

Many small planes turn upside down when they ditch in the water, so you're most likely to find yourself inverted, with the cabin filling with water. Keep composed — you probably have about 30 seconds, which is plenty of time to do this maneuver right.

Wait until the motion of the plane has completely stopped. Identify your exit (the nearest door handle) with one hand,

and with your other hand, find a point of reference inside the cabin, like the dash or the handle near the ceiling. Release your seat belt and pull yourself out through the exit you've identified. If that door is stuck, you may have to go out the other. If all the doors are stuck, break out a window. Use a heavy tool, if possible, such as a fire extinguisher. Kick with your legs; they're much stronger than your arms.

Righting a Small Boat or Canoe

Small boats and canoes are easy to tip if you're not careful. Unless your vessel is very easy to right, don't bother trying to do it on your own unless you're an expert and have practiced it a lot. Some small vessels have good flotation capabilities, so you can actually sit in a sunken canoe and paddle it to shore, even if it's 90 percent underwater. Here's what to do if your vessel capsizes.

As soon as you're in the water, be sure to put on a personal flotation device (PFD) if you're not already wearing one.

You can usually right a small sailboat that's flopped on its side by standing on the daggerboard (also known as a centerboard) and letting your weight roll the boat upright. If the boat has turned all the way over (turned turtle), you may have to step on the *gunwale* (the ridge that runs along the edge of sides of the boat), grasp the daggerboard with your hands, and lean back to slowly turn the boat on its side.

If you were in a canoe and you have a friend with you, go under the overturned boat (with your PFD still on). When you're underneath, the two of you have to push the canoe up out of the water a few inches and then throw it over to one side. Decide, when under the inverted canoe, which side you're going to throw it to, and then count, "One, two, three" to a combined upwards shove. Many times, doing this requires the two of you to kick with your legs at the same time to give yourself just enough buoyancy. If you have two canoes, one capsized and the other upright, you can lift the inverted canoe out of the water and slide it crosswise across the floating canoe; then turn it over and launch it back into the water.

Escaping a Forest Fire

Forest fires can move quickly and wipe out almost anything in their path. For humans, the main dangers are suffocation (the fire consumes so much oxygen that there's literally nothing to breathe), choking (breathing in ash or dense smoke), and of course, burning. Here's how to escape a forest fire:

1. **Make a mask from a bandana or other material to protect yourself from smoke inhalation.**

   Use it to cover your mouth and nose tightly.

2. **Try to get downhill and into a clearing with little or no fuel to burn.**

   Fire moves upward fastest, so going downhill buys you time. Sandy areas like dry riverbeds are good places to go. A forest clearing is better than a fully vegetated forest. If you find a lake or river, get in and wait for the fire to pass.

3. **If you can't find cover and a fire is coming close, dig a ditch, get in, and cover yourself with as much sand or dirt as you can.**

   Be sure the sand or dirt doesn't contain a large percentage of dead wood or *forest duff,* the soft, decaying layer of vegetation that carpets many forest floors; this material explodes into flames.

4. **When the fire has passed, stay in the areas that are burnt off and begin efforts to signal for help.**

   With nothing left to burn, the fire can't come back.

Escaping a Bee Swarm

If bees start swarming, here's how you can evade the attack:

✔ Run as fast as you can for dense vegetation; they may lose your trail there.

✔ If you have a campfire going, run to it and try to make a lot of smoke with wet vegetation to deter the bees.

✔ If you have a blanket or tarp, wrap yourself in it tightly and wait them out.

✔ If you can find a body of water, you can lie in it, on your back, breathing with just your lips out of the water or using a reed to breathe (a fun thing to practice on a hot afternoon) However, the bees may still be there when you surface.

Try not to crush bees; their dead bodies emit an alarm to others.

Surviving a Bear Encounter

Bears are common in many wilderness regions. With bears — from black bears to grizzlies and even polar bears — the best offense is a good defense. Let them know you're coming in the first place; some people wear a bell when they hike in bear country, yell, "Hey bear!" loudly every few minutes and/or hit trees or rocks with sticks. These sounds often frighten bears away before an encounter even happens. For more on keeping bears away from you, see Chapter 15.

Although bears are unpredictable, some general advice has proven valuable. Here's how to handle a bear encounter:

✔ **If a bear spots you:** Don't run, and don't make eye contact. Hold your ground for a moment and then back away slowly. You can try speaking in calm monotone voice to reassure the bear. If you're between a mother and a cub, get away from them as fast as you can without making jerky, panicky moves.

✔ **If the bear rushes you:** Hold your ground. This is important but hard to do.

✔ **If a bear attacks you:** Don't fight back. A bear is much stronger than you are. Play dead by curling up in a ball and protecting your neck and skull with your hands. (The only time to fight back is if the bear doesn't leave you alone after you've played dead for a while; then, it has decided to eat you, and you might as well fight. Go for the eyes.)

Many people venturing into bear country carry *bear spray,* a large canister containing some kind of pepper or deterrent that bears don't like to get in their snouts or eyes. Sometimes it deters bears, other times it doesn't, and sometimes it backfires when the wind blows the spray back into the human's face! All things considered, carrying bear spray is a good idea, but be sure you know how to use it, and don't let it fool you into thinking you're safe from bears.

The most unpredictable and dangerous bear is the polar bear. In a survival situation, only a high-powered rifle or a large-gauge shotgun loaded with slugs are realistic defenses. Don't get caught in the high Arctic without one of these weapons and the knowledge of how to use them effectively and humanely. If you're forced to shoot a polar bear, aim for the lungs first. If you disable the bear, be sure to kill it with a final, lethal shot, to prevent suffering.

Encountering a Mountain Lion

Mountain lions (also known as *cougars, pumas,* or *panthers*) are big cats, roughly 100 to 200 pounds (45 to 90 kilograms) in weight. In spite of constant media hysteria to the contrary, attacks on humans are rare. Mountain lions are opportunistic predators, which means that they're looking for the *easiest* thing to eat.

When a mountain lion confronts you, you want to convince it that you're the hardest thing in the world to eat. Make yourself larger by opening your jacket and spreading it out to the sides or by lifting your backpack over your head. You can also try holding up branches of trees or large boards — anything that makes you appear to be a very large animal.

Never run from a mountain lion. Instead, you want to signal to the animal that you're not a sheep or deer. Do not crouch, limp, or act in any way infirm. The cat knows the difference between strong and weak prey.

If the animal attacks, it usually goes for the neck or head. You can fight off mountain lions. A sharp blow to the bridge of the nose or to the eyes with a large stone or the blunt end of an ax communicates to the animal that you're not easy prey. Continued strikes may be necessary to get your point across, but the animal should disengage as soon as it realizes its mistake.

Surviving an Avalanche

Avalanches are sudden landslides of ice and snow that can bury you and suffocate you in the blink of an eye. The best policy is to avoid avalanche terrain altogether (see Chapter 16). However, if you are caught in an avalanche, follow these steps:

1. **Try to get your backpack off.**

   Some people say this prevents the body from being dragged down into the snow.

2. **Use a swimming motion to try to stay on the surface.**

   Swim in an overhand, freestyle motion. Some survivors say being in an avalanche is like being caught in a raging river.

3. **As you slow down, fold your arms across your face.**

   If you're lucky, this creates a breathing space as the snow settles all around you.

4. **After you stop moving, try to dig for the surface or make sounds to help rescuers.**

   If you're not sure where up is, let some drool slide out of your mouth: It heads downward, so you want to dig in the opposite direction.

Surviving a Whiteout

A *whiteout* is a thick mist or blizzard that reduces visibility to just a few feet. If you don't know exactly where you are, you may find yourself stepping off a cliff, so traveling in a whiteout is a bad idea unless you're highly experienced and have a good map and compass skills. A whiteout, though, should really just be an inconvenience. Remember that you don't really need food for the night and that things will probably look better in the morning. To wait out a whiteout, do the following:

1. **Get your hat on, and if you're going to sit down, insulate your body from the snow with anything you can, such as a backpack or vegetation pulled from a tree or bush.**

2. **Make a snow shelter (refer to Chapter 16).**

3. **Do whatever you can to keep your body temperature up.**

   Light a candle, wrap yourself in a survival blanket, huddle with another person — whatever you need to do. If it gets very cold, get active. Be sure to leave some signal outside the entrance so rescue crews don't just ski right past you.

Getting Out of Quicksand

Quicksand forms when water wells up from an underground spring and "liquefies" sand or mud to the consistency of gelatin. If you find yourself in quicksand, don't panic — your body is probably less dense than quicksand, so you shouldn't sink fast. Note that on television, survival experts have to leap into quicksand with both feet to show how to get out dramatically. You're much more likely to realize you're in quicksand when one leg goes in.

If you're walking in the country and suddenly find yourself with one leg deep in quicksand, simply sit back on the firm ground you just stepped off. Shove your walking stick down alongside your leg and work the shaft back and forth as you try to pull out your leg slowly. This breaks the vacuum formed by trying to pull your leg out. Don't try to jerk your leg out of the pool; work your leg free slowly and get back on firm ground.

If you find yourself suddenly up to your hips in quicksand, slowly bend forward at the waist to try to lay some of your body on the surface. If you have a walking stick, lay it across the quicksand in front of you and lie on it, distributing your weight across a larger area. Use your arms to slowly swim or drag yourself forward. Continue to work your way toward firm ground. If you can't see firm ground in front of you, work back toward the firm ground you last walked on.

Index

• *N* •

BUSINESS, CAREERS & PERSONAL FINANCE

**Accounting For Dummies,
4th Edition***
978-0-470-24600-9

**Bookkeeping Workbook
For Dummies†**
978-0-470-16983-4

Commodities For Dummies
978-0-470-04928-0

Doing Business in China For Dummies
978-0-470-04929-7

E-Mail Marketing For Dummies
978-0-470-19087-6

**Job Interviews For Dummies,
3rd Edition*†**
978-0-470-17748-8

**Personal Finance Workbook
For Dummies*†**
978-0-470-09933-9

Real Estate License Exams For Dummies
978-0-7645-7623-2

Six Sigma For Dummies
978-0-7645-6798-8

**Small Business Kit For Dummies,
2nd Edition*†**
978-0-7645-5984-6

Telephone Sales For Dummies
978-0-470-16836-3

BUSINESS PRODUCTIVITY & MICROSOFT OFFICE

Access 2007 For Dummies
978-0-470-03649-5

Excel 2007 For Dummies
978-0-470-03737-9

Office 2007 For Dummies
978-0-470-00923-9

Outlook 2007 For Dummies
978-0-470-03830-7

PowerPoint 2007 For Dummies
978-0-470-04059-1

Project 2007 For Dummies
978-0-470-03651-8

QuickBooks 2008 For Dummies
978-0-470-18470-7

Quicken 2008 For Dummies
978-0-470-17473-9

**Salesforce.com For Dummies,
2nd Edition**
978-0-470-04893-1

Word 2007 For Dummies
978-0-470-03658-7

EDUCATION, HISTORY, REFERENCE & TEST PREPARATION

**African American History
For Dummies**
978-0-7645-5469-8

Algebra For Dummies
978-0-7645-5325-7

Algebra Workbook For Dummies
978-0-7645-8467-1

Art History For Dummies
978-0-470-09910-0

ASVAB For Dummies, 2nd Edition
978-0-470-10671-6

British Military History For Dummies
978-0-470-03213-8

Calculus For Dummies
978-0-7645-2498-1

**Canadian History For Dummies,
2nd Edition**
978-0-470-83656-9

Geometry Workbook For Dummies
978-0-471-79940-5

**The SAT I For Dummies,
6th Edition**
978-0-7645-7193-0

Series 7 Exam For Dummies
978-0-470-09932-2

World History For Dummies
978-0-7645-5242-7

FOOD, HOME, GARDEN, HOBBIES & HOME

Bridge For Dummies, 2nd Edition
978-0-471-92426-5

**Coin Collecting For Dummies,
2nd Edition**
978-0-470-22275-1

**Cooking Basics For Dummies,
3rd Edition**
978-0-7645-7206-7

Drawing For Dummies
978-0-7645-5476-6

**Etiquette For Dummies,
2nd Edition**
978-0-470-10672-3

Gardening Basics For Dummies*†
978-0-470-03749-2

Knitting Patterns For Dummies
978-0-470-04556-5

Living Gluten-Free For Dummies†
978-0-471-77383-2

**Painting Do-It-Yourself
For Dummies**
978-0-470-17533-0

HEALTH, SELF HELP, PARENTING & PETS

Anger Management For Dummies
978-0-470-03715-7

**Anxiety & Depression Workbook
For Dummies**
978-0-7645-9793-0

Dieting For Dummies, 2nd Edition
978-0-7645-4149-0

**Dog Training For Dummies,
2nd Edition**
978-0-7645-8418-3

Horseback Riding For Dummies
978-0-470-09719-9

Infertility For Dummies†
978-0-470-11518-3

**Meditation For Dummies
with CD-ROM, 2nd Edition**
978-0-471-77774-8

**Post-Traumatic Stress Disorder
For Dummies**
978-0-470-04922-8

**Puppies For Dummies,
2nd Edition**
978-0-470-03717-1

**Thyroid For Dummies,
2nd Edition†**
978-0-471-78755-6

Type 1 Diabetes For Dummies*†
978-0-470-17811-9

---

* Separate Canadian edition also available
† Separate U.K. edition also available

INTERNET & DIGITAL MEDIA

AdWords For Dummies
978-0-470-15252-2

**Blogging For Dummies,
2nd Edition**
978-0-470-23017-6

**Digital Photography All-in-One
Desk Reference For Dummies,
3rd Edition**
978-0-470-03743-0

**Digital Photography For Dummies,
5th Edition**
978-0-7645-9802-9

**Digital SLR Cameras & Photography
For Dummies, 2nd Edition**
978-0-470-14927-0

**eBay Business All-in-One Desk
Reference For Dummies**
978-0-7645-8438-1

eBay For Dummies, 5th Edition*
978-0-470-04529-9

eBay Listings That Sell For Dummies
978-0-471-78912-3

Facebook For Dummies
978-0-470-26273-3

**The Internet For Dummies,
11th Edition**
978-0-470-12174-0

**Investing Online For Dummies,
5th Edition**
978-0-7645-8456-5

**iPod & iTunes For Dummies,
5th Edition**
978-0-470-17474-6

MySpace For Dummies
978-0-470-09529-4

Podcasting For Dummies
978-0-471-74898-4

**Search Engine Optimization
For Dummies, 2nd Edition**
978-0-471-97998-2

Second Life For Dummies
978-0-470-18025-9

**Starting an eBay Business
For Dummies, 3rd Edition†**
978-0-470-14924-9

GRAPHICS, DESIGN & WEB DEVELOPMENT

**Adobe Creative Suite 3 Design
Premium All-in-One Desk Reference
For Dummies**
978-0-470-11724-8

**Adobe Web Suite CS3 All-in-One
Desk Reference For Dummies**
978-0-470-12099-6

AutoCAD 2008 For Dummies
978-0-470-11650-0

**Building a Web Site For Dummies,
3rd Edition**
978-0-470-14928-7

**Creating Web Pages All-in-One Desk
Reference For Dummies,
3rd Edition**
978-0-470-09629-1

**Creating Web Pages For Dummies,
8th Edition**
978-0-470-08030-6

Dreamweaver CS3 For Dummies
978-0-470-11490-2

Flash CS3 For Dummies
978-0-470-12100-9

Google SketchUp For Dummies
978-0-470-13744-4

InDesign CS3 For Dummies
978-0-470-11865-8

**Photoshop CS3 All-in-One
Desk Reference For Dummies**
978-0-470-11195-6

Photoshop CS3 For Dummies
978-0-470-11193-2

**Photoshop Elements 5
For Dummies**
978-0-470-09810-3

SolidWorks For Dummies
978-0-7645-9555-4

Visio 2007 For Dummies
978-0-470-08983-5

**Web Design For Dummies,
2nd Edition**
978-0-471-78117-2

**Web Sites Do-It-Yourself
For Dummies**
978-0-470-16903-2

**Web Stores Do-It-Yourself
For Dummies**
978-0-470-17443-2

LANGUAGES, RELIGION & SPIRITUALITY

Arabic For Dummies
978-0-471-77270-5

Chinese For Dummies, Audio Set
978-0-470-12766-7

French For Dummies
978-0-7645-5193-2

German For Dummies
978-0-7645-5195-6

Hebrew For Dummies
978-0-7645-5489-6

Ingles Para Dummies
978-0-7645-5427-8

Italian For Dummies, Audio Set
978-0-470-09586-7

Italian Verbs For Dummies
978-0-471-77389-4

Japanese For Dummies
978-0-7645-5429-2

Latin For Dummies
978-0-7645-5431-5

Portuguese For Dummies
978-0-471-78738-9

Russian For Dummies
978-0-471-78001-4

Spanish Phrases For Dummies
978-0-7645-7204-3

Spanish For Dummies
978-0-7645-5194-9

**Spanish For Dummies,
Audio Set**
978-0-470-09585-0

The Bible For Dummies
978-0-7645-5296-0

Catholicism For Dummies
978-0-7645-5391-2

**The Historical Jesus
For Dummies**
978-0-470-16785-4

Islam For Dummies
978-0-7645-5503-9

**Spirituality For Dummies,
2nd Edition**
978-0-470-19142-2

NETWORKING AND PROGRAMMING

ASP.NET 3.5 For Dummies
978-0-470-19592-5

C# 2008 For Dummies
978-0-470-19109-5

Hacking For Dummies, 2nd Edition
978-0-470-05235-8

**Home Networking
For Dummies, 4th Edition**
978-0-470-11806-1

Java For Dummies, 4th Edition
978-0-470-08716-9

**Microsoft® SQL Server™ 2008
All-in-One Desk Reference For Dummies**
978-0-470-17954-3

**Networking All-in-One Desk Reference
For Dummies, 2nd Edition**
978-0-7645-9939-2

**Networking For Dummies,
8th Edition**
978-0-470-05620-2

**SharePoint 2007
For Dummies**
978-0-470-09941-4

**Wireless Home Networking
For Dummies, 2nd Edition**
978-0-471-74940-0

OPERATING SYSTEMS & COMPUTER BASICS

iMac For Dummies, 5th Edition
978-0-7645-8458-9

Laptops For Dummies, 2nd Edition
978-0-470-05432-1

Linux For Dummies, 8th Edition
978-0-470-11649-4

MacBook For Dummies
978-0-470-04859-7

Mac OS X Leopard All-in-One Desk Reference For Dummies
978-0-470-05434-5

Mac OS X Leopard For Dummies
978-0-470-05433-8

Macs For Dummies, 9th Edition
978-0-470-04849-8

PCs For Dummies, 11th Edition
978-0-470-13728-4

Windows® Home Server For Dummies
978-0-470-18592-6

Windows Server 2008 For Dummies
978-0-470-18043-3

Windows Vista All-in-One Desk Reference For Dummies
978-0-471-74941-7

Windows Vista For Dummies
978-0-471-75421-3

Windows Vista Security For Dummies
978-0-470-11805-4

SPORTS, FITNESS & MUSIC

Coaching Hockey For Dummies
978-0-470-83685-9

Coaching Soccer For Dummies
978-0-471-77381-8

Fitness For Dummies, 3rd Edition
978-0-7645-7851-9

Football For Dummies, 3rd Edition
978-0-470-12536-6

GarageBand For Dummies
978-0-7645-7323-1

Golf For Dummies, 3rd Edition
978-0-471-76871-5

Guitar For Dummies, 2nd Edition
978-0-7645-9904-0

Home Recording For Musicians For Dummies, 2nd Edition
978-0-7645-8884-6

iPod & iTunes For Dummies, 5th Edition
978-0-470-17474-6

Music Theory For Dummies
978-0-7645-7838-0

Stretching For Dummies
978-0-470-06741-3

Get smart @ dummies.com®

- Find a full list of Dummies titles
- Look into loads of FREE on-site articles
- Sign up for FREE eTips e-mailed to you weekly
- See what other products carry the Dummies name
- Shop directly from the Dummies bookstore
- Enter to win new prizes every month!

* Separate Canadian edition also available
† Separate U.K. edition also available